Regionalism and Globalization in East Asia

Regionalism and Globalization in East Asia

Politics, Security and Economic Development

Mark Beeson

palgrave
macmillan

First published 2007 by
PALGRAVE MACMILLAN
Houndmills, Basingstoke, Hampshire RG21 6XS and
175 Fifth Avenue, New York, N.Y. 10010
Companies and representatives throughout the world

PALGRAVE MACMILLAN is the global academic imprint of the Palgrave
Macmillan division of St. Martin's Press, LLC and of Palgrave Macmillan Ltd.
Macmillan® is a registered trademark in the United States, United Kingdom
and other countries. Palgrave is a registered trademark in the European
Union and other countries.

ISBN-13: 978-0-230-00032-2 hardback
ISBN-10: 0–230–00032-0 hardback
ISBN-13: 978-0-230-00033-9 paperback
ISBN-10: 0-230-00033-9 paperback

This book is printed on paper suitable for recycling and
made from fully managed and sustained forest sources.

A catalogue record for this book is available from the British Library.

A catalog record for this book is available from the Library of Congress

10   9   8   7   6   5   4   3   2   1
16   15   14   13   12   11   10   09   08   07

Printed in China

For my parents

Contents

List of Figures

List of Tables

Acknowledgements

I am indebted to a number of people who have directly or indirectly assisted in the development of this book in particular, and my thinking about the East Asian region more generally. I should, of course, absolve them from all responsibility for any errors of fact or judgement in what follows, but I am deeply appreciative of their assistance nonetheless. A number of people read drafts of various chapters and they deserve particular mention and thanks: Alex Bellamy, Bill Case, Bob Elson, Stephen Feng, David Hundt, Kanishka Jayasuriya, Matt McDonald, Aurelia George Mulgan, John Ravenhill and Richard Stubbs.

I should also like to acknowledge the support and forbearance of colleagues, especially Stephen Bell, at the University of Queensland while on sabbatical, as well as the Centre for the Study of Globalisation and Regionalisation (CSGR) at Warwick University for hosting me while in England. Jan Aart Scholte and Richard Higgott deserve particular mention and thanks in this context. Will Grant provided invaluable research assistance and help in the preparation of empirical material. I should also like to acknowledge my publisher Steven Kennedy's unfailing enthusiasm for the project and his usual efficiency in helping to bring it to completion.

I would also like to express my appreciation to the Reserve Bank of Australia, the Bank of Japan, and the Ministry of Economy Trade and Industry for permission to reproduce empirical data. Finally, I would like to acknowledge that much of the research for this project and the opportunity to spend time in East Asia has been made possible by various grants from the Australian Research Council.

MARK BEESON

The author and publishers are grateful to the following for permission to reproduce copyright material: Bank of Japan for Table 6.2; Reserve Bank of Australia for Figures 6.1, 6.2 and 6.3; Ministry of Economy, Trade and Tourism Japan for Tables 6.3 and 6.4. Every effort has been made to contact all the copyright-holders, but if any have been inadvertently omitted the publishers will be pleased to make the necessary arrangement at the earliest opportunity.

List of Abbreviations

ABRI	Angkatan Bersenjata Republik Indonesia
AFTA	ASEAN Free Trade Area
AMF	Asian Monetary Fund
APEC	Asia-Pacific Economic Cooperation
ARF	ASEAN Regional Forum
ASA	Association of Southeast Asia
ASEAN	Association of Southeast Asian Nations
ASEM	Asia-Europe Meeting
BN	Barisan Nasional
CCP	Chinese Communist Party
CMI	Chiang Mai Initiative
CSGR	Centre for the Study of Globalisation and Regionalisation
DPP	Democratic Progressive Party
DPRK	Democratic People's Republic of Korea
EAEC	East Asian Economic Caucus
EAS	East Asian Summit
EASG	East Asia Study Group
EAVG	East Asian Vision Group
EPZs	export processing zones
EU	European Union
FDI	foreign direct investment
FILP	Fiscal Investment and Loan Programme
GATT	General Agreement on Tariffs and Trade
GDP	gross domestic product
IFIs	international financial institutions
IMF	International Monetary Fund
IR	International Relations
IT	information technology
JSDF	Japan Self-Defence Forces
JSP	Japan Socialist Party
KMT	Kuomintang
LDP	Liberal Democratic Party
MCA	Malayan Chinese Association
MIC	Malayan Indian Congress
MITI	Ministry of International Trade and Industry
MNC	multi-national corporation
MoF	Ministry of Finance
NAFTA	North American Free Trade Area

NATO	North Atlantic Treaty Organization
NEP	New Economic Policy
NICs	newly industrializing countries
NIEs	newly industrializing economies
ODA	official development assistance
OECD	Organisation for Economic Cooperation and Development
OPEC	Organization of Petroleum-Exporting Countries
PAFTAD	Pacific Trade and Development Conference
PAP	People's Action Party
PAS	Parti Islam Se Malaysia
PKI	Communist Party of Indonesia
PLA	People's Liberation Army
PRC	People's Republic of China
R&D	research and development
ROK	Republic of Korea
SEZs	Special Economic Zones
SOEs	state-owned enterprises
SPDC	State Peace and Development Council
TRT	Thai Rak Thai
UMNO	United Malays National Organization
VCP	Vietnamese Communist Party
WTO	World Trade Organization

Introduction

This book provides an introduction to, and analysis of, East Asia; a region that looks likely to exert a profound influence on the course of global history in the twenty-first century. The sources of this influence are to be found in the region's remarkable economic development and increasing strategic significance. Yet, however significant East Asia proves to be in the future, one of the major arguments I develop in what follows is that we cannot understand why the region is becoming a more important global force unless we take an integrated view of economic, political and security issues, and the specific historical circumstances that shaped them. Unlike many other books on East Asia, therefore, this volume provides an analysis of regional development that is grounded in the region's long, highly distinctive and often bloody history, simply because it is not possible to make sense of the region's development without it. Many of the most striking characteristics of East Asia – the preoccupation with sovereignty and security, the close ties between business and government, and the frequently fractious nature of its internal relations – have their origins in the region's unique formative experiences; they help to explain the course of national and regional development to this day. In short, history matters.

Armed with a sense of East Asia's distinctive history, we are in a better position to make sense of the contemporary era. For all the talk of 'globalization', one of the most striking things about East Asia and the countries that compose it is its internal heterogeneity and its distinctiveness from other regions. Indeed, if there is one observation that is always made about East Asia it is about its diversity. Whether this diversity is measured in terms of living standards, political systems or religious beliefs, there is much that distinguishes one East Asian country from another. Yet, despite all this diversity and uncertainty, there is increasing interest in attempting to give political and institutional expression to a distinct East Asian region, even if its precise borders remain contested and uncertain. If a more self-consciously realized, increasingly coherent, regional development process does continue, however, it will be one of the most important regional and *global* political developments since the Second World War for, despite the East Asian crisis that erupted so unexpectedly in 1997, and despite the moribund performance of the Japanese economy throughout the 1990, East Asia remains a crucial and increasingly important part of the global economy. The intention of this book is to unpack the component parts and dynamics that are either encouraging or inhibiting this process. To develop a sense of how these complex processes might unfold, therefore, I explore East Asia's inter-connected political, economic and strategic processes in the overarching geo-political context of which they are an increasingly influential part.

That the region will be influential is no longer in doubt, despite the financial crisis of the 1990s. Overall, East Asia has regained much of the ground it lost, but the region's significance has been further enhanced by the remarkable, and seemingly unstoppable, rise of China. China's astounding growth has already had a profound effect on the global economy, but it is also forcing a major reconfiguring of international relations both within East Asia itself, and between East Asia and the rest of the world. Remarkably enough, given that China was long seen as a source of threat and insecurity, some of China's neighbours are adjusting quite quickly to the new realities. For others – especially Japan – China's rise is altogether more discomfiting: despite the fact that China's rise has been good for Japan economically, historical animosities and regional leadership rivalries mean that the adjustment process will not be easy.

The relationship between Japan and China will be the key to the region's future development, or at least to its development as a self-consciously organized and coherent region in the manner of the European Union or – more realistically, in the short term, perhaps – the North American Free Trade Area. If East Asian regionalism is to amount to anything more than a series of reports and mission statements, then it will need to find a way of accommodating an increasingly powerful China and an economically colossal, but politically marginal, Japan. This may be even more difficult than it may seem at first glance: not only does Japan's single most important relationship lie outside the 'East Asian region' with the USA, but its relations with China are poisoned by an often violent, invariably acrimonious history that threatens permanent derailment of the chances of developing an inclusive regional grouping. For this reason, one of the first chapters of this volume is an overview of the region's history, without which it is simply impossible to understand the obstacles to regional development or the bilateral relations within it.

The structure of the book

The book begins with an introduction to some of the debates that surround the growing interest in regional processes and their relationship to the processes of 'globalization'. Chapter 1 spells out just what is meant by a region, and why regions have become increasingly important even in an era in which globalization is the apparently dominant metaphor, if not material reality. This apparent paradox helps to explain and actually drives regionally-based processes: simply put, regional cooperation potentially offers members advantages that equip them to respond more effectively to 'global' pressures. Indeed, when we unpack the discourse of globalization a little more carefully, it becomes apparent that it has a very strong regional accent. Interest in regional development is consequently growing, and not just among academics. Policy-makers, too, are increasingly alive to the potential competitive advantages and sheer political clout that regional collaboration offers, and are particularly conscious that their peers in other parts of the world are undertaking similar initiatives. In this context, regionalism is an idea whose time appears to have unambiguously come.

And yet the history of 'East Asia' also serves to remind us that there is nothing new under the sun. While it may not have been described as such – especially when there were no other regions to contend with – East Asia has always had an important regional quality. For some 3–4,000 years China has been at the centre of a regionally-based order that it dominated and which was remarkably orderly for long periods of time. Chapter 2 explains how, for all the differences in the development of individual East Asian 'nations', Chinese hegemony has given an underlying continuity to much of East Asia's commercial and political relations. Indeed, it could be argued that the common experiences of more recent European colonization and integration into a world order dominated by the superpowers has reinforced rather than undermined common regional experiences. This claim is contentious, but the idea that regional coherence is fundamentally alien to East Asia is not as obvious as some would have us believe.

What *is* clear is that security issues or, more straightforwardly, war and violence, have had a profound impact on the course of development in East Asia. This is true of much of the world, of course, but there are issues and events that distinguish East Asia and make universal assumptions and generalizations of questionable value. As Chapter 3 explains, some quite distinctive ways of conceptualizing security issues have emerged in East Asia, and the region's unique history has left an enduring legacy that has given a particular shape to its evolution. The friction between Japan and China, for example, cannot be understood without the relationship being placed in its unique historical and strategic context. But security, and the thinking that informs it, also spills over into political, and even economic, issues. Consequently, it is one of the central claims and themes of this book that understanding East Asia at either the level of the individual nation, or as a potential regional actor, involves looking at not only conventional political and economic factors but also at the overall geopolitical context in which they have emerged.

The basis of this claim becomes clearer in Chapters 4 and 5. Chapter 4 looks at East Asian politics, although it is repeatedly stressed in this chapter, and those that follow, that political and economic processes are deeply integrated and ultimately inseparable everywhere, but especially in East Asia. Nevertheless, it is useful to highlight some of the formal distinctions between regimes that are democracies, such as Japan; versions of democracies, such as Malaysia; or not democracies at all, such as China. This is important not just at the national level, but also because it has implications for possible regional collaboration. Plainly, states that are radically different in terms of their internal structures, social embeddedness and basic operational styles are likely to find it much more difficult to cooperate regionally than, say, the democracies of Western Europe. The possibility of developing a collective identity is also more remote as a consequence. The final part of Chapter 4 examines the 'Asian values' debate as this is the nearest approximation to some sort of distinctive regional discourse yet developed.

Another distinctive East Asian development, if not invention, has been the 'developmental state' (see Chapter 5). Although some would argue that it is no longer effective or relevant, it remains one of the most distinctive features of East Asia's remarkable economic expansion, and its legacy endures in much of the region. Indeed, some would argue – and let me say at the outset that I am one of them – that under certain conditions effective state capacity and intervention in economic processes may still be an important part of stimulating the economic development process, especially for countries attempting this process relatively late in the day. But whatever the merits of this argument, the fact remains that the developmental state has had a dramatic impact on the region, and the distinctive relationships between government and business it encouraged have not disappeared.

The legacy – or even the continuity – of the developmental state becomes especially significant in the context of East Asia's integration into the wider international economy. It is clear that different states have responded to the complex array of challenges and opportunities associated with globalization in different ways. Much has depended on the sort of strategies individual states have pursued and the capacity of various governments to implement them. Much has depended, too, on the timing of the integration process, the scale and structure of the economy involved, and their potential attractiveness to international investors. Chapter 6 spells out the different ways this has occurred, both within the region itself, and between the region and the rest of the world. In the course of this discussion it becomes clear just how dependent East Asian economies have been on access to global markets and – in many cases – access to foreign capital. It is also clear that the rise of, first, Japan and, more recently, China is giving East Asia an economic weight and internal dynamic that is making it less dependent on, and a more powerful force in, the rest of the world.

Whether East Asia has the capacity to coordinate and increase this economic weight through a coherent, regionally-based political institution is the subject matter of Chapter 7. Here, the evidence is rather mixed. On the one hand, East Asia already has a history of institutional development, but it is patchy and generally disappointing in terms of its outcomes. On the other hand, the fact that *any* institutional development and collaboration has occurred in a region with all East Asia's apparent problems and differences is no small achievement in itself. It should also be noted that East Asia has generally been relatively peaceful since the end of the Vietnam War over three decades ago. Despite all the alarmist talk about regional 'flashpoints' and Southeast Asia's position as the 'second front in the war on terror', East Asia does not appear to be about to descend into the chaos that is so frequently predicted. On the contrary, East Asia's existing institutions, including the Association of Southeast Asian Nations (ASEAN) and the ASEAN Regional Forum (ARF), must be given some of the credit for this, and their example should be a source of encouragement for advocates of further regional integration.

The final chapter considers – somewhat ambitiously, perhaps – East Asian futures. In this regard, much will depend on the sort of political processes outlined in the preceding chapter. Much will also depend on the region's overall ability to keep the developmental process going in the (generally) highly successful way it has for decades. Nowhere is more important in this regard than China. Without continuing rapid development, the legitimacy of the ruling elite in China may be fatally undermined and the country plunged into political chaos. Unfortunately, and despite the formidable economic development that has already occurred, the success of this project may hinge on more than simply technocratic competence or continuing foreign investment. The most formidable and perhaps insurmountable hurdle to endless economic growth may be the natural environment and its capacity to sustain massive economic and demographic expansion. The final chapter considers East Asia's environmental constraints, and speculates about the possibility of addressing them.

In the best of all possible worlds, the East Asian success story continues, and East Asians find ways – possibly through effective regional institutions – of dealing with their common development, environmental and security problems. The alternative – nationally-based struggles over diminishing resources in which material power is paramount, if not decisive – is likely to destroy much more than the region's enviable and generally deserved record for unexpected and remarkable, although not quite miraculous, development.

Chapter 1

Conceptualizing East Asia: From the Local to the Global

Identifying 'East Asia' is more difficult than it might seem at first glance. One of the problems inherent in describing any region is deciding where to draw the boundaries: who's in and who's out? Which countries can be considered 'authentic', unambiguous members of a region, and which should be excluded? Upon what basis should inclusion or exclusion occur? Are there differences in the way political and economic regionalism occur? Even more problematically, is it possible that regionally based 'security communities' might overturn some of the most widely held expectations about regional security and the possibilities for cooperation rather than conflict in East Asia as a consequence? This chapter begins the process of answering these questions by providing some conceptual tools for thinking about regions. It also suggests why it makes sense to consider East Asia as potentially constituting a region in the same way we think of Western Europe or Latin America.

The main purpose of this chapter is to consider the nature of regions generally and of the East Asian region in particular. In so doing, I shall highlight one of the central themes and questions that animates this entire book: what, if anything is different about East Asia? Are such differences diminishing in the face of seemingly irresistible global forces, or are they sufficiently robust and institutionalized to remain distinctive and different from much of the rest of the world? There are no simple answers to these questions and much depends on the country and the specific issue area we consider. As we shall see in this chapter and those that follow, however, despite the existence of powerful forces actively encouraging change and reform within the East Asian region, there remains much that is very different from comparative 'Western' experiences.[1]

East Asia contains some of the world's most important and distinctive political economies. There are signs that East Asia's undoubted economic and strategic weight is gradually being institutionalized in new regionally-based organizations that have the potential to alter the global distribution of power and influence. This is occurring as part of a complex adjustment on the part of states to increasingly global pressures and

1

influences. What is especially distinctive about this process is that it has a pronounced regional dimension. States have discovered the potential utility and benefits of cooperation with their more immediate neighbours. This chapter provides an overview of some of the key forces that are driving and mediating these processes, and a framework for capturing the dynamic nature of regional interactions, development and the construction of regions themselves. The key point to emphasize at the outset is that there is nothing 'natural' or inevitable about the course of regional development; it reflects specific national and regional histories, contingent constellations of power and interest, and the wider global environment of which they are a part.

Consequently, the first part of this chapter reviews some of the more illuminating ways that regional processes have been considered. Although there are some general principles involved in regionally-based phenomena, this chapter and the ones that follow also make it clear that we need to place each regional experience in a specific historical context to capture the particular political, economic and strategic circumstances that gave it a distinctive shape. The process of identifying what is specifically East Asian about the area that is of primary concern in this book is begun in the second part of this chapter. I introduce the main countries of the region and suggest why it makes more sense to think of them as being part of 'East Asia', rather than, say, the Asia-Pacific or any of the other possible ways of describing the countries of the area under consideration. The final part of the chapter considers regional processes in the context of the all-encompassing globalization phenomenon. In particular, I consider how states everywhere are attempting to mediate between various levels of activity, and how we can understand their varying capacities to do so. The overall intention here is to provide a conceptual framework within which both the individual states of the region, and their emerging collaborative activities, can be understood.

Recognizing regions

One of the most widely noted features of the contemporary international system is the persistence and importance of regionally-based modes of cooperation and organization. The European Union (EU) is by far the most important exemplar of regional integration and cooperation, and its development is often taken as a benchmark against which other regions are measured. While East Asia is nothing like as coherent or established as the EU, especially as far as political cooperation is concerned, nevertheless there are substantial grounds for considering it as a discrete region in much the same way as we think of Western Europe.

It is important to emphasize that the prominence of regions anywhere is somewhat surprising: we live in an era that is routinely characterized as 'global', so the persistence of regional variation, let alone the self-conscious pursuit and active creation of regional organizations and identity, is not what some of the most enthusiastic observers of globalization might have led us to expect.

Historically, interactions with immediate neighbours have always been both important and more likely as a consequence of simple geography. For much of human history, what Geoffrey Blainey has famously described as the 'tyranny of distance' has meant things could hardly have been otherwise: the sheer difficulty of interacting over long distances placed fundamental constraints on the nature of possible relationships. But the advent of more reliable forms of communication and transport has led some observers to claim that we now inhabit a deeply integrated world in which global, rather than national or regional processes will predominate, sweeping aside earlier forms of political and economic order (O'Brien 1992; Ohmae 1990). And yet, not only are states proving to be highly resilient and important forms of political organization in places such as East Asia, but they are increasingly exploring ways of cooperating on a regional rather than a global basis. How are we to explain this apparent paradox?

Interest in regions at both a policy-making and at a theoretical level has really gained momentum in the period following the Second World War, although it is not an exclusively post-war phenomenon. Chapter 2 illustrates how both Japan, and especially China, have attempted to assert an influence over the region for considerable periods. But it was the development of the EU in the post-war period that really galvanized scholarly interest in regionalism. It also caused policy-makers in other parts of the world to try to emulate its success. Although the demonstration effect of the EU has exerted a powerful influence on other parts of the world, practical interest in regional cooperation is not simply a product of the rational calculation of discrete 'national interests' and the possible benefits that flow from international cooperation. On the contrary, the formation of the EU in particular cannot be understood in isolation from the particular geopolitical circumstances and regional order that emerged in the aftermath of the Second World War. Not only was there an understandable desire to ensure that the Western European powers did not engage in the sort of internecine struggles that had devastated Europe, but the emerging Cold War confrontation with the Soviet Union also meant that the United States was intent on ensuring that Western Europe would be a successful capitalist bulwark against Soviet expansion (Beeson 2005b).

Strategic considerations and dynamics have been equally important factors in shaping regional cooperation in East Asia. They have also been crucial obstacles to regional integration, too: the East Asian region was divided by the ideological and strategic cleavages of the Cold War period, effectively precluding the possibility of regional cooperation between all the states of Northeast and Southeast Asia (Cumings 1997a). Consequently, the 'first wave' of theorizing about the emergence of coherent regions in the post-war period focused predominantly on the EU experience and was strikingly 'functionalist' in tone. The leading theorists of this time were people such as Ernst Haas (1964; 1968) and David Mitrany (1965) who saw European development as an essentially technocratic exercise, in which policy-makers cooperated to create new regionally-based institutions for mutual gain. There are some well-known problems with this sort of functionalist analysis, which have seen it lose influence as a way of explaining regional dynamics.[2] Functionalist explanations have always been preoccupied with explaining how regional processes work and the benefits that flow from their capacity to generate 'spillovers', but they were less good at explaining the creation of regional orders in the first place (Hurrell 1995).

Nevertheless, the neofunctionalist analysis drew attention to some-thing of a problem for conventional International Relations (IR) theory: if the world really was composed of discrete nation-states locked in a never-ending struggle for survival in an anarchical world order, then the sort of regionally-based cooperation that the EU embodied was difficult to explain. The EU has clearly generated mutual benefits and seemingly changed the underlying logic and practice of international relations in Western Europe as it institutionalized cooperative relations and made the prospect of conflict between the European powers increasingly remote (Wallace 1995). It is precisely these sorts of tangible benefits – benefits that are sharply at odds with the expectations of conventional IR theory – that have encouraged renewed interest in regional processes.

Louise Fawcett (1995) suggests that a number of key factors have underpinned the emergence of the 'new regionalism'. Although a renewed practical and theoretical interest in regionalism was evident in the 1980s, the end of the Cold War provided a crucial impetus for regional processes. As noted briefly above (and as we shall see in more detail in subsequent chapters), it was simply not possible for a broadly-based form of East Asian cooperation to take hold while the region was divided along ideological lines. The ending of the Cold War has also encouraged the decentralization of the international system, which Fawcett considers to be a second critical factor encouraging regional processes. Economic and even security relations are assuming a greater regional character as organizations such as the North Atlantic Treaty Organization (NATO) expand, and as institutions for regional economic cooperation such as the North American Free Trade Area (NAFTA) attempt to coordinate cooperative efforts at a regional level.

The success of the EU in particular provided a further spur to regional collaboration, Fawcett argues, as countries became concerned about the implications that flowed from 'fortress Europe' for their own economic welfare. In addition to NAFTA, we have seen the emergence of organizations such as Mercosur in Latin American, and the Asia-Pacific Economic Cooperation (APEC) forum, which includes parts of Latin America, Australasia and East Asia. For some areas of the world, regional cooperation offered a way of warding off the possible negative impacts of global processes and providing a degree of insulation for regional polities and economies. This is an argument that still has some relevance for contemporary East Asia: regional processes seem to offer a way of responding to the ubiquitous challenges thrown up by globalization (Oman 1994). To understand more clearly how the global–regional interaction occurs, it is helpful to consider how regional processes have come to be understood in the most recent wave of theorization.

Theories of regional cooperation and integration

One of the most widely employed distinctions made in the theoretical literature is between regionalism and regionalization (Breslin and Higgott 2000). Wyatt-Walter (1995: 77) suggests that a basic distinction needs to be made 'between economic regionalism as a *conscious policy* of states or sub-state regions to coordinate activities and arrangements in a greater region, and economic regionalisation as the *outcome* of such policies or of "natural" economic forces' (emphasis in original). In other words, regionalism implies a degree of intentionality as states and other actors engage in an essentially political process of collaboration. Regionalization, by contrast, is a less self-conscious and coherent process, which is primarily driven by the private sector. This is an especially important consideration in the context of East Asia because – in sharp contrast to the European experience – regional integration has thus far been driven primarily by the uncoordinated impact of corporate restructuring and investment in the region (Ravenhill 1995). Although there is no reason to suppose that the European experience is the only form that regional collaboration can take, or that the success of regional projects in other parts of the world should be judged solely by their capacity to replicate the structures and practices of the EU, it is possible to identify a number of features of regional processes that give some indication of their importance, and which help to set regionalism apart from the elementary forms of regionalization associated with the private sector activities and international economic restructuring.

Regional awareness and identity, Andrew Hurrell (1995) argues, are two of the potentially most important features of regional processes. If regions are to amount to anything more than fairly arbitrary geographical demarcations, then they necessarily have a discursive and ideational component that gives some sense of what it means to belong to the region, and what factors distinguish members from non-members. Formal institutional development at the regional level is a powerful marker of this process. Consequently, identity issues are important because 'all regions are socially constructed and hence politically contested' (Hurrell 1995: 334). Equally importantly, as Benedict Anderson (1983) famously pointed out, the creation of 'imagined communities' is challenging enough within national political spaces, especially for newly independent countries such as those of Southeast Asia, let alone at a regional level where a putative sense of identity may be far more tenuous and undermined by long-running local tensions. The failure of France to endorse the EU's constitutional changes and the continuing tensions caused by Turkey's desire for EU membership serve as powerful reminders of just how contentious and enduring questions of national and regional identity can be, even for the region with the longest history of successful cooperation. And yet, without some sense of regional identity, the prospects for the sort of close political cooperation and pooling of sovereignty that has been the hallmark of the EU look remote.

This sort of regional identity or common outlook on key issues is an important determinant of the success of regional projects generally, and of what Hurrell describes as 'regional cohesion'. There are, Hurrell (1995: 337) suggests, two aspects of regional cohesion: first, when the region plays a defining role in relations between regional states and the rest of the world, and second, when the region forms the basis for policy coordination within the region itself. Although the EU has not always proved capable of playing the sort of coherent and significant role that its strategic, political and especially economic weight might suggest it could, it is clearly greater than the sum of its parts (Ash 2004). Put differently, none of the members of the EU acting alone could hope to exercise the degree of influence in international affairs that the EU can – in theory, at least – when acting on behalf of its member states. It is precisely the sort of potential leverage that political collaboration offers that makes regionalism an attractive prospect.

However, the sort of de jure regionalism, or formally organized cooperation, which is so characteristic of the EU has proved more elusive elsewhere. East Asia has thus far been associated primarily with *de facto* regionalism, which is one way of thinking about the potential for regional cooperation that flows from what Hettne and Söderbaum (2002: 41) describe as the 'real region'. Of course, this begs the question of what the basis of the 'real region' might be. But as we shall see when we consider the respective fates of APEC and its vision of an all-encompassing, but ultimately unrealizable Asia-Pacific regionalism, and the more recent 'ASEAN+3' (ASEAN plus China, Japan and South Korea) pursuit of East Asian regionalism, the latter looks to have greater potential mainly because it represents a narrower, more innately coherent underlying reality. Before attempting to substantiate this claim in specific historical terms, it is useful to look more closely at the countries that potentially constitute the East Asian region.

East Asia: unity in diversity?

One of the most frequently noted features of East Asia, and one of the principal reasons that the prospects for EU-style regional cooperation generates such scepticism, is the sheer diversity of the countries of the region. Table 1.1 gives an indication of just how heterogeneous East Asia is. Not only does the region contain every major religion and form of government, but it is also distinguished by massive disparities in wealth distribution. Even if we put to one side the troubled history of the region for a moment, and concentrate solely on contemporary indicators of GDP and per capita incomes, it is plain that there are very significant differences in the underlying economic circumstances of the region's members. Compounding the differences in economic weight are the very different demographics of the region, ranging from China's gigantic population to the micro-states of Singapore and Brunei. Even within these figures, there are major differences in the circumstances confronting Japan with its rapidly ageing population and, say, Indonesia, which continues to experience rapid population growth.

Despite all this diversity, it is helpful to make a broad distinction between the countries of Northeast and Southeast Asia. As we shall see in more detail in subsequent chapters, Northeast Asia contains two major powers – China and Japan – which have exerted a long-term influence on both Northeast Asia in particular and East Asia more generally. In China's case this influence, primarily indirect and cultural, has stretched back over thousands of years. More recently, Japan's highly successful industrialization process not only demonstrated that Asian powers were capable of becoming major economic and strategic forces in international affairs, but it initiated a process of more generalized economic development in Northeast Asia as Taiwan and Korea followed in its wake (Cumings 1984). In Southeast Asia, by contrast, industrialization and economic modernization occurred significantly later and was delayed partly as a consequence of European colonization (a fate

Table 1.1 East Asia and the USA: comparative data

Country	Area (000 sq km)	Population (million)	GDP (US$bn)	GDP per capita (US$)	Government	Main religion
Burma	678	48.3	9.6	179	Military dictatorship	Buddhism
Brunei Darussalam	6	0.36	5.2	14,352	Constitutional monarchy	Islam
Cambodia	181	12.2	4.2	310	Constitutional monarchy	Buddhism
China	9,561	1,294	1,601	1,227	Communist	Atheist/Taoist
Hong Kong, China	1	7	164	23,592	SAR*	Multiple
Indonesia	1,904	217.5	222	1,003	Democracy	Islam
Japan	378	127.5	4,621.2	36,184	Democracy	Shinto
Korea, South	99	47.4	667.4	13,806	Democracy	Buddhist
Korea, North	120	22.9	30.8	1,400	Stalinist	Suppressed
Lao PDR	236	5.4	2	362	Communist	Buddhism
Malaysia	333	23	112.5	4,418	Semi-democratic	Islam
Philippines	300	78.6	84.2	1,019	Democracy	Christian
Singapore	1	4.2	103.6	23,999	Semi-democratic	Taoism
Taiwan	36	22.5	307.5	13,359	Democracy	Buddhism, Taoism, Confucianism
Thailand	513	64.3	165.7	2,556	Democracy	Buddhism
Vietnam	331	80.2	40.4	494	Communist	Buddhism
United States	9,373	288.5	11,750.4	39,991	Democracy	Christian

* Special Administrative Region.

Sources: For area and population: *The Economist: Pocket World in Figures: 2005 Edition*; *The APEC Region Trade and Investment 2004*. For GDP *The APEC Region Trade and Investment 2004*; *ASEAN Indicators*; *ASEAN Statistical Yearbook*; *World Bank Development Indicators*; *CIA World Factbook*.

that the countries of Northeast Asia largely escaped). This also explains differences in the extent and depth of the industrialization process in Southeast Asia (Yoshihara 1988). Chapter 5 explains how the superior 'state capacity' of Northeast Asian countries such as Japan enabled them to promote and direct the course of industrialization more effectively. While a number of Southeast Asian countries (such as Singapore and, to a lesser extent, Malaysia and Thailand) have also displayed an ability to guide and facilitate economic development, there is still a distinct difference in both the timing of the industrialization process and the sheer scale of the much larger economies of Northeast Asia, which makes the basic differentiation between Northeast and Southeast Asia meaningful. The recent 'rise of China' looks set to cement this historical divergence and reinforce the economic, political and strategic dominance of the north.

Consequently, East Asia appears to lack the sort of commonalities that have distinguished the EU in particular, and which are frequently thought to help account for the relative success of the European project. And yet, we need to treat the conventional wisdom with a degree of caution. The extent of European homogeneity is frequently overstated, and the degree of identification with, and enthusiasm for, the European project is not necessarily universal. Consequently, we may need to look for other factors to explain the success of the European project which may have more to do with the 'normal' calculation of state interests (Moravsik 1998), albeit in rather unique historical circumstances. But even if we accept that historical circumstances have played a crucial role in preparing the ground, at least, for the sort of sovereignty-pooling and political cooperation that distinguishes the EU, this merely begs the question of whether East Asia has similar preconditions. Richard Stubbs (2002) has argued that the rapid emergence of ASEAN+3 owes much to common historical experiences, particularly Japan's economic and military impact on the region, common cultural traits, the impact of the Cold War, and the distinctive nature of East Asia's business and political relations. All of these factors will be explored in more detail in subsequent chapters, but the point to emphasize at this stage is that there are grounds for possible cooperation and identification that may transcend the supposedly implacable obstacles to collaboration that many take to distinguish the region (Hund 2003).

This possibility is particularly clear in the case of ASEAN which, for all its shortcomings, remains the most enduring multi-lateral institution of its kind in the developing world. More importantly, perhaps, it has arguably changed the nature of inter-state relations between Southeast Asia's highly disparate states in ways that are surprising and suggestive of possibilities for the larger East Asian regional project. As will be argued in more detail in subsequent chapters, ASEAN owes much of its importance and success to a unique set of geopolitical circumstances which provided both the impetus for inter-state cooperation between the ASEAN states, and which help to account for the organization's surprisingly high profile as a consequence. While the sceptics are right to point to ASEAN's limited record of achievement, the very existence of ASEAN has socialized its members into patterns of behaviour that are unlikely to have come about otherwise. As Charrier (2001) points out, the sheer repetition of particular models of behaviour and the routine interaction of states on the basis of their membership of a particular regional grouping has helped to further constitute and give substance to the idea of the region as a distinct, meaningful entity.

This is an especially important consideration when we remember that the idea of Southeast Asia as a distinct region is something of a historical accident and a reminder of the profound impact that external factors have had on Southeast Asia's development in particular. During the Second World War when the British fought the Japanese in Burma and elsewhere, they began to refer to 'Southeast Asia' to describe the countries of what we now think of as the ASEAN grouping (Emmerson 1984). The emergence of 'Southeast Asia' highlights a more general point about the contingent nature of regional definition on the one hand, and the process by which regions are defined on the other. Edward Said (1985) has done more than most to highlight how particular discourses effectively create the idea of an 'other' that effectively constitutes and reinforces identity – even ones with negative connotations. As far as contemporary East Asia is concerned, the significance of this insight is that it highlights what might be described as the self-reflexive element of regionalism and its inevitable connection to larger global processes: the idea of 'Asia' was necessarily an outgrowth of the interaction between an increasingly self-conscious European continent and the land mass to its east. As Korhonen (1997: 349) points out, this interaction had its greatest impact with the outward expansion of the European powers in the nineteenth century, a process that culminated in the displacement of a Sino-centric regional order by European perceptions of geographical space and political practice. Thus, regional definitions are somewhat arbitrary, mutually constitutive and politically contested, and reflect a particular distribution of power and influence in the international system. This is why the self-conscious pursuit and creation of regional institutions is such a defining part of regional orders.

Theories of regional definition

The possibility that regional definition reflects something other than simple geography can be seen in the attempts to use the idea of the

'Pacific Age' (or, more recently, the 'Asia-Pacific') as a way of self-consciously constructing an idea of regional identity that might be used to encourage particular economic or political outcomes. The idea of a Pacific Age has waxed and waned, and is a measure of American enthusiasm for engagement with Asia (Korhonen 1996) about which I shall say more in the next chapter. The more recent invocation of the 'Asia-Pacific' region was intended to promote a vision of mutually-beneficial cooperation and economic prosperity that glossed over many underlying tensions and contradictions (Beeson 2006b), not the least of which was the fact that much of East Asia was not capitalist. Even those countries that were ideologically aligned with the United States were not necessarily enamoured of the sort of liberal, market-oriented capitalism that it promoted (Woodside 1993). The all-encompassing Asia-Pacific idea has proved unable to sustain the hopes of its advocates, especially as a consequence of the Asian financial crisis of the late 1990s. As I explain in more detail in Chapter 7, the tensions and contradictions contained within the Asia-Pacific, combined with its amorphous nature, have led to a renewed interest in the more narrowly defined East Asian region.

However, even if the notion of an East Asian region has more potential resonance amongst Asian policy-makers than the Asia-Pacific idea, there are still a number of major benchmarks that need to be achieved if East Asia is to achieve what Björn Hettne describes as 'regioness' (1999). Hettne suggests that a number of qualities are needed for a region to be an effective actor and meaningful entity. In addition to basic geographical barriers and ecological characteristics, regions should contain a social system that transcends the local and which effectively constitutes a regional security community. Although some observers consider that such a community already exists in the Southeast Asian part of the region (Acharya 2001), as Chapter 3 indicates, the creation of an authentic security community at an East Asian level continues to present a formidable challenge. There are well-known internal obstacles to the development of close security ties in the region, and the continuing importance of the USA and its bilateral ties with a number of key East Asian powers such as Japan means that there are potentially insurmountable structural constraints to this aspect of regioness.

At the level of organized cooperation in the fields of cultural, political, economic and military affairs – the third of Hettne's measures of regioness – the signs are more hopeful. Not only is the basis for security cooperation institutionalized in the form of the ARF but, as Chapter 3 illustrates, there have been concerted efforts to encourage deeper economic integration at the regional level through cooperative political efforts. While it is important not to overstate this, or to exaggerate the role that governments (as opposed to the private sector) have played, sufficient progress has been made to at least give a veneer of regioness to political and economic integration. At the level of 'culture' the picture is less clear, as will be explained in Chapter 4. Certainly there are a number of commonalities, particularly Confucianism and a predilection for authoritarian government, but the attempted cultivation of 'Asian values' across much of the region during the mid-1990s was brought to a shuddering halt by the Asian economic crisis.

Consequently, the picture regarding common values – Hettne's fourth criterion of regioness – is consequently mixed and evolving. On the one hand, there are some common views about forms of political and economic organization, as well as sensitivities about Western intrusion. On the other hand, however, these views are being diluted by global processes and the expansion of civil society. And yet, despite long-established traditions of democratic rule in places such as Japan and the remarkable process of democratization that has occurred in Indonesia, much of the region remains undemocratic and civil society remains underdeveloped (see Chapter 4). Thus, there is even less potential for the rise of the sort of *transnational* civil society that Hettne takes to be a measure of substantive regional integration and consolidation (see Beeson 2001a). Nevertheless, Hettne's final suggested measure of regioness is the capacity of the region to act as a subject with a distinct identity, legitimacy and structure for decision-making. Here the signs are rather more promising, although there are limits to the development of cooperative decision-making processes, which is a legacy of the jealously guarded nature of national sovereignty across much of the region and the reluctance to pool sovereignty in the way the EU has.

Despite the fact that, by the measures of Hettne's criteria of regioness, East Asia looks to be nowhere near as developed as the EU, it still makes more sense to consider the countries of East Asia as members of a putative political and economic grouping, rather than simply as individual countries that happen to inhabit the same part of the planet. Even in the seemingly least promising area of regional interaction – security cooperation – it is important to remember that threats travel most directly over short distances and neighbours have little choice other than to attempt to accommodate each other if they wish to avoid conflict (Buzan and Waever 2003). Interpreting the rise of China is, as we shall see, critical in this context: whether China's intentions are peaceful, cooperative or aggressive will prove the central determinant of intra- and inter-regional relations during the twenty-first century. Although it is clearly impossible to predict how China's rapid rise to prominence will influence its strategic thinking and behaviour in the longer term, what we can say is that it will happen in a profoundly reconfigured geopolitical environment and regional order: the end of the Cold War means that regional cooperation within and across East Asia is no longer foreclosed by the divisions of the Cold War. As a consequence, some observers consider that the new post-Cold War environment may actually encourage a reversion to the sort of Sino-centric regional order that prevailed for hundreds, if not thousands of years before European engagement (Kang 2003a). The question is whether this underlying order and potential can be translated into an institutionalized regional framework. These issues are explored in more detail in the next two chapters.

Interest in East Asian regionalism, as I explain in Chapter 7, was given added momentum as a consequence of the East Asian crisis. A key motivating factor here was the possibility that regionally-based institutions might have the potential to provide collective regional responses to external challenges. The crisis highlighted the region's vulnerability to external economic and political forces, and many in the region wanted to develop indigenous mechanisms to manage future crises and make East Asia more autonomous (Bowles 2002; Pempel 2005b). It remains to be seen how successful such initiatives will be, but the desire to act in this manner and resist some of the unwanted impacts of 'globalization' highlights a theoretical and practical issue that will recur throughout this book: are the countries of East Asia inevitably 'converging' on Western styles of economic organization and political representation, or are the differences that distinguish the region sufficiently embedded and institutionalized that they will continue to diverge from the idealized free-market, liberal democratic model?

It was precisely such an expectation about the inevitability of convergence that informed Francis Fukuyama's (1992) celebrated predictions about the 'end of history'. Although Fukuyama's predictions look premature and Panglossian, he raised an extremely important question: is there something about the nature of contemporary global integration that makes certain types of public policy and economic organization – perhaps even strategic relations – more sustainable and feasible than others, simply because of their compatibility with transnational processes? Even more provocatively, is there something about America's political and economic practices that makes it – and, by implication, American hegemony – uniquely congruent with contemporary globalization? (see Ikenberry 2001b). These questions are taken up in the final chapter, but at this stage it is useful to pose the flip-side of Fukuyama's question: is there something about the nature of contemporary *regional* processes that continues to make them attractive to policy-makers? To put it even more starkly, is there something about the nature of socially and institutionally embedded political economies that gives regional, as opposed to global, dynamics a particular immediacy and power? The rest of this introductory chapter explores these questions and highlights some of the theoretical and practical issues that may help to answer them.

Regional divergence or global convergence?

One of the most fundamental problems in thinking about international relations of any sort revolves around which level of analysis to employ (see Buzan 1995). Interestingly enough, the regional level that is the principal focus of attention in this book is generally neglected in most analyses of international relations. Indeed, traditional IR theory tends to focus on the state and its place in a system of states, with little attention being given to either regional forces or the array of new actors that are subsumed under the rubric of globalization. But even the regional–global bifurcation is inadequate and somewhat misleading: not only are the distinctions between the global and the regional not as precise as this sort of terminology might imply, but this schema threatens to completely neglect the national level, which is of particular importance in East Asia where the nation-building project is often still in train, and where attempts continue to be made to reinforce rather than give up sovereignty to regional or global forces (Beeson 2003e). To help clarify what is an extremely complex set of interactions and processes, it is useful to add to the discussion of regional processes by unpacking the broadly conceived global and national categories, so that we can better understand how they influence each other, and how they may ultimately shape the development of East Asia as a distinct entity.

The global level

One of the problems with making sense of the idea of globalization is that the associated literature has become so vast and draws on such a diverse range of perspectives. Sociologists, geographers, political scientists and economists have all employed the term to highlight different aspects of transnational processes.[3] Given the many different uses to which the term has been put, there are grounds for questioning whether it retains much theoretical or descriptive utility. Despite the rather indiscriminate way the term is often used, I suggest that it serves a double purpose: first, if globalization is carefully defined, it serves as a useful shorthand for a range of transnational processes that have become more prominent over the last 50 years or so and which are characteristic of the contemporary era. Second, globalization serves as a convenient counterpoint to regionalization, and allows us to make better sense of the way these levels interact.

As with regional processes, globalization has distinctive economic and political aspects. Although these features are often treated separately, they are inextricably intertwined. While there is a good deal of debate about when globalization might have begun (Frank and Gills 1993), and how extensive it may actually be (Hirst and Thompson 1996), there is little doubt that the institutional order created under the auspices of American hegemony, which we now think of as the Bretton Woods regime, was absolutely pivotal in creating the sort of 'open', liberal economic order that encouraged economic integration across state borders (Eichengreeen and Kenen 1994; Latham 1997). Not only did the Bretton Woods institutions – the International Monetary Fund, the World Bank (IMF), and the General Agreement on Tariffs and Trade (GATT)[4] – encourage the development of international money markets, massive growth in trade and foreign investment, and the restructuring of corporate activities across national borders, but they were also instrumental in promoting a particular normatively-based policy agenda which came to be associated with neoliberalism (Pieterse 2004).

Historically much of East Asia has proven remarkably unenthusiastic about the neoliberal model and the agenda of liberalization, deregulation and minimal government with which it is associated (Beeson and Islam 2005). This has caused a good deal of friction between the USA and a number of East Asian countries over recent decades, and highlights the inescapably political and contested nature of globalization. Having said that, however, there is an underlying process of economic restructuring that interacts with political and regulatory initiatives, and which helps to explain the particular shape of the international order (Ruigrok and van Tulder 1995). The next chapter illustrates how such processes have unfolded over the longer term and how entire regions (such as East Asia) have been drawn into an expanding web of capitalist production structures that have profoundly affected existing patterns of social relations across much of the world. In assessing the extent of global influences and the degree of change that has occurred as a consequence, much depends on the time frame employed (Beeson 2002a). As Chapter 2 demonstrates, there has been a fundamental transformation in the political structures and social relations of East Asia as a direct consequence of its interaction with 'the West' and its associated economic and political practices.

In debates about convergence and divergence, therefore, this process of long-run change may prove to be the most significant: the fact that formerly feudal or socialist countries adopt *any* form of capitalism is ultimately the critical point, not whether they are interventionist or *laissez faire* in their public policy (see Strange 1997). However, the principal focus of this book is on the recent past, and here the evidence about the impact of globalization – especially in the narrowly defined economic sphere – is more ambiguous. Although the consolidation and increasingly sophisticated organization of multi-national corporations has been one of the most important developments of the post-war period (Dicken 1998),[5] its impact has been uneven and contradictory for a number of reasons. First, there is no such thing as a typical multi-national corporation (MNC). Different industrial sectors present different organizational challenges and company strategies differ as a consequence (Dunning 1988). Moreover, it is possible to disaggregate the entire production process and locate different aspects of the 'commodity chain' in different countries dependent on their value and the locational advantages of specific areas. Consequently, the underlying logic of production is vastly different in the textile, automotive or resource industries, let alone in some of the evermore sophisticated service sector industries that are an increasingly large part of the global economy (Gerrefi 1995). The implication of this, of course, is that some regions of the world will be integrated into the global economy differently because they offer particular attractions for potentially mobile MNCs.

However, a striking, counter-intuitive characteristic of MNCs is that they continue to display a surprising degree of national identity. For all the talk about the supposedly footloose nature of international business, the irresistible competitive pressures associated with globalization, and the need for firms to adopt 'international best practice', the reality is that corporate organization across the world continues to display distinctive local features that distinguish one part of the global economy from another (Doremus *et al.* 1999). Corporate structures in East Asia, especially Japan and Korea, continue to display noteworthy local characteristics, making any notion of rapid convergence unlikely, as I explain in subsequent chapters. Similarly, there is an array of distinctive business practices and social relationships associated with 'Chinese capitalism' that have attracted widespread attention (Redding 2002). Although these distinctive forms of business organization are coming under formidable competitive pressures (Yeung 2000b), especially as a consequence of the Asian financial crisis, they remain sufficiently entrenched and institutionally distinctive to make their rapid disappearance or replacement by Western-style corporate organization unlikely (Whitley 1999).

China also illustrates another feature of globalization that needs highlighting: because different countries offer MNCs different opportunities, they will attract different types and amounts of investment as a consequence (Dunning 2000). Chapter 6 demonstrates how China has absorbed the lion's share of foreign direct investment (FDI) in East Asia since it has opened up its domestic economy. Japan, by contrast, chose not to encourage large amounts of foreign investment during its own (earlier) development process. The point to emphasize here, therefore, is that the attractiveness of different countries as potential investment locations is not solely a function of their 'natural' endowments, such as cheap labour or natural resources, but will also be influenced by specific national regulatory environments and policies. Crucially, the experience of the EU and recent policy initiatives in East Asia suggest that such attractions may be aggregated at a regional level.

The question here is whether there is an inevitability about the sort of policy frameworks MNCs will favour and which governments will feel obliged to provide as a consequence, or whether individual countries have the capacity and autonomy to create distinctive responses to global pressures. More pertinently for our purposes, can regional agreements provide a basis for dealing with external economic actors? In this regard, it is important to emphasize just how uneven FDI flows are. Not only are the vast majority of major MNCs located in the rich, industrialized economies, but flows of FDI are concentrated there, too (Sutcliffe and Glyn 1999; UNCTAD 2005). The so-called 'Triad' of Western Europe, Northeast Asia and the United States dominates global trade, production and investment, leaving much of the developing world out of the economic loop.[6]

Much the same can be said about the other feature of economic globalization that has developed rapidly since the 1970s and transformation of the original Bretton Woods regime: cross-border flows of mobile capital. Following the US's unilateral political decision to abandon the system of managed exchange rates, other countries had little option other than to follow suit (Helleiner 1994). Significantly, there was a rapid expansion in the scale and scope of international financial markets, and an explosive growth in the level of international capital flows as a (largely unanticipated) consequence of the accompanying regulatory initiatives. Importantly, these new capital flows were unlike FDI: they were much more fluid and able to move rapidly in and out of national jurisdictions. While international capital flows can take a number of forms – foreign direct investment, international bank lending, bond and equity purchases, foreign currency transactions, new derivatives and swaps instruments, or portfolio investments – the key point to emphasize about all of these types of capital is that they have expanded at a remarkable rate. The international banking sector as a percentage of world output grew from a negligible 1.2 per cent in 1964 to 37 per cent in 1991. Foreign exchange markets have grown even more spectacularly, achieving a turnover of around US$1.5 trillion per day by the beginning of the twenty-first century (Held *et al.* 1999: 189–235).

The remarkable rise of financial capital has eroded some of the key relationships associated with the developmental state and precipitated a major crisis in East Asia; a crisis that was instrumental in undermining the stability of individual economies and the status of the region's so-called 'miracle' economies more generally.[7] It is testimony to the pervasive influence of international financial institutions (IFIs) and the neoliberal ideas they have championed that governments across the world have followed the advice of organizations such as the IMF and opened their capital accounts,[8] permitting the unregulated flow of mobile capital in and out of their economies (Cammack 2003). This is especially remarkable given that there is continuing debate about the merits of such policies, especially for smaller economies which may find themselves rapidly destabilized by adverse market sentiment (Stiglitz 2002; Strange 1998). As I explain in Chapter 6, such potential was tragically realized in the financial crisis that affected much of Southeast Asia in particular.

The general point to make at this stage is that, despite a series of financial crises that have affected much of the developing world, there has been a long-run change in the dominant international policy paradigm, broadly in line with the so-called 'Washington consensus' of deregulation, liberalization, privatization and minimal government (see Williamson 1994). Although many of East Asia's political and economic elites have evinced little enthusiasm for this model in the past, it continues to make inroads and is helping to bring about a long-run transformation in the conduct of economic policy across the region. It is also affecting the relative strength of pro- and anti-liberalization forces within individual countries as a result (Ravenhill 2006). The way such struggles between competing perspectives and interest groups resolve themselves within national contexts will undoubtedly influence the course of and rationale for regional integration (Jayasuriya 2003). The significance of globalization in this context is that it dramatically highlights differences within national economies between domestically- and internationally-oriented economic actors, raising difficult questions about the nature of public policy as a consequence. Indeed, some commentators have questioned whether it any longer makes sense to talk about a discrete 'national economy' at all in an era of cross-border production strategies and capital flows (Bryan 1995; Reich 1991).

In such circumstances, when there is no longer a necessary correlation between national economic and political identities (Held 1995), and where the effectiveness of government appears to be undermined by forces associated with globalization (Korbin 2002), it is understandable that governments should look to regional cooperation as one way of reclaiming authority and competence. In this regard, the importance of the EU exemplar cannot be underestimated, as it has overturned conventional expectations about the behaviour of unitary states and pioneered new forms of transnational governance in the process (Caporaso 1996).

It is significant that in the EU regional cooperation has been primarily focused on, and designed to facilitate, regionalization: the creation of a single market within the protected borders of the EU was a deliberate strategy designed to increase economic integration within the EU, boost local industry and make the EU as a whole a more attractive investment location (Hall 1999). Regional cooperation, in this case led by states, has succeeded in making Western Europe one of the most peaceful and prosperous parts of the planet, and helps to explain the potential attraction of regional cooperation in other parts of the world. The question is: can East Asia achieve something similar? Before attempting to answer that question, we need to look more closely at the ability of states themselves to develop and enact policies that might produce EU-style outcomes. In other words, we need to consider the nation-state level of analysis before we can assess the possibilities for regional cooperation.

The nation-state in a global context

A focus on the national or individual state level is especially important in the context of East Asia. As I shall explain in more detail in Chapter 5, the state has been at the centre of the highly successful developmental project that has attracted so much interest in the region. Indeed, the East Asian experience has been a major reason for 'bringing the state back in' to the study of comparative political and economic development (see Evans *et al.* 1985; Weiss and Hobson 1995). The historical role of the state is one of the common qualities that serves to distinguish the region, and which potentially offers, if not some form of common identity, then at least some basis for a common approach to public policy that might ultimately be transposed to the regional level. Consequently, it is helpful to have some conceptual tools with which to make sense of the role of the state generally and of its particular place in East Asian development in particular.

In the context of potential regional collaboration, there are major differences between the EU and East Asia – especially in the quantity and quality of their respective institutional infrastructures (Beeson 2001a; Beeson and Jayasuriya 1998) – which raise questions about the ability of East Asia to replicate the European experience. Such differential capacities are significant because one of the most widely noted political aspects of the globalization process has been the emergence of what some observers have described as global civil society (Lipschutz 1992). Yet, it is clear that there are significant, historically-determined differences in the extent of domestic civil society in Europe and Asia, the nature of the social formations within which states are embedded, and constraints on the sort of political outcomes that are possible as a consequence. As

Chapter 4 makes clear, the relatively limited experience of democratic rule, the influence of authoritarianism, and the continuing importance of the state as the central arbiter of political outcomes means that the influence of civil society at either the domestic or international level is relatively limited in East Asia. This has significant implications for the development of a sense of regional identity and the depth of regioness as a consequence.

The conventional wisdom in much of the globalization literature suggests that we are witnessing a profound reconfiguration of political organization which is fundamentally undermining the autonomy of the state (Ohmae 1996; Strange 1996). In this reading, the ability of the state to act independently is undermined both as a consequence of global economic processes it is increasingly unable to control, and because of a transfer of power and regulatory responsibility to a new array of actors on the global stage (Boli and Thomas 1999; Mathews 1997). If this analysis is correct, it would have especially important ramifications for the role, and even the legitimacy, of East Asian states that have been at the centre of national development projects. Certainly, there is little doubt that states generally have voluntarily ceded authority to the private sector in many key areas of economic regulatory activity (Braithwaite and Drahos 2000). It is also clear that national governments are subject to the judgement of non-state authorities such as ratings agencies in a way that they have not been before, potentially constraining their policy autonomy as a consequence (Sinclair 2005). But it is far less certain that states have lost their ability to act effectively, either individually or collectively.

Analytically, there have been a number of important contributions to our understanding of why some states have been effective and others have not. One way of conceptualizing this variable degree of effectiveness is as 'state capacity', which essentially means a government's ability to formulate and implement policy successfully (Polidano 2000). There are a number of critical factors influencing this apparently simple requirement. Peter Evans (1995) famously argued that unless states – or, more specifically, bureaucratic elites acting in the 'national interest' – enjoyed a measure of 'embedded autonomy', then there was a danger that they would either be ineffective, or they would simply act in the interests of whichever powerful domestic interest managed to capture them. The trick, then, according to Evans, was to be sufficiently embedded in society so that the plans and policies of government could be successfully implemented, but not so close to powerful vested interests that they lost their independence or became corrupted as a consequence. This is an especially relevant consideration in the case of East Asia as there is a major debate about just how independent and non-corrupt state elites across the region actually are.

Other writers have also drawn attention to the importance of state–society relations, suggesting that states must have the ability to reach down into the society within which they are embedded in order to extract the resources necessary to underpin development (Mann 1993). Joel Migdal (1988; 1994) has provided an especially useful series of analyses of state development and strength in the 'Third World'[9] that have particular relevance for an East Asian region that contains both 'strong' and 'weak' states, and different levels of economic development as a consequence. State strength is essentially a synonym for state capacity, but what is distinctive about Migdal's analysis is the link he makes between a lack of state capacity and the specific challenges of state-building and economic development in the Third World. Too often the analysis of political organization and economic management is focused on the developed world, and these circumstances have only limited relevance to East Asia as a whole. If what Migdal calls 'social control' is unrealized, and if political authority is contested and considered illegitimate, he suggests the chances for the development of effective state capacity or strength are remote. It is increasingly widely recognized that without social stability and functioning institutions, the prospects for development remain dim (Fukuyama 2004). What is significant about Migdal's analysis in this context is that he highlights the dynamic nature of the state–society interaction and their mutually constitutive effect:

> As the state organization comes into contact with various social groups, it clashes with and accommodates to different moral orders. These engagements, which occur at numerous junctures, change the social bases and the aims of the state. The state is not a fixed ideological entity. Rather it embodies an ongoing dynamic, a changing set of goals, as it engages other social groups . . . The formulation of policy is as much a product of this dynamic as it is a simple outcome of the goals of top state leaders or a straightforward legislative process. (Migdal 1994: 12)

What is distinctive and different about such processes in the contemporary era, of course, is that they occur within an increasingly influential and constraining international context. Although the state may be a more dynamic, politically-contested space than many conventional analyses suggest, and while domestic competition may continue to be a central determinant of national policy, such contests occur in a wider global environment. Understanding the relationship between individual states, their national policy-making capacities, and regional or global processes is therefore vital.

It is clear that states remain crucial parts of the contemporary international system. Without the regulatory and legal frameworks that states provide, the complex patterns of social interaction associated with capitalism simply could not survive (Heilbroner 1985). There is nothing natural or inevitable about the existence of market-mediated social relationships and modes of economic organization, as Karl Polanyi's (1957) brilliant and influential analysis of British economic and social development reminds us: even in supposedly *laissez-faire* Britain, capitalist social relations were not the spontaneous response of individuals to the hidden hand of the market, but had to be coercively imposed through state auspices. Similarly, one of the most fundamental changes in East Asia – a transformation that is still under way today – has been the incorporation of the region into an increasingly pervasive and global capitalist economy; it has completely overturned pre-existing patterns of social relations, economic organization and political authority in the process. Indeed, it is important to remember that the Westphalian state[10] that is such a central and taken-for-granted part of the international system, and which is generally charged with managing the adjustment process, was itself actually introduced to East Asia as part of the expansion of European political and economic power (a process that is described in more detail in the next chapter).

At this stage, it is useful to make a distinction between the state as part of a system of states and the state responding to global processes on the basis of more particularistic national strategies. In the contemporary global era, there is a functional requirement for the provision of various collective goods that transcend national borders. International exchange rate systems, for example, are critical parts of the international political economy that only states can ultimately underwrite, but which they can only provide by acting collaboratively (Cerny 1995). In other words, at one level the state remains fundamental, but only as a cooperative part of a system of states. As I explain in Chapter 7, it is the recognition by individual states in East Asia that mutual gains are not only possible through collaboration, but may actually be impossible to realize without it, that has spurred recent interest in regional cooperation. We might expect, therefore, that the response of individual states to ubiquitous global pressures might become increasingly similar, even if such responses have a regional dimension. Some of the most sophisticated analyses of global processes have, indeed, suggested that states are locked in a process of 'regulatory arbitrage' that leaves them very little room for manoeuvre (Cerny 1996). And yet, when we look at the responses of individual states to the challenges of globalization, we see continuing differences in terms of both capacity and in the strategies that they have self-consciously chosen in response to seemingly universal pressures

(Beeson 1999b; Berger and Dore 1996; Drezner 2001a; Hall and Soskice 2001).

There are two particularly useful general explanations of this apparent paradox, in which individual states seem to be assailed by competing centres of power and authority, and yet still able initiate policy. On the one hand, states – or some states, at least[11] – seem to have the ability to adapt to changing circumstances and adjust policy accordingly. Linda Weiss, for example, argues that globalization actually *requires* states to act proactively if economic development is to occur, and that states retain an 'enabling' capacity that allows states to develop new forms of economic management predicated on cooperation, coordination and social partnership (Weiss 2003: 308). Clearly not all states will have this sort of capacity, but even where the ideology of neoliberalism has made state 'intervention' unfashionable and controversial, the empirical record suggests that a more directive and 'hands-on' approach to economic management is still feasible. Moreover, it may not be punished by the controllers of mobile financial assets (Garrett 1998): not only do financial markets seem (for much of the time, at least!)[12] surprisingly relaxed about the specific style of economic management as long as it is predictable and stable, but the scale of domestic taxation is not necessarily a fatal fiscal flaw either. On the contrary, governmental tax shares across much of the industrialized world have actually risen (Hobson 2003).[13]

So, if one way of explaining the persistence of state effectiveness revolves around the strategies they employ and the way they are received by powerful external actors, the other is to consider the internal architecture of states themselves and their relationship with nationally demarcated societies. The fundamental dilemma confronting states today is the disjuncture between political and economic space: as a consequence of globalization, economic activity and political authority are no longer coterminous. What Ruggie (1993) calls the 'unbundling' of territoriality, in which the old relationship between nationally-demarcated political authority and economic space has broken down, to be replaced by a more complex, fluid set of relationships that transcend national borders, has transformed both the environment within which states operate and (to varying degrees) the state itself. The contemporary state occupies a 'crossroads position' in a complex network of actors, institutions and processes (Cerny 2005) as it attempts to mediate between 'domestic' and 'external' forces. In such circumstances some of IR's most foundational ideas about the nature of states and their capacities come under challenge, as does the capacity of individual states to respond to such challenges.

The tension between the old, state-centric conception of territorialization, and the new processes of deterritorialization that emerge as a consequence of economic globalization have been well highlighted by economic geographers (Agnew 1994; Brenner 1999). But if it has become clear that economic activity increasingly occurs in a space 'beyond' national borders, it is also apparent that political structures are being reconfigured as a consequence, too. As Reinicke (1998: 66) points out, globalization challenges the state's 'operational sovereignty', and forces it to develop new ways of adjusting to an array of global *and* local or national pressures that emerge as a consequence of the long-term restructuring of the international political economy. Kanishka Jayasuriya (1999; 2001) has explained how global pressures are encouraging a reconfiguration of the internal structures of the state, as various agencies and institutions – central banks are the quintessential example – assume greater independence and authority. Although this process has gone furthest in the EU, it is also apparent that policy networks and institutionalized relationships that cross national borders and integrate formerly discrete polities on a regional basis are also a central part of the processes of sovereignty-pooling that is such a distinctive part of the Western European experience (Wallace 1999). Although we should be careful not to assume Europe's past in Asia's future, or that there is either only one response to globalization or one road to regional integration, the EU experience illustrates some potentially universal issues that East Asians may have to confront if regionalism is to take hold there.

Conclusion

Despite the well-known heterogeneity that characterizes the countries of East Asia, there are a number of reasons for thinking that, when taken together, they constitute a distinct region. The story of East Asia's recent attempts to institutionalize and deepen intra-regional cooperation is told in detail in Chapter 7. This chapter has provided ways of making sense of that empirical evidence. One of the most important points that emerges from the theoretical literature is that regional processes have interconnected economic and political aspects that emerge in particular geopolitical circumstances. The strength of what we might call 'regionality' is largely dependent on how deeply political and economic processes are linked and coordinated, and how effectively coordination mechanisms are institutionalized. The EU has gone furthest in this process; it remains to be seen whether East Asians have either the desire or, equally importantly, the capacity to replicate European-style institutional structures.

It is possible, of course, that East Asian forms of regional integration will take a different form from those of the EU. Indeed, we should expect that this will be the case, given the very different geopolitical circumstances that prevailed in East Asia, the different ways and times at which regional actors were incorporated into emerging global processes, and the specific patterns of political and economic organization that emerged as a consequence. The 'thickness' of Europe's institutional infrastructure, especially at the non-state level, means that some forms of transnational coordination and cooperation are simply more feasible in Europe than they are in East Asia (Beeson 2001a). As subsequent chapters suggest, despite East Asia's association with authoritarianism, significant movement towards greater democratization is occurring across the region, and the extent and influence of civil society is expanding at both the domestic and (to a more limited extent) transnational level. But there are plainly limits to this process and the potential to replicate the EU experience, largely as a consequence of limited state capacities and concomitant concerns about state security, and the protection rather than the pooling of national sovereignty.

The East Asian experience consequently has important comparative significance for much of the non-Western European world. States everywhere find themselves subjected to an array of new pressures. Not only is their ability to develop and implement policy autonomously compromised, but expectations about what states ought to deliver for their citizens have generally grown, despite the neoliberal preoccupation with minimal government and reduced government spending. While it is clear that states are far from powerless, and that proactive responses to the challenge of globalization not only exist but help to determine the way in which different parts of the world are integrated into the global economy, one of the most striking paradoxes of this process is that states may need to sacrifice – or at least redefine – their sovereignty to do it. This has been the EU solution: collective regional action has generally proved an effective way of responding to global pressures and increasing the influence of Europe as a whole.

While it is important not to overstate the EU's subsequent international influence, or minimize the internal conflicts and coordination problems that continue to plague it, nevertheless it remains a remarkable exemplar of the benefits that accrue from successful regional collaboration. If nothing else, the EU has made the likelihood of war between its members almost unimaginable. Given that East Asia is routinely described as having some of the world's most combustible potential 'flashpoints', for this reason alone regional collaboration has important security implications in addition to the more obvious economic and political benefits. There are, however, some major, historically-entrenched obstacles to this rosy picture. To begin the process of assessing East Asia's particular national and regional dynamics, therefore, we need to place them in their specific historical context.

Chapter 2

The Weight of History

All states and societies are products of their particular historical circumstances. Even where countries or regions have been profoundly influenced by external forces, such forces are mediated by local institutions, actors and contingent factors that give a distinctive character to seemingly ubiquitous influences. The impact of contingent factors can be seen in the different responses to the impact of European imperialism in Latin America and East Asia, for example. Equally important and revealing, such forces can be seen in the very different impacts apparently similar influences had on countries within various regions. Japan and China not only responded very differently to the challenge of European economic and political expansion, but their subsequent historical development has been distinctive as a result. Consequently, if we want to understand the contemporary economic, political and strategic positions of the various countries of East Asia, and why there are important differences both between the developmental experiences of individual countries, and between Northeast and Southeast Asia, then we need to place recent developments in historical context.

In this chapter the key historical patterns and developments that underpin contemporary East Asian intra- and inter-regional relations will be outlined. Given the extent of the region's history, this is no easy task and the result is necessarily a broad brush sketch. China alone has been a distinct civilization for more than 3,000 years. While it is not possible to do justice to even China's history and its influence over what we now think of as East Asia in the course of one chapter, it is vital to have a sense of the legacy of Chinese hegemony and its place at the centre of a relatively stable East Asian order. Indeed, some observers think that the older, China-centric world order may be re-emerging and providing the basis for a more narrowly defined East Asian regionalism (Kang 2003a). Even if such analyses prove to be wide of the mark, the tensions between countries such as Japan and China, which may actually frustrate greater regional integration, cannot be understood without placing their bilateral relations in the context of some of the grimmer episodes of recent history. Likewise, the disparity in developmental outcomes that distinguishes Northeast and Southeast Asia cannot be explained unless we recognize the impact of colonial rule on countries such as Indonesia, Malaysia and the Philippines.

The central argument of this chapter is not just that history matters, but that it continues to shape contemporary relations within the region, and between the region and the rest of the world. The impact of contact with Europe is perhaps the most obvious and dramatic illustration of this possibility. China's position at the centre of an East Asian order was overturned by this process, inaugurating a 'century of shame' from which it is only just recovering. Similarly, Japan's post-war subordination to, and reliance on, the United States, and the impact this has had on its place in the world, cannot be understood without an appreciation of the historical context that has shaped Japan's recent foreign policies. The strategic implications of these developments will be taken up in the next chapter. The point to emphasize here is that historical factors have been crucial determinants of the course of economic, political and strategic developments within the region and help to account for the comparatively late development of regional processes in East Asia.

The first part of the chapter looks at the relative decline of China and the internal and external factors that brought it about. Following this, we will explore Japan's very different response to the challenge of European expansion, a story that has important comparative lessons and continuing contemporary relevance. While the sometimes violent relationship between China and Japan has been the most important bilateral interaction in the East Asian region, a historically-informed analysis also makes it clear just how influential outside forces have been – especially the hegemonic powers of the day. This observation is particularly apposite for the countries of Southeast Asia, which are examined in the final part of this chapter. Although it is not possible to do adequate justice to the complex and distinct histories of the countries of the region in a single chapter, some of the key historical influences that continue to shape the intra- and inter-regional relations of East Asia to this day will be identified.

The decline of Chinese hegemony

Lucian Pye (1990: 58) famously observed that China was 'a civilization pretending to be a nation'. While this may not be as true as it once was, it captures something important about the unique historical position of China in world, and especially regional, history. Although there is some doubt about just how far back Chinese civilization stretches, it can be traced to the Three Dynasties of Ancient China – the Xia, Shang and Zhou – which existed in the 2000 years before the birth of Christ. Many of the imperial and cultural institutions that came to be associated with dynastic rule in China were established in this period. Confucius (551–479 BC), for example, lived during the Zhou dynasty, developing a social and moral code that continues to exert an influence to this day, and which largely preceded the Ancient Greeks and the dawn of Western civilization. Despite developing the world's first great civilization, sophisticated social and cosmological perspectives, to say nothing of a series of remarkable technological innovations that would ultimately provide an important impetus to Western development (Hobson 2004), Chinese history is punctuated by often convulsive dynastic transformations and the threat of foreign conquest.

Although the principal focus of this chapter is on recent Asian history and the impact on East Asia of 'globalization' in the form of European economic and political expansion,[1] it is important to acknowledge briefly the legacy of this earlier period. During the Han dynasty (206 BC–220 AD), for example, not only was there an internal consolidation and expansion of Chinese rule and the establishment of 'imperial Confucianism' (Fairbank 1994), which incorporated the idea of the 'Mandate of Heaven' and cosmological harmony,[2] but such ideas were spreading to other parts of the region. Korea had begun to adopt Chinese writing and administrative practices by the fourth century AD, and Japan followed suit during the fifth and sixth centuries. Although this period marked the beginning of China's cultural hegemony over its neighbours, its own position was not assured. For all the disdain the Chinese have displayed for 'barbarians', it is no small irony that their history has been powerfully shaped by them.

The invasion of China in the late thirteenth century by the Mongols under Kublai Khan was the most traumatic example of external intervention. The major lasting impact on China of the Mongol interlude was to pave the way for the introverted Ming dynasty (1368–1644), which withdrew behind the Great Wall and isolated itself economically by closing land and sea connections with the West (Huang 1997). In the context of world historical change, it is difficult to overstate the significance of this period in helping to determine the relative fates of Europe and China. By 1400, Chinese ship-building and nautical expertise, as well as expanding commercial links, had made the country a major economic force in East Asia.[3] Existing trade patterns with the countries of what we now think of as Southeast Asia were consolidated. And yet concerns about renewed Mongol power, and the in-principle objections of Confucian trained scholar-officials[4] to commercial activities, helped to encourage a further turning inward and isolationism. Although there is some dispute about how complete this process was, the contrast with what was happening in Europe is striking and it is worth making a few comparative observations as they help to explain both the remarkable expansionary dynamism of Europe and the inevitability of its collision with East Asia. They also help explain the region's ill-preparedness when confronted with the European challenge.

China's ultimate inability to respond to European expansionism is all the more remarkable when we consider that China, Frank (1998) has persuasively argued, was at the *centre* rather than the periphery of world trade until at least the end of the eighteenth century. In Frank's view, China's isolationism is overstated and reflects in part the bias of the Eurocentric interpretation of world history that has occurred in parallel with European military and economic domination. According to Frank, it was only the discovery and exploitation of the Americas that really gave the hitherto backward Europeans an entrée to the emerging world economy. While this thesis is still controversial, it is clear that the massive flows of wealth – especially in the form of gold and silver – from both South America and Africa provided a crucial stimulative impact to European development and helped to establish Europe as a *capitalist* society (Blaut 1993).

While the transformation of European social relations that saw the overturning of feudalism and the emergence of a new forms of market-mediated societies was a complex process that spanned hundreds of years (see Wood 2002), it is important to highlight the contrast with China's much more rigid social order. Whereas much of Europe was experiencing profound upheaval in its domestic social relations, institutions of governance, political ideas and economic dynamics, China was comparatively more institutionally inert (Jones 1981). China's effective, but highly conservative structures of governance are widely considered to have been an obstacle to the sort of flexibility and adaptability that characterized the often convulsive social change that swept through Europe from the fifteenth to the nineteenth centuries. China, by contrast, was paralyzed by the 'ethnocentric complacency of Confucian officials and the imperviousness of Chinese culture to outside stimuli' (Hsü 1983: 106). For millennia, Chinese elites considered they had had nothing to learn from the barbarians outside their empire. When combined with an overburdened and cumbersome imperial decision-making process, it meant that by the time the Europeans had become increasingly forceful in their attempts to break into Asia, China's leadership under the final Qing dynasty (1644–1911) was 'stultified below and worn out at the top' (Fairbank, Reischauer and Craig 1965: 103).

Although market mechanisms existed within the Chinese empire, economic development remained stunted in comparison to Europe (McNeil 1982). Despite China's early lead in technological development and the spur this proved to the West (Hobson 2004), it was Europe's technological development that really accelerated its development and paved the way for its subsequent economic and military dominance (Pomeranz 2000). Crucially, China's failure to make the transition to capitalism was as much ideational as it was institutional. As Wong

(1997: 147) points out, 'Chinese rulers had no reason to imagine, let alone promote, the mercantilist policies invented by European rulers.' In other words, the competitive economic and inter-state dynamic that had underpinned both the rise of European economic *and* military power in a mutually reinforcing virtuous circle (Tilly 1990) was absent in China; China's comparative stability engendered complacency and a disdain of the sort of systematic, break-neck, inter-connected economic develop-ment that was the hallmark of Western Europe's increasingly region-wide developmental process. By contrast, East Asia would have to wait for the rise of industrialized Japan to work a similar miracle.

The end of empire

While the collapse of the Qing dynasty marked the end of the imperial system, it is worth remembering that for its first 150 years of existence the Manchu-led empire[5] experienced the greatest territorial expansion since the time of Mongol domination. Why was the subsequent collapse so rapid and inexorable? At one level, this was clearly a consequence of what David Abernathy calls European imperialism's 'triple assault' on domestic institutions of governance, on established patterns of economic organization, and on indigenous ideas and values that gave meaning to life. The combined effects and superior organizational capacities of European states' soldier-administrators, merchants and missionaries had a generally overwhelming impact on colonized countries. The net effect, Abernathy (2000: 9) argues, was the European powers' 'capacity to undermine the power and legitimacy of other expanding political systems'. Although there is still a good deal of debate about the underly-ing dynamics of imperialism,[6] there is less doubt about its impact: not only did the imperial era establish the preconditions for the most recent phase of globalization and the almost complete adoption of capitalism as a system of economic organization across the world, but it also led to the universal expansion of the inter-state system and the dominance of the nation-state as a consequence (Watson 1992).

However, even if we accept that the Europeans had developed more effective institutions with which to coordinate economic and military activities, and a technological edge with which to underwrite them, we should not jump to the conclusion either that Europe's domination of China was complete, or that it came about solely as a consequence of European, rather than Chinese, attributes. China was simply too big and difficult to conquer, and the impact of European ideas and commercial practices outside key elites is easy to overstate (especially in the Chinese hinterland). Moreover, not only did Chinese culture exert an important influence on Europe,[7] but a good deal of the feebleness of China's response to the European challenge was a consequence of internal degen-eration, rather than simple European superiority. In short, 'foreign aggression was made possible only by the weakening of dynastic leader-ship and efficiency' (Fairbank, Reischauer and Craig 1965: 81). The inflexible and overloaded nature of the imperial administrative system noted above, when combined with increased corruption, a stagnant economy and the relentless population pressures that have haunted all administrations in China, meant that the internal dynastic cycle was as much to blame for China's weakness as was Europe's comparative strength. With a more competent, vigorous and responsive leadership in the nineteenth century, regional (not to say world) history might have looked very different.

As it was, Europe's economic expansion and the demands that accom-panied it were implacable. The Opium War (1839–42) was emblematic of the new economic and strategic relationship between China and Europe, and with Britain in particular. The opium trade was dominated by private merchants and the British East India Company, and it was they who encouraged the British government to underwrite their commercial inter-ests with naval fire-power when the Chinese authorities threatened their freedom of economic action. The Treaty of Nanjing, which ended the Opium War, forced China to accept a massive increase in opium imports and cede control over a series of Chinese ports, guaranteeing foreign traders commercial access to the mainland. Why were the British so enthu-siastic about peddling addictive drugs to China's masses in violation of the wishes of the Chinese government? Because the opium trade offered a way of solving a perennial British trade deficit with China. Europe consumed Chinese silk, spices and especially tea, but exported very little in return. Britain and Europe were able to pay their bills with bullion plundered from the 'New World' and derived from the slave trade, but the systematic culti-vation of a market for opium produced in another of Britain's colonies – India – promised to solve the trade problem. The overall impact on China is pithily summarized by Pomeranz and Topik (1999: 103):

> The Chinese not only lost their battle to exclude dope and their war with the British navy; they lost their tariff autonomy, a large indem-nity, the right to subject foreign residents to Chinese law, and the land that would soon be Hong Kong. The worst was yet to come: its mili-tary weakness exposed, China entered a calamitous century of foreign aggression, domestic disorder, and civil war. Skyrocketing opium use – to perhaps 40 million addicts by 1900 – played no small role in this.

Clearly, the opium war was not the single cause of China's decline, but it certainly highlighted the fundamental military and political weakness of the Chinese state and imperial system relative to the European intruders. It also highlighted how important China's economy was to the rest of the world even at this early stage of globalization, and how far other countries were prepared to go to try to ensure that economic relations were conducted on a favourable basis. In this regard there are, as we shall see in Chapter 5, interesting parallels with China's recent accession to the World Trade Organization (WTO): although China's entry is voluntary rather than coerced by gun-boat diplomacy, the two episodes shed a revealing light on the different natures of British and American hegemony. More will be said about the latter in Chapter 8. What is important to note here is the general historical potential for even the most powerful countries to come under the sway of extra-regional powers.

Nothing highlighted the potential imbalance of influence and authority better than the 'standard of civilization' by which the European powers judged China and other states as potential members of the inter-state system. As Gerrit Gong (1984: 7) points out, the standard of civilization idea may have provided a justification and legitimacy for the global expansion of the Western powers, but 'it represented an insult, a humiliation, and a fundamental threat to the proud and culturally independent non-European countries'. In this context, the existence of the Treaty ports and European extra-territoriality came to be a badge of inferiority and subordination. This is why the reforms undertaken in the final days of the imperial system were so significant, argues Zhang:

> The Imperial reforms in the first decade of the century instituted fundamental changes in nearly every sphere of Chinese life. The changes in the Chinese values system and traditional institutions brought about by the reforms called into being a New China, similar to the rest of the world in terms of its political attitudes and values and in its legal institutions. Whether intentionally or not, this was not just a transformation of empire, but also a civilization. (Zhang 1991: 10)

Ironically, of course, the belated attempts at 'self-strengthening'[8] and modernization, which had been resisted by the Confucian elites, accelerated the Empire's demise rather than rescuing it. Education about Western ways was not confined to technical matters, but included new political doctrines which further undermined the ideological legitimacy of the old order. In little more than one hundred years, the foundations of a dynastic order that had lasted for millennia had been fatally eroded. From being at the centre of a regional order that dominated its neighbours and which accepted their tribute as a mark of its due status,[9] China found itself reduced to a subordinate power on the brink of catastrophic internal collapse.

Internal struggle

The last years of the Qing dynasty were marked by increased unrest and declining authority. The Boxer Rising (1898–1901) was one of the most important expressions of growing discontent. It highlighted widespread popular unhappiness about the impact of Christian missionaries and China's loss of face as a consequence of European and Japanese intervention in China. China was losing control of its territory to the British, Germans, French, Russians and – most gallingly, perhaps – the Japanese. In Godement's (1997: 26) colourful phrase, 'the country was being carved up like a watermelon'. While this is something of an overstatement, it does capture the sense of powerlessness and consequent humiliation that gripped many Chinese in the face of their country's apparent dismemberment, infiltration and subordination. In such circumstances, the stage was set for a major internal struggle over China's future.

Ironically, the final decade of Qing rule from 1901 to 1911 was marked by significant attempts at social and institutional reform, but they proved too late to save it. Once the reform process was under way, it proved impossible to control; the heady mixture of social transformation and ideological contestation was too much for an imperial system that was legitimated by its stability and autonomy. Not only was the need for modernization widely accepted by the beginning of the twentieth century, but the modernizing impulse was synonymous with nationalism. Even more remarkably, the revolution when it did finally come, was 'largely made in Japan' (Fairbank, Reischauer and Craig 1965: 631). Japan's remarkable – and highly successful – modernization process, and the nationalism that had been such a prominent part of it, made it a role model for other would-be modernizers across Asia. Sun Yatsen (1866–1925), one of the key figures in the revolutionary movement in China and a future nationalist leader, spent time in Japan absorbing new ideas and establishing a support base amongst Chinese students studying there. The Japanese were happy to support Sun and encourage his republicanism.

The actual revolution of 1911 was 'singularly unviolent' (Fairbank, Reischauer and Craig 1965: 640). The old order had been thoroughly undermined and discredited by the nationalists and modernizers, and the hollowed-out shell required surprisingly little to shatter. It is important to remember that the Qing dynasty had initially been established by the Manchu minority; the nationalist movement offered the majority Han Chinese a chance to re-establish their dominance, as well as the prospect of establishing democracy and institutional reform (Fung 1995: 182). Resolving questions of national identity that had been long-standing sources of tension and resentment provided a powerful underlying dynamic for the nationalist movement above and beyond the general promise of reviving China and enabling it to stand up to external challenges.[10] This was an entirely predictable consequence of China's integration into the international states system, which had the effect of making China a nation-state rather than an imperial civilization, and making nationalism a key part of the new order. Nationalism remains a potent force in Chinese politics to this day (Gries 2004).

However, the initial post-revolutionary compromise, which saw Sun Yatsen sacrifice his leadership ambitions in favour of a military strong man, Yuan Shikai, for the sake of national unity and stability, proved unsustainable. Indeed, the country collapsed into a prolonged period of warlordism and internecine conflict in which the centralized authority of the state essentially broke down. In some ways this is unsurprising: given the longevity of the imperial system, it might be expected that developing new institutions and patterns of authority would prove difficult. What is more surprising, perhaps, is the degree of intellectual disputation that accompanied the new order. On the one hand, the May the Fourth Movement[11] epitomized the desire of many modernizers to reject the traditional, Confucian order and adopt a more independent posture towards the West. On the other hand, however, the West's influence was clearly manifest in the ideological struggles that erupted between the nationalists and the communists: these divisions would eventually culminate in civil war. At the outset of this contest, however, there was a noteworthy degree of cooperation between differing factions. Initially the Kuomintang (KMT), which was led by Sun and was the main manifestation of the nationalist impulse, actually cooperated with the Chinese Communist Party (CCP), which drew its inspiration from Marxist-Leninism and the successful Russian revolution.

Following Sun Yatsen's death in 1925, the KMT assumed power under Chiang Kai-shek (1887–1975), who exploited nationalist sentiment to establish a modernizing government in Nanjing. Significantly, both the nationalists under Chiang and the communists under Mao Zedong (1893–1976) were able to exploit hostility towards Japan and its aggressive takeover of Manchuria to bolster their own positions (see Etō 1986). Chalmers Johnson (1962) has demonstrated how the CCP was able to mobilize the peasantry – traditionally a conservative and unpromising source of revolutionary potential – as a direct consequence of the war with Japan which broke out in 1937 and lasted until the end of the Second World War. Indeed, Johnson's analysis suggests that Chinese communism was primarily a form of nationalism and a response to Japanese aggression. The great achievement of the CCP was to establish a power base in the countryside, an area neglected by the more urban-oriented KMT. One of the critical failures of the KMT government was its inability to penetrate the countryside and exercise the sort of infra-structural power that is one of the hallmarks of effective state capacity. Chiang's dominance of the regime meant that although government became more centralized, the KMT became less influential and the administrative infrastructure of the Nanjing government failed to develop adequately. It relied on coercion to maintain its authority and resources were directed towards the military as a consequence. Perhaps most important, though, Chiang's failure to institute reform and win over the countryside allowed his communist rivals to survive and regroup despite his best efforts to crush them (Eastman 1986).

The great mass of China's population has always lived on the land, so they occupy an especially important place in Chinese history. Even now, 40 per cent of China's population live and work in the agricultural sector,[12] despite the major internal migration and structural transforma-tion of the economy that has occurred over the last few decades. In the first half of the twentieth century, however, the peasantry represented an even greater section of the population and one that had been destabilized by the collapse of imperial rule and the rise of warlordism. Part of Mao's genius, and part of what marked him out as a potential leader of the CCP, was his theoretical flair and his attempt to replace the patron–client rela-tions that predominated in the countryside with the ideology of class struggle. During the Long March of 1934–6, in which the CCP traversed much of western China while being pursued by Chiang's nationalist forces, the Party leadership was consolidated under Mao. It also allowed the CCP to shake off the influence of Moscow and establish a distinctive doctrine and the sinification of Marxism (a split that would have long-term implications for the future international relations within the region and beyond).

Japan's invasion of Manchuria in 1937, and the war it sparked, exposed the potential weaknesses of the Nationalist government. Although the CCP and Chiang's Nationalist government collaborated to fight the Japanese invaders, it was marriage of convenience that could not last. Significantly, it was the United States – already revealed as the key external power in the East Asian region – that attempted to unify the Chinese forces. Roosevelt's suggestion that the command of all Chinese forces should be united under the American, General Stilwell, proved too much for Chiang, however, for it revived the spec-tre of foreign domination that the nationalists had taken such pains to overcome. Yet, it should also be emphasized that American assistance for China eventually occurred only as a consequence of the wider Second World War and a calculation of the United States' own strategic interests. Before that, and despite the violation of Chinese sovereignty and Japan's brutal occupation, the USA remained isolationist and uninvolved. Indeed, it is particularly significant – and understandable, perhaps – that in the aftermath of the Second World War, and despite the emerging outline of the ideologically divisive Cold War, the Americans should have shown little enthusiasm about intervening in the resolution of China's internal struggles (see Iriye 1967).

As we now know, of course, this policy would allow the communists to triumph in their struggle with the nationalists, and contribute to the 'loss' of China to the Soviet sphere of influence. We also now know that the idea that there was a homogeneous anti-capitalist bloc was an overly-simplistic reading of the complexities of relations among the communist powers. The consequences that flowed from such ideologically-blinkered assumptions are taken up in more detail in the next chapter. What is of most significance at this stage is the historical legacy of this period: China became a communist country in 1949 and the nationalists were driven off the mainland to Taiwan,[13] setting the stage for the major strategic confrontation between the capitalist and communist powers that would distinguish global politics for the next 40 years or so.

The domestic and foreign policy history of China's communist regime is taken up in Chapters 4 and 6. There are a number of points about China's pre-war experience that emerge from this brief overview of Chinese history that merit emphasis. First, the demise of the dynastic system that constituted China's civilization and identity for millennia was always going to be traumatic and difficult to accommodate. Arguably, the process is still under way. Second, the 'century of shame' that the break-up of the old order and the intervention of external powers inaugurated also made a profound impact on both China's internal and external relations that can be seen to this day. Nationalism remains a potent force in China and one which the authorities struggle to control. Third, China's recent history has been – and continues to be – powerfully shaped by external influences. Fourth, state strength or capacity is a powerful determinant of how effectively countries will be able to manage and accommodate both external *and* internal forces. In China's case, it took decades for the old order to die and a new one to be born under communist auspices. The question now is whether those structures are any longer able to cope with the new pressures and challenges globalization generates. Paradoxically, much the same is true of Japan – China's pivotally important neighbour – which, despite a much more successful initial response to the challenge posed by the West, is also facing profound adjustment problems as it tries to reconfigure its historically embedded institutions. To see why, we need to look more closely at Japan's history, too.

The rise of Japan

The comparative historical experiences of Japan and China in response to European contact and expansion could hardly be more different. True, for a period Japan also attempted to turn inwards when confronted by the West's potentially destabilizing beliefs and practices. But, when Japanese elites did decide to learn from rather than ignore the West, they set in train a process that would see Japan become the second largest economy in the world and – for a while, at least – a formidable military power. Japan's very different response to incipient global processes is not just important in the context of intra- and inter-regional relations, but is also a powerful historical reminder that there is nothing inevitable about the impact of external forces or the way individual states will respond to similar challenges. Indeed, the Japanese experience has provided a major challenge to those theoretical perspectives that assumed that Asia was in some way incapable of developing because of inappropriate cultural values, or because the structurally entrenched dominance of the West made significant development in the 'periphery' of the global economy all but impossible. As we shall see in Chapter 4, so significant has been the experience of Japan and its acolytes, in fact, that it has generated an influential school of thought which argues that there are actually advantages in 'late' development (Gerschenkron 1966). Such possibilities were not immediately apparent in Japan's early history, however.

In 1603, Ieyasu (founder of the Tokugawa house) established the Tokugawa shogunate and national dominance after a series of civil wars throughout the fifteenth and sixteenth centuries. As in China, Japan had an imperial system, and the Shogun or principal military leader was notionally the Emperor's deputy. In reality, however, power resided with the Shogun and his central administration, or *bakufu*. Power outside the capital, Edo (now Tokyo), was held by various feudal lords or *daimyō*, who enjoyed greater or lesser degrees of independence from the centre depending on personal connections with the Shogun. The *daimyō* positions were primarily hereditary and dependent on the distribution of land by the Tokugawa. Beneath the *daimyō*, society was broadly divided between the samurai (a small but expanding merchant class) and the mass of the people who lived on the land. The samurai had originally been a warrior class dependent on specific lords for their support but, as Japan changed and became more peaceful, many samurai became civil officials, achieving social mobility and creating a cadre of skilled administrators in the process. This would prove invaluable when the modernization process began in earnest in Japan (Beasley 1993).

Before this happened, however, Japan had been deliberately cut off from the rest of the world. For around 200 years, from the early 1600s to 1854,

Japan had either rejected or attempted rigorously to control contact with the outside world. Japan's leaders were uncomfortable about the destabilizing impact of ideas that Portuguese traders and missionaries brought during the sixteenth century. Isolationist policy was feasible because, unlike China, Japan was of little interest to the Europeans, who regarded Japan as poor and inaccessible. And yet, the picture of backwardness and isolation is misleading: not only were literacy rates in Japan comparable with Europe's by the nineteenth century, but the emerging domestic capitalist class was a cause and consequence of the economic development that had already occurred during the Tokugawa period. Crucially, and in sharp contrast to China, there was not an inherent disdain of commerce in Japan, something that encouraged urban merchants and even rich peasants to invest in longer-term economic activities. Consequently, by the nineteenth century 'the Japanese probably had the most advanced and thoroughly monetized economy in Asia and were well prepared for further economic development' (Fairbank, Reischauer and Craig 1965: 191).

There are a number of other factors that help to explain why Japan was better placed to respond to Western demands to open their economy. First, the speed at which integration with the West occurred was far greater than it was in China. Rather than gradually responding to a growing threat that they initially failed to take seriously, as imperial China did, the superiority of Western arms, technology and even governmental structures was rapidly evident to Japan's ruling elites (Moore 1973: 251). Indeed, there was a greater diversity and pragmatism in Japanese thought, evidenced by the tradition of 'Dutch learning', in which Dutch traders had become an important source of knowledge and eventually a synonym for all Western scientific knowledge. Neither did Japanese elites suffer from the sort of civilizational hubris that left China fatally ill-prepared to respond to the West. Japan's leaders recognized the small, vulnerable nature of their country and were determined to learn from the West in order to overcome their weakness. In this context, they were aided by the realization that the old feudal structures were outmoded and increasingly irrelevant. The samurai, for example, had been transformed by peace and were irked by a lack of social mobility, and were in many cases psychologically prepared for the transition from feudal retainer to salaried man (Fairbank, Reischauer and Craig 1965: 192). But despite such propitious preconditions being in place, before this internal transformation could occur Japan still required a decisive prod from outside.

The opening of Japan and the Meiji Restoration

The arrival of US Commodore Matthew Perry in what is now known as Tokyo Bay in 1853 is rightly seen a defining moment in modern world history. Not only was Japan irrevocably drawn into the international system, but it heralded the arrival of the United States as a major power in the Asia-Pacific region, and one that would continue to exert a direct influence over the course of national and regional developments in East Asia. It also marked the beginning of what has come to be the largest economic, and one of the most strategically important, bilateral relationships in the world. From this point in East Asia's history, the centre of power and influence begins to shift from Europe to North America. Understanding East Asia now meant understanding American foreign policy, too.

Perry's arrival highlighted some uncomfortable realities the Japanese would have to come to terms with. First, American technology was plainly far ahead of Japan's, something the presence of Perry's new steam-driven ships made painfully apparent. Second, the USA was already part of an emerging global economy and willing to use its superior technological and military capacities to pursue its commercial interests. In this context, Japan was a potentially crucial source of coal for the steamships that conducted the rapidly growing trade between the USA and China. But underlying these commercial imperatives was an expansionist foreign policy and sense of 'manifest destiny' which, if not imperial in the British sense, certainly helps to explain the sense of moral rectitude and God-given duty that has often accompanied America's foreign affairs (McDougall 1997; Smith 1994). As Iriye points out, from the outset, America's relations with East Asia have been underpinned by something akin to missionary zeal:

> Few were so naïve to believe that America was the embodiment of perfection and that all its ideas and institutions could be transplanted abroad. But all were convinced that American society was a step nearer to perfection than other societies, and that if these latter sought to reform themselves there was much that Americans could do to help . . . the nations of Asia seemed to be waiting for precisely such help. Americans could teach the Chinese and the Japanese rudiments of technology and modern science; they could introduce Western ideas and customs; they could assist the Asian governments as they struggled to survive in a turbulent world; above all, Americans could bring Asians to a new and higher level of spirituality. (Iriye 1967: 18)

Consequently, interaction with Japan in particular and East Asia more generally has always been marked by fundamentally different – and frequently incompatible – differences of opinion about the way political, economic, social and even religious life should be organized; these have led to much mutual misunderstanding as a result. In the context of Japan–America relations, there has been an unrelenting clash of value systems and basic forms of institutional organization as a result of the different ways their societies have been organized (LaFeber 1997).

This is an important and enduring consideration, especially given that the Meiji Restoration, which occurred not long after the USA forced Japan to open up, involved a transformation of some of Japan's most fundamental institutions. Although the actual events of 1868 constituted 'little more than a shift of power within the old ruling class' (Jansen 1989: 308), the Meiji Restoration signalled the end of the feudal era in Japan and the consolidation of centralized power under a modern monarch. It was not an easy process, however. The Commercial Treaty of 1858, negotiated by Townsend Harris, marked the definitive opening of the Japanese economy, but this bland-sounding document triggered a crisis within Japan's ruling elite. The leadership of Ii Naosuke, who took responsibility for Japan's opening, was cut short by his assassination, revealing the inability of the *bakufu* to cope with foreign encroachment. Loyalists looked to the Emperor as an alternative around which to rally, under the banner of 'revere the emperor, expel the barbarians' (W. Cohen 2000). A complex struggle developed between rival *daimyō*, which culminated in an alliance against, and the eventual defeat of, the shogun. The young Emperor was re-installed as a symbol of national unity, while real power lay with a rising generation of young samurai who had usurped the old *bakufu*.

The point to emphasize here is that, unlike China, the social revolution that foreign contact was instrumental in triggering did not lead to the complete dismemberment of the old institutional order. On the contrary, the Emperor became a key element of continuity, albeit a largely symbolic and ceremonial one. What is of even greater long-term significance is that the young generation of reformers, which came to hold real power in Japan, instituted a series of reforms that would have far-reaching implications, changes that would provide the basis for Japan's highly successful accommodation to external challenge. Although the development of new political institutions to replace those of the Tokugawa era would take a generation and not be finalized until 1889 with the promulgation of a constitution (Beasley 1989), this did not stop the more broadly based modernization process, or the overarching desire to build up Japan's national strength relative to the imperialist powers.

It is a measure of how completely the Japanese were able to redefine key elements of their domestic institutions and foreign policy practice that they adapted to the European 'standard of civilization', and the specific notions of statehood and international behaviour that implied, far more successfully than China had (Gong 1984). Whether the prize was worth the effort is, of course, a moot point, but it is an important indicator of the transformation Japan had undertaken, nevertheless, and one that Japanese elites self-consciously pursued as a marker of their new status in the international system. Before this could be achieved, a series of reforms – generally drawing on European models[14] – had been undertaken in the Japanese military, legal system and bureaucratic structures. One of the most important reforms in this context was the abolition of the domains of the *daimyō*, which allowed the further centralization of power and coordination of the reform process. Six key ministries, headed by an oligarchy of court nobles or feudal lords, came to dominate an authoritarian decision-making process in the first decade of Meiji rule. Of the other reforms that were put in place, perhaps the most important was the desire to import and copy Western technology, especially in armaments and communications. This would eventually underpin Japan's dramatic rise as a regional and military power.

The reorganization of the military, initially along French lines, and the establishment of a conscript army involving compulsory national service, were major steps in this process. Subsequently, a military police was established as well as staff colleges for the army (1884) and navy (1888). The highlighting of military reforms is deliberate because they came to assume such long-term significance. As early as 1873, some were agitating for war with Korea (partly as a way of defusing the domestic tensions the rapid reform process was generating).[15] Eventually, Japan contented itself with a punitive expedition against Chinese-controlled Taiwan. This development was, in some ways, an entirely predictable part of the modernization of Japan as a distinct nation-state and the concomitant desire to define its boundaries. The slogan 'rich country, strong army' had encapsulated many of the Meiji regime's ideas about the inter-connectedness between military and economic strength (Samuels 1994). The status of Taiwan was uncertain, and Japan's forceful assertion of its position was in keeping with its overall desire to emulate European-style imperial practice and a measure of the effectiveness of the new Meiji regime (Iriye 1989). There was one other major consequence of Japan's imperial phase that needs emphasizing. Both Taiwan and Korea established deep ties with Japan in a process that Bruce Cumings argues laid the foundations for the more generalized industrialization process across Northeast Asia: both colonies experienced an early form of the 'administrative guidance' of a sort that became such a crucial part of Japan's post-war renaissance. As a consequence, Cumings (1984: 11) argues, 'a highly articulated, disciplined, penetrating colonial bureaucracy substituted both for the traditional regimes and for indigenous groups and classes that under "normal" conditions would have accompanied development'.

Japanese imperialism not only had long-term implications for the development of Taiwan: it also highlighted the changing balance of power between China and Japan. Relations with Korea assumed a similarly important symbolic quality; on the one hand, Japan was keen to ensure that Korea acknowledge its new status. On the other, the evolving regional order simultaneously highlighted China's relative decline and the end of Korea's tributary relationship with it. As a consequence of Japanese expansionism and nascent imperialism, it established colonial enclaves or dominance over parts of China, Korea and Taiwan between 1880 and 1895, in the process becoming the first country to force Korea – the 'hermit kingdom' – to open itself to foreign engagement. Whatever we may think of these achievements in retrospect, it is important to recognize that they were very much in keeping with the practices of the 'great powers' of the day. They were also a clear indicator of how successful and rapid the reform process in Japan had been: not only were the lineaments of a modern state in place by the 1880s, but Japan already had a capacity to redefine the region of which it was an increasingly influential part. Significantly, in a pattern that was to be repeated more peacefully elsewhere in later years, Japan's control of Korea was consolidated by the establishment of deep economic ties, and these links helped to drive Japan's own process of domestic industrialization (Iriye 1989).

Tensions between China and Japan over Korea culminated in the Sino–Japanese War (1894–5) and Japan's decisive naval victory over China, which eventually led to the latter's complete withdrawal from Korea. Japan's dominance over China was highlighted by its subsequent annexation of Korea in 1910, and later occupation of Manchuria. This highlighted China's diminished status and capacity, and created a long-running source of bilateral tension in the process. The subsequent Treaty of Shimonoseki (1895) confirmed China's humiliation and its failure to modernize as successfully as Japan had done. It also gave the Japanese Taiwan and the Liaodong peninsula into the bargain. Russia insisted that the Liaodong peninsula be handed back to the Chinese as it had its own imperial ambitions in China. But given that Japanese elites were by now steeped in the logic of empire and supported by an increasingly nationalistic population, it was entirely predictable that one of the principal longer-term consequences of this period was to set the scene for future conflict and the outbreak of the Russo–Japanese War (1904–5).

Japanese imperialism and militarism

Japan's growing imperial ambitions coincided with its modernization and militarization, and confirmed its status as a major power at the beginning of the twentieth century. The signing of the Anglo–Japanese alliance in 1902 was one indication of Japan's new status, but its inter-imperialistic war against Russia – and the unprecedented defeat of a major European power it subsequently yielded – highlighted just how far Japan had developed. Again, it is important to emphasize that the violent resolution of Japan's imperial conflict with Russia over their rival claims to Manchuria enjoyed widespread popular support in Japan: patriotism, militarism and imperialism were producing precisely the same sort of heady cocktail in Japan as they had in Britain and Germany; they would ultimately produce equally tragic results. It is worth noting that (at this stage, at least) questions of national prestige and relative international standing would seem to have had as much, if not more, to do with Japanese expansionism as any strictly material explanations of the sort that have distinguished influential Marxist analyses (see Hoogvelt 2001: 21–8). In Japan's case, the defeat of Russia and the destruction of its fleet fuelled the national appetite for further expansion. By 1910, Japan had completed the annexation of Korea and converted it into a fully-fledged colony, instituting governmental and organizational reforms that would have far-reaching consequences for both subsequent economic development in South Korea, and for contemporary Japanese–Korean bilateral relations.

Although Japan had begun a process of modernization that was transforming its economic infrastructure and governmental institutions, at the beginning of the twentieth century it was still a predominantly agricultural country. True, the Japanese government was assiduously trying to develop its ship-building and steel-making capacities, and establish a national rail network, but the picture of a far-sighted and competent state single-handedly driving forward Japan's industrialization process needs to be treated with some caution. As Tessa Morris-Suzuki's careful analysis has demonstrated:

> Technological change in Meiji Japan was not confined to state-owned enterprises, nor to the handful of embryonic *zaibatsu* who possessed close links to government. Instead, the really significant feature of Meiji innovation is that it was quite widely spread through many companies and craft workshops in many parts of the country. (Morris-Suzuki 1994: 85)

The debate about the importance and competence of the state and its role in Japan's development will be taken up in more detail in Chapter 4, as it remains one of the most important issues not just for Japan, but for debates about the role of the state more generally in East Asia. What we can say about this earlier period is that the 'second phase of modernization' in Japan was accompanied by an average level of government investment in the economy of more than 40 per cent per year during the period 1887–1940 (Fairbank, Reischauer and Craig 1965: 493–4). The targeting of this scarce capital to specific business groups established a pattern that would become a distinctive feature of Japan's post-war development; it also helped to establish the handful of major *zaibatsu* or industrial conglomerates that would come to dominate the economic landscape.

All this investment underpinned an accelerating transformation of the Japanese economy, and its rapid integration into the wider world system. As in Britain's early industrialization, and as China has recently demonstrated, the development of a major textile industry was a key step in the journey to industrial development. In Japan's case, textiles constituted 50 per cent of its industrial output in 1891, and an even bigger slice of exports (Fairbank, Reischauer and Craig 1965: 499). But as Japanese exports of manufactured goods took off, so did the need to import raw materials. This dilemma has been at the centre of Japanese public policy since the modernization process began, and helps to explain all that is distinctive – and occasionally tragic – about Japanese foreign and economic policies. But even before Japan's foreign and domestic policies led it inexorably into further military conflict, the ambivalent nature of greater integration into the international system had become apparent during the Great Depression, which resulted in a crippling blow to international economic activity across the world.

Japan was not as badly affected as most by this crisis, however, or at least not in terms of its immediate economic prospects. Not only were Japanese goods still cheap and comparatively attractive, even in greatly reduced international markets, but military adventurism in Manchuria in 1931 gave further buoyancy to the Japanese economy. This is an even more surprising development than it may seem, given the benefit of hindsight and our knowledge about the outcome of Japanese militarism. Between 1918 and 1931, the prospects for political reform, internationalism and peaceful coexistence had looked surprisingly bright in Japan. During the 'liberal twenties' the growth of Japan's cities, the expansion of a domestic bourgeoisie, improving levels of education and greater knowledge of Western ideas all created pressure for political reform (Beasley 1993). Party politics had become established in Japan by the end of the First World War, and men over the age of 25 were given the vote in 1925. At the same time, however, authoritarian controls were introduced to control political dissent, especially on the Left. The tensions between the move towards liberal democracy and authoritarian militarism were resolved in favour of the latter following a series of political assassinations.

These tensions culminated in a major insurrection and political crisis in 1936, which had the effects of tilting the country further towards authoritarianism, intimidating the political class, and increasing the relative power of the military. The army presented itself as a force for national unity in the face of destabilizing political contestation and extremism. The insulation of military matters – including the authority to decide questions of war and peace – reflected and consolidated the shift of power to the military and the service chiefs. A descent into warfare was the all too predictable consequence of these domestic convulsions. Equally predictably, perhaps, given long-running regional tensions, it was a war with China. We have already seen the impact of the war that broke out in 1937 on China itself, but it is also important to recognize how important China was to Japan, and what a watershed the colonization of Manchuria was in this context. Japan had established a puppet government in 'Manchukuo', as the Japanese called it, in 1932 after engineering their own military intervention. The subsequent exploitation and occupation of Manchuria provided both a model of military-style colonialism and a way of cultivating support for the army at home as well: 'in concrete ways, aggression abroad brought about the militarisation of politics at home. The bubble of enthusiasm for the Manchurian occupation restructured the balance of bureaucratic power in favour of the army, which in turn ensured the perpetuation of the new policy of military expansionism' (Young 1998: 129). The war with China generally, and the occupation of Manchuria in particular, are significant, therefore, not just because of the long-lasting impact they had on Sino–Japanese relations, but because they served as a model for what Young (1998: 240) describes as the 'advance guard of Japanese industrial capitalism'.[16] The potential significance of this development became clearer as the Second World War unfolded.

The War and its aftermath are considered in greater detail in the next chapter, but at this stage it is important to make a couple of preliminary points. First, there was a certain inevitability about the looming clash between the USA, which had rapidly become the premier power in the Pacific, and Japan, which was increasingly reliant on imports of raw materials to fuel both its industrialization *and* its militarization. As early as 1936, Japanese military strategists were looking towards Southeast Asia to provide critical raw materials. By 1940, the conflict in Europe was seen as providing a suitable distraction for Japan to expand into the region: aggressively, if necessary. Although Japanese strategists wanted to avoid a clash with the USA, the inexorable logic of Japan's distinctive military–industrial complex drove them on.

Predictably enough, the USA was becoming increasingly concerned about Japanese militarism and expansionism, not least as a consequence of Japan signing the Tripartite Pact with fascist Germany and Italy in 1940. The increasingly painful sanctions the USA imposed on Japan in an effort to rein in its expansionary ambitions during 1940 and 1941 were seen by the Japanese military as an explicit and fundamental threat to Japan's autonomy and economic security, providing the trigger for conflict. From the perspective of Japan's dominant military elites, its dependency on Southeast Asia for crucial supplies of natural resources such as oil and rubber left it with few options if it wanted to maintain economic independence and military autonomy (Willmott 1982). The tragic consequences and ultimate result of Japan's misreading of both American strength and willingness to fight are well known. Before concluding the discussion of Japan's historical legacies, though, it is important to say something about Japan's Southeast Asian empire, for no matter how short-lived it may have been, it had a profound impact on the region and continues to influence the conduct of Japan's relations with the Southeast Asian sub-region to this day.

Getting regionalism wrong

The next chapter will spell out some of the conventional, if somewhat surprising, consequences of the war between Japan and the USA. There is, however, another (generally less well understood and appreciated) aspect of this conflict that is particularly important in the context of a discussion about regional development and the prospects for future East Asian collaboration. One of the most important consequences of the war as far as Japan was concerned – and by extension, much of the rest of the putative region, as well – was its impact on Japan's sense of itself as a nation and as a member of an international order.

Even before the outbreak of the Second World War, Japanese elites were preoccupied with Japan's place in an emerging regional order, and many were actively promoting a vision of 'pan-Asianism'. For all its demonstrated capacity to learn from, and even become part of, a Western-dominated international economic and political order, by the outbreak of the Second World War the idea that Japan could and should be the leader of a regional order that incorporated the whole of East Asia (including China) was becoming firmly established. Indeed, Japanese regional leadership was seen in some quarters as a way of ridding the region as a whole of a pernicious European and American presence. Seen in this light, Japan's subsequent occupation of Southeast Asia takes on a different aspect:

> The Japanese never disguised the fact that their primary interest lay in obtaining the rich resources of the colonial region. The difference this time was that in trying to achieve this goal, they were engaged in an expulsion of Westerners from Asia . . . The rhetoric of pan-Asianism

provided a ready-made rationale for such action. At the same time, however, this rhetoric required something more substantial than defeating American and European forces. The Japanese had to develop a vision of the new Asia that they were purportedly constructing. (Iriye 1981: 64)

In reality, the vision was never coherently developed or realized. The Greater East Asia Co-prosperity Sphere was intended to be a mechanism for unifying East Asia under Japanese leadership, with the Japanese economy acting as its principal engine of growth. From its inception, however, the proposed structure was plagued by bureaucratic infighting in Japan and outright hostility in some of its critical constituent parts, especially the Philippines and Malaya. As Beasley (1993: 206) points out, in Northeast Asia the Japanese were able to use a common Confucian heritage to try to win over converts to the East Asian idea. In the southeastern part of the region, however, there was no such common cultural glue to overcome resentment of Japanese dominance. The idea of 'co-prosperity' that supposedly lay at the heart of Japan's pan-Asian vision was never realized either: the demands of Japan's war-time economy meant that it was unable to replace Western markets or supplies of consumer goods, despite the relentless exploitation of Southeast Asia's raw materials. Predictably enough, living standards across Southeast Asia declined as a consequence of its economic isolation, lack of investment, and economic dependence on Japan. Moreover, from a Japanese strategic perspective, the (often brutal and widely resented) occupation of China and Southeast Asia tied down troops that might otherwise have been occupied in fighting the enemy.

Strategically and economically, then, the Greater East Asia Co-prosperity Sphere was ill-conceived and unsuccessful. Misguided as it was, though, it is important for a number of reasons that merit spelling out. At one level, it represents the first attempt to think explicitly of 'East Asia' as a distinct region in its own right. Although the underlying rationale and motives might have been dubious and self-serving, it did have the effect of drawing attention to putative notions of 'Asianness' in opposition to a 'Western' other.[17] At another level, and despite the appalling impact Japanese occupation had on much of Southeast Asia and its people, it had the effect of demolishing the idea of European superiority and the invincibility of the white races. As we shall see, prior to Japan's violent intrusion into the region, the European powers had generally enjoyed an untroubled ability to exploit ruthlessly their colonial possessions. After the Second World War and the crushing defeats the Japanese – crucially, an *Asian* power – inflicted on Britain in particular, the days of European colonization were definitively over. Only the timing of their withdrawal remained to be decided.

Before we consider that process and the circumstances that preceded this process in Southeast Asia, it is important to spell out the long-term consequences of this period for Japan. As we shall see in the next chapter, one of the most important impacts of the Second World War generally has been Japan's military and – to a lesser extent – political subordination to the USA. In a regional context, not only were future relations between Japan and Southeast Asia (especially China) poisoned as a consequence, but any prospect of Japan's overt regional leadership being resurrected was rendered inherently problematic. As far as much of the region was concerned, Japan's image was almost irrevocably tarnished. Governments across the region, especially in China, have ruthlessly exploited Japan's awkwardness and guilt about its war-time activities to extract maximum diplomatic and material advantage. Not all countries have been able to take advantage of this, or Japan's remarkable post-war transformation, however.

The subordination of Southeast Asia

As we saw in the last chapter, considering 'Southeast Asia' as a distinct region is a relatively recent development (Emmerson 1984). The fact that it was an external power – the British – that began this practice is emblematic of a wider set of relationships and the way in which Southeast Asia has been drawn into contemporary international political and economic structures. The manner of this integration will be taken up below and in other chapters, but it is noteworthy that Southeast Asia as a whole has never really shaken off this somewhat dependent, even subordinate, position. Indonesia, for example, is the country with the largest Muslim population in the world, nearly twice that of Japan's, but it is not talked of as a prospective member of the Security Council the way Japan is, or invited to take part in G7 discussions although a much less populous and strategically important country, Canada, is. To understand why Indonesia and Southeast Asia more generally have such little influence and standing in the world's most important forums we need to look at their development and standing in historical perspective. Despite the widely noted heterogeneity of the Southeast Asian region, for our purposes it makes sense to consider the countries of the region collectively as there are sufficient commonalities in their respective historical experiences to make some degree of generalization about this sub-region possible.

One of the most important distinctions to make within the Southeast Asian region itself is in the fundamental difference between mainland and maritime Southeast Asia. This has resulted in major differences between the development of states such as Vietnam, Laos, Cambodia,

Burma and Thailand, which would ultimately emerge on the edge of the East Asian land mass, and others such as Indonesia, Malaysia, the Philippines, Singapore and Brunei, which were maritime states. Predictably enough, the first important centres of power in Southeast Asia developed on the mainland in Funan from about 100 to 600 AD, mainly in what is now Cambodia, and in Champa, from about 200–1700 AD, in what is now Vietnam. Yet, even within the broad division between mainland and maritime centres, there is a further distinction to be made between the permanent settlements that grew up around rice production in key river systems such as the Mekong, and the more thinly populated regions outside. Anthony Reid (2000: 4) describes this as the 'fundamental dualism of hill and valley, upstream and downstream, interior and coast'. The legacy of these early divisions can still be found in the hill tribes of countries such as Vietnam. Such basic geographical features of Southeast Asia help to explain the fundamental challenges of governance that have historically confronted political elites across much of the region. This is particularly true of maritime states such as the Philippines and Indonesia. Modern Indonesian governments, for example, have had to try to impose centralized order on a sprawling archipelago that encompasses thousands of small islands in addition to the main – very different – population centres of Java, Sumatra, Bali, Sulawesi or Kalimantan, not to mention the currently troublesome region of West Papua.

Indonesia may be something of an extreme example, but it highlights another surprisingly common experience amongst all the diversity: Southeast Asia has been profoundly influenced by contact with the outside world, and not just during the period of European colonization, which is the principal focus of attention here. Evidence of the influence of other cultures on Southeast Asia can be seen from the extensive impact of Hinduism and Buddhism, although the historical record of the region's early development is sketchy and imperfect. It is clear, however, that as early as the seventh century, major new centres of power and economic activity were emerging in maritime Southeast Asia, as the development of the important trading empire of Srivijaya in Sumatra demonstrates (see SarDesai 1997). What is of most significance for our purposes is that, from about the fifteenth century, access to Southeast Asia became easier as a consequence of improvements in maritime transport and technology. There had certainly been contact with Indian, Chinese and Arab traders before this period, but from 1500 to 1800 there was an intensification of trade relations. There was one other enduring and important consequence of period before European domination of Southeast Asia's trade routes we must note: the introduction and steady spread of Islam, something that was marked by the conversion of the strategically important

Malay trading port, Melaka, in the fifteenth century (Watson Andaya 1999).[18]

The effect of this period was to incorporate the region into an extant political and economic order, a process that had profound implications for the societies of what we now think of as Southeast Asia. But before considering this process in any detail, it is important to consider how life was organized before the encroachment of both European capitalism and the inter-state system that emerged alongside it, which has come to define exclusively *national* political space in the process. Although Southeast Asians have generally taken up the ideas of nationalism, sovereignty and all the other trappings of the inter-state system with great enthusiasm, there was nothing inevitable about this. On the contrary, the dominant patterns of relationships that existed before European imperialism transformed the region suggest that things could have developed differently.

Perhaps the most fundamental and far-reaching aspect of the transformative process European contact encouraged initially was the development of colonial relations and, subsequently, independent nation-states where none had existed before. Prior to European colonization, the demarcation of political space, which we take to be such a familiar part of national and international life, was unknown in Southeast Asia. While the increasingly fine-grained delineation of time and space, and the more instrumental and objective nature of authority have been hallmarks of modernity in the West (Harvey 1988), in Southeast Asia, by contrast, the extent of rule, and the nature of authority, was by turns imprecise and personal. As Nicholas Tarling (1998: 47) puts it, 'What concerned a ruler was the people not the place.' In other words, not only were the boundaries of the pre-European kingdoms of Southeast Asia generally highly uncertain, but power and authority were closely bound up with the personal qualities of the ruler. To quote Tarling again:

> The concept of a frontier was uncommon, if not unknown, in Southeast Asia. The idea that the ambit of a state was geographically fixed was rarely accepted. What counted in Southeast Asia, sparse in population, was allegiance. Whom, rather than what, did the state comprise? States might indeed advance or retreat, grow or decline, but in terms of adherents and followers, a network of familial and suprafamilial relationships. (Tarling 1998: 47)

The idea that political – and by implication, economic – life in Southeast Asia might be primarily dependent on personalized relationships is in some ways not unlike the situation that prevailed in China before its abrupt incorporation into the wider intentional system. What distinguishes Southeast Asia, though, is the importance and prevalence of patron–client ties.[19] In what Lucian Pye (1985) has described as 'the Asian view of power', consensus, paternalism and deference are the distinguishing features of a system based on personal authority. In the West, by contrast, the expectation is that authority will come to be invested in particular institutions or the specific office an individual holds. It was precisely this sort of underlying differentiation that led thinkers as diverse as Max Weber and Karl Marx to believe that capitalism could not flourish in Asia in the absence of the sort of state structures, legal systems, individual attitudes, and formal rationality[20] that had developed in the West (Sayer 1991).

We now know, of course, how wrong such assumptions were. Asia has generated some of the most successful capitalist countries ever seen, at least when judged in terms of rising per capita incomes and gross domestic product. We also know, as we shall see in more detail in subsequent chapters, that within the overarching framework of capitalist production structures great variations are possible in the way political and economic processes are organized, *and* in the interaction between them. Although we should be careful about making sweeping generalizations based on civilizational distinctions of the sort Pye, Marx and Weber claimed, it is clear that local differences in social structures and norms help to account for the way various parts of East Asia responded to external economic pressures and the spread of global capitalism. It is also clear that vestiges of these earlier patterns continue to distinguish different forms of capitalist organization in the region to this day.

It is not just our understanding of capitalist development that is modified when refracted through an Asian prism, however: the early development of Southeast Asia also reminds us that even the practice of an international relations system itself – which many IR scholars take to be a timeless, unchanging and universal phenomenon – can look very different across time and space. Because of the highly personalized nature of rule, and the great imprecision of geographical boundaries in early Southeast Asia, Wolters (1999: 29) has argued that we should think of the distribution of power in the region as being characterized by a series of overlapping *mandalas* or 'circles of kings', rather than the sort of clearly demarcated national boundaries that were becoming such a prominent part of Western Europe and their subsequent colonies. This pattern of personalized relationships helped to define relationships within and between loosely configured kingdoms across much of Southeast Asia before European colonization, argues Wolters.

Amitav Acharya (2000: 24) has drawn on Wolters' *mandala* metaphor to claim that 'one could at least imagine a *regional pattern* of inter-state relations in classical Southeast Asia based on essentially similar political forms' (emphasis in the original). While this may seem a slender reed to build too great a conceptual structure upon, it does highlight one important fact, nevertheless: when the Europeans, as the Indians, Chinese, Arabs and even Japanese that went before them, eventually did arrive and impose themselves on the region, they were not writing the subsequent history of their colonial rule on a blank page. Previously established patterns of indigenous rule, relationships and authority would be transformed rather than completely erased as a consequence of Europe's entry into the region.

The coming of the Europeans

One of the most noteworthy features of Southeast Asia before 1750 was the remarkably low levels of population density, especially compared to Northeast Asia. Even as late as 1800, around 80 per cent of the region was still covered by dense jungle, and the 20 or 30 million people of Southeast Asia were concentrated in a few scattered trading states and the agricultural centres that emerged around the mainland's major river systems and in Java. Two of the most important changes in the region over the past 200 years have been the dramatic increase in population and the startling physical transformation of the natural environment; these phenomena are clearly not unrelated. One of the most important forces underpinning these inter-connected processes was the incorporation of the region into global economic structures.

Although the Chinese played a major role in pioneering trade with Southeast Asia, their retreat into isolationism in the fifteenth century left the way open for others to fill their place. Indeed, from as early as the fifthteenth century the lure of the 'spice islands' proved irresistible for Portuguese traders, and the Dutch East India Company (VOC) established a monopoly over Southeast Asia's spice trade as early as the 1620s (Reid 1999: 116–21). Of course, trade was not the only thing the Europeans were interested in or brought with them: the Portuguese also brought Christianity. It is worth noting, in light of more recent events, that Christianity clashed with the Islamic traditions imported by Arab traders, with Islam providing an important rallying point for those hostile to European intrusion and the disruption of hitherto Muslim-dominated trade routes (McCloud 1995: 115). The Dutch were less confrontational than the Portuguese, and were thus able to profit from the enmity the latter had generated and establish themselves in the region following their capture of Melaka in 1641. Indeed, the European powers had quite different imperial styles and impacts (Parry 1971: ch. 5). In what we now think of as Indonesia in particular, the Dutch (and, more specifically, the VOC) established effective control over the archipelago, but we need to be careful not to overstate the immediate impact of this on traditional Indonesian society. As Robert Elson points out:

> A deliberately self-limiting exercise, mercantile capitalism eschewed interference with indigenous polities except to make necessary arrangements for the delivery of desired trade goods; apart from strategically placed forts and 'factories', it avoided territorial conquest and the overheads which administration and defence of such territories involved unless these were deemed necessary to protect its more important commercial interests. While sometimes it imposed itself upon the indigenous setting through its activities as tribute gatherer and trade director . . . mostly it meshed its activities into the practices and routines already well established in Southeast Asia. (Elson 1999: 132)

This is a surprisingly modern sounding approach to economic control and exploitation, and one with contemporary parallels. Although the style of rule developed by the Dutch was not as directly intrusive as we might think when seen retrospectively, the cumulative, long-term impact of integration into the general European-dominated economic and political system was profound, and 'seriously diminished the sense that the region enjoyed any substantial and inherent shared identity or characteristics or destiny' (Elson 2004: 17). Other observers go even further, and argue that Britain's belated intervention into Southeast Asia, for example, 'introduced social, economic, and political changes that left the fabric of indigenous society threadbare' (McCloud 1995: 119). When we look at the impact of British colonialism, it is clear that a number of Southeast Asian nations developed their particular social structures and economic profiles – with all the problems that have subsequently flowed from them – as a direct consequence of their position in Britain's imperial economy.

The most obvious manifestation of Britain's colonial presence was the series of trading colonies it established in Penang (1786), Melaka (1824) and Singapore (1819). These developments reflected more than the simple commercial imperatives that might be expected to flow from one country – or even, company – pursuing its interests, however. The colonization and carving-up of Southeast Asia reflected intense intra-imperial competition amongst the Europeans themselves as they jockeyed for control and influence in Asia. Under such circumstances, it becomes easier to see why the Japanese felt that this was the natural order of things and emblematic of great power status. For Southeast Asia, it meant that societies and economies were reshaped as a consequence of much larger, extra-regional forces and contests. Even where local actors proved decisive, invariably it was as a consequence of wider struggles. The complex rivalries, occasional conflicts and shifting alliances between the Dutch, British and French in Europe had their counterparts in the colonies.[21] Britain's rise and the relative decline of the Dutch had allowed the British steadily to expand its imperial possessions, frequently at the expense of the Dutch. But whichever European power was in the ascendancy, relations in the colonies were always complicated and overlaid by European imperatives and the capacity of their colonial officials.

The quintessential 'man on the spot', Stamford Raffles, was in fact the Lieutenant-Governor of Java before he helped establish Singapore as a key part of Britain's expanding trade empire in the region. Raffles was unhappy at the concessions the British government had made to the Dutch in return for their support against the French in Europe's continuing struggle for supremacy. Not only did the establishment of the Straits Settlements – as Singapore, Penang and Melaka were known – reveal the amount of autonomy colonial representatives frequently had in the far-flung outposts of the empire, but it consolidated Britain's economic position and secured the vital trade route to China. And yet, there was often a good deal of ambivalence on the part of British governments about the wisdom of accumulating additional colonial responsibilities. Despite the existence of extensive tin mines in Malaya, for example, the British government was initially reluctant to intervene in the Malay states. However, the growing importance of tin for industrializing Europe, improvements in communication and a concomitant rapid expansion in the tin trade meant that British merchants lobbied their government to establish more secure conditions and minimize foreign competition. In another revealing example of what could be alternatively described as initiative, arrogance or chutzpah, Britain's Governor-Designate for the Straits Settlements proceeded to engineer, with the more or less willing compliance of the traditional Malay chiefs, a de facto extension of the British empire across the Malay peninsula (Tarling 1966).

It is also typical of the imperial mindset of the times that the British considered that, far from exploiting native peoples and their natural wealth, they were actually introducing them to the benefits of civilization and imposing an order that they were incapable of realizing themselves (SarDesai 1997: 107). The reality was rather different. Assets such as the tin mines and the new, rapidly expanding rubber industry were not only ruthlessly developed, but they were also worked by 'coolie' labour imported from China. This pattern of importing labour from China was repeated across much of Southeast Asia, where the seemingly endless supply of cheap labour from the mainland was also put to work in the rapidly expanding, completely alien, plantations that sprang up in the sugar, rubber, palm oil and tobacco industries of the Philippines,

Cambodia, Vietnam and Sumatra (Elson 1999). In Malaysia, Chinese labour was also supplemented with large numbers of Indians and Tamils. It is not simply because the working conditions that confronted these immigrants were generally appalling and almost comically at odds with the purported civilizing mission of British empire that this period is noteworthy; for Malaysia in particular, the long-term legacy of British colonization was the profound impact it had on the ethnic and social make-up of the country, and the structural distortion this wrought on the resulting Malaysian economy. It is a legacy that has shaped public policy and hampered indigenous development ever since.

British imperial preferences also had a similarly dramatic, and ultimately even more tragic, impact on Burma. Burma's principal significance as far as the British were concerned was political: the British wanted to keep the French out and establish hegemonic influence as they had in India (SarDesai 1997). The fact that Burma also offered a potential trade link with China was an important strategic bonus. The seriousness of British intent can be gauged from the fact that there were no fewer than three Anglo–Burmese wars as they attempted to impose their authority. During the third of these, the gratuitous British humiliation of the Burmese royal family sowed the seeds of enduring enmity of the Burmese and a major guerrilla war. But bad as Britain's colonial record frequently was, it was possibly not as inept or imbued with as much hauteur as that of the French, and neither or would it prove as painful and traumatic to dislodge.

Although the French had had a presence in Vietnam since the seventeenth century, it consolidated imperial power there in the latter part of the nineteenth century. Proselytizing Catholic missionaries had been at the forefront of early French intrusions into Vietnam, but the French wanted to replicate Britain's success in opening China to foreign commerce. The persecution of French missionaries proved a convenient justification for a more extensive intervention, culminating in the signing of a treaty with the Vietnamese Emperor, Tu Duc, in 1862. This gave the French control of 'Cochin China', or the southern provinces around Saigon.[22] The French were also granted the right to navigate the Mekong as part of the settlement, something that facilitated their further expansion into Cambodia. Internecine warfare between the Thais, the Vietnamese and the Cambodians had left the latter in a vulnerable state and actively seeking the support of external allies, which helped the French consolidate their presence in the region.[23] By 1884, France had established control over the whole of Vietnam. This triumph would prove short-lived, however, and usher in a period of turbulent colonial government that would ultimately culminate in France's expulsion from the region. Paradoxically, France's 'superior' state capacity and the heavy-handed use of military repression would undermine traditional village life and organization in Vietnam, instituting unpopular administrative reforms that would fan peasant unrest and eventual rebellion (Trocki 1999: 103). Although it would prove to be the most traumatic and drawn-out, France's experience was not uncommon as Southeast Asia became swept up in series of revolutionary, nationalist and independence movements in the first half of the twentieth century.

Nationalism, revolution and insurrection

The circumstances in which some of the most important countries of the region achieved independence are considered in more detail in subsequent chapters. At this stage, it is important to outline the circumstances behind the independence movements and the way relations between the what might be described as the 'centre' and the 'periphery' developed before the Second World War.[24] Although it is difficult to disentangle all the factors that encouraged the steady, unstoppable progress towards independence in the new, post-war Asian order, it is possible to identify a number of pivotal influences that were prominent in the period between the First and Second World Wars.

One of these, of course, was the First World War itself. There were a number of major consequences of this period for East Asia as whole, and for the Southeast Asian sub-region in particular, that merit emphasis. In the north, China was able to escape the most intense European predations and Japan to confirm its status as a great power (Edwardes 1961). In Southeast Asia, the First World War helped undermine the idea of a united, superior European civilization, revealing the potential vulnerability of the European empires, fuelling an upsurge of anti-colonial organization and thinking in the process (Christie 1996: 11). Likewise, the potential perils of economic integration into the expanding international system – a recurring theme of Asia's relationship with the economies of the West – were also vividly illustrated during the Great Depression. Southeast Asia's increased exposure to capitalist vicissitudes increased social instability and political unrest across the region. More immediately, the Europeans themselves provided Southeast Asians with a new nationalist conceptual framework and vocabulary around which to mobilize in opposition to colonial power.

Nationalism was not an entirely novel force in East Asian political life: the Vietnamese and the Burmese had employed 'nationalist' sentiment in opposition to Chinese rule at various times, for example. But it is the steady introduction of the distinctively modern and European form of nationalism that is the really distinctive feature of this period. As we shall see in more detail in Chapter 6, nationalism has been a crucial force in the evolution and consolidation of, first, the European nation-state (Smith 1998), and subsequently the very idea of a national polity where none existed before in Southeast Asia. Ironically, it was the introduction of Western forms of education, and especially political ideas, that really paved the way for the emergence of a nationalist discourse across the region. Not only were European notions of liberty, equality and justice imported from Britain and France, but so, too, was the even more incendiary doctrine of revolutionary Marxism.

Marxist ideas would prove especially influential in Indo-China, but their eventual ascendancy was not a foregone conclusion. The commercialization of rice production and integration of Vietnam into the global economy exacerbated the impact of France's colonial administration noted above, creating the conditions for potential conflagration (Wolf 1969). Yet, the peasantry was a conservative rather than a revolutionary force, and generally preoccupied with maintaining rather than overturning the status quo. Unsurprisingly, given the peasantry's social circumstances and lack of education, there was little ideological content in the mass rebellions that were engendered. As Godement (1997: 38) observes: 'In Asia, nationalism and communism both came into being not in a blaze of fire, but with a spark which needed intellectual momentum and organizational power to fan the flames.' It was the capacity of middle-class intellectuals such as Ho Chi Minh (who absorbed these new ideas while in Paris and who provided the revolutionary leadership and doctrine) which was able to interpret and take advantage of the combustible aftermath of, first, French colonialism, and then world war. In the same way that the Chinese communists had gathered strength during the Second World War, Vietnam's revolutionary leaders established themselves in the hinterland before launching an independence movement that would eventually expel the French.

In light of recent events and the attention given to Islamic movements in Southeast Asia, it is also important to note that Marxism was not the only doctrine available to those disenchanted with colonial rule. On the contrary, Islam's role as a force for political mobilization against perceived oppressors is far from unprecedented. In Indonesia, during the first decades of the twentieth century, Low (1991: 26) argues that it was Muslim movements such as *Sarekat Islam* (Islamic Union) that were more powerful vehicles for political mobilization than strictly nationalist organizations, which did not develop until later (see Elson 2005). It is also clear that, as with Ho in Vietnam, Indonesia's eventual independence leader, Sukarno, was educated by the Dutch and absorbed the political ideas of the West as a consequence. But Sukarno's particular genius lay in his ability to wed the secular, modernizing impulse he derived from Europe to customary Javanese notions about the nature of power and leadership. As in Vietnam, traditional Javanese village life was overturned by the penetration of Western political (and especially economic) practices, once again preparing the way for an independence movement; in Indonesia's case, it was given extra momentum by the impact of Japan's war-time colonization (Anderson 1972). We shall look more closely at the role nationalism has played since Indonesia's independence in Chapter 4. At present, though, it is necessary to say something about two countries that have as yet played little part in this narrative: Thailand and the Philippines.

Both of these countries are distinctive, even amongst all the heterogeneity that is Southeast Asia. Thailand was the only country in Southeast Asia to avoid direct colonization by an external power, and the Philippines is unique in that it was the latter-day champion of anti-colonialism – the United States – which exercised colonial authority most recently, and which continues to cast a long shadow over contemporary developments in that country. Despite the fact that Thailand escaped direct colonization, from the nineteenth century onwards the European powers exercised 'considerable indirect control' (Vandergeest 1993: 139). The Thai monarch was compelled to sign a series of treaties with European and US governments which limited autonomous control of trade and taxation. As in Japan, the perception of weakness and vulnerability encouraged Thai elites to undertake far-reaching reforms, including an expansion of the bureaucracy. Significantly, the ethnic Chinese that had arrived in earlier waves of migration to Southeast Asia, and which had now established themselves as an increasingly powerful force within Thai society, played a growing a part in this process. These domestic reforms culminated in the end of the absolute monarchy and the moral and intellectual order that had previously prevailed. The cultivation of a national language, the extension of universal education and the development of a national rail system were key elements of the deliberate process of nation-building that Thai elites undertook. Perhaps the most enduring legacy of this period was the emergence of the military as the most powerful force in Thailand. As Chai-Anan Samudavanija puts it: 'During the first three decades after the overthrow of the absolute monarchy in 1932, the military was the most powerful political actor, dominating every facet of Thailand's political life and keeping in place a dictatorial regime that ruled almost unchallenged for most of that period' (Chai-Anan Samudavanija 1993: 271).

As in Thailand, the high colonial period had long-lasting impacts on the Philippines that are still working themselves out. It is important to note that, in the case of the Philippines, the history of anti-colonial resistance is longer than anywhere else in Southeast Asia. As early as the eighteenth century, there was a series of revolts against the rule of the Spanish colonists. As the Philippine economy was inexorably drawn into the wider international system during the nineteenth century, the basis of domestic production and class relations changed. As in other parts of the region, the country was exposed to new ideas and values. In part, this was a consequence of the revolutionary changes that were gripping Spain itself, but the ending of the short-lived Spanish republic led to political repression rather than liberalism in the Philippines. And yet, the demand for greater political rights had established a foothold in the Philippines: the demand for greater political freedom championed by the indigenous leader, José Rizal, and the nascent sense of national consciousness it engendered would prove difficult to suppress, despite Rizal's death. But the events that decisively transformed the status of the Philippines were occurring on the other side of the world as a consequence of the Spanish–American War which broke out in 1898.

When the Americans inherited remnants of the Spanish empire as a consequence of their victory, they were uncertain quite what to do with them. This was an especially acute dilemma as the Filipinos themselves had launched a revolution designed to overthrow Spanish rule before the Americans arrived, and which the US government found itself having to suppress when it assumed control. The subsequent war – or insurrection, as the Americans preferred to think of it – between the USA and the local population was surprisingly drawn-out and costly (Boot 2002). The eventual result of America's first imperial venture was a 'structure of accommodation, or collaboration' (Thomson, Stanley and Perry 1981: 117), in which the US government cultivated indigenous elites to deal with the local people and run the Filipino economy,[25] while the Americans guaranteed order and imposed overall leadership. This arrangement proved agreeable to all parties as it was predicated on the idea that the Philippines' eventual independence was guaranteed (although this became a less important issue as time went on). However, the USA's dependence on a small group of local intermediaries helped to create an enduring social structure that has been at the heart of many subsequent political and economic difficulties:

> America's reliance upon collaboration and suasion to maintain its insular empire made the collaborators a privileged group. Positioning themselves between the two real loci of power and authority in the islands, the American government and the mass of the Filipino people, they became indispensable mediators. Since the only credible collaborators – the only people with the authority, outlook, and education necessary to deliver the allegiance of the people – were members of the established elite, the imperialism of suasion thus became the bulwark of class interest . . . While protecting and institutionalising the power

of the Filipino elite, the Americans allowed themselves to be used as an external device for deflecting criticism of their regime. (Thomson, Stanley and Perry 1981: 119)

The pattern of relations established between the USA and the Philippines has not entirely disappeared even after independence; the USA remains a critically important partner of contemporary Philippine governments as a consequence. The nature of the relationship also highlights a more general feature of American power and influence: the preference for arm's-length, rather than direct, control. This issue is explored more extensively in the next chapter, but it is important to highlight just how jarring America's role as an imperial power was for many in the USA, which then, as now, saw itself as a beacon for freedom, democracy and independence (Smith 1994). The contradictory nature of American policy was further highlighted by the fact that the USA locked the Philippines into a highly restrictive set of trade agreements during the first three decades of the twentieth century, effectively cementing its dependence on the USA. Moreover, the predominantly agricultural exports that went to the USA failed to benefit the mass of the population and entrenched the power of the large-scale rural landholders (Hawes 1987).

The Philippines has subsequently become something of an anomalous outlier in many ways, including its economic and political development. Indeed, the Philippines has performed significantly less well than most of its contemporaries in Southeast Asia, including Indonesia; but the roots of this underperformance can be traced back to this colonial period. Spain's initial colonization did little to integrate the Philippine economy into the developing international trading system. There was consequently little development of indigenous bureaucratic capacities to manage increased commercial activities, as happened in Thailand and even Indonesia (Crouch 1985). This comparative handicap was compounded by subsequent American colonization. The Americans had little sympathy with, or interest in, the development of indigenous government and the sort of extensive state structures that would become synonymous with much of the region. Consequently, the main impact of American colonialism, Paul Hutchcroft (1998) argues, was to consolidate the position of an indigenous oligarchy which was able to opportunistically enrich itself and use the state as a vehicle to maintain its own position, rather than as a vehicle for nationally-based economic development.

Given the importance of the colonial period in enabling (and possibly foreclosing) subsequent paths of development for all the countries of the region, it is worth highlighting a few general comparative points. With the exception of Thailand, which was also not immune to imperial pressures, all the colonial powers needed to establish working relations with indigenous collaborators if they were to maintain control and exploit the economic resources of the colony. But the style of rule and the manner of exploitation varied as a consequence of both the nature of the colonizer and the colonized. As Trocki (1999: 83) points out, the Dutch empire in the East Indies and that of the Spanish in the Philippines were 'pre-modern creations' that were established as early as the sixteenth and seventeenth centuries. The attenuated nature of colonial control meant they were more reliant on coopting local elites into their administrative enterprises. But the consequences of colonial power could be quite different: the declining status of Java's administrative class stands in stark contrast to the experience of the Philippines where colonial rule strengthened the position of the *mestizo*[26] classes.

When the ruling power was Britain, with its multiple colonies, noteworthy differences of administration and state formation could emerge even within one empire. In Malaya, the British worked with the existing Malay rulers to prop up at least the façade of traditional rule. Throughout the Straits Settlements, the actual implementation of British rule relied heavily on the Straits Chinese, who had established themselves as an increasingly important bureaucratic and economic force. In Burma, by contrast, 'the British were prepared to risk dramatic change' (Tarling 2001: 173). The fact that this change was frequently ill-conceived, and the country difficult to pacify, should not obscure the larger point about colonial differentiation. The distinction is captured in the notion of direct and indirect rule (see Trocki 1999: 90–7). The former refers to the attempts to impose 'rational' governmental practices on indigenous peoples, who were invariably conceived of as inferior and incapable of achieving effective self-rule. The British in Burma and the French in Indo-China came closest to this model. Indirect rule, by contrast, described the sort of collaborative relationships that existed between the British in the Straits Settlements, and the Dutch in some parts of Indonesia. The Americans in the Philippines attempted the first and entrenched the latter.

In short, the consequences and style of colonial rule in Southeast Asia are highly uneven and contradictory. Nicholas Tarling (2001: 199) suggests that 'the overall impression of the imperial regimes must be one of fragility and lack of penetration. Indeed, greater penetration was likely to increase fragility.' And yet, if we need to be careful about over-emphasizing the immediate consequences of colonial rule, we need to be equally alert about the possibility of understating the long-term impact of the colonial period. However resilient some indigenous beliefs and patterns of social relations may have been, the reality is that the countries of Southeast Asia are now part of a larger international system that has unambiguously affected domestic political and economic development.

At a very minimum, the countries of Southeast Asia are now part of a globe-girdling system of states and a ubiquitous capitalist system. One of the most important and enduring consequences of this transformation has been the consolidation of the domestic state in Southeast Asia, something that has generally been accompanied by a growth in the size, penetration, competence, centralization and range of functions of national governments as a consequence (Elson 1999). The development and relative strength of this sort of state capacity has been at the heart of the entire region's subsequent development.

Conclusion

Even a long chapter such as this can barely scratch the surface of a regional history that goes back thousands of years and encompasses such a diverse range of countries and experiences. Nevertheless, a few important points that emerge from the discussion are worth highlighting as they help to explain the course of the region's subsequent development, and the different trajectories of the countries that comprise it. The first point to make is that despite all this diversity, the countries of the region were all forced to come to terms with the impact of European imperialism, even if they were not directly colonized as were Japan and Thailand. Consequently, there is at least one common historical experience that they all share, which may prove the basis for at least some form of collective regional understanding, if not identity.

The second important general historical development to highlight during the period up to the Second World War has been the decline of China and the rise of Japan. As we saw, China had been at the centre of regional affairs – even if not strictly 'East Asian' regional ones – for several thousand years. Its toppling from this accustomed pinnacle was the cause of internal upheaval and national shame. The humiliation was all the greater given that Japan (its smaller, hitherto subordinate, neighbour) was not only instrumental in bringing about its downfall, but directly prospered as a consequence. Despite the fact that we appear to be in the midst of another long-term change in the relative fortunes of these two regional giants, this time in China's favour, the earlier humiliations continue to rankle, or at least to provide useful ammunition for diplomatic leverage.

Japan's rise and its own imperial phase is the third point to emphasize. Japanese capital has played a pivotal role in underpinning the widespread process of economic development that has occurred across much of the region in the post-war period. But even before the Second World War, Japan's imperial presence helped establish the conditions for economic take-off in Korea and Taiwan. Even more fundamentally, Japan's own successful industrialization before the war demonstrated that Asia could be a major centre of economic development and an important player in the inter-imperial geopolitical contests that were such a feature of the period. Seen in this historical context, Japan's post-war renaissance is less 'miraculous' and unprecedented than it might seem.

Southeast Asia's later economic take-off, albeit on a smaller, less successful scale is, nevertheless, rather more surprising. It is testimony to the effectiveness of some of the developmental strategies that were eventually put in place that so much development has occurred as rapidly as it has. As we have seen, while the colonial experience may have had the effect of modernizing and centralizing some political structures, it left the economies of the region heavily reliant on a limited number of commodities. Independence leaders would consequently face the double challenge of trying to encourage economic development and nation-building at the same time. Chapters 4 and 5 consider how they fared. Before that, however, we need to place the entire region in the context of the unfolding geopolitical contest that developed in the post-war period and that would, somewhat surprisingly, provide the enabling conditions for the rise of the developmental state and the 'East Asian miracle'.

Chapter 3

Geopolitics and Security

Most analyses of the East Asian region tend to focus on the security sphere, economic development or politics. Despite the deeply inter-connected nature of economic and political processes everywhere – espe-cially in East Asia – it is unusual for even political and economic issues to be considered simultaneously as part of an integrated whole.[1] It is rarer still for such analyses to be explicitly linked to the historical development of the region's security or geopolitics. I shall suggest, however, that it is simply not possible to understand either the region's remarkable economic development, or the distinctive form political relations have often assumed in East Asia, without placing them in the larger context of the region's unique geopolitical circumstances. We have already seen how inter-state and domestic level conflict were major influences on the course of regional development in the colonial period, and we have also seen how this dramatically affected the relative standing of Japan and China as a consequence. In this chapter, I shall explain how strategic factors are continuing to affect intra- and inter-regional relations, and helping to determine other political and economic outcomes as a conse-quence. One of the most important but counter-intuitive impacts of war and conflict on much of East Asia has been to encourage the development of the 'strong' states that are such a distinctive feature of the region more generally (Katzenstein 2005; Stubbs 2005). For this reason alone, an examination of security issues is essential if we are to develop a richer understanding of the evolution and importance of East Asia's distinctive political structures.

One of the central contentions of this chapter is that it is not possible to understand East Asian development without considering the influence of its relationship with the United States. As a result, the first part of this chapter considers the nature of American hegemony and its impact on the post-war global and regional systems. Explaining the USA's impact and continuing role in East Asian affairs involves saying something about the most obvious manifestations of traditional security concerns: inter-state war and domestic conflict. In this regard, there is no doubt that East Asia has been more affected than any other region – save possibly sub-Saharan Africa – by the ravages of war and conflict. Even the 'Cold' War was anything but in much of Asia. And yet, the remarkable reality is that there has not been a major conflict in the region since the end of the Vietnam War. Even more noteworthy, perhaps, is the fact that there has not been a recent major conflict in East Asia that did *not* involve the United States. For a country that is routinely considered to be an indispensable force for regional stability (Joffe 1995), without which chaos would supposedly ensue, this is an interesting paradox that needs investigating. In addition to providing a fairly standard, if brief, account of East Asia's principal conflicts, therefore, this chapter also critically interrogates the nature of America's role and its supposed indispensability, and raises the question of whether East Asia represents a putative independent security community.

Although the idea that East Asia could either resolve some of its internal differences or do without America's direct strategic involvement will strike some readers as outlandish, it may not be as fanciful as it first seems. Just as many East Asian ideas about economic development, business organization and the role of the state are noticeably at odds with the prevailing Western wisdom so, too, are ideas about security. In much of East Asia, policy-makers pursue a much more 'comprehensive' form of security that includes economic and social factors, in addition to the standard military capabilities that tend to preoccupy many Western observers. Even more strikingly, some countries in the region (Japan is the most important exemplar) have placed a much lower priority on military as opposed to economic security, and given responsibility for much of their conventional security needs to another power: the United States. At the very least, such behaviour represents a fundamental challenge to prevailing Western beliefs and expectations about what motivates states and how they will behave as a consequence; they are simply not supposed voluntarily to give up much of the responsibility for their own security. As we saw in the last chapter, Japan's unique historical circumstances help to explain its possibly anomalous behaviour, but it is not alone in developing an orientation towards security issues that is distinctive and at odds with practices elsewhere. Consequently, the second section of this chapter examines the very different national circumstances that influence security outcomes across the region. The final section provides a more conventional analysis of inter-state security relations and the principal possible sources of tension in the region. The overall focus of the chapter will not be on the minutiae of various weapons systems and comparative military strengths, of which there are already very many (see, for example, Huxley and Willett 1999), but on the distinct nature of East Asia's general strategic circumstances and thinking; these factors will provide the backdrop for the discussions that follow in other chapters.

Before we start, I want to explain my use of the term 'geopolitics' in the title of this chapter. There are two quite distinct ways in which this term is currently used. First, it is associated with a form of thinking about relations between states and empires that became influential at the beginning of the twentieth century. In this version, the primary concern was with relations between the 'great powers', their control of physical space, and the grand strategies they employed to this end (see Ó Tuathail 1996). More recently, as a result of the work of political geographers in particular, an altogether more critical use of the term has come into prominence, which uses the term geopolitics to describe the social practices and discourses that effectively create particular understandings of space and spatial relations (see Murphy 2004). It is this latter term that is of most significance here, as the active, social and political construction of regions is an issue of central importance to this book, and one in which, as we shall see, security issues have played a crucial part.

American hegemony and its impact

To describe the United States as 'hegemonic' is simply a way of trying to describe the nature and extent of its influence in the international system. It is not necessarily to make a judgement about whether this is a good or a bad thing; although it is possible to make argument in favour of either of these positions, and many people have done so. However, it is important to try to clarify precisely what the term means and why we are talking about American hegemony at the present time, rather than, say, Chinese. In short, what makes the United States so powerful that we need to consider it in the context of a discussion about East Asia, and how has its influence been manifest in the region?

The last chapter considered the history of East Asia until the end of the Second World War. The periodization is convenient and not accidental: the end of the Second World War definitively marked the beginning of American dominance of the international system, despite the existence of another formidable 'superpower' rival in the form of the Soviet Union. It will be recalled that there was relatively little mention of the United States in the last chapter, and this was also not an oversight. In fact, throughout the nineteenth century the centre of global power lay in Europe rather than North America, and with Britain in particular. But Britain's position had steadily declined along with its economy – bled white by two cataclysmic World Wars – to a point where it was 'simply no longer able to bear the cost of Empire' (Ferguson 2002: 352). And yet, despite the fact that the United States had rapidly become the largest economy in the world by the twentieth century, and a potentially decisive military force, it remained preoccupied with its own concerns, 'isolationist', and reluctant to assume the mantle of hegemonic leadership in the inter-war period (Lake 1999). Indeed, in one of the most influential contributions to debates about the nature of hegemonic leadership, Charles Kindleberger (1973), famously argued that the principal reason for the duration and intensity of the Great Depression during the 1930s was the failure of the United States to play a hegemonic role in leading the international economic system and ensuring it did not collapse into mutually destructive autarky and isolation.

Since Kindleberger's seminal contribution to the debate about the nature of hegemony generally and of America's position in particular, there has been a growth in analyses of hegemony from a number of disparate positions (see Beeson 2006a). Although there is general agreement that hegemony refers to the dominance of an individual country at a particular historical moment, there is less agreement about the precise nature of that hegemony or the way it operates. For the purposes of this discussion, the important feature of these debates is that they highlight different aspects of hegemony that have potentially important implications for political, economic and strategic outcomes in East Asia. Some of the most sophisticated and influential analyses of America's relationship with rising powers such as China have viewed East Asian–US relations through the prism of realist readings of hegemony, which emphasize the possession and pursuit of material power, and the likely eventuality of conflict that this implies (Mearsheimer 2001).

Yet, one of the most striking facts about the East Asian region over the last several decades has been the *absence* of conventional inter-state conflict of a sort that was widely expected to have occurred by now (Friedberg 1993/4). Even more dramatically, some scholars have claimed that East Asia has actually spawned a new type of state which has self-consciously relinquished, or at least downplayed the importance of, what realists take to be the inescapable, defining state function of military security. Richard Rosecrance (1986), for example, has argued that Japan represents a new type of 'trading state' that is able to take advantage of the new 'open' international order to become an economic giant while allowing another power to underwrite its security and the stability of the overall system.

Before considering Japan's – possibly unique – circumstances and experience, it is necessary to spell out another aspect of American hegemony, because it is central to the development of the sort of liberal, 'open' economic order that may have allowed Japan to behave in such an apparently aberrant way. American hegemony in the post-war period has been notable not only for its military dominance, but also because the USA was instrumental in creating a particular sort of economic system as well. Crucially, and in keeping with this chapter's major thesis, these developments were not coincidental but deeply inter-related. Because the

USA became a hegemonic power in the context of the emerging Cold War with the Soviet Union and the spectre of communist expansion in the immediate aftermath of the Second World War, from the outset American dominance was about more than simply military might. On the contrary, ideological contestation with what was then an apparently credible, centrally-planned Soviet economic system meant that it was essential that capitalism as system was successful and desirable (Hobsbawm 1994). The consequence for Western Europe, and to a lesser extent East Asia, was massive American economic assistance to prop up wobbly allies (Kunz 1997).

The most significant consequence of this period (other than America's direct bilateral aid for a number of key allies) was the creation of an enduring institutional architecture to facilitate and lock-in a specific type of international economic order (Ikenberry 2001a; Latham 1997). But the creation of the so-called Bretton Woods institutions needs to be seen in a larger geopolitical context that includes both security and political/economic issues as part of an integrated whole. Not only is it debatable just how generous the USA would have been in propping up its putative capitalist allies in the absence of a communist challenge, but it is also not clear whether American policy-makers would have been so tolerant about deviations from their preferred liberal ideal. As we shall see, successive US administrations have been prepared to turn a blind eye to political and economic practices of which they may not have approved in the context of the wider conflict with the Soviet Union and the possibility of defection (a situation that has completely changed in the post-Cold War period: see Beeson 2005a).

Consequently, American hegemony has been associated with the promotion of a specific institutional and ideational order. Until very recently, American hegemony was realized through multilateral institutions and the promotion of a set of norms and ideas associated with economic liberalism (Beeson and Higgott 2005). The way in which particular ideas have the potential to become the ruling orthodoxy and profoundly constrain the choices available to individuals and policy-makers alike is a major part of the operation of contemporary hegemony (Gill 1995). Despite the fact that 'the US' is in reality a disparate array of centres of power and influence that encompass not just the foreign policy-making elite, but an array of historically powerful domestic interests and lobbyists (Wittkopf and McCormick 2004), it has been persuasively argued that the principal manifestation of American hegemony overall has been the promotion and widespread emulation of what John Agnew (2005: 2) calls 'marketplace society', or the 'progressive universalisation of capitalist commodification and accumulation'. In other words, market-based economic systems and the social relations they generate are ubiquitous and at this moment in history there are no serious alternatives. Philip Bobbitt (2002) reaches a similar conclusion, albeit from different premises,[2] when he claims that the emergence of the 'market-state' represents the eventual triumph of the capitalist powers in the 'long war' with socialism over the form of the state during the twentieth century.

These are major claims of the utmost importance about long-term macro-historical change, or the evolution of 'big structures and large processes' (Tilly 1984: 61). The transformation that is occurring in China at present is powerful evidence of the transformative impact of globalization and the concomitant integration of formerly discrete and different social systems into an America-centric, capitalist international order. As far as East Asia as a whole is concerned, it is equally important to ask how individuals and groups respond to these larger processes and how such changes are manifest at the micro-historical level. Subsequent chapters will draw on the rich literature that details the very different ways in which essentially capitalist modes of economic organization are actually realized in different ways across East Asia. The big question that emerges from these analyses is about the rate of change that global processes are causing in places such as East Asia, which either may have little history of marketplace society, or may have domestic institutions that are so entrenched and powerful that they mediate and reshape global forces, making any 'convergence' process incremental rather than dramatic (Beeson 2002b).

These questions will be explored in more detail when the political and economic dimensions of these processes are given more explicit consideration. What we can say at this stage is that given such underlying differences within long-run macro-historical change, it becomes easier to understand why the potential incommensurability of American and Asian ideas about political practices and economic organization has been at the heart of seemingly interminable debates and conflicts over policy. While the possibility that ideational differences exist in the areas of politics and economics is increasingly widely recognized,[3] the remarkable thing about East Asia is that even in the security arena – where much traditional theorizing would suggest that the issues and imperatives are universal – relations between the USA and East Asia have been characterized by misunderstandings, divisions and fundamental differences in the way security is conceived. These divisions, and the ideological differences that effectively precluded any possibility of regional collaboration or integration, were most dramatically evident during the Cold War.

The Cold War in Asia

The conventional wisdom has it that Europe was the principal focus of superpower attention during the Cold War. Certainly, in the immediate aftermath of the Second World War when the future of Europe hung in the balance, and when it was not at all obvious that much of Europe would even become capitalist economies, let alone highly successful ones, the preoccupation with Europe was understandable (Milward 1984). After all, Europe had been at the centre of global power for centuries, and recent world history had been shaped by struggles that had their origins there. And yet, when we think about the dramatic shift from isolationism to global engagement, which underpinned a transformation of American foreign policy, it is important to remember that one of the seminal events that encouraged this reorientation was Japan's attack on Pearl Harbor, an event that unambiguously ended American isolationism and propelled it into war. The pre-eminent historian of the Cold War period, John Lewis Gaddis (1972: 353–4), argues that:

> From then on, American policy-makers would seek security through involvement, not isolation: to prevent new wars, they believed, the whole system of relations between nations would have to be reformed. Assuming that only their country had the power and influence to carry out this task, United States officials set to work.

The scale of this undertaking, especially the construction of the Bretton Woods regime, has already been touched on. However, it needs to be emphasized that the impact of American hegemony was – and is – uneven (Beeson 2005b). Europe was the principal focus of America's post-war reconstruction efforts; the levels of assistance provided, and the creation of a specific security architecture in NATO, was a reflection of this. In East Asia, by contrast, not only was there no attempt to institutionalize a similar multi-lateral security organization, but American attitudes towards the region were distinctly different, too. As Hemmer and Katzenstein (2002) point out, in Europe American policy-makers considered they were dealing with equals, and the multi-lateral post-war security architecture that emerged there reflects this. In East Asia, by contrast, American policy-makers felt they were dealing with an alien, inferior set of polities and the bilaterally-based, 'hub-and-spokes' security architecture they effectively imposed on the region expressed this. While it may seem rather shocking to contemporary audiences, it is important to note that racist attitudes towards Asia were reinforced during the conflict with Japan (Dower 1986), but surprisingly commonplace long before that, even amongst senior American policy-makers (Hunt 1987).

The net effect of the hub-and-spokes system that emerged in the aftermath of the Second World War as far as prospective East Asian regionalism was concerned was that any possibility of region-wide cooperation, or even meaningful dialogue, was foreclosed. Not only did key security relationships go through Washington rather than neighbouring capitals, but this underlying bilateralism was further reinforced by the fundamental cleavage that resulted from the rapidly intensifying Cold War. The ideological divide between the capitalist and communist powers, Cronin (1996: 6) claims, had rapidly become 'essential to the structure of the international system'. Essential or not, it had certainly become defining, with many countries aligning themselves with one superpower or the other. In an East Asian context, the emerging structure of bipolarity – or the nuclear-armed stand-off between the Soviet Union and the United States, which defined the international relations system for over four decades – was complicated by the 'loss' of China to communism as a consequence of the CCP's triumph on the mainland under Mao Zedong. This event 'caught everyone by surprise' and had the effect of suddenly propelling East Asia to the forefront of the evolving Cold War struggle (Gaddis 1997: 54). It is important to place this development in the context of the Truman Doctrine and the strategy of containment that informed much of America's Cold War policy and thinking.

Harry Truman's open-ended Presidential commitment to support free people threatened by internal or external oppression articulated and accelerated the development of America's post-war role. The Truman Doctrine not only provided a blueprint for America's foreign policy, but set in train far-reaching changes in the nature of the US bureaucracy and military as well (Hogan 1998). This period established a primacy that the USA has never relinquished, and gave a particular character to the Cold War period in the process (Leffler 1992). At the centre of the USA's Cold War strategy was the idea of 'containment', which was predicated on the assumption that only an unambiguously robust, militarily credible posture that made no concessions to an implacable foe could hope to curtail Soviet expansion (Gaddis 1982: 23). As far as China was concerned, at a time when non-alignment was unheard of, and when the pressing, inter-connected imperatives of economic development and national security made the Soviet Union an almost inescapable ally, it was equally inevitable that China would also find itself being 'contained'. But as Nathan and Ross (1997: 36) point out, the (relatively short-lived and tense) 'tilt' towards the Soviets was a direct consequence of the perceived 'need for security against the United States'.

This perception of vulnerability on the part of China's new communist leaders was perfectly understandable given the behaviour of the European imperial powers that I described in the last chapter, not to mention the USA's implacable ideological hostility to communism which intensified during the Cold War; and yet, given China's decisive, unexpected, high-profile participation in the Korean War (1950–3), it is worth spelling out the circumstances that precipitated it. Most importantly, neither the Soviets nor the Chinese expected the Americans to intervene in the way they did, given that Korea was not inside the 'perimeter fence' that defined the outer limits of America's strategic commitments. Consequently both were supportive of North Korean leader Kim Il Sung's goal of reuniting the Korean peninsula under the control of the Democratic People's Republic of Korea (DPRK): (see Yahuda 2004: 25).[4] It is also important to point out that 'even by world-beating Korean standards, [the DPRK] were fierce hard-bitten nationalists', who had formed an alliance with the CCP during their joint struggles against the Japanese and the Chinese Nationalists (Cumings 1990: 375). The North Koreans had fought with the Chinese communists and China was returning the favour. This was something that was never recognized by the Americans; neither was the importance of nationalism rather than communist ideology as a motivating factor in the North Koreans' pursuit of what Yahuda argues was 'essentially a domestic or civil war that had unanticipated international consequences' (Yahuda 2004: 27).

For the purposes of this discussion, it is this wider context, rather than the detail of the Korean War, that is of primary concern. The most important effect of the Korean War as far as the Americans were concerned was to make Asia a pivotal part of the wider Cold War contest, and to leave an unresolved problem that is routinely cited as a potential 'flashpoint' and source of instability. Before considering how dangerous the Korean peninsula actually is, it is important to note that one of the principal beneficiaries of the original Korean conflict was – somewhat surprisingly, perhaps – Japan. Not only did the Korean War bring about the end of the Occupation of Japan by the Americans, but it also saw its strategic importance increase. As a consequence of America's involvement in the Korean War, and of Japan's enhanced strategic significance as a potential bastion of successful capitalist democracy in East Asia, Japan became a crucial component in America's war efforts. As Richard Stubbs' (2005) analysis of the impact of war in East Asia demonstrates, Japan was a particular beneficiary of a process that simultaneously encouraged state strengthening across much of the region and gave a dramatic boost to Japan's post-war economic recovery. While the war may have been a disaster for Korea, it provided a crucial stimulus for a number of allied non-combatants, as did the Vietnam War in the following decade. Unless we recognize the inter-connected nature of these strategic and political/economic factors, we shall miss an important part of the region's development and the crucial preconditions for the subsequent economic 'miracle'.

The impact of the American Occupation on Japan's domestic institutions is considered in the following chapters, but one other inter-state consequence of this period merits emphasis. The emergence of the 'San Francisco system' was a central part of the evolution of Japan's distinctive approach to security policy. The peace treaty with Japan that was concluded in 1951 inaugurated a new structure of inter-related political, military and economic commitments between the United States and its allies in the Asia-Pacific (Calder 2004: 136). Its significance lay in the consolidation of the primarily bilateral security relationships mentioned earlier. Crucially, allies were offered the prospect of economic assistance to lock-in their support against the potential rise of communist China, and in favour of a 'soft' peace agreement with Japan, which some key allies (such as Australia) still viewed with hostility (Millar 1978). Japan in particular was offered preferential, asymmetrical trade and investment arrangements in exchange for security trade-offs. This period is especially important for, as Calder (2004: 146) observes, 'what is remarkable is how minor the structural changes in Pacific affairs have been' despite major changes in the region's political economies in the intervening half-century.

Security at the national level

Given the persistence of Japan's very distinctive security relationship with the USA, it is worth spelling out in more detail just how it has worked and what its implications have been. Japan's approach to security and foreign policy in the post-war period was shaped by its own recent, traumatic past, and by the emerging logic of the Cold War and American grand strategy. There were revealing tensions in the American camp over policy towards occupied Japan, with some (including Occupation Commander General Douglas MacArthur) wanting to concentrate on dismantling Japan's *zaibatsu* business groups, while others, such as the architect of the USA's containment policies, George Kennan, were pre-occupied with stabilizing Japan and reviving the economy. The implications of these sorts of divisions are drawn out in Chapter 5. Suffice to say at this stage that the concentration on economic revival which emerged from this period established a larger pattern that would come to define Japanese policy over the next several decades.

The evolution of 'comprehensive' security

The key figure in developing Japan's distinctive post-war policies was Yoshida Shigeru, Japan's first post-war prime minister and the architect of the 'Yoshida Doctrine' that bears his name. It was Yoshida who proposed permanently stationing American troops on Japanese soil as he wanted to 'ease Japan back into the world community without incurring the costs of rearmament or alienating the United States' (Schaller 1997: 27). In the context of the unfolding Cold War, an expansionist Soviet Union, a shaky Korean peninsula, a hostile China, and an East Asian region that had fresh memories of Japanese brutality and occupation, it was a shrewd move. It also gelled with a basic antipathy towards militarism on the part of a Japanese population that remained traumatized by the war and the nuclear devastation it brought to Japan itself (Katzenstein 1996). In such circumstances, the American imposition of the 'peace constitution' of 1947, including the celebrated Article 9 in which the Japanese renounced the sovereign right to use force to resolve international disputes, was less remarkable than it might seem initially. As Hughes (2005: 21) points out, the most enduring impact of the war had been the development of a 'strong strain of anti-militaristic sentiment amongst Japan's policy-making elites and general citizenry, and a genuine ambivalence about the centrality and efficacy of military power in ensuring security'.

The essence of the bilateral relationship that developed between Japan and the United States in the aftermath of the Second World War was one in which Japan relied on the USA to underwrite its security while maintaining a low diplomatic profile and concentrating on the job of reconstructing the Japanese economy. Although contingent circumstances may have provided the preconditions for a fundamental shift in Japanese policy goals, 'the fundamental orientation toward economic growth and political passivity was also the product of a carefully constructed and brilliantly implemented foreign policy' (Pyle 1988: 452). In other words, Japanese foreign policy in the post-war period may have been in part 'reactive' and affected by bureaucratic rivalries within the policy-making establishment, as Calder (1988b) has argued, but it also reflected a careful and highly original calculation of what Japan's 'national interests' actually were and the best means for pursuing them.

In short, nothing about Japan's post-war foreign and domestic policy suggests that it has been driven by essentialist, immutable, culturally-derived factors, or by the ineluctable, universal structural logic of the international system. On the contrary, Japan's foreign policy-making has evolved over time and reflected shifting balances of domestic forces and foreign pressures, in much the same way as it does anywhere. What the Japanese experience does remind us of, though, is that national policies are products of unique geopolitical circumstances and histories, and it is these factors that give national policies their distinctive qualities and delimit the range of possibilities open to policy-makers. In addition to the constraints placed on Japan by the war and American occupation, Japan's post-war leaders were keen to ensure the economic security of a country that lacked the basic resources to fuel its rapidly expanding reconstruction and industrialization. The disastrous consequences of Japan's aggressive wartime expansion into Northeast and Southeast Asia had demonstrated the dangers and futility of the military option as a way of securing Japan's economic future. The consequence of the long-term redefinition of Japanese security and the best means to achieve it was the formalization of the doctrine of 'comprehensive security', which emerged in 1980 under Prime Minster Ohira Masayoshi.

Japan's vulnerability to major economic and political changes in the international system was highlighted by the twin 'oil shocks' of the 1970s. Adding to Japan's sense of insecurity was the pronouncement of the so-called 'Nixon Doctrine' in 1969. Richard Nixon, chastened by America's ruinously expensive and strategically futile involvement in the Vietnam War, warned America's Asian allies that the USA was no longer prepared to commit troops to Asia and that they must assume greater responsibility for their own defence. This led to an emphasis on 'self-help' in Japan, and a gradual rethinking of the role of the Japan Self-Defence Forces (JSDF).[5] While this may seem conventional enough, the other noteworthy aspect of Japan's new security thinking was the development of 'resource diplomacy', in which the Japanese government employed an elaborate array of official development assistance (ODA) packages, and assisted Japanese corporations to secure access to vital resource supplies overseas (Arase 1995; Hatch and Yamamura 1996). The long-term significance of these strategies will become more apparent when we look at the expansion of Japanese business into East Asia.

Overall, Japan's notion of comprehensive security is far more encompassing than the notion of security generally proffered in IR theory, or the security practices of Western counterparts. Comprehensive security goes beyond conventional military security to include political, economic and sociocultural factors. As Alagappa (1998: 624) puts it, 'underlying the notion of comprehensive security is the belief that survival and prosperity are better served by all-round strength than by reliance on military power alone'. This basic insight not only allows us to make sense of the specific content of Japan's multi-dimensional, integrated developmental strategies, which emphasized the control of strategically important technological processes (Heginbotham and Samuels 1998), but it also helps to explain the attractiveness and emulation of such policies in other parts of East Asia.

While some observers have flatly denied the idea that there is any such thing as an 'Asian' approach to security (Segal 1995), it is clear that there is a range of concerns in East Asia that go beyond a narrow preoccupation with military matters (Harris and Mack 1997). Plainly, they are products of the region's specific historical circumstances. While it is difficult to generalize about such a disparate group of countries, it is evident that 'for most states, the core component of comprehensive security is still political survival' (Alagappa 1998: 625). True, this may be a concern of all states everywhere, as conventional IR theory might suggest, but this observation has particular significance in an East Asian context because of the region's unique history. As we have already seen, East Asia was profoundly affected by imperialism, an episode that revealed the region's vulnerability to Europe's superior military technology, and which galvanized Japan in particular into a rush to modernization. But the decolonization and independence processes have been equally influential in shaping the more broadly conceived notions of security that have come to distinguish the region.

Southeast Asian security dynamics

The more explicitly political aspects of the post-war decolonization process are considered in Chapter 4, but at this point it is important to sketch briefly how the military has developed in the region, as this has had major implications for both the type of political regimes and even the nature of the development processes that have emerged as a consequence. In much of Southeast Asia, it is possible to make a general observation about the legacy of the colonial period on the region's militaries: 'rather than imbuing the armed forces with military professionalism which required absolute obedience to the civil authority, colonial rule left behind armed forces more often oriented towards maintaining internal order than to external defense, and therefore implicitly attuned to domestic politics' (May, Lawson and Selochan 1998: 1). Consequently, the military has often assumed a uniquely powerful role, sometimes as a force for liberation from colonial oppression; sometimes as a vital tool of nation-building and development; almost always as one of the most powerful institutions in the country.

Indonesia is the most complete exemplar of these inter-connected possibilities and the highly distinctive role that the military has played in the nation's political and economic life as a consequence. Not only did Indonesia's army have its origins in the revolutionary struggle against the Dutch colonialists, but they played a crucial role in unifying 'Indonesia' from the highly disparate elements that had made up the Dutch East Indies. The pivotal nature of the ABRI's[6] role in Indonesia's development was captured in the notion of *dwifungsi* or dual function, which describes its military and *non*-military 'ideological, political, economic and socio-cultural roles' (Emmerson 1988: 115). I explain in more detail in subsequent chapters the impact of the Indonesian military on economic and political development, but at this stage it is important to emphasize a number of aspects of its role, some of which have wider implications. First of all, the military has been the most powerful, effective, extensive and penetrative organization in the country. In terms of effective state capacity, ABRI has been one of the most important expressions of political as well as more directly coercive power. Second, the Indonesian army is deeply involved in economic activities. To some extent, it had little choice: by some estimates 60–65 per cent of the military's operating expenses come from 'off-budget sources' rather than the central government (Cochrane 2002). This has not only encouraged the development of close ties between political, economic and military elites in Indonesia, but it has also encouraged the growth of corruption, illegal activities and cronyism (see Chapters 4 and 5). While the extent and institutionalized nature of some of these problems may be uniquely Indonesian, the final point that country highlights is more general: the military in Indonesia, as its counterparts across Southeast Asia, has been almost entirely preoccupied with *internal* threats to the survival of the state.

The preoccupation with internal security helps to explain the remarkably infrequent clashes and inter-state conflicts, despite widespread concern about the numerous supposed flashpoints and threats to Southeast Asian security and stability (Tan 2000). It is not simply because this sort of behaviour is sharply at odds with what much Western theorizing and policy practice might lead us to expect that the Southeast Asian experience is interesting; it also represents very different ways of accommodating specific historical circumstances and geopolitical pressures. Variations on the Indonesian theme can be multiplied throughout Southeast Asia. In Thailand, for example, the military was at the centre of national politics from the time it overthrew the monarchy in 1932 until the actions of a newly assertive civil society appeared to have significantly curtailed its influence in 1992. That the military should have assumed such a large place in the political life of the country for so long is explicable by the fact that Thailand's modern military has, from its inception, been 'explicitly political'; it was 'modernised to protect the regime from domestic enemies and enforce its policies, and was not intended for external defence' (Ockey 2001: 191).

The growth of civil society in Thailand and elsewhere in the region has potentially major implications for both the military and regional development more generally, and these are considered in more detail in Chapter 4. The potential tensions between military and civil society are also evident in other parts of the region, especially those with a history of authoritarian rule. Although the Philippines currently has one of the most vibrant civil societies in Southeast Asia, it has not always been so, and neither is it clear that the military's role in politics has been permanently ended.

Again, it is important to emphasize how important the historical legacy of the colonial period and the subsequent geopolitical context has been in shaping both the form of the military itself and its relationship to other social and political institutions. Not only was the military preoccupied with internal threats (in this case communist insurgency), but it also became a direct extension of the authoritarian rule of Ferdinand Marcos following his imposition of martial law. Significantly, under the guise of enhancing national security, the military became a deeply institutionalized part of the Philippine economy and politics, as well as gaining control over the legal system and media (Hedman 2001). As in Indonesia, power and patronage became increasingly concentrated in the hands of an authoritarian leader. Loyalty was given to Marcos rather than to the state, cementing the ties between political and military power. All of this was tolerated, if not encouraged, by the USA in the context of the Cold War and the perceived need for 'strong' allies (Berger 2004b).

Although the concern with domestic threats to national security is one of the defining characteristics of the Southeast Asian region, the precise role the military plays in achieving this varies. In Malaysia and Singapore, for example, despite the persistence of non-democratic political practices and rather repressive forms of rule, the militaries are generally professional and not directly involved in maintaining domestic order.[7] At the other end of the spectrum is Burma, where a military dictatorship, in the form of the grotesquely misnamed State Peace and Development Council (SPDC), completely dominates every aspect of national affairs, allowing no political freedom and jailing Burma's principal champion of democratic reform, Aung San Suu Kyi. The SPDC has, in one form or another,[8] been running Burma since 1988 when General Saw Maung seized power and crushed a nascent 'people power' movement. The military also controls Burma's principal export industry and cash crop, and supplies something like 70 per cent of the world's opium and heroin as a result (Neher 2001: 161). While this is clearly an extreme example, it highlights the importance of acknowledging specific national and historical circumstances in attempting to explain both the role of the military in Asia, and the sorts of institutionalized links to political and economic activities that may explain both the nature of their conception of security and the style of foreign policy it engenders, as well as the difficulty of instituting regime change.

It might be objected that while these sorts of national-level contingent factor are of interest in countries with little strategic weight or international significance, they matter less when it comes to the universal and timeless concerns of the 'great powers'. And yet, we have already seen that Japan, which clearly has the potential to become a major power if it so chooses,[9] has – until recently, at least – chosen to renounce aggressive militarism. Japan serves as a powerful reminder that nationally-embedded values and ideas about the appropriate role of the military can help to determine the role of the military in particular, and the nature of foreign policy more generally. Recent history suggests there may be limits to this process and that Japan may indeed be becoming a 'normal' country. But, before we consider this possibility in any detail, it is important to say something about China's military, since China is a country that everyone agrees is a 'rising power', and some believe it is on an inevitable collision course with the current hegemon (Carpenter 2006).

Security and the People's Republic of China

If there is agreement about China's increased significance in regional and global affairs, there is less consensus about what this might mean, or what informs China's security perspective. As we saw in the last chapter, the humiliation inflicted on a weak China by the European powers (in particular) sparked a transformation of the country's key institutions, and profoundly influenced the People's Republic of China (PRC) leadership's views about China's place in the international system. From the outset of PRC rule, much of China's inter-linked foreign and security policies have been driven by the essentially nationalist desire to regain its place among the great powers. While this might seem a conventional enough aspiration, and one that is perfectly in keeping with much standard IR analysis, the fact that China is notionally a communist country may make its policies and goals different, too. Indeed, history seen through the lens of Marxist-Leninism *ought* to look rather different from what was seen by Thucydides or Hans Morgenthau.[10] Thus, one of the enduring questions about China's place in the international order is whether it is, or may become, a 'normal' country, or whether its unique historical legacy – especially the century of shame, its more recent revolutionary origins and the seemingly non-negotiable status of Taiwan – means that it is inevitably a non-status quo power.[11]

Despite the fact that the Chinese case has sparked a good deal of interest in the impact of different, nationally-based 'strategic cultures' (see Booth and Trood 1999), the most exhaustive study of China's strategic culture, and one of the principal triggers for much of the ensuing debate, came to a slightly paradoxical conclusion: while individual strategic cultures do make a difference and influence the views of policy-makers, in China's case such views are 'long-term, deeply rooted, persistent and consistent' (Johnston 1995: 258). In other words, broadly similar views about security can be found in China both before and after the revolutionary period in which the PRC came to power, and – equally importantly – historically they are not significantly different from the views of other major powers, Johnston claims: 'Chinese strategic culture – with its stress on the overall efficacy of force for achieving state security, and on careful, capabilities-based assessments of opportunities for applying force – arguably predisposes those socialised in to it to make strategic decisions roughly along realpolitik expected utility lines (Johnston 1995: 260).

This may help to explain why realist theoretical perspectives initially became so popular amongst Chinese IR specialists (Shambaugh 1994: 44). Of late, however, it is significant that liberal and even constructivist perspectives have come to exert a bigger influence over IR scholars in China, a development that helps to account for the emphasis placed on China's 'peaceful rise' and the benefits of inter-dependence (Shih 2005). This is not an entirely unprecedented or inconceivable development: it is clear that the PRC leadership has operated in an environment where non-material factors have been important. China's communist leadership found itself confronted by a formidable opponent in an international and regional order that was divided primarily along *ideological* lines. Mao in particular saw American hegemony in ideological terms, reflecting a Marxist-inspired reading of history, which was cognizant of the inherent contradictions that supposedly drive imperial powers. While the end result may have been the same – potential conflict between major powers – the possibility that it might have been the consequence of the ineluctable workings of long-run historical-materialist forces made the prospects for the diplomatic resolution of difference infinitely more problematic. The fact that the PRC leadership actively aspired to become a leading in force in, and role model for, the Third World compounded the ideological divide.

It would be remarkable if there were not major differences in the way Chinese policy-makers and strategists view the world, especially when compared to America's. Since its inception, the United States has been blessed by a uniquely favourable set of strategic circumstances, with weak and/or friendly neighbours to its north and south, and oceans into which to project power to its east and west. To this benign picture can be added resource wealth and self-sufficiency, to say nothing of a remarkably productive combination of relative social stability and underlying dynamics. China, by contrast, is bordered by poor, unstable, frequently hostile countries, has been torn apart by foreign intervention and domestic upheaval within living memory, and is struggling to deal with a rapidly expanding population and growing environmental problems that threaten to overwhelm the country's capacity to manage them. Just how China is actually coping with some of these problems will be taken up in more detail later. At this stage, it is sufficient simply to note the hugely different geopolitical circumstances that have confronted the two principal protagonists in the unfolding strategic drama in East Asia.

Before considering how US–Chinese relations are evolving, and how this is affecting the wider East Asian region, it should be noted that not only are the views of China's strategic thinkers different from those of the USA, but they are much closer to the notion of 'comprehensive' security developed by Japan. Like Japan, Chinese conceptions of security incorporate both an economic component and a recognition of the importance of technological development (Shambaugh 1994). Wu Baiyi argues that there has been a major shift in the thinking of Chinese strategists over the last 20 years or so, in which there has been a notable shift from a preoccupation with national survival to a position in which there is a greater emphasis on national economic development. Crucially, this process is increasingly seen as dependent on integration with the wider, capitalist world economy. As a consequence, Wu (2001: 281) argues that security policy has become 'accommodative rather than confrontational'.

It is difficult to overstate the importance of this rather understated claim, if accurate. In a manner that liberal theorists of international political economy might find entirely predictable, China's governing elites appear to have undergone a major transformation in their thinking as a direct consequence of the 'opening'-up of the Chinese economy and the benefits that this has generated. As Johnston (2003a: 17) points out, 'Chinese leaders realise that this economic growth – and hence their legitimacy – comes from integration into the global capitalist institutions, not isolation from them or attempts to alter them fundamentally.' Rather than being a threat to the international economic order, China has, as I explain in Chapter 6, become one of its central pillars and a critically important source of capital for the USA itself.

Although it is true that many in China are concerned about the potentially negative impacts of globalization (Garrett 2001), it is also accurate to say that 'the most fundamental change in the dynamics of foreign policy decision-making has been the shift of emphasis since 1978 on the part of the central leadership from the nation's physical security to its economic development' (Lu 2001: 57). This merits re-emphasis because so many conventional accounts of Chinese security concerns and their possible impact on the region and the world focus primarily on military hardware (see Office of the Secretary of Defence 2005), rather than on the thinking of the people that control them. Clearly, the fact that the Chinese economy has expanded and allowed for the modernization of the military is a not insignificant factor in East Asia's overall development, but it is not determinative either. Indeed, the limitations of this sort of missile-counting approach can be seen by considering the proportion of government spending that China devotes to defence acquisitions. The reality is that despite alarmist predictions on the part of American strategic planners, China actually spent *less* on defence as a proportion of GDP and government expenditures in the 1990s than it did in the 1980s (Johnston 1999: 267; Nathan and Ross 1997: 147). This pattern looks set to continue as demands for spending on social services increase, leaving Chinese defence spending as a modest fraction of the US (see K. Crane *et al.* 2005).

At one level this might be seen as a pragmatic – realist, if you will – response to strategic realities: given the technological lead the US enjoys and the fact that, unlike China, its defence spending has continued to expand, then any attempt to maintain parity, let alone catch up, is futile (Segal 2003). At another level, though, China's accommodation of changes in the international system and its own place within it reflects, and has been manifest in, longer-term changes in the role of the People's Liberation Army (PLA). Although there have been significant attempts to streamline and modernize the PLA since the 1980s, not only is much of the military hardware vastly inferior to that of the USA in particular (Nathan and Ross 1997), but much of its senior leadership seems unsophisticated about the nature of both the contemporary international system and some of the latest weapons technologies (Shambaugh 1999). More importantly in the long term, the importance and political influence of the PLA has diminished as a consequence of broader changes in the Chinese polity, especially the increased institutionalization and bureaucratization of security policy-making, a process that gathered pace under Jiang Zemin (Tai 2001). Simply put, absent a major conflict, the military is nothing like as influential a force as it once was in China's policy-making processes.

Of course, it is precisely the supposed potential for conflict and crisis that alarms so many observers and which continues to inform American policy towards China and the region as a consequence. Before we consider this in any detail, however, let me briefly highlight a number of issues that emerge from this national level analysis of East Asia's security concerns. First, the particular preoccupations that galvanize specific national elites invariably have local roots. True, the wider geopolitical context has provided a critical, overarching conditioning environment within which strategic calculations have been made, but the latter have always been deeply overlaid by contingent factors and domestic sensibilities. The second striking thing to note is that such contingencies can have a regional component: not only did East Asian countries suffer similar historical challenges and traumas, but some of their responses show some degrees of commonality. The prevalence of a comprehensive approach to security – even where the detail or ideology that informs it may vary as a consequence of distinct national experiences – is a surprisingly common feature of East Asia's approach to security and has influenced the way the region's nascent security architecture has developed as a consequence.

Regional international relations and security

Having looked primarily at the national basis of security issues in East Asia thus far, it is time to turn to a more conventional examination of East Asia's intra- and inter-regional relations. There are, however, some limitations in the state-centric approach that dominates conventional analyses, and these need to be acknowledged at the outset. Most importantly, many of the most influential interpretations of state behaviour entirely neglect the sort of domestic level analysis presented above, considering that the actions of states are the entirely predictable consequences of the structure of the inter-state system itself (Waltz 1979). And yet not only have these sorts of prediction about the inevitable nature of state behaviour in the post-Cold War period not materialized (Waltz 1993), but the very structure of the international system itself has undergone a profound metamorphosis as well. On the one hand, the predicted return to a 'normal', multi-polar system has not occurred, while on the other, we are currently living in an era which is dominated by the United States and routinely characterized as 'unipolar' (Krauthammer 1990–1).

This is a largely unexpected turn of events. Although some observers have always emphasized the inherent structural power of the United States (Strange 1987), the conventional wisdom during the 1980s was that the US was in a state of inexorable decline, partly as a consequence of economic competition from Asia and its inability to sustain its hegemonic ambitions (Kennedy 1989). The political economy of the United States' relationship with Asia and the durability of American hegemony remain live issues (Beeson and Berger 2003), as we shall see in greater detail in Chapter 6. What is of greatest significance at present juncture is that the belief that America possessed historically unprecedented power but simply lacked the political will to apply it has become one of the core beliefs of the so-called 'neoconservative' thinkers associated with the administration of George W. Bush (Beeson 2006e; Kristol and Kagan 1996).

Consequently, two initial points merit emphasis before we begin to look at the impact of this transformation in the application, if not the underlying durability of, American power. First, current assertiveness and the direct commitment of American military might to remake political regimes and security structures across the world stands in stark contrast to recent American history. A little more than 40 years ago, the United States was making a humiliating retreat from active engagement on the Asian mainland following the Vietnam War. For our purposes, the principal significance of the Vietnam War is that it brought about a period of national introspection in the USA, a recalibration of American foreign policy, and an apparent reluctance to undertake large-scale military interventions overseas.[12] The renewed willingness to act 'pre-emptively' against perceived threats to American power has become a central part of the emerging Bush doctrine (see US Government 2002). As a consequence of this largely unexpected development,[13] the second point to make is about the impact of this changed policy stance on allies and potential foes alike. In the wake of the 'war on terror' and the USA's increased willingness to act unilaterally, other countries are being forced to respond to an unparalleled assertion of extra-regional power in a post-Cold War, unipolar era that leaves smaller countries in particular with little room for manoeuvre, other than possibly collaborating on a regional basis.

One influential view of East Asia suggests that such cooperation is unlikely because the region is 'ripe for rivalry' (Friedberg 1993–4). Europe's past could be Asia's future, the argument goes, but in the sense of nineteenth-century-style regional, multi-polar competition, not the increased levels of transnational cooperation and institutionalization, that characterized the twentieth. While Friedberg is right to highlight the increased salience of the region as a focus of security concern, inter-state conflict has of late been the rare exception in East Asia, not the rule. It is also important to note that cooperative approaches to security issues have progressed furthest in Southeast Asia, where the United States is least engaged, and remained underdeveloped in Northeast Asia, where the US is heavily involved in directly managing intra-regional relations (Alagappa 2003: 594). Consequently, the basic premise that is found in so much North American scholarship in particular – that America's strategic presence is the necessary glue that stabilizes an otherwise combustible region – may not be as self-evident as many observers seem to think.

However, there is no doubting the 'intense' animosity that exists between Japan and China, which some claim is only prevented from destabilizing the region by America's strategic presence in general and the USA–Japan alliance in particular (Christensen 1999: 51). But, while the depth of the historically-based animosity and mistrust between China and Japan is significant and arguably the largest single obstacle to meaningful East Asian cooperation of a European type, the scale and rapidity of their economic integration, detailed in Chapter 6, places major constraints on both governments.[14] In short, both countries have much to lose and little to gain from outright conflict. If this seems an unrealistically optimistic reading of relations between China and Japan, it should be remembered that the degree of cooperation and trust that currently exists between Germany and France would have seemed equally unimaginable 60 years ago. Times change, and so can attitudes – even when they are as historically entrenched as they clearly are in East Asia.

Two major factors stand in the way of any dramatic improvement in Sino–Japanese ties, however. First, Chinese and, more recently, Japanese governments have been able to make significant domestic political capital by appearing to stand up for national interests.[15] The Chinese have turned Japan-bashing into something of an art form, using it to extract endless apologies and aid from Japan, while simultaneously improving their own standing in the region.[16] For both countries, though, playing the nationalist card carries significant domestic risk, and thus far there has been a degree of pragmatic continuity in the bilateral relationship despite all the rhetorical bluster. The economic reality is that both countries need each other, not least because their economies are 'strikingly complimentary' (Emmott 2005: 14).

The second obstacle to closer ties that is especially pertinent in a strategic context is Japan's enduring reliance on the USA as its principal ally and security guarantor. As we have seen, the close strategic relationship between Japan and the USA is a consequence of the American Occupation and the culture of anti-militarism that emerged in Japan in the war's aftermath. Although the closeness of ties with the USA places inherent constraints on Japan's policy-making autonomy and regional leadership ambitions,[17] most observers of the USA–Japan relationship see the alliance strengthening (Hughes 2005), and remaining the 'indispensable core of Japan's position in the world' (Green 2001: 3). While this may seem to guarantee the existing status quo in ways that some argue even China welcomes (Johnston 2003a: 40–3), the development of the Bush Doctrine and the insistence that closer allies play a more active part in the 'war on terror' may be accelerating a major reconfiguration of Japan's strategic position. Richard Tanter (2005) suggests that those Japanese policy-makers who have long argued that Japan should become a 'normal' country, abandoning the constitutional constraints on its military role and developing a more independent military capability, have been given a major boost by recent events. And yet, despite the revamping of Japan's military capacity and the abandonment of its commitment to a strictly defensive security position, its tight allegiance to the Bush regime and the latter's willingness to exploit its structural dominance may leave it less room for manoeuvre than ever (George Mulgan 2006). In this regard, Japan highlights the possible incompatibility between bilateral obligations, and the development and institutionalization of an authentic regional security architecture.

Hubs and spokes or regional security communities?

We have seen that two factors have predominantly shaped security policy in East Asia in the period since the Second World War. First, the countries of East Asia have been powerfully influenced by the region's distinctive historical experiences and the challenge of integration into an international strategic, political and economic order dominated by the West. Second (and the principal contemporary manifestation of the first), there has been the role played by the United States. Two further implications of this general situation merit emphasis: on the one hand, the countries of East Asia have developed an – understandable – preoccupation with shoring up national sovereignty, security and the integrity of the state. On the other hand, the region has been fundamentally divided. The principal instance of these divisions was the ideological splits of the Cold War, which occasionally became 'hot', but which were invariably reinforced by older enmities and suspicions. It is, of course, in the interests of the hegemonic power that things should remain this way. As Michael Mastanduno points out:

> since the United States does not want to encourage a balancing coalition against its dominant position, it is not clear that it has a strategic interest in the full resolution of differences between, say, Japan and China or Russia and China. Some level of tension among these states reinforces their individual need for special relationships with the United States. (Mastanduno 2002: 200)

Some observers go further and argue that the hub and spokes strategy that the USA has employed in East Asia is both in America's interests and necessary for regional stability (Joffe 1995). Given existing regional tensions and a hegemonic power that currently displays little enthusiasm for either multi-lateralism or relinquishing its structurally-embedded dominance over the region, there are clearly some formidable, possibly insurmountable, obstacles to greater region-wide cooperation in the security sphere. Nevertheless, there has been a growth in regional security cooperation, and there is some persuasive evidence as to its efficacy.

The most important attempt to institutionalize security cooperation in the region thus far has been the development of the ARF. The ASEAN grouping, which was instrumental in bringing this about, is considered in more detail in Chapter 7, along with what is potentially its most important off-shoot thus far, ASEAN+3. However, it is important to make a couple of preliminary observations about ASEAN as they help us to understand the potential significance of the wider geopolitical context in shaping security relations in the region. Although ASEAN was notionally intended to 'accelerate . . . economic growth, social progress and cultural development' (ASEAN 1967), it was very much a product of the Cold War and the geopolitical imperatives that it generated. Shared concerns about the rise of China and the spread of communism, combined with anxieties about the USA's long-term commitment to the region, provided the impetus for regional cooperation (Frost 1990). Nearly 30 years later, the ending of the Cold War and the redefinition of the overarching international security situation provided a similar stimulus for the formal establishment of the ARF in 1994.

It is significant that from its inception the ARF was designed to engage, and if possible manage relations with, the major regional powers. Its membership consequently includes all the key countries with a capacity to shape security outcomes in the region.[18] Equally significantly, the ASEAN governments conceived of the ARF as 'ASEAN writ large' (Leifer 1996: 25). In other words, the sorts of operational practices, norms and behaviours that were part of the ASEAN grouping's modus operandi would form the basis of the ARF's as well. As we shall see in Chapter 7, this mode of operation has some decided weaknesses, and the ARF has also suffered from the same problems. But given that there was a perceived need to make sure that all the participants – especially China – felt 'comfortable' with the format, it was perhaps inevitable that membership of the ARF would have limited implications and obligations. But as critics have been quick to point out, consensus, voluntarism and inclusiveness (the hallmarks of the 'ASEAN way') have their limitations.

The major criticisms of the ARF in particular, and ASEAN's security initiatives more generally, centre on their apparent ineffectiveness, or on the necessity of there being a congruence of interest with the major powers. ASEAN initiatives such as the 1971 Zone of Peace, Freedom and Neutrality (ZOPFAN), for example, are frequently seen as contradictory and unrealizable, intended to limit extra-regional intervention while simultaneously recognizing and even encouraging the involvement of the major powers in the economic and security affairs of the region (Collins 2003: 161). Likewise, the resolution of the 'Cambodian problem',[19] which is frequently cited as ASEAN's finest hour and the pre-eminent exemplar of its diplomatic effectiveness, is seen by others as wholly dependent on a coincidence of interest between the United States and China, thus allowing the ASEAN grouping to play a prominent role (Smith and Jones 1997). Both the USA and China wanted to see Vietnam withdraw from Cambodia following its invasion to remove the murderous Pol Pot regime. It was this confluence of interests – rather than the effectiveness of ASEAN diplomacy in influencing either its neighbours or the major powers – that was decisive, critics claim.

However, it is the potentially crippling ineffectiveness of ASEAN-style approaches to conflict management that has drawn some of the sharpest criticism. Smith and Jones (1997: 147; emphasis in original) claim that ASEAN 'is not really a conflict avoidance organisation. It is rather an *issue* avoidance organisation.' In other words, ASEAN is primarily a mechanism for sidelining problems regional leaders consider politically too difficult or sensitive. Equally problematically, there is a potentially irreconcilable difference of approach between the ARF's East Asian and 'Western' members that mirrors the sorts of division that have hamstrung APEC and made the concept of an 'Asia-Pacific' grouping inherently problematic. With the noteworthy exception of Japan, ASEAN members and China prefer general, non-binding discussions about security issues, whereas the likes of Australia and the United States want to develop specific confidence-building measures (CBMs) capable of rapid implementation (Simon 1998: 207). While the divisions between ARF members may not augur well for agreement and cooperation, it may have the effect of encouraging closer ties between China and at least some ASEAN members of a sort that China is assiduously trying to cultivate (Ba 2003).

Although the prospects for China's diplomatic initiatives are uncertain, it is possible to make a number of observations about both the ARF and the evolution of strategic thinking in East Asia that suggest that the institutionalization of security relations can have important effects. At its boldest, this is thought to have created a situation in which the ideational construction of particular security orders is neither simply a manifestation of brute material preponderance, nor a one-way street. Amitav Acharya (2004), for example, has suggested that ideas about security are not simply mediated by local actors and 'grafted' onto local circumstances, but may in fact come to shape the behaviour of major, extra-regional powers. Acharya suggests that the Americans' acceptance of ASEAN's and the ARF's norm of 'cooperative security' – which was based on a non-legalistic inclusiveness and rejection of deterrence-based security systems – is indicative of the way in which the less powerful Southeast Asian states were able to influence the behaviour of the hegemon. Given the low priority the USA has given to both ASEAN in particular and to multi-lateral institutions more generally of late, it remains to be seen how binding these norms will be.[20] However, the possible impact of socialization and ideational learning seems clearer in the case of the USA's principal rival for regional leadership.

The great hope at the heart of ARF initiative was not only that China could be engaged, but that it might be socialized into 'good' behaviour as a consequence. Although we should remember that, as we saw earlier, there are multiple (frequently competing) interests at work in the construction of China's foreign policy, and that this is necessarily an elite-level process, there is evidence that 'China' is being socialized in precisely the way ASEAN desired. As Johnston (2003b) points out, 'China's involvement in the ARF and related processes seems to have led to the emergence of a small group of policy-makers with an emerging, if tension-riddled, normative commitment to multilateralism because it is "good" for Chinese regional security'.

In revealing and stark contrast to recent American efforts (see van Ness 2006), there seems to be an increasingly sophisticated recognition on the part of Chinese elites that multi-lateral institutions offer a way of consolidating their position, pursuing their interests, and reassuring a nervous neighbourhood about their long-term intentions (Goldstein 2001). Indeed, some observers suggest the United States is 'ceding regional leadership while seeding regional rivalry' (Heginbotham and Twomey 2005: 244). In other words, America's heavy-handed unilateralism, predilection for military solutions, and increased unpopularity within the region[21] is creating a leadership vacuum which China is attempting to fill. This is not meant to imply that China's policy is necessarily 'better' than that of the USA, although it may more adroit and alert to regional issues. Neither is it meant to imply that China will be motivated primarily by regional rather than national concerns. On the contrary, as Lampton (2001: 36) points out, 'China's elites will show no less dedication to the PRC's interests in the future than in the past, but gradually, by fits and starts, even narrow calculations of national interest may produce progressively more cooperative behaviour'. What it does imply, therefore, is that China's elites may have undergone a profound shift in their thinking about regional and international relations, changes that extend beyond security issues and which reflect some of the central assumptions about the nature of inter-dependence (Yahuda 1997).

There are, however, some apparently non-negotiable issues that threaten to cloud this potentially bright picture and undermine the idea of China's 'peaceful rise' which has been so carefully cultivated by China's ruling elites.[22] The biggest potential obstacle to harmonious regional relations, of course, is Taiwan which, as we saw in the last chapter, was taken over by the Chinese nationalists in the aftermath of the civil war. Consequently, the PRC regards Taiwan as a 'renegade province', an internal matter, and sees its eventual reunification with the mainland as a core goal of foreign policy. The principal reason that it is routinely cited as one of the key East Asian flashpoints is because 'China will not commit itself to rule out the use of force . . . and has the right to resort to any necessary means' (PRC 2000: 18). Although it has been plausibly argued that China is happy with the face-saving status quo and unlikely to act pre-emptively against an American-backed Taiwan (Swaine 2004), the unambiguous nature of the PRC's language, and the significance of the Taiwan issue in China itself, is grist to the mill for those in the USA who advocate the 'containment' of, rather than 'engagement' with, China (see Shambaugh 1996).[23] And yet, even those analysts who believe China still subscribes to an essentially 'realist' view of the world recognize the potential importance of institutions in modifying China's behaviour and decreasing the risk of conflict, especially if such institutions can incorporate Taiwan as well (Tow 2001: 120).

Clearly, conflict over Taiwan cannot be ruled out. Miscalculation, misunderstanding, accident or – more likely, perhaps – ungovernable nationalism on the mainland (Gries 2004; Miles 2000–1), could all overturn 'rational' calculations of advantage and plunge the region into a potentially catastrophic conflict with entirely unforeseeable consequences. The reality thus far, however, has been that China has shown an increasingly nuanced capacity to calculate its national interests and the best ways of pursuing them. This includes both an adroit use of diplomacy and a willingness to 'acquiesce' to America's preponderant position (Roy 2003: 57); the ultimate goal may be to displace the USA as the regional hegemon, but the means for getting there are incremental and non-confrontational. It is important to remember that, from Beijing's perspective, it is the USA that is the expansionary hegemon with a proclivity for using its military advantage to get what it wants, not China (Deng 2001).

By demonstrating a willingness to engage in multi-lateral diplomacy, China may also make a contribution to the resolution of two of the region's other notorious flashpoints: the Korean peninsula and the Spratly Islands. As China itself, Korea was divided by war and stands as enduring testimony to the impact of the Cold War period. Resolution of the 'Korean problem' is made inherently more difficult by the opaque, unpredictable nature of the North Korean regime. It has developed a quite distinctive and different identity compared with its Southern counterpart, and this is something that ought to give significant pause to those who advocate culturalist explanations of Asian politics and security. Indeed, it is striking how influential the construction of national identities has been in entrenching the divide between the two Koreas; it is also important to recognize how such identity-based assumptions remain an obstacle to improving relations between both the North and South, and between the DPRK and the United States (Bleiker 2005). The persistence of unhelpful stereotypes in both the USA and the DPRK has made relations difficult, especially since the North was included in what George W. Bush famously described as the 'axis of evil'. What is noteworthy in this context is that it has been China that has played a key role in convening the so-called 'six-party talks' that have been charged with trying to find a diplomatic solution to the current impasse (Yuan 2005).

A number of features of the Korean situation merit emphasis. First, as noted earlier, American unilateralism and a willingness to use its military strength have made it far less likely that the DPRK will want to give up its nuclear capability. This is not to defend or justify DPRK policy or the regime itself, but simply to point out the non-productive nature of American policy, and the reality that the North has pursued nuclear weapons as a way of ensuring its own survival (Kang 2003b). Given the potential importance of distinct national experiences and strategic cultures noted above, the DPRK's traumatic recent history and its reliance on the aggressive use of military force has tended to reinforce its pursuit of strategic autarky (Kang 1999). Second, the USA's heavy-handed approach to the North undercut the Republic of Korea's (ROK) own 'sunshine policy' and attempts to establish a rapprochement with the DPRK. As a consequence of this, as well as wider concerns about American militarism and its role in the management of the East Asian financial crisis, attitudes towards the North in the ROK have become more positive, while the relationship with the United States 'is rapidly and perhaps irreparably deteriorating' (Chaibong 2005: 70).[24] Third, American policy allowed China to position itself as a regional peace-maker despite its long-standing support for the DPRK, while Japan in a rare display of independence initiated its own overtures with the North as Japanese Premier Koizumi travelled to Pyongyang (Rozman 2004). Even in the event that the six-party talks remain inconclusive, China has cemented its place as a pivotal part of Northeast Asian diplomacy.

Whether China can improve its position in relation to Southeast Asia is a moot point. In this context, competing jurisdictional claims in the South China Sea present a potentially intractable problem in themselves, and also highlight a longer-standing nervousness on the part of the ASEAN grouping about their increasingly powerful neighbour. At the centre of the competing claims over the Spratly Islands is not the islands themselves, which are minuscule, but the potential resources that lie beneath and around them. China's gargantuan appetite for oil means that it has become increasingly concerned about securing vital resource imports. While it is unclear precisely how much resource wealth might be associated with control of the Spratly and other islands on the South China Sea, their dubious legal status means that they are the subject of conflicting claims. The way their status is ultimately resolved will be something of a benchmark for future regional relations (see Collins 2003: 189–200). Thus far, it has proved difficult to establish binding agreements between the competing claimants,[25] which in addition to China include Vietnam, the Philippines, Malaysia, Brunei and Taiwan. However, thus far there has not been any serious conflict either,[26] and China's simultaneous attempt to woo the ASEAN states with economic linkages and diplomatic overtures suggests that there is much to constrain China from behaving unilaterally, not least the possibility that it might drive the ASEAN countries into the arms of the Americans (Odgaard 2001).

The emergence of 'new' security issues

The dispute over the potentially resource-rich South China Sea also highlights a more fundamental set of problems that affects all of East Asia directly or indirectly. The most noteworthy aspect of these problems is that they are 'non-traditional'. For all the attention that is given to high-profile issues such as Taiwan, North Korea and the South China Sea, the reality is that the most likely long-term threats to East Asian security come not from the threat of traditional inter-state conflict, but from a new array of transnational issues that transcend national borders and which may be beyond the control of individual states. At one level, this has triggered an overdue debate about the very nature of 'security' in the broadly conceived Asia-Pacific area, and a welcome refocusing on human rather than state security as a result (see Burke and McDonald 2006). At another level, however, the focus on the new security agenda serves as a powerful reminder of just how challenging and multifarious the new security issues are likely to be, and raises serious questions about the capacity of states in the region to manage them.

Alan Dupont (2001) has provided perhaps the best and most extensive survey of the new security challenges and their possible impact on East Asia. Most fundamentally, the region's relentless population expansion and urbanization drives a series of inter-connected environmental problems: soil erosion, deforestation, declining air quality and increasing water scarcity, to say nothing of a looming energy crisis that threatens to put a fundamental constraint on the region's prospects for continuing rapid economic development.[27] Even more problematically, some observers think it inevitable that conflict over diminishing resources will be the trigger for future wars (Klare 2002).

Energy and environmental issues will be addressed in more detail in the concluding chapter, as they have the capacity to derail the entire development-oriented East Asian project. At this stage, it is worth briefly noting other problems highlighted by Dupont which are caused by unregulated population movements, people-smuggling and environmental refugees, as well as transnational crime, drug trafficking and the AIDS pandemic (to which we can now add SARS and bird flu, of course). This is a formidable and intimidating list of problems which inspires little optimism about their easy resolution, especially in parts of Southeast Asia where less effective structures of governance are the norm (Elliott 2004). Challenging though such problems may be, they highlight an enduring reality that conventional analyses of security relations generally neglect: 'transnational threats are primarily non-military in nature and constitute a broader set of security considerations relating to survival, resource allocation and the health of the planet. They are therefore unlikely to be resolved by military force or ameliorated by traditional security approaches' (Dupont 2001: 32). Many of the traditional analyses of East Asian security that remain preoccupied with the relative strength of rival militaries – an approach that continues to inform policy at the highest levels[28] – generally fail to acknowledge the importance of either the underlying trends that Dupont and others have identified or the redundancy of military options. The key security threat posed to states such as Indonesia, for example, is not invasion by a foreign power – what possible incentive could there be to do so? – but the disintegration and collapse in authority in what is already a fragile state.

At its most dramatic, this can lead to a process that Mary Kaldor (2001: 5) has described as 'more or less the reversal of the processes through which modern states evolved'. This internal fragmentation of the state and concomitant inability to govern is most pronounced in sub-Saharan Africa, a region dotted with 'failed' states, ineffective governance and consequently appalling economic development outcomes (Duffield 2002).[29] Ironically, parts of Africa cannot persuade foreign governments to become involved in their countries under any circumstances; the fear of invasion is the least of their problems. While Southeast Asia has not reached anything like this point as yet, and while it is rightly known for its highly impressive development outcomes, there are other threats that have the potential to place additional pressure on regional governments, and which may undermine both their legitimacy and their capacity to govern effectively.

One of the key challenges for the governments of Southeast Asia in particular comes from their association with the spread of terrorism across the region. The perceived need to combat terrorism has been given particular prominence as a consequence of the American-led 'war on terror' that began as a consequence of the attacks of September 11. This issue has attracted so much (frequently inaccurate and negative) attention that it is important to put the issue in perspective. Consequently, the first point to make is that there is nothing new about insurrectionary movements in Southeast Asia. There have been long-running struggles with an assortment of independence movements, rebellions and separatists in the Philippines, Southern Thailand and Aceh (Chalk 2001). What distinguishes the war on terror is the focus on *Islamic* terrorism, and the assumption that 'the West' is threatened by an implacable enemy bent on establishing a Muslim Caliphate across Southeast Asia. While there may, indeed, be some in the region who would like nothing better, and who would stop at nothing to achieve their ends, it is important to maintain a sense of proportion about this. The second point to make, therefore, is that much of the commentary on terrorism in the region is necessarily based on unreliable secondary sources, hearsay and supposition. Natasha

Hamilton-Hart claims this is a symptom of the same sort of 'ideological blindness' that characterized depictions of communism during the Cold War, with the further consequence that 'when anti-American hostility figures in explanations of terrorism it is pathologised as psychologically deviant rather than understandable in secular, non-fanatical terms' (Hamilton-Hart 2005: 316).

The debate about terrorism is often not just tendentious as a consequence, but assumes a remarkable prominence in public policy discourse given the very small numbers of people that have been killed as a consequence of terrorist activities.[30] This is not to trivialize the impact of terrorist activities on those directly affected by them, not the least of which is the dramatic economic impact such actions can have on places such as Bali. Rather, the intention is to highlight the disproportionate attention such threats are given compared to the other, very tangible, problems facing the region noted above. The principal reason for this is that Southeast Asia, as a consequence of its large Muslim populations and an assumed propensity for militancy, has become a possible threat to Western interests. It has been depicted as the 'second front' in America's war on terror, despite the fact that the extent of the threat and the organizational capacity of terrorist networks may be seriously overstated (Gersham 2002). David Wright-Neville (2004) has gone some way towards correcting the more alarmist and imprecise depictions of radical Islam by constructing a continuum running from 'activists' to 'militants', and making the important point that unhappiness about American foreign policy or a commitment to Islamic beliefs does not automatically translate into radicalism, let alone terrorism. The numbers of militants involved in terrorist activities in Southeast Asia is unknown, but appears to be small (Wright-Neville 2004).

If radical Islam's importance was confined to its ability to directly threaten the security of states such as Indonesia, then it would not be much of a threat at all. As noted earlier, parts of Southeast Asia have been living with the reality of insurrection and armed rebellion for decades. What makes the war on terror significant is that it has been instrumental in redefining relations between East Asia and the United States, as the latter has insisted that other states make it clear whether they support or oppose American foreign policy. Not only does such an uncompromising, unilateral position threaten to undermine the legitimacy of the United States itself (Kagan 2004; Tucker and Hendrickson 2004), but it makes life very difficult for the leadership of countries such as Indonesia, with a predominantly Muslim population that is increasingly sceptical about the rationale for, and impact of, American policy.[31] Given that Indonesia is in the first stages of a difficult process designed to entrench democratic governance, the authority and credibility of the government risks being undermined if it is seen as being too compliant in following the wishes of an unpopular foreign power. More importantly, in the longer term perhaps, 'we may be witnessing a return to one of the features of the cold war, namely a high level of tolerance for political regime variation in the interests of security' (Rodan and Hewison 2004: 397).

Certainly the USA's suddenly improved – for a while, at least – relationships with Malaysia and China, and re-established links with the militaries of Indonesia and the Philippines, were palpable expressions of America's new foreign policy priorities. And there was, indeed, a familiar willingness to turn a blind eye to regimes of which the USA might not have approved in other circumstances. Overall, the American preference for acting through bilateral channels and the privileging of security issues had the effect of undermining the region's multi-lateral security architecture on the one hand (Acharya 2005), whilst inhibiting the development of civil society in Southeast Asia on the other (Beeson 2004a). This latter issue is dealt with more extensively in Chapter 4. What matters here is the impact that the region's shifting security priorities have had on intra- and inter-regional relations and the nascent security architecture's capacity to manage them. In this regard, the USA's lack of enthusiasm about, and support for, the ARF has contributed to the latter's marginalization in the management of regional security relations, despite some observers claiming that American support for the ARF might shore up the USA's position as an 'Asia-Pacific' power (Goh 2004: 63).

Implications of the evolving security agenda

Where do the combined effects of a renewed regional preoccupation with security, the war on terror, American pre-emption and the rise of China leave East Asia? According to one long-time critic of US foreign policy, not only have America's misguided Cold War strategies been directly responsible for the emergence of new security threats including Al-Qaeda, but its rather overbearing and insensitive approach to Southeast Asia in the Cold War's aftermath means that some believe it is 'only a matter of time until the small nations of East Asia get tired of this American bullying and find a suitable leader to create an anti-American coalition' (Johnson 2000: 227). Although such views remain in a minority, Chalmers Johnson has been one of the most perceptive and best informed observers of East Asia for many years, and the idea that the USA is an obstruction to, rather than an instigator of, more effective regional coordination is becoming an increasingly common scholarly position (Alagappa 2003: 595). More importantly, it is also an idea that many of East Asia's political elites have begun to take seriously as well.

As we shall see in Chapter 7, it is precisely this recognition that underpins the emergence of ASEAN+3 and the Asian Economic Community, entities that intentionally exclude the USA.

The key question, of course, is which nation might provide alternative leadership in the region, and the obvious candidate is China. From a traditional realist point of view that focuses primarily on material power and comparative military strengths, there is a certain inevitability about both China challenging US dominance and the prospects for conflict as a consequence (Mearsheimer 2001). Even more sanguine analyses take the view that 'the United States is and will remain a crucial determinant of the stability of the Asia-Pacific' (Ikenberry and Mastanduno 2003: 423). And yet we have seen that the United States has been involved in both major wars in East Asia since the Second World War, and is currently the driving force in the war on terror and the major realignments this is generating in the region. Even if we take a broad view of the nature of 'stability', the idea that the region is unambiguously more secure as a consequence of American involvement is contentious.

This raises the question of whether the region might be more stable in the absence of the USA, and whether China might be able to supply such stability. In some ways, the question is misconceived and implies a rather narrow focus on conventional notions of security. Ironically, one of the most enduring elements of American hegemony and one of the principal sources of its legitimacy and the stability of the overall system of which it was a part was not military at all, but a consequence of the sort of 'soft power' that is such a crucial feature of its political dominance. This possibility will be explored in more detail later, but it is important to mention it here because many conventional analyses fail to make this connection to the multi-faceted nature of hegemony. And it is in this context – not in the narrowly conceived military arena – that China has most ground to make up.

Intriguingly, though, an historically-informed analysis that focuses on what Braudel famously described as the *longue durée* reminds us that the possibility of Chinese hegemony and a stable regional order is far from unprecedented or unimaginable. As we saw in the last chapter, for thousands of years China was the centre of a generally stable and remarkably durable 'international' order, in which the other nations of what we now think of as East Asia accepted its dominant position and frequently benefited from it. At a time when it seems inevitable that China will again become the dominant economic power of the region and a major strategic force, it is not unreasonable to ask whether an older and more enduring regional order may also be remerging. It is precisely this possibility that informs David Kang's (2003a: 57) contention that 'a rich and strong China could again cement regional stability'. Not only does Kang reject the assumption that an American withdrawal from the region would necessarily generate instability, but he suggests that Japan would have little to gain from initiating the sort of great power competition that many Western analysts consider inevitable.

While it is clear that Japan's post-war behaviour has been far from 'normal' and not what much Western IR theory might lead is to expect, it is not clear that it can reorient itself as easily as Kang implies. As Gavan McCormack (2004: 30) points out, George W. Bush 'could not have hoped for a more cooperative opposite number' in his bid to get Japan to play a more active, deeply integrated role in American grand strategy. Significantly, this involves not just overturning constitutional constraints on the use of Japan's military, but locking Japan into new weapons systems which make it 'overly dependent on the US, to the position where it cannot extricate itself from the alliance' (Hughes 2005: 144). While much of the legitimating rhetoric for these initiatives revolves around either the war on terror or – in the case of the Ballistic Missile Defense system – 'rogue states' such as North Korea, the real driver of the USA–Japan alliance is the rise of China. From a situation in which Japan was relatively relaxed about China's strategic potential during the Cold War, there has, claims Mochizuki (2004: 90), been a growing 'convergence' of views between policy-makers in Japan and the USA.

Thus, at the level of strategic policy, there are clearly major links between the USA and Japan which make the possibility of closer ties between China and Japan inherently problematic. Indeed, the development of enhanced security ties between Japan and the USA were formally announced in February 2005 and included a statement about joint US–Japanese efforts to resolve 'Taiwan Strait issues'. This was an especially provocative gesture as far as China was concerned (Boucher 2005). Likewise, Koizumi's insistence on honouring Japanese war criminals by repeatedly visiting the Yasukuni shrine in Tokyo was guaranteed to further inflame Beijing, not to mention Korea, which also suffered at the hands of the Japanese (Masaki 2005b). There are, then, a number of material and ideational obstacles that make the possibility of a good working relationship, let alone close ties, between China and Japan look fairly remote. And yet, the rapid expansion of economic ties between the two countries and the concomitant necessity for cooperation may make closer links inevitable and inescapable. In short, the fundamental dynamic interaction between coercion and capital that has been at the heart of both the development of the Western system of nation-states (Tilly 1990), and of the post-war development of East Asia (Stubbs 2005), will continue to shape relations across the region for the foreseeable future.

Conclusion

Most analyses of security in East Asia focus on relative military capacities. This is clearly a crucial determinant of the significance of individual states. Despite having an enormous army, North Korea would plainly not have the same strategic significance were it not for the fact that it has nuclear weapons. Similarly, the fact that China's economic development allows it to purchase new weapons systems is not unimportant; but we also need to remember that its still lags far behind the USA in terms of defence spending and technological sophistication (Crane *et al.* 2005). Indeed, Beijing's strategic planners are painfully conscious of their strategic inferiority and vulnerability relative to a far superior power that has shown an increased willingness to use its military might in pursuit of foreign policy goals. Given this American dominance and assertiveness, as well as China's recent traumatic history, it becomes easier to understand why its leaders might consider that a strong military is a prerequisite of independence in the contemporary international system. What is more remarkable, perhaps, is that they have not made this an even *greater* priority.

What this chapter has demonstrated is that national security policies and perspectives are simply not the same everywhere. True, there are some basic considerations that inform the strategic calculations of all states (the most important of which is the preservation of the state itself), but the way states go about this and the way they prioritize security issues varies as a consequence of distinct, historically contingent circumstances. Indeed, the very definition of 'security' continues to display noteworthy national and even regional variation. This latter point is potentially especially significant: despite all the well-known variations in the circumstances that influence strategic thinking in the countries of East Asia, there is a widely held belief that the achievement of security is a more 'comprehensive' process than it is generally seen to be in the West. Although such distinctive, regional orientations to security questions are no guarantee that East Asia's security relations will either be orderly or revert to some sort of pre-existing order centred on China, it does suggest that even in the contentious, seemingly non-negotiable security arena there may be some common ground.

Whether this will prove sufficient to overcome historically-entrenched animosities and suspicions, let alone provide the basis for an institutionalized, region-wide, authentically East Asian security architecture is a moot point. Certainly the construction of an East Asian 'security community', or a 'transnational region comprised of sovereign states whose people maintain dependable expectations of peaceful change' (Adler and Barnett 1998: 30), looks some way off. Even some of the most persuasive advocates of this possibility concede that such a community is 'nascent' at best (Acharya 2001: 208). Similarly, Buzan and Waever (2003: 177) argue that despite the increased importance of China at the heart of East Asia's intra-regional relations, unless and until China becomes democratic the development of a regional security community is simply not feasible. Such conclusions only serve to reinforce one of the underlying themes of this chapter: national differences remain crucially important determinants of both domestic security arrangements and external relations. The distinct histories and patterns of social relations that distinguish East Asian nations will continue to delimit the range of possible relations within and between the countries of the region. To see whether such distinctive histories will, indeed, prove insurmountable barriers to greater regional cooperation, we need to look more closely at the political development of the countries of the region and at the prospects for change.

Chapter 4

Nationalism, Domestic Politics and Asian Values

Some of the most powerful ideas about the course of history, about the prospect of future convergence for disparate national systems and about the dynamics of regionalism revolve around 'domestic' politics. As we have seen, it has become commonplace to argue that forces associated with globalization are systematically undermining the power of the state, making borders increasingly porous, if not irrelevant, and presenting a profound challenge to the idea that nationally demarcated communities of fate are still the most important political entities or sources of identity (Held 2004). Even more radically, it has been argued that the nation-state itself is destined to be supplanted by other – possibly regionally-based – actors (Ohmae 1996). More nuanced, but no less radical in its implications, is Francis Fukuyama's (1992) widely-known contention that in the present era, only systems that are economically and politically liberal are capable of answering the needs of contemporary citizens. In this case, there is some powerful support from Samuel Huntington (1991) and his claim that democracy has become an ever more irresistible and omnipresent force in world affairs.

East Asia's historical association with very different forms of political rule – ones frequently characterized by authoritarianism and political repression, the protection of sovereignty and the abuse of human rights – makes claims about the inevitability of change and convergence of more than academic interest. Indeed, if the arguments of Huntington and Fukuyama in particular are accurate, then the very existence of East Asia's traditional political order and that of the political elites who have benefited from it is in question. Given that political elites the world over are generally resistant to change that disadvantages them or threatens their power, we might expect such apparently ineluctable historical forces to be vigorously resisted. In much of the region, that is precisely what has happened. And yet, it is also clear that democratic forces are making progress across the region, too. Once again, there is no single 'East Asian model' or experience. There are, however, some important continuities and commonalities that distinguish the region, and these could conceivably serve as the basis for a common approach to regional integration. At the very least, East Asia's national political structures and traditions will effectively delimit the range of possible regional outcomes and thus merit detailed consideration.

Although it is not possible to provide a single, all-encompassing explanation for East Asia's political heterogeneity, or even to elaborate a consistent set of variables that accounts for specific national circumstances, it is possible to identify a number of key issues and forces that are common across the region. In this context, the legacy of history and the impact of the distinct set of geopolitical and strategic circumstances detailed in earlier chapters have exerted a powerful influence across East Asia. More recently, individual countries have been attempting to accommodate the challenges of 'globalization' and the array of external pressures that are encouraging, sometimes compelling, changes in the internal regulatory architectures of individual states and the socio-political milieus within which they are embedded. Economic development and integration are reconfiguring domestic class structures and political relationships in unpredictable ways that defy easy generalization, but which reflect the particular history of each country and the manner in which it has responded to, and articulated with, the wider international system. As we shall see in this chapter and those that follow, the success of this adaptation depends in large part on the 'strength'[1] of the state and the sort of capacities discussed in Chapter 1. As we shall see, there are a variety of ways of responding to the inter-connected challenges of internal transformation and external pressure.

The primary concern of this chapter is with the internal changes and accommodations found in East Asia. Consequently, it surveys the different political structures found in the region, which run the gamut from genuine democracy to military dictatorship, with various forms of authoritarianism and 'semi-democracy' in between. It also explains the specific circumstances that have made authoritarian rule such a common part of East Asia's collective history, and why nationalism continues to exert such a powerful appeal despite the emergence of apparently universal pressures for change and emancipation. As we shall see, political repression has left a powerful legacy, and civil society in much of East Asia remains underdeveloped as a result. Even where it has developed, in places such as the Philippines, this is no guarantee of either good governance or immunity from military takeovers. Even global forces are filtered through domestic institutions and may not have the impact we might expect.

This chapter is the first of two inter-connected discussions of the political economy of the region. Although political and economic forces are thoroughly meshed and cannot be understood in isolation from each other (Underhill 2001), for the sake of convenience I shall initially examine some of the more formal expressions of political activity across the region, before looking at how this has affected national patterns of governance and economic development in the next chapter. Consequently, after examining the theoretical claims about the nature of democratization, globalization and their potential impact on authoritarianism, the particular circumstances that have led to the wide variety of political outcomes across the region will be explained. This will be done by initially considering Japan and the countries of Northeast Asia, followed by Southeast Asia, and then finally China. (A similar structure is employed in the next chapter as well.) Finally, we shall consider whether there is any basis for a pan-Asian discourse of identity and political development; the idea of 'Asian values' provides an especially illuminating framework through which to explore such possibilities.

East Asia's democratic moment?

Before looking at specific East Asian experiences, it is worth putting these general developments in historical and theoretical context. It should be emphasized at the outset that much of 'our' thinking about the prospects for East Asia, and the sort of political and economic trajectory it *ought* to follow, is a consequence of the bias of Euro-centrism (Hamilton 1994). Because the West has come to dominate much of the rest of the world through imperialism – be it the older economic variety or the more recent cultural version – it becomes easy to believe that this is the 'natural' order of things and that no other outcomes were, or are, possible. This was certainly implicit in the writings of the so-called 'modernization' theorists who were so influential during the Cold War period.[2] However, it is plain that there is a good deal of resistance to the some of the most pervasive and insidious expressions of globalization (Barber 2001). Moreover, it is not at all clear that there is only one way of responding to global forces politically. As the next two chapters demonstrate, there are still distinctive, nationally-based ways of managing economic development and integration, even in an increasingly global economy. The questions we need to consider in this chapter are whether the very diverse political regimes that are found across the region are likely to persist in the face of global pressures, and whether they are likely to provide fundamental obstacles to more regionally-based relationships if they do.

The temptation to view the East Asian experience through Western lenses may be strong, but it needs to be resisted. It is important to remember that 'the rise of the West', and the distinctive political practices, belief systems, and economic relationships it generated were products of a very specific set of historical circumstances (Hall 1986; Spruyt 1994;

Tilly 1990). The transformation of social relations that the development of capitalism inaugurated in Western Europe was not replicated in what was then a more stable China or other parts of Asia until much later. It is important to keep this in mind because the transformation in European social structures that was associated with the rise of a domestic capitalist class, and in the sorts of concomitant changes in the distribution of political power that the rising classes demanded, simply did not happen in the same way in Asia. In terms of political development, this was a double blow: not only did much of Asia not experience the kind of improvements in living standards and technological development that occurred in much of the West, but they did not receive the same impetus for political emancipation and democratization either. This is crucial, because the development of more 'progressive', economically dynamic class structures appears to be one of the prerequisites for any move towards more democratic political practices (Rueschemeyer, Stephens and Stephens 1992).

One of the crucial factors that came to distinguish parts of Europe, and which stands in sharp contrast to the East Asian experience, is what Held (1995: 69) calls the 'reciprocity of power'. The growing dependence of national governments on cooperative subject populations brought about a long-term change in state–society relations. This change was consolidated by the growing legitimacy of emerging nation-states, ultimately entrenched in systems of representative democracy, and codified in new regulatory architectures. In Western Europe's case, the accommodation between economic and social forces has proved remarkably durable, adaptive and capable of encompassing significant variations on the overall theme of capitalist democracy (Boyer and Hollingsworth 1997; Jessop 2003). The ubiquity of the capitalist-democratic form in Western Europe has evidently made the development of regional cooperation much easier as well. This resilience, and the historical tendency for the capitalist state to supplant all rivals, is undoubtedly a major reason that observers such as Fukuyama have claimed that there is a certain inevitability about the technically superior form of Western political organization sweeping all before it. Yet, not only is the ascendancy of the state not as assured as once thought, but the associated triumph of democracy – or at least a democracy worthy of the name[3] – is even more uncertain.

Again, it is important to emphasize how unexpected and counterintuitive this all is. The state has rightly come to be seen as the dominant political institution of the modern period, and its association with economic development has underpinned expectations about the course of political reform. However, while economic development may make the transition to democratic patterns of government more likely, in that it has the capacity to encourage the growth of new class forces that may undermine non-democratic or authoritarian forms of rule and demand greater emancipation (Huntington 1991: 72), this does not guarantee political reform. On the contrary, not only are some forms of non-democratic authoritarian rule actually positively associated with economic development (Bertrand 1998; Leftwich 2000), but there is no necessary link between democracy and development either (Przeworski *et al*. 2000: 271). Moreover, it has been argued that the emergent middle classes of East Asia, which might be expected to demand greater political rights, may be prepared to trade them off for more economic development and security (Jones 1998). What we can say is that forms of corporatism, characterized by state bureaucratic domination, monopolistic political representation, ideologically exclusive executive authorities and anti-liberal, authoritarian or mercantilist states (Schmitter 1979: 22), have been surprisingly prominent across much of East Asia.

These are issues that need to be explored by looking at the very different accommodations that have been arrived at in East Asia. Before doing so, however, it is possible to make a few generalizations that will help to make sense of the ensuing discussion. First, although the path to democracy may still be more uncertain and varied than some of the Fukuyama-esque analyses might have us believe, there does seem to be strong evidence to suggest that if the transition is made, 'democracy is almost certain to survive in countries with per capita incomes above [US]$4,000' (Przeworski *et al*. 2000: 273). This matters because many of the countries of the region – including large parts of China – have either achieved such income levels, or have them in sight. Consequently, the prospects for democratic consolidation, all other things being equal,[4] look good if the initial hurdle of transition can be safely negotiated. The second point to emphasize is that while stable growth and democratic consolidation may have the potential to become a virtuous circle, its realization 'depends on the development of political institutions that can effectively mediate policy debates and coordinate relations among contending social and economic interests' (Haggard and Kaufman 1995: 335). The state's ability to manage these contests and their direct impact on the development process will be taken up in the next chapter; most attention will be focused on the more narrowly conceived political structures and struggles in this one. One final point merits brief consideration before we look at political life in the region in any detail: the enduring importance of nationalism.

That nationalism is such a powerful force in East Asia, and has the capacity to influence the course of development there, should not surprise us. After all, nationalism was a central part of the earlier

European experience and an essential part of the nation-state coupling in particular and the dominance of Europe more generally (Hobsbawm 1987). Indeed, nationalism has been considered one of the essential qualities of European-style modernity and a prerequisite for the development of industrial economies and societies (Gellner 1983). Although the importance of nationalism and the purposes to which it has been put vary across the region, for some countries – Indonesia is, perhaps, the most important exemplar – it potentially offered the glue with which to bind together the disparate and arbitrary remnants of the Dutch empire. As Anderson (1983: 12) observed: 'It is the magic of nationalism to turn chance into destiny.' Put more prosaically in the language of social science, nationalism provided what Giddens (1985: 219) called the 'cultural sensibility of sovereignty'. In other words, if the emergent independent states of Southeast Asia – and the liberated, reconstituted states of Northeast Asia for that matter – were to amount to more than lines on a map and notional claims to jurisdictional authority, then their leaders needed the support of the populations they claimed to represent and the populations needed to recognize themselves as part of the same collectivity.

When seen in this light, it becomes easier to understand why so many of East Asia's political elites have been preoccupied with developing national myths, protecting sovereignty, and generally resisting external intrusion: the nation-state was often a fragile entity, but one that (if successfully realized) held out the prospect of more effective governance and control within politically demarcated boundaries, however arbitrary, contested and contingent their origins may be. The great paradox for East Asia is that, at the very moment when it might be expected that nationalism would come into its own, the entire nationalist project is being undercut by global processes that are systematically undermining 'national' borders and bringing the authority and competence of national governments into question. Moreover, in many parts of the world there is a growing tension between the national identities that were established in the original nation-building period, and the sorts of local (and even transnational) identities that have become more prominent or reconstituted by processes associated with globalization. At a moment when – in much of the trail-blazing West, at least – individual identities are becoming much more contingent, reflexive and detached from national boundaries, there are important questions to be asked about the future of nationalism and even its possible mutation into 'supra-nationalism' (see Smith 1998: ch. 9) These are questions that are central to the future of East Asia and its constituent parts. Before considering them, however, it is necessary to look back at the evolution of the various political regimes in the region.

Japan and Northeast Asia

This section examines the political development of Japan, the two Koreas and Taiwan. Most attention is given to Japan, partly because it is one of East Asia's unambiguous major powers, but also because it has played such a central role in shaping the overall region's post-war development. (An equal amount of attention is given to China later for similar reasons.) Japan is especially important as an exemplar of a highly successful *Asian* state, and a capitalist one at that: whatever problems Japan may have experienced recently in attempting to adjust to competing regional and global pressures, the fact remains that it pioneered a very distinctive way of accelerating the developmental process. The nature of Japan's early successes and its more recent problems is in part a reflection of its political system and the competence of its political class.

The riddle of Japan

Even by East Asia's remarkably diverse standards, Japan is something of an anomaly. It is, of course, the region's most enduring democracy and frequently cited as proof that 'Western' forms of democratic rule can be successfully transplanted to other parts of the world.[5] Even though the formal mechanisms of democracy have been established in Japan, it is a fairly unusual variant. Not only has Japanese democracy been associated with a form of what Johnson (1987) calls 'soft authoritarianism', but it has also been a virtual one-party state: with the exception of a brief interregnum in 1993 when a coalition government led by Hosakawa Morihiro held power, the Liberal Democratic Party (LDP) has enjoyed an unbroken period of rule since 1955. If the regular turnover of ruling elites really is considered to be a defining part of democratic life, then it is an open question how well Japan actually qualifies.[6]

Those analysts enamoured of culturalist explanations of what Pye (1985: ch. 6) calls the 'riddle of Japan' attribute its distinctive political development to factors including the influence of Confucianism and 'traditional' social values based on merit, respect, filial piety and so on. Such views have been given renewed currency as explanations of East Asia's more general political and economic development with the promotion of 'Asian values' – despite the fact that, as I suggested earlier, the very same values were once widely thought to have *inhibited* development in Asia. Be that as it may, there are some rather more tangible, specific and mundane explanations of Japan's distinctive patterns of political life, reasons that have as much to do with war and peace, and the familiar staples of interest-driven politics, as they do with anything distinctly 'Asian'.

A number of specific events helped to give a particular shape to Japan's post-war politics. Most decisive, of course, was the fact that Japan not only lost a major war, but lost it to the United States (Johnson 1999). That Japan might have lost enthusiasm for militarism and been amenable to a new national paradigm was understandable, given that over 2 million Japanese were killed during the Second World War and their country was left economically devastated. What was equally important, though, was America's vision of itself as an instrument of political emancipation (Smith 1994), which rapidly allowed America's forces to adopt a paternalistic role once Japan had been peacefully occupied (Dower 1986: 305). That such attitudes were often racist and ill-informed did not make them any less effective. Significantly, the demilitarization and democratization of Japan were seen by the Americans as deeply intertwined, with the latter guaranteeing the former. Equally significantly, in the early phases of this process, political change was 'fundamentally progressive' (Dower 1995: 166): even the Communist Party was legalized, and trade unions were allowed to organize freely.

However, this pattern of political mobilization, openness and expanding civil society – which is what we might expect a genuine democracy to look like – could not survive in the bleak atmosphere of the Cold War and the geopolitical constraints it imposed. Although the Americans had only limited success in modifying Japan's bureaucratic and corporate structures, they were far more effective in crushing Japan's post-war labour militancy.[7] The significance of this process should not be underestimated for the eventual triumph of Japan's distinctive, highly cooperative, managerial style of labour relations is anything but a 'natural' expression of underlying social harmony (Gordon 1993). Likewise, the eventual course of Japanese politics and its crystallization into its distinctive one-party dominance owes much to the overarching imperatives of this period.

At a formal level, the most significant changes in post-war Japan revolved around the imposition of the 'peace constitution' discussed in the last chapter, and the shift of sovereign power from the Emperor to Japan's parliament, the Diet. The intention was to create a Westminster-style political structure in which executive power would reside with the Prime Minister and Cabinet. The other goals of the reforms were to broaden participation in the political process by allowing women to vote and curbing the power of big business and rural landlords. There were also attempts at bureaucratic reorganization and decentralization, which are discussed in greater detail in the next chapter, but which can be simply characterized at this stage as rather ineffectual. Nevertheless, as far as the formal trappings of democratic rule were concerned, Japan experienced a major post-war restructuring (see Stockwin 1999).

At the same time as these changes to the formal structure of the political system were being enacted, major developments were occurring within Japan's political parties that were to give such a distinctive cast to Japanese politics. In the first decade after the war, Japan experienced a number of short-lived coalition governments between socialists and conservatives. Predictably enough, these coalitions proved unstable. In 1955, in one of the defining moments of Japan's post-war political history, the various conservative parties came together to form the LDP. As noted earlier, it has hardly been out of office ever since. The key to the LDP's dominance has been its ability to attract support from big business, the agricultural sector and Japan's expanding urban middle class on the one hand, and skilfully to manage and accommodate internal disagreements on the other (Jain 1997). The other factor that consolidated the position of the LDP, and which allowed it permanently to eclipse its rivals in the Japan Socialist Party (JSP), was American support for the LDP over its Soviet-oriented socialist opponent. Again, the Cold War context proved pivotal.[8] Overall, one of the most striking features of the LDP has been its ability to accommodate internal differences. This is primarily because internal divisions are non-ideological, but revolve around power struggles between different factions within the LDP itself (Eccleston 1995). The absence of internal ideological competition mirrored a wider social consensus that emerged during the 1960s: the primary objective of the government (and the people more generally, for that matter) was an unrelenting focus on economic growth.

As we shall see in the next chapter, this allowed key bureaucratic agencies to take responsibility for planning Japan's economic renaissance. It also consolidated a basic division of labour amongst Japan's elites and further encouraged the growth of factional politics within what was effectively a form of one-party rule. This helps to explain some other novel features of Japanese politics. One of the most striking aspects of Japan's post-war political system is not just the very prominent role assumed by unelected officials within the bureaucracy, but the comparatively uninfluential role of the political class that is notionally in charge. Japan's political class simply has not played anything like the same sort of active, policy-making and implementing role that similar groups have elsewhere. There are signs that, after many false starts, this relationship may be finally changing, and the key institutional actors, such as the prime minister, may be acquiring the sort of power enjoyed by their counterparts in the West.[9] However, this is a relatively recent development, and for most of Japan's post-war history things were very different. In the so-called 'iron triangle', a mutually rewarding division of labour and responsibility was maintained between the bureaucracy, professional politicians and business elites. Some of its style is captured in van Wolferen's bleak assessment:

> The bureaucrats tinker with the economy, making adjustments to facilitate further growth. The politicians and almost everyone else keep out of their way. Parliamentary representatives, largely chosen for their pork-barrelling skills, attend mainly to the business of getting re-elected. Since this depends largely on their ability to spread national wealth politicians are perpetually indebted to the bureaucratic guardians of the budget. The industrialists continue to expand their foreign market shares, and enter new markets with the help of the bureaucrats. They are kept in line by their peers and they pay the politicians. Nobody is boss, but everybody, in some way or other, has leverage over somebody else, which helps maintain an orderly state of affairs. (van Wolferen 1989: 54)

While this has become a somewhat dated caricature, it does capture something important about the nature of Japan's post-war politics, and suggests what can go wrong with the idealized notion of the developmental state. Before we consider that, however, it is important to explain how the political system operated in Japan, why it became so dysfunctional and impotent, and why – as it has done elsewhere in East Asia – 'money politics' mattered so much.

If one individual epitomizes much that is unique about Japan's post-war politics, it is Tanaka Kakuei who, despite being dogged by corruption scandals throughout his career and being forced to resign the prime ministership in 1974 after being accused (and ultimately convicted) of taking bribes from the American Lockheed Corporation, still exerted a powerful influence over the LDP as a 'shadow shogun'. He was able to do this by making his own faction the largest in the LDP and ensuring that it 'became impossible for anyone to become prime minister without the support of the Tanaka faction' (Curtis 1999: 82). Tanaka was the quintessential kingmaker to whom any prime minister was beholden, and who could insist on control of key cabinet posts in proportion with the strength of his faction. Tanaka was able to influence the selection of prospective LDP candidates, which ensured their loyalty was to him personally, rather than to the LDP as a whole (Schlesinger 1999). The depth of such ties cannot be underestimated: even after his conviction and disgrace, prominent younger generation politicians such as Ozawa Ichiro remained publicly loyal to their former mentor. The cost of competing in Japan's complex electoral system meant that such ties were often reinforced through the direct distribution of resources. The consequence of this, of course, was to entrench the role and importance of money politics.[10]

While this depiction of Japan's political system may seem unremittingly negative, I should emphasize two things. First, this very same system was also at the heart of Japan's dramatic, historically unprecedented post-war recovery and rise to economic prominence. One of the things that has changed, though, has been the standing of the hitherto revered bureaucracy, elements of which were revealed to be either corrupt or (possibly even more damagingly) incompetent. Not only has this 'dramatically undermined its credibility' as a consequence, but it has contributed to the further unravelling of the integrated post-war regime (Pempel 1998: 141). The second point to stress is that recent initiatives by Koizumi Junichiro, and his preparedness to confront various factions within the LDP and the interest groups they are aligned to, has led some observers to declare that 'Japanese politics has changed forever' and the 'days of weak leaders are over'.[11] While it is too soon to determine how far-reaching Koizumi's reforms are likely to be, his policies may at least curtail the influence of the factions and reduce the amount of pork-barrelling or distribution of resources to special interest groups. However, critics argue he is less likely to reform the bureaucracy, which will ultimately have responsibility for implementing his initiatives (George Mulgan 2005; Mishima 2005).

The great paradox that the Japanese case reveals is that corrupt politicians are not necessarily obstacles to development, but neither is it clear whether more competent ones will be able to institute needed reforms. The impact of the reform process in particular, and the changing nature of Japan's integration into the global economy more generally, are taken up in subsequent chapters. At present, it is necessary to consider political activity in other parts of Northeast Asia, a region that displays some surprising commonalities and some revealing differences.

Korea and Taiwan

The first point to make about both Korea and Taiwan is that, as with Japan, the political histories of both countries directly reflect the wider geopolitical context of which they are a part. Both countries are divided, either internally (as in Korea's case) or from the larger entity of which they were originally a part (as in Taiwan's). The consequences for their respective political development and structures have been profound and cannot be understood without reference to this wider historical legacy. As we saw in earlier chapters, both countries owe their existence – in their current forms, at least – to struggles that occurred more than half a century ago. The division of Korea in particular directly reflects an initial post-war superpower compromise that was consolidated by the Korean War. The most enduring consequences of this period have been both the tragic, anachronistic division of Korea itself, and the creation of the world's last Stalinist outpost. North Korea (the DPRK) is, indeed, so bizarre and *sui generis* that it is as well to deal with it first.

Chapter 3 made clear that the DPRK's principal significance – other than being a unique comparative case study for social scientists – is strategic. Because the DPRK has nuclear weapons, because its very existence poses a continuing threat to the South, and because it has the capacity to plunge the region into a major conflict with unforeseeable but inevitably catastrophic consequences, we need to take it seriously and try to understand it. The defining characteristic of the DPRK is that it has become a family dynasty, perpetuating a style of charismatic, strong man leadership that is disappearing from much of East Asia. Despite the fact that the current leader, Kim Jong Il, is a seemingly much less impressive figure than his father and founder of the DPRK, he was able to inherit the leadership on the latter's death. The insular, opaque nature of the regime means that it is difficult to know quite how the DPRK operates under Kim the younger, or what his prospects are for sustaining the regime his father created and dominated. What we can say is that Kim Il Sung dominated every aspect of life in the North, centralizing power in a form of what Bruce Cumings (1997b: 399) describes as 'conservative corporatism', and establishing a personality cult the like of which has rarely been seen (Suh 1988).

Initially, Kim Il Sung was a creature of the Soviets. It is indicative of Kim's views that Khrushchev's de-Stalinization of the Soviet Union prompted a split with the DPRK's former sponsors and a closer alignment with China. Kim Il Sung developed the ideology of *chuch'e*, or self-reliance, which continues to exert an influence to this day, with disastrous consequences for the North's economy. Although Kim consolidated his control through the apparatus of the Workers' Party, it is, as Chung (1986: 35) points out, 'more a personalised system than a communist state'. The difficulty of implementing socialist principles is something that continues to confound other regimes in the region, too, as we shall see, and serves as a reminder that we should not expect 'communist' regimes to behave in predictable, ideologically orthodox ways. Interestingly, in the DPRK's case, Kim's ideology drew on older, romanticized, traditions to create a regime in which power radiated outwards in concentric circles (Cumings 2004: 124), much like the *mandalas* of traditional Southeast Asia discussed in Chapter 1. 'Asian values' or modes of governance of one sort or another can, it seems, be put to diverse purposes. However, the potentially fragile nature of such ideational constructions is generally revealed at moments of crisis, something the North's manifold problems mean is an increasingly permanent regime characteristic. Indeed, astute observers have concluded that 'the disintegration of the present system seems merely a matter of time' (Bleiker 2005: 98). The key question, of course, is just when and how this will happen, and whether the transition is manageable or catastrophic. What is clear is that the regime presides over an especially brittle system that is especially incapable of accommodating the multi-faceted challenges subsumed under the rubric of globalization.

Perennial uncertainty and insecurity has not only affected the North, it has also been the overarching reality within which development in the South (the ROK) has occurred. Chapter 2 illustrated how Korean insecurities are long-standing. Sandwiched between Japan and China, Korea has found itself continually subject to long-term pressures from its more powerful neighbours. When combined with the later traumas of civil war, the seemingly never-ending Cold War, foreign occupation and the social upheaval caused by rapid industrialization, it is perhaps unsurprising that the history of the South, as with the North, has been marked by fairly extreme politics of one sort or another. The fact that for much of the South's post-war history this should have taken the form of repressive authoritarian rule is not surprising either. After all, not only was the ROK attempting to achieve stability and development in unpromising conditions, but it was also building on the foundation of Japanese authoritarianism and military rule established during the colonial period. Interestingly, the American military government that took control of the South after the Second World War used the bureaucratic machinery created by the Japanese to suppress socialist *and* nationalist forces (Sohn 1989: 14). Not only did this mean 'salvation' for those who had collaborated with the Japanese, but it also marked a systematic attempt to 'depoliticise civil society, and to destroy the social foundations on which a unified nation-state could be established' (Choi 1995: 18).

That the first leader of the new Republic of Korea – Syngman Rhee – was an authoritarian who also used Japan's coercive apparatus to maintain control, was consequently an entirely predictable artefact of the emerging Cold War. The Americans wanted to establish strong, anti-communist leaders across the Third World (Gaddis 1982: ch. 6), and Rhee's election was in keeping with this goal. Indeed, in some ways the Korean War, for all its trauma, was instrumental in shoring up Rhee's position as it effectively eliminated Leftist opposition in the South, while anti-communism provide the ideological basis for the First Republic established in the war's aftermath. The state became the key to stabilizing the regime and driving development, but it was a state that was established in very different circumstances and much more rapidly than had been the case in Europe, or even Japan. Thus, from the outset, the ROK was a product of American hegemony and defined in opposition to the 'communist' regime in the North.

In a significant harbinger of future social struggles, however, Rhee's downfall in 1960 came about as a consequence of student unrest and mounting opposition to his regime in a nascent civil society. Given that at this time the overwhelming majority of the South's population was still involved in agriculture, this development is all the more remarkable. But the limited extent of the ROK's civil society at this time makes it less surprising that the initial foray into democratic rule proved short-lived, and a military coup installed a new authoritarian leader, Park Chung Hee. The distinctive features that came to characterize the South throughout the 1960s and 1970s – authoritarianism, political repression, and state-led developmentalism – were laid down at this time. In the next chapter, we shall consider how the regime was able to accelerate the course of economic development from these foundations. The point to emphasize at present, though, is that these economic initiatives had a profound impact on the ROK's domestic social structures: by the mid-1970s, the bulk of the population had moved off the land into the cities, and had become part of the emerging export-oriented industrial economy. In short, the class structure of the ROK rapidly evolved, creating the basis for a general expansion of civil society and the often violent labour struggles that became such a high-profile part of its subsequent development.

Evidence of this potential was seen following Park's assassination in 1979 and the subsequent imposition of martial law, when labour unrest became even more widespread and intense. Significantly, opposition to the government of Chun Doo-hwan, which was installed by another military coup, included students, workers, religious groups, and the expanding 'middle class' of urban professionals. This coalition of forces engineered a major social uprising in 1987 which eventually brought down the Chun government. The capacity of the new government of Roh Tae-woo to deal with the underlying social unrest was made more complex by the emergence of a reunification movement in 1988, but somewhat easier by the 'demobilization' of the democracy movement itself. The middle-class pro-democracy forces believed they had achieved their principal goal and transformed the formal political structures of the South. However, despite the fact that the ROK adopted all the trappings of democracy and the military appeared to have relinquished its interventionist role in Korean politics, many considered that the post-1987 changes were 'only cosmetic' (Chin 2003: 204).

Nevertheless, there have been a number of elections in the intervening period and a peaceful transfer of power from one democratically elected civilian president to another. Even more significantly, despite both being associated with the political opposition at various times, Kim Young-sam and Kim Dae-Jung represent different political groupings in the South, and the transfer of power between competing elites in the 1990s is a substantial indicator of the durability of democratic forms in the ROK. Paradoxically, however, although most observers agree that the formal trappings of democratic rule appear to be firmly established and that alternatives are increasingly unthinkable, there is some doubt about the degree to which individual Koreans have internalized the norms that go with democratic processes (Shin *et al.* 2003). Moreover, there has been a much higher tolerance of 'corruption' in the ROK, and an expectation that politicians will use their office to enrich themselves personally (Morriss 1997). Legitimacy in this context is much more about performance than probity. The possible significance of such 'cultural' variations will be explored when we consider Korea's developmental state. At this stage, it is useful to make one final point about the South's political development that provides a useful counterpoint to Taiwan's: in South Korea organized labour – despite its militancy and high profile – has been excluded from what Buchanan and Nicholls (2003) consider its corporatist governance structures. In Taiwan, by contrast, organized labour has been closely aligned with the state and is much less of an independent political force as a consequence.

That labour would be effectively nullified as an independent political force, and that other forms of civil society might be subdued is unsurprising, given Taiwan's recent history. It needs to be remembered that the modern Taiwan was established by the defeated KMT nationalist forces under Chiang Kai-shek. The manner in which the 1.5 million new arrivals established their hegemony over the 7 million strong indigenous population established a pattern of rule that was to endure for decades: the KMT supplanted Japanese officials, brutally subdued local opposition to their rule and created a socially insulated corporatist-style state apparatus that was unrepresentative but which enjoyed significant capacity. Significantly, the new regime was able to initiate major land reform which removed a potentially obstructive landlord class. When combined with the incorporation of labour, noted above, the 'authoritarian corporatist'[12] governments of the KMT were able to dominate the policy-making process and institute the sort of economic initiatives that are discussed in more detail in the next chapter.

For all the remarkable success of Taiwan's economic development, though, many indigenous Taiwanese regarded mainlander rule as 'a foreign imposition akin to colonial domination' (Alagappa 2001: 12). For the first four decades of KMT rule, it was possible to neutralize the pursuit of democratic reform because of the overall geopolitical context: the threat of invasion by the mainland gave the nationalist leadership a convenient rationale for authoritarian rule and the privileging of national security. However, when the larger international climate began to change in the 1980s political reform became more feasible, if not inescapable. Decades of rapid regional expansion, the increased stability it seemed to generate, and a more generalized international movement towards democratization all helped to create the preconditions for change. Even for Taiwan's authoritarian leadership, democratic reform was potentially attractive as it gave an increasingly internationally isolated Taiwan a way of positioning itself as a beacon of regional democracy in contrast to the autocratic mainland (Lu 1991). The birth of the Democratic Progressive Party (DPP) in 1986 was a tangible manifestation of the democratizing impulse.

However, it was not until the opposition actually won an election and there was a handover of power by the entrenched KMT elite that public confidence in the substance as well as the form of democracy became stronger. When long-time KMT President Lee Teng-hui's nominated successor, Lien Chan, was defeated by the DPP challenger Chen Shui-bien in 2000, it represented something of an 'electoral earthquake' that consolidated democratic rule and gelled with the wider international climate (Diamond 2001). More immediately, the KMT's defeat can be attributed to what Diamond calls its 'moral and political exhaustion': after so long in office, the growth of corruption and factionalism had become an electoral liability. When added to Chen's charisma and the plodding performance of Lien Chan, the KMT's fate was sealed. While these domestic transformations are hugely important in the context of Taiwan's domestic politics, they also have a wider geopolitical significance: Chen has subsequently emerged as a champion of greater independence for Taiwan,[13] something that has potentially major implications both for Taiwan's relationship with the mainland, and for the triangular relationship that includes the United States as well (notionally Taiwan's single greatest guarantor of continuing independence).

Paradoxically, therefore, Taiwan is both important and marginal when thinking about the impact of domestic political conditions on regional development. On the one hand, Taiwan is generally conspicuously absent from major regional and global forums such as the United Nations and – in a regional context – the emergent ASEAN+3 process. Deference to the increasingly powerful mainland has meant that the ranks of Taiwan's allies, especially those that are willing to express support for Taiwanese independence, have grown remarkably thin. Even the USA, the avowed champion of democracy and free speech, has traditionally maintained a position of 'strategic ambiguity' regrading its intentions towards Taiwan and its status as an independent entity (see Tow 2001: 108). All sides prefer to maintain the polite fiction that Taiwan remains an 'internal' problem for the PRC that will be resolved at some point in the future. On the other hand, however, Taiwan's increased penchant for democracy and freedom of speech threatens to puncture this politically convenient, if somewhat farcical, arrangement by pursuing its independence. In that case, Taiwan has the capacity not simply to make regional cooperation and confidence-building more difficult, but to destabilize the entire international system.

Consequently, while it is difficult to see how the more independently-minded Taiwanese will achieve their goal of independence, Taiwan's position highlights an issue with wider ramifications: regional and extra-regional powers will continue to turn a blind eye to authoritarian regimes, human rights abuses and inter-state bullying, even if this means snubbing a genuinely democratic regime to do so. The relationship between external and internal pressure for political reform is a function of the overarching geopolitical context (something that also helps to explain the durability of authoritarianism and the distinctive patterns of political order in Southeast Asia).

Southeast Asia and the making of nations

Heterogeneity may be the leitmotif of East Asia, but the diversity of political systems found in Southeast Asia makes generalization difficult, if not foolhardy. And yet, it is possible to identify historical patterns and commonalities that, if they do not entirely explain the course of subsequent political development, at least give us a sense of the parameters in which it occurred. The overwhelming common historical reality that – with the exception of Thailand – distinguished Southeast Asia was that they were newly independent states confronted with the dual challenge of national political consolidation and economic development. In such circumstances, when the very boundaries of nascent states were not always certain, and where the capacities of the emergent independent governments remained underdeveloped, it is hardly surprising that newly empowered elites across the region would turn to nationalism as the glue with which to bind frequently disparate communities together (Stockwell 1999).

The Second World War provided a decisive break with the colonial era. Not only were the Europeans encouraged to leave the region by increasingly effective independence movements in Indonesia, Burma and Vietnam, but they did so at the urging of the USA, too. The geopolitical imperatives of the gathering Cold War meant that, from a US perspective, it was essential to cultivate pro-capitalist allies in Southeast Asia lest they fall like so many dominoes to communist expansion.[14] While this may have betrayed a remarkably unsophisticated grasp of both the diversity of regimes within Southeast Asia and of the long-standing intra-regional rivalries that prevailed there, it did have one noteworthy effect: the USA was prepared to tolerate, even encourage, the development of 'strong man' leaders if they were anti-communist. Even the somewhat erratic, independently-minded Indonesian independence leader, Sukarno, was initially wooed by the USA as a potential bastion against communist expansion (McMahon 1999: 85). That these expectations were not realized should not blind us to the reality that geopolitical contestation and the fragile nature of the post-independence regimes provided an environment within which autocrats could flourish, and concerns about democracy became second-order issues.

The other point that emerged from the discussion of security issues in Chapter 3 concerned the prominent, sometimes dominant, role the military has played in a number of Southeast Asian countries, especially Indonesia, Burma, the Philippines, Thailand and, of course, Vietnam (a country that has spent much of its modern history fighting one external power or another). Indeed, in Vietnam's case it is hardly surprising that, given the army's pivotal role in the life of the nation and its independence struggles, it continues to occupy a major place in a communist regime with limited state capacity and an underdeveloped civil society (Kolko 1997). In some other parts of the region, what is more surprising perhaps is that there has been a shift away from modes of governance that were dominated by strong man leaders and/or the military, to those in which some form of democratic rule appears to be consolidating. This is remarkable and somewhat unexpected, even if its extent and significance are sometimes overstated. Although there are some general trends emerging, there are also significant continuing differences in the nature of political regimes across the region. It is worth briefly spelling out what these are in the most important and illuminating countries.

The democracies

That Indonesia and the Philippines should be considered Southeast Asia's most genuine democratic regimes is remarkable and rather surprising. Given their often traumatic histories, internal divisions, limited state capacities and prominent positions in the 'war on terror', the omens were not good. Indeed, the current status of the other country I shall consider here – Thailand – serves as a salutary reminder that the process of democratic consolidation is fragile, unpredictable and without guarantees.

Indonesia's new-found democratic status is especially noteworthy given its history since independence. Both of Indonesia's most important post-independence leaders – Sukarno and Suharto – put their own distinctive mark on Indonesian 'democracy'. Sukarno instituted 'guided democracy' in 1959 in response to domestic unrest. He also banned elections, suspended the constitution and consolidated his own pre-eminence in the process. The ostensible motivation for this was achieving national stability but, in a familiar regional pattern, the trampling of political liberty was justified with reference to Indonesian 'cultural values' (Vatikiotis 1996). It was a pattern of rule that was to be entrenched and given unique expression by his successor, Suharto. The precise details of Sukarno's downfall in 1965 remain uncertain,[15] but it is clear that his increasingly erratic behaviour, his closeness to China, and his support of Indonesia's domestic communist party, the PKI, made him a liability in the eyes of many. By contrast, Suharto's vehement anti-communism and antipathy towards China made him highly acceptable to the United States and its strategic and economic interests (Tanter 1990), despite Indonesia's prominent place in the non-aligned movement.

Suharto's 'New Order' established a form of authoritarian corporatism that became a more widespread part of East Asia's political landscape during the Cold War. The specific challenges of political consolidation and economic development in Indonesia were crystallized in the ideology of 'Pancasila'. The next chapter illustrates how these ideas underpinned the distinctive nature of Indonesia's state-led economic development project. What is important at this juncture, however, is the structure of the political regime that made this possible. The five principles of Pancasila were initially propounded by Sukarno,[16] but under Suharto they were turned into 'the basic credo to which all Indonesians had to adhere' (Liddle 1999: 40). Although the People's Consultative Assembly had formal responsibility for electing the President,[17] and while the People's Representative Council has notional responsibility for authorizing the budget and legislation, under Suharto there was only the form and not the substance of popular control. Pancasila provided a theoretical justification for the rejection of Western-style political pluralism by appealing to an 'integralist or organicist stream of thought' (Elson 2001: 240). In other words, in a pattern that would distinguish much of Southeast Asia, Suharto justified political repression in the name of supposedly traditional Indonesian cultural values and practices. When reinforced by a military that the ex-soldier Suharto kept under close control, and a political party that dominated stage-managed electoral processes,[18] the New Order achieved a remarkable degree of ideological and social control in what was a new, developing country.

The other key qualities that distinguished the Suharto regime were his ability to 'personalize' control of the military (Elson 2001: 244), and to place himself – and eventually the rest of his family – at the centre of a dense network of political and business relationships. These relationships were central to the web of patronage-based connections that consolidated Suharto's power (Robison and Hadiz 2004: 43). The impact of these relationships on economic development in Indonesia will be examined in the next chapter. The point to emphasize, in the context of a discussion of explicitly *political* considerations, is that the multi-faceted domination of Indonesia by the New Order regime not only militated against the development of an independent civil society, but meant that the authority and legitimacy of the regime was fatally undermined by the East Asian economic crisis and its aftermath. Moreover, the collapse of the regime was sudden, unanticipated and left little in the way of effective alternative structures of governance and coordination. Two further points merit emphasis: first, the regime collapsed despite, not because of, an effective, organized opposition, Robert Elson (2001: 293) argues. Second, in the absence of a such an internal opposition, external global forces in the shape of international controllers of mobile capital and the newly assertive IFIs created an irresistible economic and political momentum for change (Beeson 1998).

The ever more integrated international economy of which Indonesia is necessarily a part, and in which the IFIs continue to exert such influence, forms the increasingly influential environment within which Suharto's successors must operate (see Beeson 2006d). When added to the rising popular expectations that have accompanied the transition to democracy, it becomes easier to understand why governance has proved so difficult in Indonesia, and why there has been such a rapid turnover of leaders in the new democratic environment.[19] The sad irony is that, despite successfully establishing the mechanisms of democratic rule, they have not made the sprawling, ethnically diverse, economically underdeveloped archipelago any easier to govern. On the contrary, some of the neoliberal initiatives urged by external agencies (such as decentralization, for example) have actually exacerbated problems of central control and fuelled corruption in the provinces (Hadiz 2004a). It is revealing that although the Indonesian electorate appears enthusiastic about the idea of democratic rule, after three relatively unsuccessful short-term leaders they have now opted for another former military man in the hope of restoring stability and economic development. Despite remarkably high hopes and approval ratings, the report card on Susilo Bambang Yudhoyono's first year in office was mixed (Guerin 2005b). The prospects for a greater military role as a consequence of internal tensions and the 'war on terror' have also sparked more general concerns about a possible diminution of political liberties and human rights, which are taken up below.[20] Indonesia's dilemmas are, however, far from unique: the Philippines also highlights the tensions between security and political liberalism.

If any country in Southeast Asia ought to be democratic and in possession of a robust, independent civil society, it is the Philippines. After all, the Philippines were colonized by not just the most powerful country in the world, but also its most ardent champion of democracy. And yet, the tragic paradox of the Philippines is that, while it may be democratic at present, its independent history has been punctuated by military coups and authoritarian rule. Indeed, the Philippines can often lay claim to having had one of the most corrupt, repressive and incompetent regimes in the whole of Asia. Adding a further layer of irony to this doleful picture is the fact that the American colonists must shoulder much of the blame. As Hutchcroft (1998: 26) points out in his definitive study of (non) development in the Philippines, 'the legacy of US colonialism was considerable oligarchy building, but very little in the way of state building'. Put differently, the Americans' antipathy to the sort of 'strong' states that abounded elsewhere in the region meant that they gave little attention to establishing an effective state apparatus with which to oversee the developmental project following independence.

The Philippines' woeful economic performance is considered in more detail in the next chapter, but it is important to note that the enfeebled state the USA left behind was captured by local elites and 'so lacking in autonomy from dominant economic interests that even the most basic regulation of capital is continuously frustrated' (Hutchcroft 1998: 15). The pivotal moment in independent Philippine history that entrenched and institutionalized this state of affairs was the declaration of martial law by Ferdinand Marcos in 1972. Prior to this, the Philippines were 'one of the last strongholds of civilian control over the military in the Third World' (Hernandez 1986: 262). It is all the more remarkable, then, that the reversion to a repressive, militarily-backed authoritarianism that occurred under Marcos should have happened in a former American colony. The reason the USA took an indulgent view of the Marcos dictatorship was the same as it was elsewhere: better a pro-capitalist dictator than even the most progressive, possibly pro-American, Left-wing leader.[21] Whatever the overarching strategic rationale for this policy was, the net effect of such policies was clear in the steady erosion of the Philippines' domestic political institutions, a centralization of power around the presidency, and an increasing reliance on coercion to maintain order (Doronila 1985).

And yet, the coercive apparatus that underpinned the patterns of corruption, cronyism and patronage that were central to Marcos' rule ultimately proved just as brittle in the Philippines as it had in Indonesia. At one level, the outbreak of 'People Power' that swept Marcos from office in 1986 was a remarkable expression of popular discontent and capacity for social mobilization. At another level, however, the installation of Corazon Aquino as the new president was not a decisive break with the past. On the contrary, Aquino was 'a member of one of the wealthiest and most powerful dynasties within the Filipino oligarchy' (Anderson 1988: 3). The diverse coalition of forces that rallied behind Aquino following the murder of her husband Benigno Aquino in 1983 began to unravel when she became President. Given the nature of the problems she faced – dealing with internal insurrection movements, attempting to implement land reform, keeping the military on side and under control, to say nothing of finally kick-starting development in the Philippines – it is perhaps not surprising that the high hopes that accompanied her arrival remained largely unfulfilled.

Aquino has much in common with present incumbent, Gloria Arroyo, beyond their gender. Both are from privileged backgrounds and closely connected to the dominant oligarchy, and both have been associated with attempts to engage the Philippines' comparatively extensive civil society. But the so-called GRINGOS (government-initiated non-governmental organizations) that are one of the principal manifestations of this impulse are not simply oxymoronic: they are often more preoccupied with maintaining control of decentralized resources and pork-barrelling (Gonzalez 2001: 279) than with promoting more widely-based, 'progressive' social causes. The only post-Marcos administration widely considered to have made some progress in both igniting domestic economic activity and in confronting some of the powerful vested economic interests that have made economic reform and development so problematic was led by Fidel Ramos during the mid-1990s. Yet, even Ramos was not able to reform key elements of the economy, such as the banking sector (Hutchcroft 1999), and neither was his administration free of accusations of electoral malpractice of a sort that has led William Case (2002: ch. 6) to describe the Philippines' political system as a 'stable but low quality democracy'. Ironically, the candidate Ramos anointed in the Presidential elections at the end of his term was defeated by an ex-movie star, Joseph Estrada, a populist and economic nationalist whose administration ended in scandal and corruption. The increased importance of 'people power' and civil society actually created the conditions in which a political novice and populist such as Estrada could rise and ultimately fall. Unfortunately for the Philippines, the one major continuity of the Estrada regime was the consolidation of networks of patronage and privilege (Hutchison 2006).

Although there are continuing questions about the nature of electoral processes and constitutional manoeuvres in the Philippines,[22] they are arguably more in keeping with democratic principles and constraints than those of Thailand. Case (2002) describes Thailand as an 'unconsolidated' democracy, which explains the doubts about its claims to be included in the line-up of Southeast Asia's more authentic democratic nations. As we saw in Chapter 3, Thailand has a long history of military rule and periodic coups in which rival elites established their relative pre-eminence. But, in 1992, it seemed that Thailand's own version of people power had ensured that there had been an irrevocable transformation in the nature of domestic politics. And yet, while the military may not be the threat to civilian political authorities that they once were, the nature of the political process itself is still far short of the democratic ideal. 'Money politics' or, less euphemistically, the outright bribing of large numbers of the electorate, continues to be prominent part of the elections that have occurred since the 1990s. When combined with political violence and intimidation, especially in rural areas, and a history of domination by a 'bureaucratic polity' (Riggs 1966), it is not surprising that Maisrikrod and McCargo (1997: 132) conclude that 'power remains the preserve of the few. The mass of the population continues to be excluded from a significant say in the way the country is governed.'

The impact of corrupt relationships on the course of economic development will be considered in more detail in the next chapter, but it is impossible to ignore its pernicious impact on the political process in Thailand as well. Corruption has been a fundamental part of the political and bureaucratic processes for decades, but has become especially prominent and pervasive since the 1980s (Pasuk and Piriyarangsan 1994). What is distinctive, noteworthy and – from the perspective of genuine democratic consolidation, at least – slightly alarming is the way that a number of centres of political, bureaucratic and economic power have come together in the government of Thaksin Shinawatra. Chapter 5 explains why there are serious concerns about the basis and stability of the 'Thaksinomics' that has seen an apparent resurrection of Thailand's crisis-battered economy since his election in 2001. The point to make at this stage is that the organization with which Thaksin has sought to guide his developmentalist agenda, the Thai Rak Thai (TRT) party, is hardly a vehicle for political emancipation. Pasuk and Baker highlight these contradictions and it is worth quoting at length from their authoritative study:

> Thaksin and the TRT recognize the need to share more of the benefits of growth, and to get rid of the country's remaining poverty. But at the same time they try to delegitimize all non-formal politics and close down political space. 'The people' stand at the centre of Thaksin's rhetoric, but their role is passive. Thaksin sees democracy as a tool of growth, a historical partner of capitalism, not as an ideal. He mentions rights only as an irritating foreign imposition. He views the rule of law as subordinate to 'management'. The government tries to suppress protest politics through above-board law and legislation, and also through old covert methods of the security state. It controls the media through rules, money, and intimidation . . . Behind these factors lies a

conviction that the nationalism stirred up by the 1997 crisis can be channelled into support for economic growth, while other agendas which might distract from the single-minded focus should be allowed no play. (Pasuk and Baker 2004: 228)

Thus, the Thai case illustrates a number of more general comparative points that merit emphasis: first, despite Thai politics assuming a democratic form, the substance is frequently rather different. Second, the structural transformation of the Thai economy and the rising living standards that are associated with it did not lead inevitably to an authentic democratic transformation (Hewison 1999). Third, Thaksin provides an especially illuminating example of a more generalized East Asian pattern in which there is a fusion of political and business interests. In Thaksin's case, he also highlights the way that domestic economic restructuring has fed directly into political realignments: having made a fortune in Thailand's rapidly developing telecommunications industries, Thaksin had the economic clout to underwrite his political ambitions. Fourth, Thaksin was able to mobilize nationalist sentiment in the post-crisis environment to gain the support of domestic business, the banking sector and even the rural population, although in the latter's case the offer of direct financial incentives may have been more decisive.[23] Fifth, despite the growth of key civil society organizations such as the trade unions since the 1980s, the reality has been that, as in the Philippines, organized labour has been fragmented and ineffective (Hadiz 2004b). Finally, the changing geopolitical environment, especially the 'war on terror', has provided the legitimating rationale for a crackdown on domestic opposition, a realignment with the USA, and a return to more authoritarian patterns of governance (Connors 2006).[24]

If the potential for a return to authoritarian politics remains a significant risk in Thailand, the prospects for genuine democratic reform may be even more fragile for those countries that have never actually achieved real democracy in the first place.

Semi-, non-, and putative democracies

Whether we call them 'semi' or 'pseudo' democracies, Singapore and Malaysia share common historical legacies that help to explain their distinctive political accommodations. The fact that both were former colonies of Britain and briefly part of the Federation of Malaysia gives them some significant commonalities, but the nature of their subsequent political and especially economic trajectories since Singapore left the Federation in 1965 suggests some important differences, too. Perhaps the single most significant political reality that helps explain Singaporean development has been the dominance of the People's Action Party (PAP) generally and the pivotal role of played by Lee Kuan Yew in particular. Lee was prime minister from 1959 to 1990, and has established something of a family dynasty as his son, Lee Hsien Loong, is the present incumbent. Although the PAP's dominance under the Lees and interim premier, Goh Chok Tong, has been so complete it seems difficult to imagine any other possibility, at the outset its hegemony was not so assured.

The PAP was originally an uneasy alliance between English-educated middle-class nationalists such as Lee, and indigenous Chinese labour and student movements. Lee Kuan Yew's great achievement, if that is the way to describe it, was to not only oversee the transformation of Singapore's economy, but the island's political system as well. Following the break with Malaysia, the PAP began to develop a corporatist regime that conferred a good deal of autonomy on the state itself, whilst simultaneously coopting potential sources of political opposition, including organized labour (see Brown 1994). The net effect of a process that was perfected over the ensuing decades was, as Garry Rodan (1996a: 95) describes it, a reconfiguring of 'the expanding realm of the state through the extension and refinement of the mechanisms of political co-optation, not the evolution of a more expansive civil society'. The PAP has skilfully nullified or deflected potential sources of political opposition by incorporating business, civil society and labour leaders into corporatist networks.[25] Similarly, effective political opposition has been marginalized through initiatives such as the Societies Act (1967), which makes political mobilization outside of government-approved boundaries all but impossible.

More recently, the PAP has maintained its tight grip over the population in general and possible sources of political opposition through a number of innovative strategies. On the one hand, supporters of the PAP are rewarded with government largesse through the up-grading of public housing estates; on the other, the Singaporean government has made increasing use of a compliant judiciary to bankrupt political opponents and to intimidate the local and international media (see Rodan 2006). Indeed, it is important to make a general comparative point about the legal system in countries such as Singapore with more authoritarian traditions: while the liberal tradition sees legalism as a restraint on the excessive powers of the state, 'in East Asia, it is employed as a managerial and technocratic device for the effective organization of the market and the state' (Jayasuriya 1996: 377). While this may not be quite as accurate a description of the entire region as it once was, the main point to make about the Singaporean experience is that there is no easy, straightforward or inevitable relationship between rising living standards and the achievement of genuinely democratic government: populations may be compliant and willing to trade political freedoms for economic growth, and states may prove themselves adept at developing new modes of social and political control.

It might be thought that the fate of a small island economy with a population of less than four million is not of great historical consequence or comparative significance, yet Singapore has assumed a surprisingly important place in debates about economic development in the region, and an even more prominent place in discussion of the possible significance of cultural values in that process. It is striking that Malaysia also took a major role in the Asian values debate, and also has a political system that is generally characterized as authoritarian. This common political background suggests that an interest in the supposed cultural basis of particular political and social formations is more than coincidental. But before we explore this possibility, it is important to spell out the background to Malaysia's distinctive political practices, especially as Malaysia's greater population (over 23 million) and more difficult developmental challenges make it more useful for comparative purposes.

Malaysia is perhaps the quintessential regional exemplar of a contemporary political trajectory being determined by a colonial experience. British imperialism not only skewed Malaysia's subsequent economic development, but it determined the distinctive ethnic mix that has been such a central feature of its concomitant political policies as well. As we saw in Chapter 2, the British solved their labour shortages by importing workers from other parts of Asia. As a consequence, about 53 per cent of Malaysia's population are indigenous Malays or *bumiputeras*, with the rest being made up of Chinese (26 per cent), Indians (8 per cent) and other indigenes.[26] The distribution of these ethnic groups is not even, though, and some areas are dominated by particular groups, such as the Chinese in Penang and 'other indigenes' in Sarawak. Malaysia's ethnically-based communities were not evenly distributed spatially, and neither were their relative incomes. The more commercially-minded Chinese had rapidly come to dominate economic activities in Malaysia, as they have in other parts of the region. This economic ascendancy generated great resentment amongst the majority Malays, and despite generally rising living standards post-independence, ethnic tensions culminated in major riots in 1969. This social upheaval led to the abandonment of gradualist development policies and the inauguration of the New Economic Policy (NEP) that was explicitly designed to positively discriminate in favour of the hitherto economically marginalized Malaysian majority (see Khoo 1995).

The economic impact of the NEP is considered in the next chapter; what is important at this point is its political impact. One of the most immediate consequences of the 1969 riots was that the Malaysian political system 'turned in a markedly authoritarian direction' (Crouch 1996: 26). The government claimed it needed more coercive powers to maintain social stability and to ensure the economic development which, it was hoped, would raise all boats. One of the principal mechanisms with which the Malay majority ensured its political hegemony was through the United Malays National Organization (UMNO), which was the dominant component of the Barisan Nasional (BN) alliance governments which have enjoyed unbroken power. The BN allowed UMNO, which principally represented the interests of Malays, to bring other ethnic communities into the alliance, through the Malayan Chinese Association (MCA) and the Malayan Indian Congress (MIC). The fact that UMNO dominated the alliance and the key levers of political power, and thus also control of economic resources, meant that as far as the Malay community was concerned 'much of its appeal lay in its patronage-dispensing function' (Crouch 1996: 37). This gave an implacable economic logic to UMNO's political activities as its power was determined and dependent on not just successful economic development, but also control of the economic resources it generated.

The underlying logic of the NEP had been developed by the dominant political figure of post-independence politics in Malaysia: Mahathir bin Mohamad. In *The Malay Dilemma*, Mahathir (1998 [1970]) spelled out why he thought the indigenous population merited preferential treatment. But Mahathir did not become prime minister until 1981, and arguably did not unambiguously cement his position until 1987, when he finally saw off internal rivals for the leadership of UMNO and, thus, the country (Case 2002: 116). What made Mahathir so dominant, however, was his ability to personalize his power and the authoritarian nature of the regime he led through what Dan Slater (2003: 82) describes as 'packing, rigging, and circumventing'. Mahathir strengthened potentially authoritarian institutions and undermined more democratic ones, systematically 'packing' key bodies (such as the judiciary) with compliant allies. The potential importance of this strategy became clear when Mahathir was able to use the legal system to destroy his former deputy and leadership rival Anwar Ibrahim.[27] The 'rigging' Slater describes refers to Mahathir's ability to manipulate UMNO's rules and procedures which determine leadership positions to his advantage. 'Circumventing' refers to the way resources are directed towards loyal allies in 'packed' institutions, making potential centres of opposition more difficult to develop. As with Singapore, Malaysia has a similarly cowed media that offered little criticism of these developments (Rodan 2005).

By winding back civil liberties, manipulating UMNO elections (where the 'real' competition for political power occurs), and changing the procedures governing general elections, Mahathir was able to retain the trappings of democracy without running the risk of regime change (Case 2002). As a result, Mahathir developed a dominant, authoritarian position within Malaysian politics; and yet, it was never entirely hegemonic and there were always potential sources of opposition and tensions within the regime (Hilley 2001). Indeed, the Anwar affair revealed major divisions within UMNO itself (see Khoo 2003). These divisions were exacerbated by the different perspectives Mahathir and Anwar developed regarding the Asian crisis and links with 'the West'. Of late, however, there have been significant changes in Malaysian politics that may mark the beginning of a less authoritarian era. One of most significant acts of Mahathir's successor – Abdullah Badawi – was to release Anwar Ibrahim from prison. While this was a highly symbolic gesture, it may be his pursuit of 'good governance' and domestic reform that will prove of greatest long-term significance, *if* it can be successfully pursued (see Khoo 2006). Although it is too soon to make a definitive judgement about the impact of the new regime and Badawi's ability, indeed desire, to break up entrenched, institutionalized networks of power and patronage, and the strong ties between business and politics that are so characteristic of Malaysia (Gomez and Jomo 1997), the fact that he employs the rhetoric of the IFIs' reformist agenda is significant and at odds with his predecessor.[28]

The new administration can also expect to have a more amicable relationship with 'the West' generally and the United States in particular, although it is important to note that the war on terror saw a notable thawing of relations between Washington and Mahathir, and a relaxation of criticism of his authoritarian rule (Nesadurai 2006). Likewise, Badawi's 'unquestioned devotion to Islam' is thought likely to blunt the influence of Parti Islam Se Malaysia (PAS), the principal expression of political Islam in Malaysia and a potentially important source of political opposition.[29] Although it is difficult to be certain about the extent of support for PAS or its long-term significance as a political and ideological force (but see Martinez 2001), it is noteworthy that it has become one of the most important potential sources of opposition to UMNO dominance (Case 2002). Malaysia's prominent position in the so-called war on terror means that the intersection of domestic and external forces will require skilful management and make the smooth transition to greater democracy more problematic.

Malaysia's authoritarian past and potential notwithstanding, it can at least lay claim to being some sort of democracy. The rest of the region's diverse polities are even further from the democratic ideal. Although it is not possible to do justice to the variety of political forms in the rest of the less politically prominent and economically significant parts of Southeast Asia, it is worth making a few very brief remarks about the non-democracies. We have already seen in Chapter 3 how the recent political fate of Burma has been completely shaped by the existence of a brutal military junta that has ruled the country since 1988, and until it collapses or is overthrown there is little to say about it in terms of political development. Simply put, there is none. Much the same could be said about the micro-state of Brunei which, while run by a Sultan rather than a military junta, shows little sign of change or political development. The key to the ruling family's domination is oil and gas wealth, which allows them effectively to buy the support of the general population. Similarly, Southeast Asia's newest potential member – East Timor – is so small and new that its significance at this stage is primarily as a focus of intra- and inter-regional concern and manoeuvring, rather than as a major actor in its own right.[30]

The main point to make about the political development of the former French colonies in Indo-China is that they are marked not just by imperialism, but by the colossal impact of the Vietnam War. Unbelievably enough, tiny Laos lost 50 per cent of its population during a 20-year civil war that ended in 1975 with the declaration of the communist-led Lao People's Democratic Republic (Lao PDR: see Fry and Faming 2001: 147). Any country faced with that sort of demographic collapse might struggle to cope, let alone one with very limited state capacity. Cambodia has been similarly ravaged by internal conflict, most notoriously at the hands of the tyrannical Pol Pot, who managed to murder perhaps one-sixth of the population during less than four years in power in the late 1970s. Although elections now occur, they are marred by violence and intimidation, and have seen power consolidate around the strong man leader, Hun Sen. Vietnam is by far the most important of this group of countries, its population size (over 80 million) and economic potential making it a potentially major force in Southeast Asian and perhaps, eventually, East Asian politics: it is rapidly integrating into the international capitalist economy, but its political system remains dominated by the Vietnamese Communist Party (VCP). In many ways, Vietnam faces the same sorts of problem as its giant neighbour China, in that it must make the transition from a rather ideologically rigid, authoritarian form of communist rule to a political structure that can accommodate the demands of global economic integration (see Beresford 2006). To get a sense of the problems ahead, it is time to turn to China itself, the politics of which have the potential to change not just the region, but the world.

Battering down the Chinese walls?

In one of the most famous passages of the *Communist Manifesto*, Karl Marx and Friedrich Engels (1978 [1872]: 477) suggested that:

> The bourgeoisie, by the rapid improvement of all instruments of production, by the immensely facilitated means of communication, draws all, even the most barbarian, nations into civilisation. The cheap prices of its commodities are the heavy artillery with which it batters down all Chinese walls, with which it forces the barbarians' intensely obstinate hatred of foreigners to capitulate. It compels all nations, on pain of extinction, to adopt the bourgeois mode of production; it compels them to introduce what it calls civilisation into their midst, i.e., to become bourgeois themselves. In one word, it creates a world after its own image.

At one level, this is a remarkably prescient description of the spread of globalization generally and capitalism in particular. At another level, however, it highlights just how unpredictable, paradoxical, even ironic, the evolution of the international system has been (something Marx's well-known, Euro-centric contempt for the 'Asiatic mode of production' made him temperamentally ill-equipped to foresee). Yet, not only is it a 'communist' country that is currently the source of cheap commodities, but it is the 'barbarians' who are snapping them up. History simply should not have turned out this way. China has got the development process all wrong (by the precepts of historical-materialism, at least). Capitalism is supposed to come *before* socialism, not after it. By reversing this process, China has undermined the intellectual foundations of the entire Marxist-Leninist project that gave birth to the PRC itself. This is not just a cheap debating point, but a fundamental problem for PRC ideologues as they attempt to explain China's place in the world and its developmental history. It becomes easier to understand the emphasis on 'pragmatism' that characterizes so much recent political discourse in China as a consequence. To borrow a famous aphorism of Deng Xiaoping, 'It doesn't matter whether a cat is black or white as long as it catches mice.'

To understand what a profound transformation the current accommodative attitude towards capitalism represents, it is important to consider China's earlier, more authentically revolutionary and socialist history. But before we do, it is also necessary to make a few preliminary points that justify the more extensive consideration of China's domestic politics. Simply put, China is such a demographic colossus, and the economic and strategic implications of its rise are so immense, that it demands greater attention as it has the capacity to 'shake the world', as Napoleon Bonaparte famously put it. But it is also important for comparative purposes: unlike most of the countries I have discussed so far, it is not a democracy of any sort, and does not look likely to become one in the foreseeable future. This is important because the United States under

George W. Bush (2005) has renewed a campaign of criticism aimed at encouraging precisely such a transformation, and reignited Chinese fears of containment as a consequence. The final reason for giving particular attention to China is because it highlights so many of the issues that recur in this book, especially the domestic response to 'globalization' and its concomitant impact on regional processes. China, in short, reveals and, indeed, increasingly determines, the dialectical relationship between the local, the regional and the global. So Marx and Engels were right, but not for the reasons they expected.

Politics in China

The fact that China is a 'communist' country means that ideology plays – or ought to play – a far more important part in the political life of the nation than it does elsewhere. And yet, while Lawrence (1998: 1) may be right to suggest that, under Mao, China was 'the largest, and arguably the most devout, Marxist regime', this does not tell the whole story. As we saw in Chapter 2, part of the genius and originality of the early CCP leadership was to mobilize the peasantry (in ways that would have astounded Marx) by appealing to their innate nationalism (Johnson 1962). As we also saw, Chinese history is punctuated by massive, traumatic upheavals, to which the communist period has not been immune. What is distinctive about the era of communist rule is that while ideology played an important part in its early phases, nationalism has become more prominent in the contemporary period (Gries 2004; Yahuda 2000). Although the comparatively recent Cultural Revolution (1966–76) demonstrated that social convulsions are still possible within the PRC, and that ideology could play a major part in their legitimation,[31] recent leaders – including Jiang Zemin – have recognized the importance of nationalism and systematically attempted to utilize nationalist sentiment and a mythologized reading of China's past to shore up support for the CCP. This was a strategy of particular importance at a time when the ideological legitimacy and practical purpose of the CCP were being undermined by rapid economic and social transformation (Terrill 2003: 147–50). The success of this project remains moot, but it serves to highlight the continuing central challenge facing the CCP in an era when its leadership has overseen its integration into a global *capitalist* economy.[32]

Despite Marxist ideas no longer having the sort of practical importance or ideational purchase they once did, the central social fact about China is that it remains a 'communist' country. This is important not just for China's intra- and inter-regional relations, but because it is predicated upon a distinctive mode of governance and a particular role for the state. Indeed, it is important to remember that the CCP emerged from the ashes of a long, destructive civil war; the construction of a 'strong' state with which to ensure domestic control and ward off possible Cold War external predations was consequently a key goal of the revolutionary leadership. This was (and is) no easy task, of course: the sheer scale of China, and the rapidity with which the communist victory was finally achieved, meant that centralizing power was in itself a major undertaking.[33] While the administration of China's vast regions was initially given over to Military Administrative Committees, the CCP set about systematically creating an entire state apparatus.

The upshot of these efforts was the development of two parallel hierarchies, the Party and the government, which shared interlocking memberships. The Party's job was primarily to provide the ideological rationale for policies, and the government's job was to implement them. Although not formally part of the decision-making process, the military, especially in this early period, was also a key political actor. The role model for China's political system was its key ally, the Soviet Union. Consequently, its supreme political body – in theory, at least – was the National People's Congress, which was empowered to enact laws, ratify treaties and select the president and vice president. In reality, it has been the National Party Congress and the central committee it notionally elects that has been at the centre of power in China. The central committee elects a politburo, which in turn selects a Standing Committee, whose chairman is the most powerful man in China. Importantly, however:

> While the chair normally exercises enormous authority, he is not, and never has been, a totalitarian dictator. It would be more accurate to describe him as first among almost equals. Decision-making appears to take place through coalition formation among Standing Committee members; the voice of the chair is generally, but not always, decisive. (Dreyer 2000: 88)

It is worth dwelling on these rather arcane and opaque structures because they are so different from those of the West, and attract such criticism on the grounds of their non-democratic nature as a consequence. But it is also worth remembering that the Party had revolutionary origins, and was initially seen as the only mechanism with which to transform China's pernicious, feudal class structures[34] and the social forces that had oppressed and exploited Chinese workers for so long. It was this historical role as the vanguard of the people that gave legitimacy to the overarching political apparatus and justified the 'dictatorship of the masses' and the paradoxical, concomitant lack of popular sovereignty. However, the net effect of the Party's attempts to institutionalize this ideology has been to entrench power and leadership struggles among a handful of senior officials (Lieberthal 1995).

The nature of the Chinese political system under communist rule, and the concentration of power that occurred under dominant leaders such as Mao and Deng, has parallels with the imperial system described in Chapter 2 (Salisbury 1992). Both leaders dominated their respective eras in ways that have few real parallels with Western democracies. The transition between Mao and Deng, and the vicissitudes of Deng's career that preceded it,[35] also illustrate the potential volatility of Chinese politics, the importance of personalities and personal loyalties, the informal nature of the political process, and the fluctuating fortunes of rival leadership factions in determining political outcomes (Dittmer 2002). The main achievement of Mao's chosen successor – Hua Guofeng – was to counter the 'Gang of Four's'[36] attempt to promote policies that were more in keeping with the spirit of the Cultural Revolution. This was a pivotal moment in China's post-war history as it marked a decline in the importance of revolutionary ideology and principles, and a turn towards pragmatism. The Eleventh Party Congress in 1977 marked Deng's re-ascent to the summit of Chinese power and a recognition that Hua lacked the authority and capacity to modernize the Chinese economy (something that was confirmed by Hua's resignation in 1981). Crucially, however, Deng's economic reforms were feasible because they did not threaten the CCP itself, and 'communist' bureaucratic institutions proved surprisingly flexible mechanisms with which to implement them (Shirk 1993: 17).

In addition to the economic reforms instituted by Deng (which are considered in more detail in the next chapter), one of the most important tactics employed by Deng and his supporters was to dismantle the personality cult surrounding Mao (Saich 2004). From that time forward, the legitimacy of the CCP would be tied less to an inherited ideological dogma and more to the Party's ability to deliver economic development. This was to be the era of 'socialism with Chinese characteristics'. Significantly, the preoccupation with economic reform that has distinguished Chinese politics since Deng became leader was not mirrored by similar political reforms. On the contrary, the tide of democratic reform that was sweeping through Eastern Europe, and igniting hopes of similar initiatives amongst Chinese students in particular, was seen by the Party as something that needed to be actively suppressed. The tensions between student activists, reformists such as Hu Yaobang and Zhao Ziyang, and the PRC establishment came to a head in the demonstrations in Tiananmen Square in 1989. Although the PLA played a major part in brutally suppressing these demonstrations, it is important to note that the military's influence and power had been significantly reduced as a consequence of initiatives instituted by Deng. What Deng was less successful in addressing was widespread official corruption, a major source of student discontent.

The year 1989 was also significant because Jiang Zemin became General Secretary and largely continued the reformist agenda pioneered by Deng. The importance attached to economic development and the downgrading of Marxist orthodoxy was evident in Deng's rather surreal, but highly revealing, claim that 'Leftists' were inhibiting the reform process and slowing China's development (Saich 2004: 76–7). Significantly, the thrust of the Dengist approach and the development of a 'socialist market economy' were endorsed by the Fourteenth Party Congress in 1992. What was significant about Jiang's role in this period was that he attempted to reimpose greater CCP control on the civil society that was developing as a consequence of economic liberalization and social transformation. And yet, it is important to note that 'many of the controls have proved impossible to implement for any length of time, testifying to the decline in state capacity and threatening to result in continuing friction between the state and elements of society' (Saich 2004: 79). In short, China's elites are forced to confront a more widespread dilemma that is one of the hallmarks of a 'global' era as discussed in Chapter 1: greater international economic integration of the sort promoted by Deng inevitably compromises the autonomy of the state. China's accession to the WTO and the domestic reforms this has necessitated are a dramatic example of this possibility (this is taken up in more detail in the next chapter). In China's case, the dilemma created by diminished autonomy is especially acute as the state has had a crucial, ideologically-legitimated role as the defender of the proletariat and vanguard of progressive social development.

The degree of political and ideological change that has occurred in China can be gauged from the fact that the so-called fourth generation of leaders are generally technocrats such as the current President Hu Jintao, with engineering backgrounds and seemingly little interest in ideology (Nathan and Gilley 2002). Indeed, it is noteworthy that capitalists are now not only seen as important elements in the development of China's productive forces, but have actually been invited to join the CCP; these developments have sparked a major internal debate about the role and purpose of the party itself.[37] The glue that binds various factions together in China's ruling elite is not ideological, as in former times, but 'corruption' and the distribution of resources (Dittmer 2003). Unsurprisingly, therefore, there are limits to which the regime is willing to go to accommodate the reformist pressures that are being placed on it,[38] especially as this affects the role of the CCP itself. In a major statement on the prospects for, and view of, democratic development in China, the PRC government argues that democracy must reflect particular national circumstances. In

China's case, this means that rule by the CCP is a continuing 'objective requirement' for the country's future development, stability and unity (PRC 2005).

This should come as no surprise. Hu Jintao has proved anything but a political modernizer. On the contrary, Hu as President and Communist Party chief has combined with former leadership rival and Vice President, Zeng Qinghong, to reinforce the power of the CCP, and clamp down on more liberal elements in the Party and in the wider civil society.[39] An even more telling indication of the limits to political liberalization on the mainland, perhaps, has been the manner in which Hong Kong has been incorporated back into the PRC following its return from Britain in 1997. Under Deng's formula of 'one country, two systems', the people of Hong Kong had been led to believe that the democratic reforms belatedly encouraged by the British would be continued under mainland rule. In reality, the British government cooperated with the PRC in drastically limiting democratic freedoms in Hong Kong, a reality that was constitutionalized in the Basic Law and its limited democratic representation (Roberti 1996). Simply put, Hong Kong became a Special Administrative Region with limited autonomy and democracy, controlled by the mainland. As the PRC has moved to tighten its grip over Hong Kong, the prospects for the restoration of democratic institutions and values are generally considered 'remote' (Thomas 1999: 263).

Although this episode is plainly something of a tragedy for Hong Kong's aspiring democrats, it has a wider significance in the context of intra- and especially inter-regional relations, and raises a number of important questions about the nature of East Asian polities: first, is the proclivity for illiberalism in China and other parts of East Asia a passing phase or a historically-engrained manifestation of fundamentally different values? Second, are such values and political regimes a potentially irreconcilable source of future tension between the region and the USA in particular and the West more generally? Finally, could such values, whatever their origins may be, provide the basis for regional ideas and identities that might bind the region together? To begin to answer this question, the final part of this chapter briefly examines the debate about 'Asian values' and human rights in East Asia.

Asian values and human rights

When the 'Asian miracle' was at its height in the mid-1990s, policy-makers and scholars around the world looked to East Asia for answers to the puzzle of economic development. The precise strategies that attracted such attention are considered in more detail in the next chapter; what is of interest at this stage is the political and ideological discourse that accompanied the region's rapid economic development. In Southeast Asia, in particular, a number of prominent figures – including Malaysia's Mahathir and Singapore's Lee Kuan Yew – were trumpeting the merits of 'Asian values' as an explanation for the region's economic take-off. Although there is much less talk of such distinctive values in the aftermath of the financial crisis of 1997, the debate is worth revisiting as it throws a revealing light not only on the socially constructed nature of this revisionist discourse, but also because it also raises important, enduring questions about both the nature of societies in the region and their compatibility with international human rights norms.

The idea that some societies are likely to be more economically productive than others has intuitive appeal and academic credibility. Plainly, societies that are peaceful, stable and governed in predictable ways are likely to have lower 'transaction costs' than those without such qualities. An increasingly influential stream of economic thought has long argued that some institutional frameworks and national jurisdictions are more conducive to profit-oriented activities than others (Williamson 1985). This basic assumption has been extended to suggest that some societies have greater 'social capital' (Putnam 1992), or enjoy greater degrees of 'trust' (Fukuyama 1995), as a consequence of their specific social and cultural histories. In both cases, these qualities are thought to account for superior economic performance. The general claim is that to a non-trivial extent, 'culture matters' (Harrison and Huntington 2000). But, as we shall see in the next chapter, in East Asia's case economic development became a region-wide phenomenon in ways that transcended specific national borders and circumstances, and appeared to owe more to particular policy regimes and wider geopolitical circumstances than it did to specific cultural values. Nevertheless, what matters at this stage is the way such cultural explanations were championed by regional elites.

According to Lee Kuan Yew (in Zakaria 1994: 114), for example, Singapore's remarkable economic development was attributable to 'thrift, hard work, filial piety and loyalty in the extended family, and, most of all, the respect for scholarship and learning'. Speaking at a time when East Asia appeared to be on an unstoppable ascending economic trajectory, Lee also claimed that the comparatively poor performance of the United States in particular was a direct consequence of the fact that 'Westerners have abandoned an ethical basis for society' (Zakaria 1994: 112). These basic assumptions came to be elaborated and associated with what was variously described as Asian values, an 'Asian Way' or 'Asian ethic'. Whatever they were called, there was broad agreement that they contained a number of implicit or explicit features:

- a number of core civilizational values broadly associated with Confucianism;
- a belief in, and pursuit of, social harmony as consequence of such underlying values;
- the family, rather than the state or the individual ought to be the focal point of social organization;
- political decision-making through consensus rather than confrontation and competitive politics;
- a preparedness to sacrifice individual interests in favour of the collective good;
- respect for age, authority and hierarchy;
- an emphasis on personal relationships, especially in business;
- a rejection of 'Western' preoccupations with individualism and human rights.[40]

A number of general observations can be made about these claims. The major point to make about the entire Asian values discourse, perhaps, is that it is pitched at such a high level of generalization and draws on such stereotypical notions of cultural difference as to be almost meaningless. The depictions of 'Asia', or indeed 'the West', are not sufficiently differentiated to capture the vast differences not just in East Asia, but also between, say, continental Europe and the Anglo–American nations (E. Friedman 2000). It should also be noted that some prominent Asian leaders have explicitly rejected the entire Asian values discourse as self-serving, and attributed the slow adoption of more authentically democratic practices to 'the resistance of authoritarian leaders and their apologists' (Kim 1994: 194). For all the attention given to the need for consensus and harmony there are, as Robison (1996: 311) points out, few mechanisms for allowing a widespread consensus to develop or to be expressed in the region's state-dominated polities. More fundamentally for the purposes of this discussion, there is no evidence to support the idea that greater political liberty is an obstacle to economic development (Sen 1999). On the contrary, as I noted earlier, the 'traditional' values that have been recently rediscovered and posited as the key to East Asia's economic transformation were long considered to be incompatible with the competitive dynamism of market capitalism and the primary reason for the region's *non*-development.

Nevertheless, as a consequence of what advocates of Asian values took to be the superiority of this value system, they believed that economic (and, indeed, political) competition in the twenty-first century would 'see a struggle between an Atlantic impulse and a Pacific impulse' (Mahbubani 1995: 105). When seen in this light, criticisms of Asian values by the West were seen as self-interested attempts to protect extant competitive advantages and prop up decadent social systems, rather than as genuine concerns about human rights violations. Indeed, supporters of Asian values adopted a position of unabashed cultural relativism in making a two-pronged claim that, first, there was no 'objective' position from which to judge the relative worth of different cultural and social systems. In other words, all values were contingent and dependent upon specific historical circumstances. The second claim that flowed from this was even more contentious: because different societies have different histories and thus different values, there are no universal forms or values that apply equally across all cultures at all times. The implication of this point was stated unambiguously by Mahathir: not only could democracy look and operate differently in different societies as a consequence, but 'not all forms of democracy are productive. There is good and productive democracy as well as bad and destructive democracy. Democratic freedom must go hand-in-hand with democratic responsibility' (Mahathir 1997: 9).

Given what we have already seen about the way politics in Malaysia operated under Mahathir, this kind of reasoning looks entirely self-serving and designed to deflect external criticism. While the precise meaning of democracy may not be as unambiguous or clear cut as we might like, there are plainly procedural minimums that must be realized if the term is to have any meaning at all. At one level, then, the arguments of Asian values advocates such as Mahathir can be seen as an attempt to accommodate a new, transnational 'standard of civilization' in which democratic principles are seen as *de rigueur*. Indeed, it is a measure of the implicit acceptance that there *are* universal standards of behaviour and human rights principles that Mahathir felt obliged to address such issues at all. At another level, however, the attraction of the overall Asian values discourse, in which the state effectively defines the nature and quality of democratic processes, is entirely domestic and a consequence, as Rodan (1996b: 329) points out, of 'its potential to marginalise views within Asia that pose some sort of challenge to authoritarian rule'.

Apologists for 'Asia's different standard' argue that 'trying to impose pet Western definitions of "freedom" and "democracy" is an incitement to destructive conflict, best foregone in the interest of promoting real human rights' (Kausikan 1993: 40), the 'real human rights' in this case being the rising living standards that, to some extent, at least, legitimated the dominant, interventionist, even authoritarian role of the state before the economic crisis of 1997. Once some degree of economic development was achieved, however, these sorts of argument looked increasingly threadbare and self-serving. Consequently, the question for many of Asia's political elites is this: having engineered economic development in the region, are they now inhibiting a similar process of political development?

This is an especially important issue for the region generally, as the historical record in Asia suggests there is nothing inevitable or teleological about the relationship between economic and political development, especially where particular regimes have been able to control and define debates about the nature of political processes.

At one level, these are national issues that are ultimately likely to be decided by the particular composition of domestic social forces (Rueschemeyer, Stephens and Stephens 1992). At another level, however, the region's continuing non-compliance with international standards of political practice means that human rights issues will continue to complicate inter-regional relations. There are two especially prominent examples of this possibility. First, the ASEAN grouping has come under considerable external pressure over its general human rights policies and those of Burma in particular. As we shall see in Chapter 7, ASEAN's institutional shortcomings and sensitivities leave it poorly placed to address these issues and socialize Burma into 'good' behaviour. As a consequence, the activities of high-profile inter-regional summits such as the Asia–Europe Meeting (ASEM) have been plagued by long-running differences of opinion about the importance of human rights issues (Eldridge 2002).

As the most prominent and influential champion of global democratic reform, the USA plays an especially critical role in placing reformist pressure on *some* of the governments of the region. In this regard, it is important to note that the USA's concern about human rights abuses and the importance of democratic procedures is highly selective, and determined by a wider strategic calculus. Consequently China, which is still viewed primarily as a strategic competitor, a challenger for regional influence, and associated with major trade imbalances, is subjected to much hectoring about its human rights record.[41] By contrast, because of the war on terror, the USA has taken a much more indulgent view of human rights abuses and non-democratic processes in countries such as Thailand and Malaysia, which have cracked down on supposedly subversive elements or discouraged radical Islamism (Glassman 2006).

Despite the continuing importance of the United States in shaping East Asia's strategic and even institutional landscape, its influence may be declining, especially at the level of 'soft power'. America's moral authority has been seriously undermined by its own actions. Not only is there a recognition that the concern expressed by policy-makers in the USA about human rights abuses is selective, but there have been a number of prominent scandals about America's own systemic abuse of human rights. As *The Economist* puts it, 'Mr Bush has a duty to press China on its systematically abysmal human-rights record – although America's own ambivalence on torture and lapses at Abu Ghraib and Guantanamo

Bay have made its lectures easier to ignore'.[42] More importantly in the long run, perhaps, major questions have been raised within the USA itself about the quality of America's own democratic practices and institutions of governance (Zakaria 2004), the impact and origins of American unilateralism (Prestowitz 2003), and the dynastic nature of an American presidency that is beholden to particular economic and religious interests (Phillips 2004).

America's declining moral authority and the inconsistent nature of its engagement on human rights issues is important for a number of reasons. First, and most importantly, perhaps, at a time when democratic processes and the competence of governments are regarded with growing cynicism in the West (Cerny 1999), this may make the promotion of democracy more difficult and provide ammunition for supporters of 'Asia's different standard'. If the promotion of human rights and democracy becomes associated with the opportunistic pursuit of strategic or competitive advantage, then the credibility of the entire project will be compromised and advocates of alternative visions will gain ground. At one level, this may only be manifest in the long-standing call for the 'Asianisation of Asia' (Funabashi 1993), or the promotion of values and practices that are more in keeping with 'traditional' notions of political process in the region. At the very least, though, this might provide precisely the sort of ideational commonality that many suggest is the missing ingredient in East Asian forms of regionalism.[43] At another level, the perception that external pressure is being applied to East Asia in ways that are designed to transform cultural values and practices for geopolitical reasons is likely to encourage precisely the sort of radical political Islam that so concerns the USA. After all, as Mohammed Ayoob points out: 'For most Muslims, antipathy towards America is not based on opposition to "American values" of democracy and freedom. It is fundamentally grounded on particular aspects of American foreign policy, especially the perception of Washington's operation of blatant double standards in relation to the Middle East (Ayoob 2005: 960).

At a time when some of the more radical forms of political Islam are widely taken to be a threat to democratic processes, this is potentially a major constraint on democratically-oriented reform in the region. Given Southeast Asia's prominence in the war on terror, there is the real danger that a preoccupation with security threats and the need to shore up allies will recreate precisely the same sort of logic that prevailed during the Cold War (Rodan and Hewison 2004), with all the negative consequences for democratic rule that implies. Once again, East Asia's political fortunes seem to be inextricably caught up in a wider geopolitical context that will shape, if not determine, the course of political development in the region for the foreseeable future.

Conclusion

East Asia encompasses a bewildering array of political practices and traditions that makes generalization difficult, and yet it is possible to identify persistent broadly-based historical patterns of political organization in which 'strong' states have played an important role, authoritarianism has been commonplace, civil society has been underdeveloped, and democracy of any sort has been the exception rather than the norm. The distinctive conditions that prevailed during the Cold War and the challenges of nation-building and development help to explain some of the common features of the region's evolution. Of late, however, there has been a noteworthy spread of democratic forms, albeit ones with distinctive local features that place a question mark over their quality. Nevertheless, one might be forgiven for thinking that, to borrow a colourful phrase from George W. Bush, 'freedom is on the march', or one *might* have thought that until the beginning of the war on terror and the renewed regional preoccupation with security issues. Now the prospects for further democratic reform in East Asia look mixed.

For those Asian political elites that have been unenthusiastic converts to democratic reform processes which inevitably threaten their own undemocratically obtained positions and power, the pressure for reform – from external sources, at least – is less intense. Even criticism of China, which has been the focus of particular attention by the USA, has become slightly more muted as a consequence of the USA's growing reliance on continuing Chinese capital flows to underpin its budgetary position and military commitments.[44] The nature of this relationship will be explored in more detail in Chapter 6, but it is important to note that there are clear limits to America's influence and its desire to exercise it that have potentially important implications for the course of future political processes in East Asia. When combined with America's declining moral authority and the frequent repudiation of multilateral mechanisms, the attractions of East Asian institutions that reflect and possibly champion regional perspectives on the world stage become more apparent.

That such perspectives exist in East Asia and that regional elites might be keen to promote them is not in doubt. The Japanese in particular have made great efforts to promote a more positive view of their own developmental experience and its potential utility for its neighbours (Terry 2002; Wade 1996). But before we consider how such initiatives have played out and how they fit into wider debates about international public policy, we need to take a closer look at the way Japan engineered its own spectacular rise, and the degree to which this model has been emulated elsewhere in the region.

Chapter 5

East Asia's Developmental States

One of the most distinctive and original features of East Asia's political and economic history since the Second World War has been the emergence of what has been described as the 'developmental state'. Although discussions of the developmental state are less prominent than they once were, it remains such an important feature of the East Asian experience that it merits revisiting if we are to understand how different countries of the region have developed and why the state remains a potentially pivotal element of the development process. Not only will the legacy of the developmental state continue to shape national, and possibly regional, outcomes in the area, but the East Asian experience has potentially important lessons for other parts of the world where development is still sorely needed (Fukuyama 2004; Sachs 2005).

At its simplest, the developmental state has become a generic term to describe governments that try to actively 'intervene' in economic processes and direct the course of development, rather than relying on market forces. As we saw in Chapter 1, the ability of states to influence the course of development and business activity depends in large part on state 'strength' and capacity, and the ability to establish effective relations with economic actors. Although the developmental state is predominantly associated with East Asia because of its association with the so-called East Asian miracle (World Bank 1993), it is important to note that some scholars have claimed that the developmental state pre-dates the East Asian experience and has been around for a long time in some form or other (Bagchi 2000), and that successful economic development *everywhere* has required major state assistance (H.-J. Chang 2002).

Of late, however, one country in particular has been considered as the pioneer of both rapid economic growth and industrialization in East Asia, and of the developmental state itself. Japan has come to epitomize all that was most successful and remarkable about economic take-off in a region that was once associated with inescapable backwardness. For this reason, Japan's experience will be given extensive consideration. A noteworthy aspect of the discussion of Japan – and the rest of East Asia, for that matter – is that precisely the same structures, practices and values that were once thought to be part of the 'secret' of Japan's success and the cause of the 'East Asian miracle' are now considered the cause of its economic problems. One of the primary tasks of this chapter is to try to make sense of recent debates about the rise and apparent fall of the developmental state (Beeson 2004a), and to identify what went right and wrong in Japan's case, and in some of the countries that followed its lead. One possibility to keep in mind is that Japan's developmental experience in the high-growth era[1] and the strategies that underpinned it may still have much to tell us, despite any problems it has recently experienced. It is important to remember at the outset that both Japan's rapid industrialization and that of the other 'newly industrializing countries' (NICs) that followed in its wake was remarkable, unparalleled and unexpected. Although the region's developmental states were clearly not solely responsible for this process – the fortuitous historical circumstances described in earlier chapters combined with the activities of local and international capital plainly helped – the state's role is sufficiently distinctive and the outcomes generally so successful that they merit detailed analysis.

Although there are important variations in the way developmentalism has been approached, and significant differences in state capacity, most of the states of the region have attempted to pursue some form of state-led development. Consequently, it is important to understand how and why this happened, not only because it is at odds with much of the prevailing Western wisdom, but because it provides an important element of commonality in the political and economic practices of the East Asian region as a whole. However, this chapter is not concerned solely with the historical experience; I also consider the possible future of the developmental state as part of the region's political and economic architecture. A crucial question emerges from this discussion: even if it is conceded that the developmental state once played a decisive role in East Asia's economic expansion, can it (or, indeed, *should* it) continue to play such a role? More fundamentally, perhaps, is the developmental state actually compatible with a more integrated, not to say globalized, international order? The Japanese experience suggests that there may be significant limits to what developmental states can, or indeed ought to do, but the situation is much less clear cut in other parts of the region. Whatever we may think about their contemporary role, however, the fact remains that activist, interventionist states have been a crucially important, highly original, and deeply institutionalized part of political and economic activity across much of the region: the course of future change and the degree of any convergence on Western models of capitalism will be determined in part by its legacy (Beeson 2002b).

The Japanese exemplar

Before considering how Japan's post-war recovery was actually engineered, it is worth spelling out what makes the developmental state conceptually distinctive and why it is so contentious as a consequence. Nearly everything about the developmental state is sharply at odds with the conventional economic wisdom that prevails in the Anglo–American nations and in the policy prescriptions of the IFIs. Consequently, the developmental state has been both a direct intellectual and ideological challenge to the dominant economic orthodoxy associated with the Washington consensus or neoliberalism (see Hall 2003), and a practical challenge because of the rapid rise of highly competitive East Asian economies.

Thinking about the developmental state

Neoclassical economics, which still provides much of the intellectual foundation for the dominant economic orthodoxy that has come to be associated with neoliberalism, emerged at the end of the nineteenth century and continues to exercise a powerful influence over contemporary economic thinking. At the heart of neoclassical economics is a belief in the efficacy of markets, which are considered to be the most efficient means of allocating economic resources. There is an assumption that individuals are best able to make 'rational choices' about their own interests, and that these will intersect with the decisions of producers to ensure the most efficient distribution and production of goods and services. The key point about this highly simplified sketch of conventional economic thinking is that economic well-being is seen as dependent not on the state or the collective actions of human beings, but on individual decision-making in response to spontaneously occurring market forces. On the contrary, in this highly abstract, historical reading of the nature of economic activity, states were seen as a potentially major *obstacle* to the efficient production and allocation of economic resources (Stilwell 2002: ch. 18).

This remarkably benign view of market processes, in which the 'laws' of supply and demand enable informed consumers to make individual consumption choices, which are then rapidly responded to by competitive, entrepreneurial producers leading to a state of 'equilibrium' and harmony, is noticeably at odds with historical reality. Capitalism has been repeatedly punctuated by profoundly disruptive periods of massive economic *dis*equilibrium (Kindleberger 1996), and the very adoption of capitalist social relations was frequently resisted and traumatic not just in East Asia, but also in its European heartland (Polanyi 1957).

Moreover, the neoclassical vision of frictionless markets, well-informed consumers and competitive producers pays little heed to the constraining impact of the initial distribution of power, privilege and property rights in society, to say nothing of the impact of consumerism (Milliband 1991). More fundamentally, the neoclassical model has little to say about the lack of competition in, and the strategic significance of, key industrial sectors – an area that is central to understanding East Asia's different approach to industrial development (Chang 2000).

Before considering why Japanese policy-makers came to such a different understanding of the basis of economic development and wealth creation, it is worth saying something about the importance of economic ideas themselves, and the specific socioeconomic circumstances that engender them. The first point to make is that the reproduction of economic ideas and the dominance of particular theories owes as much to the way such ideas are reproduced as it does to the inherent brilliance of the ideas themselves. Consequently, ideas have the capacity to shape policy whatever their intrinsic merits (Woods 1995), even when they may no longer be appropriate or relevant (Milner and Keohane 1996). At one level this is a function of the content and style of economics teaching in different countries (Gordon 1994), but at another level it reflects the proselytizing role of influential transnational agents such as the IFIs, and their capacity to tie aid to the adoption of specific policy prescriptions (Barnett and Finnemore 2004; Wade 2002). Seen in such circumstances it is striking that Japan developed a different ideational framework in the first place, and this is a reminder of the importance of the sort of contingent local factors discussed in the last chapter. Whether such differences will persist is a moot point and something I explore below; but first we need to consider what the 'Japanese model' actually looked like and where its inspiration came from.

Economic ideas and national 'visions'

George Bush senior famously said that he did not do the 'vision thing'. By contrast, Japanese public officials do, or at least they used to. There are two senses in which the notion of 'vision' matters when thinking about why different countries have very different views not just about what appropriate policy looks like, but what an economy is, the way it should be thought of, and the purposes to which it should be put. The first sense is well captured by Warren Samuels who suggests that: 'To the extent that an economy is an artefact, what is important to the social (re)construction of the economy is not so much what is "true" in some epistemological sense, but what people believe and act upon' (Samuels 1991: 518). In other words, 'the economy' is not some universal essence that can be touched or directly acted upon in the same way everywhere, but a way of thinking about a wide range of inter-connected *social* processes. The discourses such practices generate help us to make sense of economic activity and the social forces that drive it. This leads directly to a second consideration in thinking about economies and economic activity: 'What is important is to see all visions as expressions of the inescapable need to infuse 'meaning' – to discover a comprehensible framework – in the world. Visions thereby structure the social reality to which economics, like other forms of social inquiry, addresses its attention' (Heilbroner 1990: 1,112).

Two further points emerge from these claims. First, despite its well-known pretensions to 'scientific' status and methodology, economics remains an imprecise social science subject, with all the difficulties this implies. Put differently, understandings of economic processes are contingent and socially determined; they are consequently also value-laden and reflective of a specific set of social circumstances, even if it is one in which international factors play an increasingly influential part. The second point to make is that the socially-constructed understanding of economic 'reality' will both reflect and *help to construct* the very economic processes and forms policy-makers and theoreticians seek to comprehend and manage. The major methodological failing of the domi-nant neoclassical model, therefore, is not just that it generally remains uninterested in its own ontological and epistemological status, but that its universalizing, ahistorical abstractions are incapable of dealing with the wide varieties of economic forms that continue to distinguish 'global' capitalism (Hodgson 1996). This failing helps to explain why the Japanese model has proved so difficult to explain for many Western economists, and why it has aroused such hostility.

Economic thought in Japan, by contrast, is a good deal more heterodox and pragmatically-oriented (Morris-Suzuki 1989), and consequently not driven by a particular economic philosophy. The relatively obscure German political economist, Friedrich List, is a far greater influence than Adam Smith on Japanese policy-makers, and their view of themselves and the potential role of the state is profoundly different as a consequence.[2] Rather than relying on what Smith described as the invisible hand of the market to determine the production and distribution of goods and services, List's ideas reinforced and legitimated a proclivity for industrial targeting in Japan that began in the late Tokugawa period and which was reinforced from the Meiji period onwards (Beasley 1993: 103). Such poli-cies were especially important as a direct consequence of the fact that Japan was a comparatively 'late' developing country. Because Britain, Western Europe and the United States had already successfully industrial-ized, there was a proven developmental template that Japanese planners could draw on and use to accelerate the course of economic development. The key insight of Alexander Gerschenkron (1966) was that late-developing states could utilize existing technology and developmental techniques to compress the rate at which the industrialization process took place.

There are a couple of other major assumptions that inform the state-led approach to economic development that are widely recognized in the literature, and which provide the rationale for the 'interventionist' approach. First and most fundamentally, perhaps, it is clear that some industries and productive processes are inherently more valuable, wealth-generating and consequently 'strategic' than others (Krugman 1986). This is the basis of the claim that 'manufacturing matters' (Cohen and Zysman 1987): manufacturing provides higher productivity gains, and greater technological 'spillovers' in the form of skill development and economic linkages across the economy in a way that other sectors, such as agriculture and resource extraction, simply cannot. While the nature of economic activity has become a good deal more complex and disaggregated of late, this basic insight still has a good deal of validity, especially when considering the initial development of the industrialization process.

There is a further salient point that flows from this basic claim, however, which has both policy and ideological implications: the assumption that some forms of economic activity are intrinsically more valuable would – or possibly should – suggest that governments have an interest in seeing them occur within their national jurisdictions. The key question then becomes whether such activities occur 'naturally' as a consequence of market forces, or whether they can be actively encouraged through government incentives or policies. Japan plainly chose the latter course; it needs to be emphasized that this amounts to a direct refutation of the conventional economic wisdom. Economic orthodoxy suggests that, following the nineteenth-century British economist, David Ricardo, countries are best advised to follow their 'comparative advantage' and do what they are 'naturally' best at. In other words, countries with large labour forces such as China should specialize in labour-intensive production, while resource-rich countries such as Australia should exploit the bounty of nature. This is fine up to a point, but it becomes a problem when – as has been the case – manufacturing in particular, and industrialization more generally, have been the key to economic growth, greater participation in global trade and rising living standards (Peet 1991). Plainly, this is a problem for those countries or producers that specialize in the production of primary products and helps to explain their relative development failures (Hoogvelt 2001: ch. 8). This is one of the major problems affecting places such as sub-

Saharan Africa, but it is something that also affects parts of Southeast Asia, too, as we shall see shortly.

Japan's elite bureaucrats have long recognized the impact on national power and security implications that flowed from the possession of an indigenous manufacturing capacity (Heginbotham and Samuels 1998). Without industrialization and borrowing from the West, Japan would not have risen to the front rank of imperial powers before the Second World War. But it was equally apparent to Japan's post-war technocrats that the wealthy countries of the world were also complex, industrialized nations with a number of key economic sectors with self-sustaining domestic linkages. Once in place, such technologically-rich industrial processes had the capacity to 'lock-in' increasing returns and rising living standards in a virtuous circle (Arthur 1989). A failure to industrialize and adopt productivity-enhancing technology threatened an equally path-dependent vicious circle of declining returns and living standards.

The key point that has emerged from some of the most sophisticated analyses of why some countries are highly successful in encouraging technological innovation and industrial development is that it requires a supportive institutional order, which states can play a major part in helping to determine (Boyer and Hollingsworth 1997). Consequently, Japan's economic bureaucrats set out, quite self-consciously and intentionally, to *create* a comparative advantage in industrial production in defiance of Western economic 'laws' and orthodoxy. While Japan's pre-war industrialization meant its policy elites were not starting from a blank sheet, the extent of war-time damage to the Japanese economy meant that the scale of the reconstruction and development was enormous and the results equally staggering. It was Japan's ability to 'custom design policy instruments to fit the differing priorities, needs, and circumstances of individual industries' that was central to the 'industry policies' its bureaucrats implemented (Okimoto 1989: 9), and the rapid expansion and development of the overall economy more generally (Weiss and Hobson 1995).

As we saw in Chapter 2, Japan's ability to respond to the challenge of Western expansion was completely different from that of China. Although contact with the West caused social turmoil and transformation in Japan too, once the Meiji Restoration was accomplished and a new generation of modernizers was in power, the basis for subsequent economic development was in place. Crucially, the willingness to borrow assiduously from the West and utilize both its technologies and its social innovations distinguished the Japanese response. From the outset, however, the Japanese state, which was increasingly centralized and effective, was at the heart of the developmental efforts. One of the reasons that the Japanese state became so effective and powerful was because of its importance in Japan's simultaneous military modernization.

Consequently, the idea of a powerful, interventionist state playing a pivotal role has not been as problematic as it might have been in parts of the West,[3] but has from the outset actually enjoyed a good deal of legitimacy.

From the latter part of the nineteenth century, Japan's political elites were preoccupied with actively drawing on the American and European industrialization experiences to plan a similar process of economic development in Japan. As a result, many of the techniques and strategies that would become synonymous with 'Japan Inc.' and the development state following the Second World War were already well developed in the first half of the twentieth century (Terry 2002). In other words, a particular view of the appropriate role of the state in economic development was in place even before the Americans arrived at the end of the Second World War. Nevertheless, when the Americans occupied Japan in the aftermath of that war it had a profound impact on Japan's political system and values, but not on its traditions of interventionism and the position and structure of the bureaucracy.[4]

The traumatic impact of the war itself ingrained a remarkably enduring antipathy towards warfare amongst the Japanese population and led to the long-term reconfiguring of Japanese foreign and security policy as a consequence. At the level of public policy and corporate organization, however, America's ability to remake Japan in its own image was much less clear cut and the legacy of pre-war institutionalized relationships was much more enduring. As Chalmers Johnson (1982) points out in his seminal work on Japan's capitalist developmental state, although the Americans wanted to reform both the bureaucracy and the *zaibatsu* system in Japan, they were constrained by geopolitical imperatives, and by the sheer difficulty of penetrating the bureaucracy itself. As a result, not only did the *zaibatsu* return to prominence in the post-war period (albeit re-badged as the *keiretsu* networks), but key agencies such as the Ministry of International Trade and Industry (MITI) and the Ministry of Finance (MoF) were in position to guide the process of industrial regeneration.

Development in practice

Thus, the American occupation had only a limited impact on the bureaucratic and corporate structures that had been consolidated before the Second World War. Consequently, established relationships between the bureaucracy and business played a prominent role in shaping the direction of Japan's subsequent, unprecedented economic renaissance. At the centre of Japan's post-war reconstruction efforts was what Johnson (1982) described as the 'plan rational' or, more commonly now, the developmental state. The key word here is 'plan', for that is precisely what Japan's political elites did: rather than waiting for the market to determine the most 'efficient' allocation of available economic resources, Japanese policy-makers made a judgement about precisely which industries and economic sectors they considered to be most strategically important, and set about encouraging their long-term development. Some of these judgements had been made before the war, when the demands of militarism and the perceived need for industrial self-sufficiency meant that a number of key industries (including ship-building) were targeted for development. The logic of targeted economic development through the use of specific industry policies was taken up again after the war, when key bureaucratic agencies were given responsibility for directing the development process.

In Japan's case, the possibility that the state would play a dominant role not just in economic planning, but society more generally, was made more likely by its specific historical circumstances. On the one hand, the Japanese had already become accustomed to the highly successful role played by its reformist elite in the nineteenth and early twentieth centuries. On the other hand, the overwhelming need to reconstruct the economy in the wake of war-time devastation gave a further impetus to the state-led reconstruction project and a broad social consensus about its legitimacy.[5] Consequently, the Japanese state was overwhelmingly preoccupied with encouraging the development process for more than 50 years, so that 'Japan's achievements were the result of a torturous learning and adaptation process that in the present context began with the financial panic of 1927 and ended with the adjustments in the wake of the oil shock of 1973' (Johnson 1982: 306).

As Johnson points out, while this was the most successful and important period of the developmental state in Japan, it was not without its disasters, not the least of which was the Second World War and the abortive attempts to develop the East Asia Co-prosperity Sphere discussed in Chapter 2. Similarly, there have been some noteworthy errors of judgement and industrial failures that serve as salutary reminders about the fallibility of Japan's economic planning elite and the limitations of industry policies and state-guided development after the initial 'catching-up' phase had been accomplished (Callon 1995). Nevertheless, in the immediate aftermath of the War, the Japanese pioneered particular relationships and policy tools that allowed its bureaucratic elites to guide the course of economic development. A number of these are very distinctive and have figured in both theoretical accounts of the developmental state, and in its active emulation in other parts of the region, so they are worth spelling out.

Some of the most significant early initiatives taken in the 1950s involved limiting the import of finished manufactured goods, but encouraging the import and transfer of new technologies. Significantly, Japanese planners also borrowed selectively from Western management practices, leading to the development of Japan's life-time employment system and the more systematic utilization of labour force skills; these initiatives were long thought to give Japan a distinct competitive advantage over Western rivals (Johnson 1982: 216). Perhaps even more important than the distinctive labour relations and corporate practices that evolved in post-war Japan were the sorts of relationships that developed between the state and business. Both these terms need unpacking because, in reality, 'the state' was primarily agencies such as MITI, the MoF and the Bank of Japan, and 'business' was the handful of mega-corporations that came to dominate Japan's post-war economic landscape. There is some contention about where the balance of power in these relationships lay, with some emphasizing the power and autonomy of agencies such as MITI (Okimoto 1989: 112–13) in precisely the way that Peter Evans suggested defined 'embedded autonomy' (see Chapter 1), and others who stress the 'reciprocal' nature of business–government relations (R.J. Samuels 1987: 2–8). However we describe it, though, there are a number of institutionalized elements of the relationship that made it productive and facilitated the development process.

In one sense, the nature of Japan's explicitly political processes we considered in the last chapter helps to account for the bureaucracy's extraordinary power and authority: the political class was preoccupied with politicking and raising money, and content to leave the management of the economy to the technocrats. The dangers of this process would eventually become all too apparent, but initially this arrangement worked well and opened up a regulatory space which the bureaucrats were happy to occupy. But this does not explain the willingness of Japan's capitalist class to go along with the initiatives that emerged from the likes of MITI. The state's dominance was partly a consequence of Japan's 'late-developer' status and the catalytic role the technocratic elite had played even before the war. But MITI and the other elements of the bureaucracy were able to exercise what came to be known as 'administrative guidance' – that is, 'informal regulatory power or indirect control' (George Mulgan 2005: 23) – in the war's aftermath because they had the policy tools and regulatory authority which gave them political and economic influence.

In the early phases of Japan's post-war recovery, MITI's control over access to foreign currency and the overall tariff regime was crucially important, and gave the bureaucracy powerful leverage over companies that wanted to operate overseas or receive government protection. Likewise, MITI's endorsement of a company or industry made it far easier for it to obtain relatively scarce capital through low-interest rate loans (Krauss 1992: 50). This was an especially important consideration given that, unlike most Western economies, Japan's system is much more dependent on bank finance rather than equity markets for raising capital (Zysman 1983). One of the key innovations that facilitated bureaucratic control and industrial development was the remarkably bland-sounding Fiscal Investment and Loan Programme (FILP), which utilized the substantial funds deposited in the Postal Savings System to channel cheap capital to targeted industries. The FILP and its policies were ultimately controlled by the MoF and were intended both to encourage Japan's already substantial savings rate, and to reinforce the overall direction of developmentalism (Tabb 1995: ch. 4). It is also important to note for comparative purposes that Japan restricted foreign investment and preferred to rely on domestic sources to fund its industrialization push; this policy stands in stark contrast with a number of other East Asian nations, and helps explain both the impact and origins of the Asian financial crisis, and the different patterns of development elsewhere in the region, as we shall see below.

Reinforcing this economic leverage were a series of more direct, personal relationships that allowed Japanese policy-makers to implement their plans and encourage the growth of targeted industries; initially petro-chemicals, steel and ship-building, and subsequently the electronics and automotive sectors. What is common to all, of course, is that they are industries that were essential to the development of a sophisticated industrial economy with complex, mutually reinforcing linkages across various sectors of the economy. In Japan's celebrated (or reviled) system of *amakudari*, senior civil servants join the boards of private sector companies upon their (generally early) retirement. This is in part compensation for the nugatory legitimate rewards given to bureaucrats, but more importantly a potentially crucial conduit for the transmission of advice from the state and the reception of feedback from business (Schaede 1995). Once again, this is in line with the idealized concept of embeddedness which Peter Evans (1995) considered to be a part of effective state capacity.

However, these arrangements are not without their potential dangers and pitfalls. While close connections between business and government can be important mechanisms for the transmission of information, they can also become mutually-rewarding 'circles of compensation' or reciprocal networks designed to further the material goals of participants (Calder 1988a). This potential is especially likely to be realized when such networks become increasingly self-serving and endure beyond their original purposes (Beeson 2003d). It is precisely this possibility that has given rise to some of the – frequently highly generalized and imprecise –

claims about 'crony capitalism'. Despite the fact that such accusations were often little more than caricatures and part of a broader attempt to destroy the credibility of the developmental state more generally, there were nevertheless major problems with (and inherent dangers in) the state-led approach to development, and Japan illustrates many of them.

Japan in crisis

Although the conventional wisdom has it that Japan has been mired in crisis for more than 10 years, it is important to remember that, even in the midst of Japan's 'lost decade' in the 1990s, unemployment was generally less than 5 per cent, and frequently significantly lower than comparable Organisation for Economic Co-operation and Development (OECD) countries. Compared to Japan's own, (earlier) break-neck economic development, growth rates in the 1990s looked anaemic. But, for all the concern about deflation that took hold at this time, this was no Great Depression.[6] Now that the Japanese economy appears to have rebounded, it is possible to make a more balanced judgement about Japan's economic problems and the wider lessons for developmental states more generally.

The first point to make about Japan's economic problems is that they were tied to domestic *and* international political forces and conditions. In Japan, and in most of the other East Asian developmental states, changes in the *international* political economy have either undermined or highlighted weaknesses in the domestic political economy. In Japan's case, it did both. On the one hand, there were, as I shall explain, major systemic weaknesses that had developed within an increasingly dualistic domestic economy. However, these vulnerabilities and potential flaws might not have been exposed quite so dramatically, or become such liabilities, had it not been for the operation of the wider international order generally and the actions of American foreign policy-makers in particular. The key development in this regard was the so-called Plaza Accord of 1985, in which Japanese policy-makers – under intense pressure from their American counterparts[7] – agreed to allow the yen to appreciate in the belief that this would solve the 'problem' of America's ballooning trade deficit with Japan (Murphy 1997).

Given that history is currently repeating itself, as the Americans try to talk the new trade villain – China – into revaluing its currency, it is worth spelling out some of the implications of this process. At the very least, it is a timely reminder that the most powerful country in the world has a capacity to compel compliance with its policy preferences, no matter what they may be.[8] Conventional economic wisdom suggests that America's problems have domestic causes and are primarily attributable to low savings rates.[9] Nevertheless, the Japanese felt compelled to go along with the policies of the Reagan administration if they wanted to ensure continued access to America's vital domestic market. Between 1985 and 1988, in a process the Japanese called *endaka*, the value of the yen increased by 56 per cent in trade-weighted terms, and by 93 per cent against the US dollar (Brenner 2002: 106).

This sort of dramatic currency appreciation would have been a problem for any economy, but it was especially acute for Japan because of the nature of its domestic economy and the logic of its developmental model. Paradoxically, some of Japan's seemingly greatest strengths – high savings rates and a phenomenally successful export-led developmental strategy – eventually became liabilities as the economy matured. 'Excessive' domestic savings led to 'underconsumption' and an ever greater reliance on exports to underpin the overall national growth strategy (Katz 1998). This highlighted another strength that seemed to have become a weakness: 'dedicated capital'. At the peak of the developmental state's powers, it had been able to redirect Japan's high levels of domestic savings to targeted companies through a process of 'financial repression'. Financial repression occurs when governments keep interest rates 'artificially' low, or lower than market-clearing rates. This affords one way of providing targeted industries or borrowers with cheap capital, gives policy-makers leverage over private industry, and helps to account for the high investment and growth rates in much of East Asia.[10] But the steady liberalization of the financial sector and the growth of domestic savings meant that firms no longer needed to rely on the government or even local financial institutions to access capital (Leyshon 1994). Consequently, the effectiveness of a major policy tool of government from Japan's high-growth era was permanently undermined.

That the power of the bureaucracy has been undermined may be no bad thing, according to some observers. Aurelia George Mulgan's detailed analysis of the Ministry of Agriculture, Forestry and Fisheries (MAFF) demonstrates all that can go wrong with powerful bureaucracies and the dangers inherent in interventionism. As George Mulgan makes clear, Japan's various economic bureaucracies have developed their own autonomous interests, which are frequently more concerned with the preservation and expansion of the Ministry itself than they are with any notion of the wider 'national interest'. In this context, intervention is not necessarily a tool for industrial development or efficient economic management, but something that 'shapes the individual ministries into independent fiefdoms, supreme over all they survey' (George Mulgan 2005: 27). As a consequence, it becomes easier to understand why the liberalization of Japan's agriculture sector has proved so difficult and contentious, despite intense external pressure and the declining importance of the sector itself:

there are simply too many organizations 'living off the agricultural support and protection industry for radical liberalisation of the agricultural sector to be a feasible prospect' (George Mulgan 2005: 214). One of the key problems that Japanese interventionism highlights, therefore, is the way that potentially effective aspects of state capacity can become corrupted, self-serving obstacles to needed reforms.

Thus, if the net effect of changes in the financial sector had simply been a diminution in the effectiveness of governmental industry policy and economic leverage, all might have been well. Unfortunately, however, the MoF made what is widely regarded as a major policy mistake in not raising interest rates and controlling credit growth as the currency appreciated. They may have done so for the best of reasons – understandable concern about the impact of the rising yen on the economy and the all-important export sector – but the net effect of this was to inflate the 'bubble economy' of the late 1980s and early 1990s. The consequences of this period of 'free money', when the combination of low interest rates and banks desperately searching for new customers made credit all too easily available are well known: a (temporary) stratospheric rise in the equity and real estate markets, a dramatic increase in the number of non-performing loans held by Japanese banks, and an outpouring of Japanese capital overseas (Wood 1992).

The implications of this latter development were not all bad, and were crucial in driving the regionalization process in East Asia, as will be explained in the next chapter. In Japan, however, the impact of the bubble economy was not only profound in economic terms, but also politically damaging as well. As T.J. Pempel (1998: 148) makes clear, as the bubble started to deflate, 'government policies were no longer a cohesive strategy directed at national improvement, but rather an eclectic mixture of ad hoc efforts to plug holes in competing dikes'. Public officials, who had formerly been held in high public esteem, were seen as increasingly incompetent and even corrupt (Hartcher 1997: 42–8). From experiencing a state of national self-confidence bordering on hubris during the boom years, a mood of introspection and doubt took hold as the difficulties involved in resolving Japan's economic problems became clearer, and confidence in the competence and honesty of public officials declined.

The ineffectiveness and compromised nature of public policy exacerbated underlying problems in the Japanese economy that had been disguised, but which were largely created by the high growth, developmental state era. In Richard Katz's extensive analysis of Japan's economic problems, he argues that at the centre of Japan's domestic difficulties was an industrial policy that had 'degenerated into little more than political pork barrelling and logrolling', designed to prop up uncompetitive industries (Katz 1998: 31–2). Again, what had been a source of strength, and central to Japan's unambiguous developmental success, gradually degenerated into self-serving networks bound together by mutual obligation and patronage (at least in the uncompetitive domestic sector).[11] Two aspects of this process were especially damaging: first, public policy reflected and helped to entrench the 'dual economy' in which uncompetitive domestic industries were protected by government, actually encouraging a shift of workers from more efficient, export-oriented industries. Indeed, many of Japan's most competitive and successful companies moved off-shore during the 1990s, exacerbating the lack of domestic competitiveness and increasing the need for greater government support (Katz 1998: ch. 3).

This latter trend contributed to the second problem that emerged from the corruption of and in Japan's government–business relations: public money that might have been used to reignite economic activity and lift the economy out of the doldrums in an orthodox Keynesian fashion was more often siphoned-off to industries that were politically, rather than economically, important. The most egregious example of this possibility occurred in what Gavan McCormack (1996: ch. 1) calls the 'construction state'. Not only were most of the major public works initiatives such as dams and roads frequently of dubious benefit, but the bidding process was corrupt and resulted in greatly inflated costs which were ultimately borne by Japanese taxpayers. How did such a system come about?

> The answer is not that Japan's mountainous lands need much more civil engineering than do other countries, but that during the long period of one-party rule in post-war Japan, a collusive system of exploiting the public by massive corruption evolved . . . in which construction is incidental to the production of power and the distribution of profit. (McCormack 1996: 33)

This is a long way from the idealized notion of a developmental state intervening to guide the course of economic development in the putative national interest. While this might seem indictment enough as far as the developmental state is concerned, there is one more, possibly even more fundamental, reason for believing that – in Japan's case, at least – the developmental state is no longer capable of playing the role it once did. There is compelling evidence that the nature of contemporary technological innovation is simply not responsive to the sort of highly interventionist, state-directed strategies employed by generations of Japanese planners (Fong 1998). Contemporary advances at the technological frontier of the most strategically important, wealth-generating industries are, it seems, more likely to occur in the sorts of diffuse networks of independent producers found in Silicon Valley (Saxenian 1994) than they are in the sort of highly centralized projects favoured by the Japanese government (Drezner 2001b). Simply put, state-sponsored innovation processes seem to be effective for generating the sort of incremental innovation associated with the catching-up phase of industrialization, whereas liberal market economies seem to be better at generating the sort of 'radical' innovation that occurs at the technological frontier (Hall and Soskice 2001: 41). Significantly, it seems as if this possibility has been recognized even by MITI as the limitations of some of its interventions and the declining effectiveness of some of its policy tools have become more apparent. As a consequence, MITI – re-badged in 2001 as the Ministry of Economy, Trade and Industry as part of a general reorganization and renaming of Japan's ministries and agencies – has become something of a champion of deregulation as its seeks to reposition itself in the intra-agency struggles that have been such a surprising but important part the operation of the developmental state (Callon 1995).

Japanese lessons?

Given Japan's importance as both a historical role model for other aspiring industrial economies in the region (Amsden 1995: 796) and the principal motor of regional economic integration (Hatch and Yamamura 1996), it is worth highlighting some of the implications of the developmental state's rise and fall before considering more briefly how some of its imitators have fared elsewhere. The first point to make is that, despite the claims by some orthodox economists that the rise of Japan and the rest of East Asia is explicable simply by reference to the working of market forces (Balassa 1988), evidence about the extent – and frequently the effectiveness – of state intervention in the early phases of Japan's pre- and post-war industrialization is simply overwhelming (Dore 1986). Whatever problems Japan may have experienced during the 1990s, it is clear that for several decades after the Second World War Japan's economic renaissance was planned and – to a significant degree – realized as a consequence of the efforts of a bureaucratic elite working in tandem with the indigenous capitalist class. While there is some debate about the degree of autonomy and influence enjoyed by the bureaucrats, and about the self-serving nature of some of the relationships and strategies that developed, Japan's post-war development occurred at a hitherto unprecedented pace and achieved a global prominence that cannot be explained without taking into account both the activities of Japanese public officials and their links to domestic large-scale industry.

However, there are aspects of Japan's developmental trajectory that are unique and make its replication difficult, even if there is a desire to do so. Japan's specific historical experience, especially the pattern of state intervention dating from the Meiji period, coupled with the existence of established large- and small-scale industry even before the Second World War, may make this style of intervention hard to emulate. Because the Japanese economy is dominated by a handful of corporations or *keiretsu* (Gerlach 1992), close cooperative relations with government were relatively easy to organize: this was facilitated by the practice of appointing ex-bureaucrats to corporate directorships. It is also important to recognize that alongside the massive corporate conglomerates such as Mitsui and Mitsubishi was an array of small-scale producers that provided much of the dynamism, flexibility and competitiveness of the manufacturing sector more generally (Friedman 1988).[12] It should also be acknowledged that the remarkable growth of these smaller-scale enterprises was not a consequence of direct government assistance, even though they may have benefited from the overall growth in economic activity. Part of Japan's success, therefore, was because its planning elites had something to work with in a way that is frequently not the case in other countries.

One of the most distinctive features of the Japanese model during the high growth era was the relative insulation of the Japanese economy. Indeed, in the first few decades after the Second World War it still made sense to speak of discrete national economies in a way that it may not now (see Bryan 1995): many of the factors outlined in Chapter 1, especially increased transnational trade and capital flows, the disaggregation of production and the growth of cross-border equity holdings and corporate control, have undermined the idea of clearly demarcated national economic boundaries. Even Japan, which scrupulously avoided dependence on inward FDI, and which contentiously maintained a range of highly effective formal and informal trade barriers (Lincoln 1990), has become increasingly affected by external economic forces. The most important change in this regard has been the integration of Japan's capital and equity markets with the wider international economy (Lapavitsas 1997). This gradual integration has made Japanese corporations more independent of government and less reliant on their own 'main banks' for capital,[13] and changed the ownership structures of Japanese corporations in the process. Not only have foreign ownership and equity holdings become more common in Japan, but the mutually-supportive cross-shareholdings between different branches of large *keiretsu* have begun to break down, too.[14]

At one level, then, the policy tools that the Japanese state employed, especially through the control of capital, have become largely unimportant and ineffective, at least as far as Japan's most competitive, internationally-oriented firms are concerned. Although Japan's industrial

policies were clearly central to the country's overall economic renaissance, a principal shortcoming, especially in more recent times, has been
a failure to discriminate between competitive and uncompetitive industries (Porter, Takeuchi and Sakakibara 2000: 44). Companies and industries often received assistance or preferential treatment on the basis of
their political connections or importance, not their economic efficiency
or contribution to overall national development. As a consequence,
government policy exacerbated what Pempel (1998: 212) calls 'the most
central economic cleavage confronting Japan ... between its internationally competitive and non-competitive sectors, firms, and groups'.
The extent of this tension and the transformation that has occurred in
business–government relations in Japan can be gleaned from the fact that
the *Keidanren* – Japan's most influential and important business federation – has actively lobbied the Japanese government both to open up the
economy through free trade agreements (Yoshimatsu 2005), and to
undertake greater deregulation of the economy and administrative
reform (Carlile 1998: 89). As we shall see, Japan's experience highlights
a more general trend: the restructuring of domestic industry and the
greater integration of formerly nationally-based economic activity that is
occurring across East Asia is also reconfiguring political relationships as
well, breaking down former alliances and creating new, pro-liberalization
forces within former bastions of mercantilism (Jayasuriya 2003;
Ravenhill 2006).

In Japan's case, however, the deeply entrenched nature of its unique
patterns of political and economic relations have proved resistant to
change, despite the apparently dysfunctional or simply corrupt nature of
some of these practices (Carpenter 2003). There are two possible explanations for this. First, as we saw in the last chapter, there is often a higher
level of tolerance for, and less strict definition of, corruption by business
and economic elites in some parts of East Asia. Moreover, in certain
circumstances – the absence of secure property rights, for example –
corruption may actually play a vital, functional role (Hutchcroft 1997;
Kang 2003c). It should also be noted that in Japan's case corruption was
widespread even when the developmental state was most effective,
although not part of its formal operations. As we also saw in the last
chapter, the former premier, Tanaka, did more than anyone else to institutionalize corruption in Japan, but this did not stop effective
business–government policy coordination (Beeson 2003d). In other
words, the existence of corruption may not be a sufficiently compelling
trigger for reform, even if it undermines the legitimacy and authority of
the participants. At a time when the Japanese economy is generally
considered to be over the worst of its economic problems (Emmott
2005), it is possible that direct pressure for reform will actually decline.

The second reason that there has been a relatively limited transformation of some of the structures of the developmental state is simply that so many have a stake in its continuing existence. As Lincoln (2001) points out, many Japanese private and public sector employees have a vested interest in the continuation of the existing system and little enthusiasm for radical policy change and the potential upheaval it would inevitably bring. Clearly, there would be losers (especially in Japan's hitherto protected domestic sector) as well as winners, should wholesale reform and economic opening occur. Likewise, the benefits of reform may be long term while the short-term effects may be socially divisive. Moreover, the failings of the present system may be less obvious to many Japanese than they are to outside observers. After all, Japan still enjoys one of the highest standards of living in the world, low levels of unemployment and impressive social stability. As we saw in the last chapter, many East Asians are unconvinced about the superiority of an Anglo–American model that is widely associated with economic polarization and social instability. All of this helps to explain why, despite the much-discussed need for major administrative reform in Japan, 'the regulatory reform measures implemented so far have had a relatively small, marginal impact with respect to increasing competition and the role of the "market" in the Japanese economy' (Carlile and Tilton 1998: 206). Indeed, the bureaucratic apparatus consolidated under the rubric of the developmental state is actually overseeing and regulating the reform process itself, reminding us that, paradoxically enough, freer markets may need more rules (Vogel 1996). Bureaucrats threatened with reform will find ways to protect their turf, and 'if necessary will pursue functional aggrandisement for the purpose of organisational survival' (George Mulgan 2005: 37).

The final lesson to emerge from Japan's overall developmental experience is perhaps the most important: Japan was in the right place at the right time. On the one hand, this meant that Japan was able to take advantage of the remarkable recovery in economic activity that occurred in the aftermath of the Second World War. North American consumer markets continued to expand and Europe's recovered rapidly, providing the perfect backdrop for Japan's export-oriented industrialization strategy. On the other hand, a second consequence of good timing was more paradoxical: because the Cold War intensified at the very moment Japanese planners were attempting to rebuild its economy, Japan benefited from both American aid and demand, but also from a more indulgent American attitude towards Japanese mercantilism and interventionism. The Americans may not have liked the Japanese approach terribly much – it was, after all, diametrically opposed to everything the Americans stood for normatively and practically – but they were prepared to tolerate it in the context of the wider geopolitical and strategic confrontation with the Soviet Union and its East Asian allies (Beeson 2004a).

If this interpretation of the Japanese experience and the importance of historical contingency is correct, it has potentially important implications for other countries that might want to emulate Japan's success. Not only is the international economic order significantly more competitive than when Japan undertook its post-war reconstruction (something to which Japan's own success has contributed), but there is far less chance of getting much assistance from external powers such as the USA. On the contrary, the USA is likely to take a much more 'interventionist' role itself, encouraging developing nations to adopt neoliberal policies that are not only at odds with Japan's successful strategies, but also with the policies the USA adopted itself (Chang 2002). But before we consider the overall utility and functioning of the developmental state in an increasingly globalized environment, it is useful to look briefly at how other parts of the region have attempted to follow Japan's lead and kick-start the developmental process.

The rise of the newly industrializing countries

The reason it became common to refer to the 'East Asian miracle', rather than simply Japan's, was because Japanese-style rapid development became more widespread across the region (World Bank 1993). It is possible to identify two broad waves of development in this process. First, the NICs of South Korea, Taiwan, Singapore and Hong Kong followed Japan's lead during the 1960s. Latterly, the countries of Southeast Asia, and also eventually China, have all attempted with varying degrees of success to follow in their wake. As we shall see, although there are significant differences between and within the various developmental waves, it is possible to detect some important commonalities and continuities, not the least of which is the role played by the state. While none of the states considered below replicated the Japanese experience in every way, the developmental state pioneered by Japan was a model for a number of countries in the region and provides a useful comparative exemplar with which to consider developmental experiences elsewhere in East Asia.

Of the first wave of industrializing economies in the region, it is noteworthy that two were former colonies of Japan's, and Singapore emulated a number of Japanese policy initiatives in its own industrialization push. Among the NICs that attracted such attention, only Hong Kong is generally thought to have deviated from the Japanese interventionist path. Even in Hong Kong, though, Castells (1992: 45) argues that 'a careful analysis of the process of economic development of Hong Kong since the mid-1950s reveals a decisive role by the state in creating the conditions for economic growth', albeit more 'subtly' and 'indirectly'. At one level this should not surprise us: as I suggested earlier, it is simply inconceivable that any form of capitalism could operate without the sort of regulatory framework that, for the last several hundred years, has been provided primarily by states (Heilbroner 1985). Even if we accept that globalization may be altering this picture in important ways that I shall take up below, and that alternative forms of regulation have existed at various times (Spruyt 1994), the fact is that during the economic take-off in East Asia states did play a decisive role. In Hong Kong's case, and despite the British influence, the colonial administration played an important role in creating the preconditions for the development of small-scale manufacturing through the creation of a supportive regulatory framework and the direct subsidization of labour costs (Castells 1992).

In Korea and Taiwan, the state's role and the influence of the Japanese model was more direct and unambiguous. As we saw in Chapter 2, both countries were colonized by Japan and, despite the trauma this caused and the damage it has done to subsequent relations in the case of Korea, both countries underwent important changes that paved the way for subsequent rapid economic development. In Korea's case, in particular, the impact of Japanese colonialism in creating the preconditions for a Korean developmental state cannot be overemphasized (Amsden 2001: 101). The Japanese created a large, centralized bureaucracy with the infrastructural capacity to reach the peripheral areas of Korea, the power of which was reinforced by a colonial police force. The net effect was a state with a 'highly centralised apex with near absolute powers of legislation and execution – and thus of setting and implementing "national" goals – and pervasive, disciplined civil service and police bureaucracies [that] constituted the core of the new state' (Kohli 1999: 105). A similar tale can be told of Taiwan, where the Japanese colonizers replaced traditional patterns of rule and authority with a centralized state. Again, despite the brutality that frequently accompanied Japanese occupation, the net effect was a radical transformation of Taiwan's existent social, economic and political structures and 'demonstrate to the Taiwanese the potential of capitalist industrialization' (Gold 1986: 45).

This common heritage notwithstanding, thereafter the histories of capitalist development in Korea and Taiwan display some noteworthy differences, as well as some important continuities. The major continuity, of course, was the prevalence of authoritarian rule (something that also distinguished Singapore, as we shall see shortly). However, one of the most important differences between Korea and Taiwan lies in the nature of the business organizations that came to dominate the industrial landscape in each country. The *chaebol*, the major corporate entity in Korea, is very similar to Japan's *keiretsu* networks. There is one major difference between Japan's *keiretsu* and Korea's *chaebol* that needs to be emphasized: in Japan there is a clearer separation of ownership and control, and good deal of management autonomy as a consequence. In Korea, by contrast, the *chaebols* are dominated by the handful of families that control them. As a result, decision-making processes are highly centralized, despite the fact that the breadth of activities undertaken by the *chaebols* is generally much greater than that of their Japanese counterparts (Whitley 1990). The reason for the distinctive character of Korea's corporations is not 'Asian values' or Confucian traditions, but something rather more ubiquitous and mundane: political power. The Korean state that Japan helped to establish subsequently became the architect of Korea's corporate development and actively encouraged the growth of the *chaebols*. As Woo (1991: 66) puts it, 'politics, and not innovative drive, has always been considered the umbilical cord nurturing big business in Korea'.

Taiwan also has a distinctive form of corporate organization and is perhaps the most important concentrated exemplar of the 'Chinese capitalism' phenomenon (Redding 2002). The key points that emerge from stylized depictions of the corporate form associated with the 'overseas Chinese'[15] are its generally small scale (especially when compared to Japan and Korea), its flexibility, and the importance of personal relationships (*guanxi*). Significantly, in Taiwan, as in Korea, the state was involved in the systematic *creation* of an indigenous capitalist class where none had previously existed, a situation that Gold (1986: 64) considers 'offers a text-book case of elite-led revolutionary social transformation'. The impact of these efforts is not in doubt: from a position where agriculture accounted for over 90 per cent of economic activity in 1951, by 1987 it was down to barely 6 per cent; manufacturing was a mirror image, having gone from less than 10 per cent to over 90 per cent (Prybyla 1991: 53). One of Taiwan's key policy innovations – as it had been in Korea, as well – was to shift from a strategy of import substitution and protectionism in the 1950s to one of export-oriented production from the 1960s onwards. Taiwan's economic take-off was also given a major economic boost by the 'massive' American aid that poured in during the Korean War, and this was something Singapore, Malaysia, Thailand and even Korea itself would also eventually benefit from as well (Stubbs 2005: ch. 3).

Paradoxical as it may seem, the Korean War consolidated the position, and underpinned the success of, the developmental state in Korea, although it is important to note that this truly developmental regime was not consolidated until Park took power in 1961 (Hundt 2005). Prior to this, aid was the 'key' to Korea's initial import-substitution strategies of the 1950s. Significantly, the war itself reduced American reformist pressure on the authoritarian leader Syngman Rhee (Haggard 1990: 55–6). The limitations of the import-substitution model, especially in terms of market size and competitiveness, became clearer in the 1950s, partly as a consequence of the comparatively poor performance of Latin America (see Gereffi and Wyman 1990). The crucial factors that allowed Korea to make a successful transition to export-oriented development were 'the concentration of power in the executive, the rationalization of the economic policy-making machinery, and the development of new instruments for steering industrialization' (Haggard 1990: 62). In other words, Korean elites developed precisely the same sort of institutional innovations that had allowed Japanese policy-makers to guide development.

One of the most widely noted innovations Korean policy-makers undertook to promote development was what Alice Amsden refers to as 'getting prices wrong'. Rather than relying on market signals to allocate resources and determine economic activity, Korean officials deliberately intervened to 'distort' prices and thus encourage business to move into specific activities. Subsidies were available to those that could meet specific performance standards in a business–government relationship that was defined by reciprocity (Amsden 1989: 139–47). As in Japan, the state used the financial system as a mechanism for allocating credit and encouraging business cooperation through patterns of reciprocal obligation (Amsden 2001: 147–8). Consequently, 'the effectiveness of government policy in dealing with large enterprises depended crucially on the effectiveness of this instrument' (Lee 1992: 188). This is why the gradual liberalization of the financial sector in Korea was not simply an important element in the unfolding of the Asian crisis, as we shall see in the next chapter, but it also marked what Woo-Cumings (1997: 58) describes as the 'historical eclipse of a developmental political economic regime'. The liberalization of the financial sector represented more than just a diminution in the effectiveness of an important policy lever as far as the state was concerned: it marked the unravelling of the state–business accommodation more generally. In sum, liberalization meant that:

Korea's financial market would be *internationalized* and not protected ... To compete at the world level, Korean firms had to behave like capitalists and not bureaucrats, think profit and not control; and this meant the *privatization* of banks. But since banks cannot thrive in situations of financial repression, finance would have to be *deregulated*. (Woo-Cumings 1997: 80; emphasis in original).

Despite the dramatic impact these changes would ultimately have on Korea, there are a number of comparative points that can usefully be made about the Taiwanese and Korean experiences while their respective developmental states were at their most powerful. First, the Korean developmental state was a good deal more centralized and bureaucratic than Taiwan's. In Taiwan, responsibility for industrial policy was dispersed through more agencies, and public officials had less decision-making authority in their relations with private firms. Taiwan has also used public investment to encourage particular activities, rather than the more directive approach towards domestic capital favoured in Korea which was facilitated by the limited numbers of actors in big business noted above (Wade 1990: 324). In Korea's case, this strategy had long-term implications and dangers as far as the state was concerned though: the very success of a state strategy designed to create large corporations inevitably changed the relationship between government and business as the *chaebols* gained more 'structural power' within the Korean political economy. By the 1990s, it was becoming apparent that the *chaebols* had the capacity to resist government attempts to introduce neoliberal reforms or restructure key industries such as automotive manufacturing (Hundt 2005: 141–2). In Taiwan, by contrast, where the extent of political change has (until recently, at least) been more extensive, the state was also compelled to respond to business pressure. But while successive Taiwanese governments wound back their 'statist' approach, they found new ways to assist business through low-interest loans, research and development (R&D) off-sets, and improved policy coordination with the private sector (Noble 1999: 153), despite the apparently ubiquitous practical and ideological constraints implied by globalization.

The capacity of governments to respond to changing circumstances is at the centre of contemporary debates about the role of states generally and developmental states in particular, as we shall see below. The final member of the original NICs – Singapore – provides a useful reminder of both the variety of state strategies and situations that confronted developmental states even before the 'global' era, and of the ability of states to take advantage of changing circumstances. Indeed, like Japan, Singapore might be said to have been in the right place at the right time, particularly as far as the emerging 'new international division of labour' was concerned (Froebel, Heinricks and Kreye 1980).[16] In Singapore's case, its geographical location at the cross-roads of Asian trade and its historical role as a crucial entrepôt of the British empire meant that it was well placed to take advantage of the expanding world economy. The key to its success, Garry Rodan (1989) argues, was an interventionist state that was able to take advantage of the opportunities offered by the international restructuring of productive capital. Singapore's limited internal market meant that the import-substitution route to development was not an option, especially after the collapse of the Malay Federation. The absence of a strong domestic capitalist class meant that the Singaporean government had little choice other than to rely on FDI and multi-national corporations if it wanted to integrate itself successfully into the expanding international economy.

The essence of the strategy the Singaporean government adopted was to make itself an attractive investment location for mobile international capital.[17] At one level, this resulted in the development of the sort of authoritarian regime described in the last chapter. A crucially important aspect of this process was a crack-down on the labour force. Simultaneously, an Economic Development Board was established in 1961 and charged with attracting multi-national capital in accordance with a preferred model of industrial development and deepening (Haggard 1990: 112–13). Through a range of incentives including tax breaks and infrastructure provision, the government attempted to 'shape Singapore's comparative advantage in the production of labour-intensive manufactures', an export-oriented industrialization strategy that proved 'a spectacular success' (Rodan 1997: 153). The Singaporean government recognized the limits of this strategy in the 1980s as neighbouring economies with lower-cost labour forces jumped on the industrialization bandwagon, and successfully converted itself into a regional finance and business hub. Singapore has become an important node in regional 'growth triangles', and in the activities of the so-called 'overseas Chinese'.[18] Part of the success of these strategies and the state's capacity to respond to changing economic circumstances is attributable to the role played by government-linked companies. These notoriously non-transparent entities continue to play a large role in the expansion of the Singaporean state's economic activities (Rodan 2006), in a pattern that has more in common with some of its neighbours in Southeast Asia.

Singapore's somewhat fortuitous circumstances and small scale mean that – like Hong Kong – it is difficult to draw too many conclusions from its experience. What we can say about Singapore, as in Korea and Taiwan, however, is that it is not so much the incorruptibility of the state, or even its complete autonomy from particularistic interests that seems to matter, so much as the recognition that 'even imperfect governmental machinery, operating with normally venal human beings, can still be moulded into an instrument capable of facilitating high rates of economic growth' (Evans 1998: 73). In other words, state capacity is a necessary but not sufficient cause of successful developmental outcomes. The critical variable underpinning the rise of the first generation of NICs would seem to be the willingness of states to 'intervene' to direct the course of economic development in ways that frequently defied the conventional, predominantly neoliberal, economic wisdom. In Robert Wade's view, what distinguished East Asia's developmental states was:

> a consistent and coordinated attentiveness to the problems and opportunities of particular industries, in the context of a long-term perspective on the economy's evolution, and a state which is hard enough not only to produce sizable effects on the economy but also to control the direction of the effects, which is a more demanding achievement. (Wade 1990: 343)

A major question that emerges from these different (but related) experiences, therefore, is whether such a role is any longer possible or appropriate, and whether states are capable of 'controlling the direction of effects'. Even if the state–business relationship remains relatively uncorrupt and capable of serving some sort of 'national interest', the impact of the Asian financial crisis on the Korean economy in particular suggested that integration into the international financial sector may fundamentally undermine state-led development strategies (Wade and Veneroso 1998). Before we consider this question in any detail, it is instructive to examine the experience of Southeast Asia, an area with a patchier history of economic development.

Southeast Asia: the maligned miracles?

Once again, the diversity of the developmental experience in Southeast Asia defies easy generalization, but it still makes sense to consider the most important states in Southeast Asia – Malaysia, Thailand, Indonesia and the Philippines – together. Not only are they the largest economies and most strategically significant countries in the region, but they all attempted to kick-start the industrialization process at about the same time and, with the noteworthy and instructive exception of the Philippines, they have done so rather effectively (Amsden 1995; Jomo 2001). Thus, they constitute a distinct second wave or tier of industrial development after Japan and the first generation NICs. The other reason for considering these countries together is because, notwithstanding some significant and enduring differences in developmental outcomes, their collective performance has not been as good as the NICs; indeed, in the case of the Philippines it has been strikingly poor. The Philippines is the quintessential exemplar of what Yoshihara famously described as Southeast Asia's 'ersatz capitalism', by which he meant its technological dependence and (especially) the poor quality of government intervention in the development process (Yoshihara 1988). Because the Philippines is something of an outlier, even in a Southeast Asian, context it is instructive for comparative purposes, and thus useful, to consider it first.

The first point to make about the Philippines is that things ought to have been different. After all, as an English-speaking ex-American colony with relative political stability and comparatively good growth rates following independence, it looked set to be the star performer in an entire East Asian region associated with chronic economic underdevelopment. One factor working against the Philippines and any rapid economic transformation was the legacy of the colonial period, and a trade structure that revolved around a limited number of products, especially sugar. But given that, with the exception of Thailand, both generations of aspiring industrializing economies that followed in Japan's wake had to cope with some sort of colonial handicap, why was the Philippines' response so inadequate? One reason was the negative impact of Japanese occupation. Whereas Taiwan and Korea benefited from vital bureaucratic reform and a transformation of existent class structures, the principal impact of Japanese contact as far as the Philippines was concerned was the destruction of its economy. And yet, during the 1950s, the Philippines actually experienced some of the highest growth rates in the region (Hutchison 2006: 43). So what went wrong?

As we saw in the last chapter, one of the most distinctive characteristics of the Philippines' political economy is the enfeebled nature of the state and its vulnerability to capture by particularistic interests. In contrast to the developmental capacities of the 'strong' states of Northeast Asia, 'the Philippines presents an insightful study of precisely what kinds of economic problems can result from insufficient development of the state apparatus' (Hutchcroft 1994: 219). Because the state was so weak, its resources were systematically plundered. Crucially, and unlike elsewhere in Southeast Asia, it was effectively looted by actors external to the state itself. The state has only been able to survive at all with the assistance of international aid from the USA and the IFIs. Its primary function as a consequence has been as a conduit with which to redirect external assistance to privileged insiders, rent-seekers and cronies within the wider Philippines' political economy. Tragically, the developmental process in the Philippines has been made more difficult because so much government expenditure is directed to servicing the resultant foreign debt obligations (Bello 2000: 241).

Part of the problem in the Philippines was the nature of the bureaucracy itself: whereas in much of the region state bureaucracies were staffed by competent, relatively uncorrupted officials, in the Philippines the bureaucracy was riddled with corruption, and appointment depended more on patronage and contacts than competence (Kang 2002: 76).

Although economic activity in the Philippines is, as in Korea, dominated by a relatively small number of families, in the Philippines there are more of them, in more economic sectors. Consequently, while competition exists, it is generally not the sort advocated by orthodox economists, but a struggle over 'the spoils of the state, with power shifting rapidly between groups' (Kang 2002: 145). In short, the Philippines represents the nadir of bureaucratic competence and effectiveness in Southeast Asia.

However, even though the Philippines is something of an extreme case, both in terms of the ineffectiveness of the state and its consequent negative impact on development, there are parallels with some of Southeast Asia's other economies. Indonesia, for example, has until recently been dominated by Suharto, another archetypal 'strong man' leader, whose grip on power was consolidated by networks of patronage and personal links to cronies and family members. And yet, for all the undoubted corruption, nepotism and lack of transparency that distinguished the Indonesian political economy under Suharto, for the three decades before the Asian crisis hit, Indonesia experienced significant, sustained economic growth and development. Indeed, it is remarkable that, Suharto's military background notwithstanding, economic development became his ideological mantra and the key to a broader notion of security. What is less surprising, perhaps, is that the army should have been 'permitted, even encouraged, to establish or extend businesses to provide new sources of funds for their operations and, indeed, for the private gain of the officers concerned' (Elson 2001: 191). As we saw in Chapter 3, the distinctive idea of security that prevailed in Indonesia, the army's position as one of the few institutions with national reach, and Suharto's own extensive connections and control within it all help to explain the military's prominent involvement in the economy. What is more remarkable is the way key elements of the Indonesian economy (the oil industry, for example) came under military control and became the principal source of funding for the army.

This is even more surprising when we remember that, from the outset, the Suharto regime has been closely associated with both the IFIs, and the so-called 'Berkeley mafia' of Western-trained economists who played a major role in the first Suharto cabinet following the overthrow of Sukarno. In 1966, the World Bank and the IMF played a prominent role in setting the economic policy agenda and approach of the first Suharto government as it attempted to establish its economic credentials and reassure potential international investors. But, despite this initial willingness to adopt the rhetoric of reform, one of the defining features of the Suharto period has been a continuing tension between technocrats and the nationalists. The relative power of each faction was directly related to the price of Indonesia's most valuable resource: oil. When the price of oil was low and the Indonesian government was more dependent on international aid and investment flows, the Western-oriented technocrats were in the ascendancy; once the price rose, the nationalists held sway. As Jeffrey Winters (1996: 96) puts it, 'not only the onset but also the depth and intensity of the country's policy changes can be linked to changes in the Suharto regime's access to windfall oil profits'. The general point to make is that, in contrast to some of the more effective Northeast Asian states, policy implementation of any sort in Indonesia was compromised by a lack of bureaucratic competence and capacity on the one hand, and by the patrimonial nature of ties between government and business on the other (MacIntyre 1994: 262–3).

In some ways, Indonesia seems to confirm the paradox of the 'resource curse', or the counter-intuitive idea that the possession of immense resource wealth can have detrimental impacts on development and governance (Ross 1999). At one level, this is plainly true: oil wealth greased the wheels of patronage politics and the distinctive, corrupt, personalized networks of power that grew up around them. And yet, the Indonesian economy grew by more than 7 per cent a year between 1968 and 1981, and industrial output expanded from 13 to 42 per cent of national economic activity between 1965 and 1995 (Booth 1999: 112–13). Importantly, not all of the oil wealth disappeared in conspicuous consumption or foreign bank accounts. On the contrary, for all its faults, the Suharto government's distinctive form of what Richard Robison (1997: 111) calls 'authoritarian state capitalism' was a major investor in steel, aluminium, fertilizers, petroleum-refining, cement and paper; in other words, some of the basic building blocks of an industrial economy. In short, the Suharto regime was highly 'interventionist' and, despite the fact that investment decisions and policies may have invariably profited particular cronies and state-sponsored business conglomerates, significant development did occur, not all of which was swept away by the Asian crisis.

One thing that was overthrown by the crisis was the Suharto regime itself. Given that the bases of the New Order regime's successful interventions in the economy were the authoritarian nature of the government and the state's manifold involvement in economic activity, it might be supposed that even the possibility of, let alone the desire for, extensive state intervention might be a thing of the past. The reality seems to be more complex and ambiguous: on the one hand, many of the old economic and political interests associated with the former Suharto regime appear to be reconstituting themselves within the new democratic order, and severely limiting the capacity of the state to impose systemic reform as a consequence. On the other hand, decentralization initiatives, coupled with the growth of democracy and political pluralism, mean that 'authority over the allocation of resources, contracts and monopolies ha[s] been shifted from a highly centralised system of state power to a more diffuse and chaotic environment of political parties, parliaments and provincial governments' (Robison and Hadiz 2004: 215). Paradoxically, enough, therefore, while the downfall of the Suharto regime may have been welcome politically, it may – in the short term, at least – have further undermined the already limited capacity of the Indonesian state to drive the developmental process.

Of all the Southeast Asian countries, Malaysia has arguably come closest to approximating the Japanese exemplar. This is both predictable and surprising. It is predictable because Mahathir had adopted a 'look East' policy which self-consciously set out to emulate the Japanese model, with all the nationalist, mercantilist and interventionist under-pinnings that implied. Mahathir saw state-led economic development as the key to breaking the shackles of Western colonialism and contempo-rary economic domination that were to become such prominent parts of his anti-Western rhetoric (Khoo 1995: 65–74). Japan has played a more direct and tangible role in Malaysian development, too, as Japanese multi-national corporations and investment have been central to the industrialization and structural transformation of the Malay economy (Machado 1992). But while this might explain the Japanese influence on Malaysian public policy, it is also important to note that Mahathir has been disdainful about the capacity of the Malaysian state bureaucracy and has systematically wound back its influence and independence (Leigh 1992).

To understand the trajectory of Malaysia's very distinctive economic development strategies we need to remember two things. First, the New Economic Policy that was the centre-piece of Malaysia's development plan was as much driven by ethnic factors as it was by economic ones, and it *necessitated* major state involvement in the economy if it were to achieve its aims (Rasiah and Shari 2001). The intention was to create an indigenous capitalist class that might compete with the dominant Chinese business groups (Jesudason 1989). This complex amalgam of racial and economic goals, and the way it has been mediated by Malaysia's ethnically divided political system, explains much about the growth of 'crony capitalism' and the sorts of defensive economic policies the Malaysian government has subsequently pursued (Beeson 2000). The NEP's goal was to place 30 per cent of share capital in *bumiputera*, or native Malay, hands by 1990. To achieve this, trust agencies were estab-lished by the government to accumulate shares on behalf of the Malay community with the intention of redistributing them at some future date. Consequently, the public sector and state-owned enterprises expanded dramatically during the 1970s and early 1980s, establishing the basis for the fusion of government and business interests that is so characteristic of the Malaysian political economy. The second point to emphasize about economic development in Malaysia, then, is that not only are politics and economics in Malaysia deeply enmeshed in ways that are at odds with, and anathema to, much Western thinking, but that 'involvement in politics increasingly came to be viewed by *bumiputeras* as a quick means to obtain profitable business opportunities' (Gomez and Jomo 1997: 26).

As Indonesia, Malaysia was the beneficiary of windfall oil revenues, which allowed the government to accelerate the development process. Also as with Indonesia – despite pervasive corruption, political interference in economic processes and a 'massive expansion of the state sector' (Searle 1999: 77) – Malaysia experienced consistently high growth rates from the 1970s onwards, as the economy switched to an export-oriented development strategy. However, while this growth and development is impressive and (at least, in part) testimony to the effectiveness of government policy, it remains constrained by history and hostage to the imperatives of ethnic accommodation. At one level, this is manifest in the emergence of a 'rentier class'[19] and the growth of money politics. At another level, it has raised fundamental questions about the quality of the industrialization process that has emerged from Malaysia's compromised industry policies. As Jomo (1997: 106–7) points out, the Malaysian economy has a number of structural vulnerabilities: it remains dominated by a limited number of manufactured products (primarily electronics); MNCs dominate exports; local content and value-adding is low; and the degree of industrial deepening and complex linkages within the domestic economy remains limited. As we shall see in the next chapter, the depth of the industrialization process and the nature of integration into the global economy remains an issue for all of Southeast Asia's 'late-late' industrializing economies.

Malaysia, as we saw in the last chapter, has been through a series of major political changes recently, which suggest that economic policy may well change, too. At one level, this is almost inevitable as the very structural changes that Malaysian economic policy sought to engineer, especially the shift to export-oriented production and greater integration into the global economy, have induced a similar reconfiguration of political relationships, too. There is now a significant domestic constituency enthusiastically lobbying for greater economic liberalization (Stubbs 2000). Consequently, there is doubt about the government's capacity to direct the course of development or – more fundamentally in a Malaysian context, perhaps – its willingness to underwrite the ethnic basis of the wider social compact and distribution of economic resources it was predicated upon.[20] Indeed, there appears to be a groundswell of support in

Malaysia for a winding back of positive discrimination on ethnic grounds in favour of a greater reliance on market mechanisms to determine economic outcomes (Stafford 1997).

The final major Southeast Asian economy it is important to mention is Thailand, a country that has also enjoyed a remarkable economic transformation. As Malaysia, the Thai economy has been dominated by ethnic Chinese but, unlike Malaysia, this has not led to such racially motivated policies. On the contrary, Chinese ethnicity in not an obstacle to political or economic success in Thailand, as the remarkable rise of current prime minister Thaksin Shinawatara and his 'unprecedented fusion of political and economic power' reminds us (Wingfield 2002: 284). What Thailand does have in common with Malaysia is both the familiar transition from an import-substitution to an export-oriented development strategy and, since the 1980s, an increasing reliance on Japanese investment to underpin it. But, while Japanese FDI has been important, it is also important to recognize that the majority of investment capital has come from domestic sources (Hewison 2001: 86–7). However, despite the fact that much capital formation was local, as in the Malaysian case, there is lingering concern about the quality and depth of the industrialization process that has occurred, and the dependency on foreign capital generally and Japanese multi-nationals in particular that has accompanied it (Bello and Poh 1998).

Thailand also has similarities with Indonesia, too, in that public policy has been affected by an underlying and enduring struggle between nationalists and technocrats about the course of development. Unlike Indonesia and Malaysia, however, energy-poor Thailand has been particularly vulnerable to fluctuations in global oil prices. Significantly, this encouraged a more interventionist policy stance on the part of successive governments in the 1970s and 1980s (Bowie and Unger 1997: ch. 6). Deciding how to cope with external pressures over which domestic policy-makers have no control remains one of the defining issues in Thailand and the rest of the region. While there are currently doubts re-emerging about the stability of the Thai economy that make generalization difficult, a few comparative points can be made.

First, as in much of the rest of the region, the state has played a 'pivotal' role in the development of the economy and an indigenous capitalist class (Hewison 1989). Second, as in Indonesia (and Korea in Northeast Asia), the emergence of major business conglomerates in Thailand owes much to government policy and the political connections of the handful of families that dominate them. Third, and directly following from the previous point, 'the power and authority of the bureaucracy – both civilian and military – has been eclipsed by the wealth and power of business interests' (Wingfield 2002: 263). The balance of power between government and business – indeed, the very distinction between the state and capital – is an underlying dynamic and contradiction that is common to the region as a whole, but which has become especially acute in Thailand. All of which leads to a final point: for all the talk about the levelling effects of globalization, the irresistible nature of competitive forces, and the other neoliberal shibboleths that have become so commonplace, in Thailand, at least, there has been a decisive shift back to the politics of economic nationalism. In short, 'Thaksinomics' is predicated upon the '"developmentalist" view that in catching-up economies, government has to play a positive role in protecting and promoting firms and sectors to overcome the disadvantages of competing against more advanced economies' (Pasuk and Baker 2004: 100; see also Amsden 2001).

Whether this will prove politically sustainable will depend in large part on the economy and the legitimacy that rising living standards confer (see Alagappa 1995). This is clearly an issue of vital interest and importance to Thais. In China's case, the way in which the performance–legitimacy dynamic plays itself out and the strategies China's elites employ in the process has implications for the entire region, if not the world.

China: more market, less plan?

As I have suggested on a number of occasions, China merits more extensive and separate attention simply because of its size and the implications of its rise. At this juncture, it is the fact that it is 'rising' at all that it is noteworthy. Not only does China's economic development have direct implications for the fifth of humanity that actually resides within its borders, but if it can be sustained – a rather large 'if', as we shall see in the final chapter – this has profound implications not just for East Asia but for the international political economy as well. Importantly, such implications go beyond the all too predictable, if contentious, concerns about the supposed inevitability of conflict and hegemonic contestation that flow from economic development. On the contrary, if China's growth endures and living standards continue to rise it may have some potentially important lessons for other parts of the world that have hitherto been primarily associated with economic backwardness and underdevelopment. The key questions, in short, are first, how did China do it? Second, is China a developmental state? And finally, what implications does China's experience and that of the region more generally have for other countries? The third question will be taken up in the final part of the chapter; at present, we need to try to answer the first two.

Given that China is, as we saw in the last chapter, still notionally a 'communist' country, it might be supposed that questions about whether the state is or is not 'interventionist' are somewhat redundant. How could it be otherwise, given the continuing importance of state-owned enterprises (SOEs) in the economy, the absence of non-state-dominated governance structures, and the underdeveloped nature of civil society? But, the most important aspect of China's developmental experience since the 1970s has been its increased integration into the global economy, and the embrace of market mechanisms that has accompanied it. At first blush, this would seem to be at odds with state control and interventionism. Inevitably, a greater embrace of market mechanisms *has* involved a different role for the state, and often a diminished one. Yet, despite this apparent transformation, it makes sense to think of China as a developmental state, albeit a reconfigured one that is replete with potential internal contradictions, and without the same level capacity as its Northeast Asian counterparts. As Gordon White puts it:

> The post-Mao era of market reforms has been seeking a new type of socialist developmental state . . . This involves a redefinition of the state's role in the economy in ways which bring it closer in many ways to the 'state capitalist' model to the extent that it disengages the state from direct economic involvement and increases the autonomy of productive enterprises, while retaining an integument of socialist political ideas and institutions. This project of 'market socialism' thus involves significant change in the developmental aspect of the state, but not its political aspect. The contradiction between these two dimensions of change is at the root of the politics of economic reform in contemporary China. (White 1993: 6)

Although he was writing more than a decade ago, the essential dilemma of reconciling Marxist ideas with market mechanisms still haunts the PRC leadership, as we saw in the last chapter. However, the necessity of rethinking the state-led developmental strategies that had prevailed in the more ideologically-orthodox 1950s and 1960s had been highlighted by the failure of the Maoist developmental state generally and the 'Great Leap Forward' in particular.[21] Nevertheless, we need to acknowledge that the Maoist era left some important, albeit unintended, legacies that made China's subsequent economic take-off more feasible and dramatic. On the one hand, the mass mobilization of the peasantry during the Great Leap Forward brought about major improvements in China's infrastructure. On the other, Mao's policies of self-reliance meant that when China did eventually embark on market-oriented reform in the 1970s, it did so unencumbered by foreign debt

(So 2003: 9). The actual catalyst for the radical change of direction that culminated in China's economic 'opening' and the embrace of market forces is complex, but Mao's death, the political upheavals it induced, and the failure of agricultural collectivization and the growing discontent in rural areas it created, were clearly central factors (Lin 2003: 35–6).

These changes would culminate in the ascendancy of the economic pragmatist, Deng Xiaoping, the principal architect of China's economic reorientation. Significantly, Deng was also politically pragmatic, too, something that was evident in his emphasis on the continuing importance of CCP leadership in achieving his vision of 'four modernizations' in agriculture, industry, defence, and science and technology. This compromise was captured in his speech to the Twelfth Party Congress in 1982, when he declared that 'We must integrate the universal truth of Marxism with the concrete realities of China, blaze a path of our own and build socialism with Chinese characteristics' (cited in Chang 1988: 58). At the centre of the 'concrete realities' confronting Deng was the centrality of the state-owned sector, which dominated manufacturing production – potentially the core of economic development – and which, by world standards, was hopelessly inefficient and uncompetitive (Lardy 1998: ch. 2). Not only did China's elites face the practical challenges of off-loading the SOEs, introducing price mechanisms to their operations, and coping with the rises in unemployment this inevitably caused, but there was also the additional ideological problem of squaring this with the precepts of Marxist-Leninism. Given the fact that the state theoretically remains the political instrument of the proletariat and guarantor of the 'iron rice bowl',[22] this was potentially no easy task, especially given that worker unrest has been a constant in China even since Mao's time (Liu 1996: ch. 3).[23]

It is, perhaps, testimony to the extent of the transformation that has occurred in China that such problems are rarely addressed in ideological terms or sources of doctrinal discontent.[24] On the contrary, one of the principal targets of worker and peasant enmity is the extent of corruption in China, especially amongst Party cadres. So pervasive is this unhappiness that some observers consider it will undermine the legitimacy of the CCP and eventually bring down the entire regime (G.G. Chang 2002). In this respect, China highlights a more general challenge confronting developmental states: the very success of the state-led developmental strategy means that there is increased wealth-generation and thus greater scope for corruption and cronyism. How this is managed is one of the defining challenges for state officials everywhere. In China's case, this problem has been exacerbated by the difficulty of making the transition from state to private ownership. Aspiring entrepreneurs remain highly dependent on connections with public officials to ensure the success of their business, and this entrenches corruption as a consequence (Young 1997). The privatization process has also intersected with China's increased integration into the international economy, allowing Party officials to use foreign investments and connections among the 'overseas Chinese' to take over former state assets. As Ding (2000: 122) puts it, 'many of the international investment projects from China have been made primarily to serve the purpose of informally transferring property from state ownership to de facto or de jure private possession, or put briefly, informal privatisation'.

The official state attitude to the SOEs and privatization was enunciated by Prime Minister Zhu Rongji in his strategy *zhuada fangxiao* ('grasp the big, let go the small': cited in Ahmad 2004: 13). The intention was to maintain control of the 'commanding heights' of the economy, while allowing small-scale enterprises to survive in an increasingly market-driven economic environment. While the desire to retain control of strategically important economic sectors as the basis of a more generalized process of industrial up-grading and deepening reflects the influence of the earlier Japanese approach (Ciccantell and Bunker 2004), the capacity of the Chinese state to play a similarly decisive, directive role may be compromised both by the quite different nature of the Chinese economy's integration into the wider international order and by China's lack of equivalent state capacity. Consequently, China's economic development has been quite unlike Japan's in that it has been highly dependent on massive inflows of foreign capital. When combined with a continuing selling-off and rationalization of SOEs, this clearly limits the control the state can have over business.

Exacerbating this problem as far as state elites are concerned, and sharply distinguishing China from East Asia's more authentic developmental states, has been the problem of what Lieberthal (1992: 5) called the 'fragmented authoritarianism' that characterized the Chinese state. Lieberthal identified six functionally defined 'clusters' of bureaucratic responsibility within the Chinese state – economic; propaganda/education; organizational/personnel; 'civilian coercive'; military; and CCP territorial committees – in which no single body had authority over the others. Consequently, decision-making was invariably contested, uncertain and far less coherent than we might expect in an ideal-typical developmental state. Importantly, these tensions and competing interests within the state continue, and have increasingly come to revolve around pro-market supporters of greater economic liberalization versus more mercantilist/protectionist forces who remain sceptical about the manner of China's integration into the global economy (Bell and Feng forthcoming). Despite the fact that China has 'tried rather self-consciously' to emulate the state-led developmental experience of its Northeast Asian neighbours (Moore 2002: 302), it has confronted fundamental capacity constraints. As Moore points out: 'the institutional culture of policy networks in post-Mao China has provided neither the degree nor the kind of bureaucratic autonomy and corporate coherence necessary for pursuing state-led policies like those often ascribed to the East Asian Trio' [Japan, Taiwan and Korea]' (Moore 2002: 285). Not only did China lack the same ability coherently to plan the course of development as some of its Asian neighbours, but it was unable to enforce the sort of 'reciprocity' for government support that is so vital in getting business to cooperate with government (Amsden 2001). This problem has been compounded by higher levels of foreign ownership and the need to divert capital to loss-making SOEs. Consequently, China's recent economic development has been increasingly market-driven and responsive to external rather than internal pressures (Bell and Feng forthcoming; Moore 2002)

The influence of external forces has been reinforced as China has been increasingly drawn into a series of multi-lateral agreements that constrain its autonomy. In Chapter 3, we saw how China's elites have been increasingly socialized into new thinking and behaviour as a consequence of their participation in multi-lateral forums. In the case of WTO accession, this ideational influence has been reinforced by specific provisions, protocols and commitments that 'far surpass those made by founding members' (Lardy 2002: 104). The extensive nature of these commitments, which even involve revising the PRC Constitution (Potter 2001: 603), is significant for a number of reasons. First, it will produce winners and losers in China: while it may generate increased employment in more competitive firms in the long term, initially it may add to unemployment and unrest (Liew 2001). At the same time, though, the provisions of WTO accession may actually provide the PRC with a legitimating rationale for off-loading inefficient SOEs (Fewsmith 2001: 574). However, it is a strategy that is not without costs, both in terms of vulnerability to further external pressure and regarding the state's capacity to direct the course of development. As Tony Saich points out:

> Rightly or wrongly, WTO regulations and practices try to prevent the kind of development strategy that was practised throughout East Asia from the 1960s onwards. It is clear that international pressure will force the Chinese government to undertake a more market-based strategy. Should China not adjust its policy it will run the risk of substantial friction with the world trading body and especially from the USA. (Saich 2004: 37)

China's accession to the WTO and the impact of globalization more generally have sparked intense debates in China about the costs and benefits of international integration (Feng 2006; Garrett 2001). Nevertheless, it seems certain that, as more people and institutions develop a stake in the internationalization process, the balance of domestic political interests will change in the same way it has in other parts of the region, consolidating the overall pro-liberalization trend in Chinese public policy (Fewsmith 2001: 591). One of the key indicators of the long-term direction of policy and the competence of policy-makers will be the manner in which China manages the financial sector. Because the domestic banking sector has been the primary supplier of capital to the inefficient, loss-making SOEs, state banks have acquired 'a huge portfolio of non-performing loans' (Saich 2004: 264).[25] Although such financial relationships are reminiscent of the policies of directed credit and financial repression employed elsewhere in the region, in China's case the unprofitable nature of many SOEs means that the policy of state support via the banking sector is unsustainable (Lardy 1998: 4–5). This has become an even more acute problem, since many SOEs have used bankruptcy as a means of off-loading existing debts and preparing themselves for privatization (Green and Liu 2005: 22–3). All of these problems are compounded by external pressures for further reform that have the potential to unravel domestic political, economic and social relationships with potentially profoundly destabilizing consequences.

In China's case, much – perhaps too much – depends on keeping the developmental process going and ensuring that living standards continue to rise. Unlike some of the industrializing East Asian economies that went before them, China's policy-makers are reliant on, and exposed to, the decisions of foreign multi-nationals and financial institutions for much of the investment that has driven recent growth. The challenge for the Chinese state is to develop a mode of governance that allows it to maintain a degree of control over the course of development, whilst simultaneously accommodating the explicit and implicit practices and agreements that effectively constitute the international economic order of which it is an increasingly integrated part. Although the contradictions inherent in being both a 'communist' and a non-democratic government mean that China's 'performance legitimacy' is especially important and dependent on its successful management of the development project (Zheng and Lye 2005), it is a challenge facing all the nations of East Asia that have followed the interventionist path. The question now is whether the practices associated with the developmental state and a more general East Asian predilection for interventionism are any longer feasible in the contemporary global order.

What now for the developmental state?

In this final section, I consider what changes in the nature of international economic activity and ideas about appropriate economic policy might mean for political practice and the possible role of governments. Although it is a discussion that focuses on the developmental state, it has wider ramifications and relevance, especially for those states that may wish to try and emulate East Asia, a region in which even the pro-market World Bank (1993: 6) conceded, 'government interventions resulted in higher and more equal growth than otherwise would have occurred'.

As we saw in Chapter 1, some commentators believe that the state's capacity to influence economic activity has been profoundly and irrevocably undermined by changes in the international political economy: either capital has become too footloose to tame and direct, or the prevailing regulatory and ideational order has entrenched 'market-friendly' policies to such a degree that alternatives are increasingly infeasible or unthinkable. And yet, we have also seen that, even in a global era in which transnational economic forces and political entities play an increasingly influential part, states still play a critical role in underpinning and implementing the regulatory frameworks within which capitalism is realized (Jessop 2003). But while there may still be a necessary relationship between political and economic forces in the realization of capitalism, it is equally clear that this relationship can be realized in significantly different ways, as the very different forms of capitalism that exist in East Asia and elsewhere remind us (Beeson 1999b).

Yet, at the very moment that the varieties of capitalism literature is belatedly alerting us to the importance of these differences in national political, economic and social forms, it is apparent that the one-to-one relationship or identification between state and capital is breaking down as the latter becomes increasingly 'deterritorialized'. This has particular implications for the state–capital relationship. As Neil Brenner puts it, 'capital's drive to diminish its place-dependency does not entail the construction of a quasi-autonomous, placeless 'space of flows' . . . but rather a complex re-scaling and reterritorialization of the historically entrenched, state-centric geographical infrastructures that have underpinned the last century of capitalist industrialization' (Brenner 1999: 64). Put differently, it seems that the increased mobility of capital, especially financial capital, is not eliminating the need for national authorities to collaborate in its realization, but it *is* helping to shape the regulatory environment within which that realization occurs. Again, this dialectical process is complex and continues to be shaped by contingent, historically-determined factors, not the least of which is the timing of the industrialization and state development processes themselves. One of the key difficulties facing policy-makers in developing economies is that they must attempt to compete in an international system that is already dominated by other powerful, established political economies (Beeson and Bell 2005a). But whether the primary dynamic shaping state–capital relations has been changes in domestic policy settings or the structural evolution of the international political economy, it seems that the capacity and willingness of states to intervene in the way they once did has declined, if not ended.

If some of the old policy tools such as financial repression and trade protection have been eroded, however, does this mean that the state has simply become an impotent cipher and transmission belt serving the 'needs' of international capital? At the most general level, the continuing variations in capitalist forms strongly suggest that this is not the case. True, all states must perform – or at least, attempt to perform – certain basic regulatory tasks if they are to appear attractive sites for potentially mobile investment, but they will continue to do so in ways that reflect specific national political contests, circumstances and capacities (Underhill and Zhang 2005). Particular national accommodations will strongly reflect specific, historically-determined relationships and contests between political and economic forces; such accommodations will subsequently give a shape to the dominant capitalist form and impart a degree of path-dependency to its evolution (Hall 1986; Zysman 1996). In other words, state behaviour is necessarily determined and constrained by its particular history in ways that will limit what is politically possible and institutionally feasible. One way to think about the evolving and differing role of the state is to consider the sorts of strategies and techniques states have developed to respond to, and to take advantage of, wider transformations in the international political economy (Beeson 2005a). One possibility is to cooperate with other states and non-state actors in the development of new modes of governance, either at the global or the regional level. The latter development will be considered in Chapter 7.

At the national level, where the developmental state has traditionally been such a decisive force, the East Asian crisis was clearly something of watershed, not least in undermining the *legitimacy* of state intervention that had been such an important, distinctive and 'un-Western' aspect of the developmental state (Woo-Cumings 1999: 20). Against this backdrop and the apparent intellectual bankruptcy of interventionism and the ascendancy of neoliberalism, some observers have suggested that not only is the developmental state finished, but that its primary function now is to entrench market-enhancing reforms, rather than state-led development. Iain Pirie (2005: 25–6), for example, has suggested that 'the contemporary Korean state has not simply engaged in a process of policy adjustment and adopted selected neoliberal policies, but rather is consolidating a whole new and unambiguously neoliberal mode of regulation'. Building on Kanishka Jayasuriya's (1999; 2001) path-breaking work, Pirie (2005: 27) argues that elements of the Korean state, such as the central bank, have become key agents in embedding neoliberal reform and the 'creation of a "new" state'.

While the evolution of the internal architecture of the state is an important part of the contemporary state-capital dialectic, as we saw in Chapter 1, it is also important to recognize that the forces associated with globalization may have enabling as well as constraining features. Linda Weiss (2003: 298), for example, argues that 'however much globalization throws real constraints in the way of state activity . . . it allows states sufficient room to move, and thus to act consonant with their social policy and economic upgrading objectives'. Recently Thurborn and Weiss (2006) have fleshed out this claim in the context of Korea's recent public policy and demonstrated that 'interventionism' is alive and well in Korea, even if the policy tools and style have evolved in keeping with wider changes in the international political economy. Indeed, even in the area where most observers think global forces and pressures have developed furthest and policy-makers' 'room to move' is most constrained – monetary policy and the management of the financial sector – Stephen Bell (2005) has demonstrated that even in a relatively small economy such as Australia's, with a predilection for market-friendly policies, policy-makers retain a good deal of policy autonomy and are frequently prepared to exercise it.

Bell's work is a salutary reminder that even 'neoliberal states' are interventionist in some ways and necessarily help to determine the way in which economic activities occur. Indeed, at some level *all* states are developmental in that no government – with the possible contemporary exception of aberrations such as Robert Mugabe's Zimbabwe – seeks to actually inhibit development. The key question, of course, is how best this will be achieved, and what sort of role governments should have in realizing it. In this regard, much will depend on the normative and institutional milieu within which economic activity occurs; in other words, on ideas about what 'appropriate' policies look like, and the specific national capacities that are available to realize them. But the possibility that states may still continue to play a critical role in underpinning the developmental process is something that is widely recognized (H.J. Chang 2002; Leftwich 2000), even by apparent champions of neoliberal orthodoxy and the Washington consensus (World Bank 1997). The significance of the East Asian experience in this regard is that it demonstrates all that can go right and wrong with the developmental state: it *can* be a (possibly indispensable) catalyst for growth and development;

and it *can* be a mechanism for self-enrichment, corruption and the wasting of public money, especially where the initial catching-up project has been more or less realized (Beeson 2003d; 2004a). Yet, for all the developmental state's possible defects, without effective state capacity and some sense of what to do with it, the prospects for significant economic development, especially in the earlier phases of the 'catching-up' process, seem remote. As far as the late-late-developing economies of Southeast Asia are concerned, the logic that underpinned the developmental state may still have some relevance, even if some of its specific strategies may need to be rethought.

Conclusion

The remarkable economic development that occurred in East Asia in the post-war period was unprecedented and largely unexpected. Although there are some important differences in the extent of the economic development that occurred and the precise strategies that were employed to encourage it, there is widespread agreement that activist state policies played an important part in most of the countries considered above. Indeed, the comparatively poor development record of the Philippines provides an illuminating example of the consequences that can flow from the absence of, at least, a minimally effective state. It is also clear that much can go wrong with the government–business relationship, especially where it endures beyond the 'catching-up' phase and becomes self-serving, or where it becomes the centre of corrupt, politically unrepresentative and even repressive regimes.

It is also clear, though, that the existence of either authoritarianism or corruption are not of themselves necessarily an obstacle to the development process. This is not to advocate either, but simply to point out that arguments that claim that events such as the East Asian crisis were a consequence of 'crony capitalism' need to explain why such relationships, and non-transparent, undemocratic (even authoritarian) regimes more generally, were not an obstacle to development before the crisis and have endured during the recovery phase. It is has also become evident, of course, that corruption is not a uniquely East Asian phenomenon. On the contrary, a series of scandals in high-profile American companies such as Enron – a major financial supporter of George W. Bush – remind us that 'crony capitalism' is potentially a ubiquitous problem where powerful economic and political interests intersect (Beeson 2003c: 318–19). The point to emphasize is that, even where the extent of corruption threatens fatally to undermine renewed developmental efforts, as in Indonesia, reform will prove difficult where it is opposed by entrenched networks of power and interest, and where alternative institutions of 'good governance' are inadequately developed (Beeson 2001a; Dick 2002).

However, even if it is accepted that the state in East Asia frequently played a crucial role in mobilizing domestic savings, directing credit to strategically important industries, and generally attempting to guide the course of the developmental processes, it is not clear that states can or should play such a role in the contemporary, increasingly integrated, international economic and regulatory order. But, as we have seen, states are inescapably still key components of even the transnational, market-enhancing regimes. In other words, there is no such thing as a truly deregulated economy (Cerny 1991); the important issue is the *type* of regulation and the outcome it is intended to produce. It is, perhaps, the degree of intentionality in public policy, and the belief that the course of development could be significantly and positively influenced, that really distinguishes much of East Asia. The question that the East Asian governments must now confront is whether the type of market-friendly, 'hands-off' regulatory frameworks they have been adopting are appropriate (Stiglitz 2002). It is a question that is especially relevant in the context of East Asia's integration with the global political economy.

Chapter 6

East Asia in a Global Economy

One of the principal reasons that the East Asian region has attracted such attention has been because of its generally spectacular economic performance. This was something of a surprise given much of the region's prior association with underdevelopment and poverty. Indeed, for the first two-thirds of the twentieth century much academic analysis was preoccupied with explaining the failure – indeed, the impossibility – of development occurring in what was described as the Third World. The 'dependent' nature of development in the 'periphery' and the structural dominance of the 'core' economies[1] meant that there were simply too many obstacles for would-be developing nations to overcome: existing patterns of exploitation meant that such countries were condemned to permanent underdevelopment. The great theoretical and comparative significance of the historical transformation that has occurred in much of the East Asian region in this regard has been to overturn many of the prevailing views about the nature of development, and about relationships between core and periphery, or developed and underdeveloped parts of what was becoming an increasingly integrated and global economy. In one sense, then, the significance of the East Asian experience is as much ideational as it is material, although it is the latter that is the primary focus of this chapter.

As we saw in early chapters, East Asia has been steadily incorporated into an expanding capitalist economy for a couple of hundred years. This chapter builds on that analysis by considering the long-term evolution of economic relationships and organizational patterns within the East Asian region itself, and between East Asia and the rest of the world. One of the most striking things in this regard has been the way that East Asia has become increasingly open to the wider global economy. Expanding trade relations have been at the centre of East Asia's integration into the international economic system since European contact. Indeed, as we saw in Chapter 2, trade was one of the principal reasons Europeans came to Asia in the first place. What is noteworthy more recently, however, is the rapid expansion in the flows of capital into and out of the region. As we shall see, this latter development has been something of a mixed blessing: while inflows of FDI may have been welcome and central to the take-off of much of Southeast Asia and latterly China, some of the more mobile flows of capital have had much more debatable consequences. But, before examining the impact of these new capital flows and their role in the Asian financial crisis of 1997, I provide some historical and empirical background which spells out some of the most important aspects of East Asia's internal and external economic relations.

Unsurprisingly, three countries loom large in the subsequent discussion. The USA has, of course, played a particularly important role as the hegemonic power of the era, effectively establishing the rules and regulations within which global commerce occurs, but also acting as an important source of investment and an indispensable market for the region's export-oriented economies. This latter role remains critical, but has become more complex and controversial as a consequence of ballooning trade deficits, first with Japan and more recently with China. These two countries are regional economic giants and have acted as important sources of growth and dynamism. Their individual historical roles and their mutual economic interaction are central parts of the story of East Asia's internal integration, but also of the region's relationship with the outside world. Japan's corporate networks and the development of 'greater China' as a centre of production have, at different periods, profoundly influenced the course of region-wide development, and merit detailed analysis in their own right. To understand why they have been so important it is necessary, once again, to place these relationships in their specific historical contexts.

Japan and the growth of East Asian regionalization

One of the key points to reiterate at the outset is that, although Japan emerged as the principal regional engine of economic development and integration after the Second World War, it did so as a consequence of a unique, possibly unrepeatable set of historical circumstances. Without the direct aid and assistance of the USA and the latter's expanding domestic markets, it seems inconceivable that regional development would have occurred in the manner or at the speed at which it did. The potential importance of the intersection between economic development and geopolitics became even clearer in the aftermath of the Vietnam War when Japan, having already engineered its own industrial renaissance, was ideally placed to expand into the region. Crucially, as Richard Stubbs points out in his definitive analysis of the historical origins of the 'Asian miracle':

> Japan's economic 'embrace' of East and Southeast Asia in the years after the Vietnam War could not have gone so successfully had it not

been for the commitment by successive US governments of men, money and material, in a massive effort to contain the spread of communism and defend what were seen as America's vital interests. (Stubbs 2005: 154)

Economic development in the East Asian region in the post-war period has, therefore, been a consequence of a complex dialectical interaction between intra- and inter-regional forces. Although the latter may have initially been crucial in providing the catalyst for both the re-emergence of the Japanese economy, and for the politically permissive policy environment that underpinned it, we need to recognize that once under way, Japan's expansion into the region was something that was largely driven and managed by the Japanese themselves in line with domestic imperatives. It is also important to recognize that when Japanese companies, trade and investment began to expand outwards into the region, it was a case of *re*-engaging with the region, rather than starting from scratch. Painful and problematic as the Japanese imperial period proved for much of the region, it is clear that such pre-existing trade patterns facilitated regional integration (Cumings 1984; Petri 1992).

In retrospect, it is striking how early the triangular structure of Japan's relationship with the rest of East Asia on the one hand, and with the USA on the other, was established. In the immediate aftermath of the War, Japan imported industrial goods from the USA and exported simple manufactured goods to the region. But, as Japan re-industrialized and labour costs rose, industries such as textiles were unable to compete and shifted offshore to take advantage of lower labour costs (Steven 1990). In some ways this may be thought of as the 'normal' pattern of industrial restructuring as countries move up the value chain.[2] What is distinctive about Japan's approach to this process is that, as with its domestic development process, the course of Japan's external expansion has occurred with the extensive involvement and oversight of public officials. The tendency for the state to become involved in directing the course of Japan's external relations (as well as its internal ones), was given additional impetus by a decidedly unexpected catalyst for economic restructuring and adjustment: the first 'oil shock' of 1973. Not only did this lead directly to the development of the policy of 'comprehensive security' detailed in Chapter 3, but it triggered a burst of outward investment and aid as Japan sought to guarantee the supply of critical resource inputs on which its economic expansion was so dependent (Nester 1992).

Two points are worth emphasizing about these developments. First, the state and business generally worked collaboratively in pursuit of the 'commercial agendas of private sector actors and the strategic economic agendas of the economic ministries' (Arase 1994: 173). In other words, this cooperative approach was an extension of the domestic regime that underpinned Japan's developmental state, and was one from which both sides could expect to benefit. The Japanese government was able to encourage the offshore migration of declining industries and facilitate the control of strategically important resources through the sophisticated deployment of official development assistance (ODA) packages for host nations, and by supporting Japanese business with technical assistance, advice, insurance and capital. Although there is no doubt that much of this investment has been welcomed by the recipient countries and played an important part in accelerating the course of development across the region, there are widely held reservations about its overall impact and intent. In one of the most persuasive and detailed analyses of Japan's economic integration with the region, Hatch and Yamamura (1996: 5) claim that Japan's business– government cooperation amounts to 'nothing less than a coordinated effort to lock up the productive resources of the world's most dynamic region'. This highlights a second important aspect of Japan's economic integration with the region that merits emphasis: although Japan has been a central element in East Asia's economic take-off, the impact of Japanese investment remains controversial.

Ambivalent attitudes towards Japanese investment have persisted despite the best efforts of Japan's political elites, who have done what they can to ensure that its role in the region is perceived positively. The preferred way of describing Japan's economic relationship with the rest of East Asia – at least as far as many of Japan's economic and political elites are concerned – is the 'flying geese' metaphor, in which Japan plays the role of lead goose, pulling along the other industrializing nations of the region in its wake. It should be noted that the flying geese idea predates the most recent phase of Japanese re-integration into the region; indeed, 'in the 1930s, the flock was commandeered by militarists who saw it as a neat emblem of Japanese ethnic superiority' (Terry 2002: 53). While the association with Japanese imperialism might help to explain why the flying geese idea has been treated with caution, there is a more fundamental reason for doubting its validity: much of the region simply has not 'caught up' in the way that might have been expected. On the contrary, a number of Southeast Asian economies seem destined to remain locked in a subordinate position in a regional production hierarchy dominated by Japan (Beeson 2001b). One of the critical flaws in the flying geese model, and a major potential obstacle to industrial upgrading of a sort that the Japanese themselves achieved, has been the conspicuous reluctance of Japanese MNCs to transfer technology to would-be competitors (Bernard and Ravenhill 1995; Mochizuki 1995).

As a consequence of the advanced nature of Japan's industrialization and the ability of Japanese companies to utilize other parts of East Asia as export platforms, countries in the rest of the region, especially Southeast Asia and latterly China, have become highly dependent on Japan for capital goods with which to produce manufactured products for markets in the USA and Western Europe. As a consequence, Japan has invariably enjoyed trade surpluses with both the emerging economies of Southeast Asia[3] and the wealthy industrialized nations of North America and Europe (Gangopadhyay 1998). The migration of Japanese capital offshore may have been a predictable consequence of a maturing economy and the rising cost of production in Japan, but it was given a further boost by a number of other factors. First, protectionist pressures from the United States in particular during the 1980s made it increasingly attractive for particular economic sectors in Japan (such as the automotive industry) to invest directly in the USA and to a lesser extent the EU, thus circumventing trade barriers. As a consequence, the USA has been by far the largest recipient of Japanese FDI, experiencing a major surge as a direct consequence of Japan's bubble economy (Farrell 2000). The second factor to boost outflows of Japanese capital was the Plaza Accord agreement discussed in the last chapter: the dramatic appreciation of the yen made foreign investment increasingly attractive and encouraged many of Japan's most successful large and small companies to move parts of their operations offshore (Katz 1998).

Despite the fact that East Asian countries were not the primary targets for Japanese investment during the 1980s and 1990s, the smaller size of the recipient economies, especially in Southeast Asia, necessarily meant that Japanese investment had a substantial impact. The general patterns and principal sources of investment in the East Asian region can be seen in Table 6.1. Perhaps the most important development revealed in these figures is the relative decline in the importance of Japan as a source of investment in the post-crisis period. Japan has been eclipsed by the EU in a number of countries, and the EU has become a more important source of bank lending than Japan as well (Hamilton-Hart 2004: 141). Likewise, for a number of countries – Korea, Taiwan, Singapore, and the Philippines – the USA is a more important source of FDI than Japan (see Hsiao, Hsiao and Yamashita 2003: 223).

This becomes significant when we think about Japan's potential role in the region and its capacity to translate economic weight into political influence. The main point to emphasize about Japan's relationship with East Asia is that flows of capital from Japan have declined by something like 80 per cent since the mid-1990s. By contrast, capital outflows to the USA have continued to grow. Consequently, regionalization sceptics argue that 'the past several years have drawn Japan closer to the United States and weakened the relative importance of its flows to Asia – hardly the picture of a nation heading toward closer embrace of its Asian neigh-

Table 6.1 FDI from Japan, the USA and the EU to China and Southeast Asia, US$ million, (per annum average)

Source	Period	China	ASEAN	Indonesia	Malaysia	Philippines	Singapore	Thailand
Japan	1980–89	289.7	1,715.1	468.5	200.2	85.43	491.7	290.6
	1990–99	1,723.58	3,902.02	1,519.26	685.25	220.45	960.47	1,067.25
	2000–3	1,821.325	2,563.68	483.95	257.53	1,85.37	621.33	741.2
US	1980–89	54.2	401.4	214.2	21.3	2.1	67.7	96.1
	1990–99	782	3,522.9	690.8	359.4	224	1,807.6	509.4
	2000–3	1,542.25	6,934.75	736.75	489.5	132	4,839.25	737.25
EU	1980–89	19.05	370.39	39.13	−20.07	18.92	296.74	35.26
	1990–99	895.66	2,733.37	372.91	556.2	322.31	840.28	566.72
	2000–3	2,307.9	5,689.95	−123.8	214.93	−21.25	4,851.43	720.65

Source: Data from *International Direct Investment Statistics Yearbook* (Database edition), vol. 2004 release 1, via SourceOECD. Paris: OECD. http://oecdnt.ingenta.com/OECD/eng/TableViewer/wdsview/dispviewp.asp

bors' (Lincoln 2004: 78). While such flows are in keeping with the historical evolution of the global economy discussed in Chapter 1, in which the developed 'Triad' regions have dominated trade and investment flows, they have important implications for East Asian regionalization. At the very least, Japan's pattern of capital outflows is a powerful reminder that for what is still the region's most important economic actor, its most important economic relationships – as its political relationships – lie outside the East Asian region. Japan's potential importance was further undermined by its failure to turn its economic weight into political influence at the height of its power, which might have been accomplished if it had provided a larger market for regional exports or attempted to internationalize the yen.[4]

There are two further aspects of Japan's general relationship with the region that merit emphasis. First, at the level of productive capital or FDI, the disaggregation of many manufacturing processes noted in Chapter 1 has allowed Japanese corporations involved in key industries such as car manufacturing and electronics to spread their operations across the region, exploiting specific locational advantages and enjoying a good deal of political leverage as a consequence (Hatch and Yamamura 1996).[5] Toyota, for example, sources different vehicle component parts in Thailand, Malaysia, the Philippines and Indonesia, while coordinating the entire process from Singapore (Gangopadhyay 1998: 44–5; Legewie 1999: 59). Such corporate strategies help to account for the growth of intra-regional trade, which has expanded dramatically since the 1990s (see Isogai and Shibanuma no date). Significantly, the restructuring of international manufacturing in particular, and the competition for mobile investment capital more generally, has also triggered important cooperative trade- and investment-related initiatives within Southeast Asia (Yoshimatsu 2002). While developments in the production process might seem to entrench the position of Japan's corporate giants in Southeast Asia, it is important to note that technological changes, the necessity of exploiting increasingly skilled labour, and competition from foreign rivals are all forcing some Japanese companies to open up production processes in their established offshore centres and transfer technology and know-how in the process (Ernst 2000). The other critical development that merits mention is Japan's rapidly growing investment in China, which amounted to over $32 billion by 2001, and helped China become Japan's largest single source of imports (Kakuchi 2003).

The final point to make about the nature of Japan's integration with the region is that although the bulk of Japanese capital flows to East Asia have been FDI, not all were (Ministry of Economy Trade and Industry 2005: 12). On the contrary, during the early 1990s in particular, Japan became a major source of portfolio or financial capital as Japanese banks not only grew, but actively chased new customers as a consequence of the domestic restructuring engendered by the bubble economy discussed in the last chapter, and the prospect of achieving higher returns offshore. Again, the pattern of portfolio capital flows has been one of a rapid rise, followed by a fairly dramatic retreat from the region in the wake of the Asian crisis. Indeed, some consider Japanese banks were partly to blame for the way the financial crisis unfolded in East Asia (Bevacqua 1998), as inflows of mobile capital initially contributed to asset inflation, before intensifying the downturn as they abruptly exited. The conclusion that Ed Lincoln (2004: 84) comes to about this is that, as with FDI flows, the decline in the volume and relative share of Japanese lending 'diminishes Japan in the eyes of other Asian nations as a close regional partner'.

The general points to make about Japan's economic role in the region are that it has played a crucially important historical role in acting as an engine of regional growth and source of capital, but one that has been in relative decline since the mid-1990s. However, as far as Japan itself is concerned, East Asia has become an *increasingly* important trade partner (Kwan 2001: 50). Indeed, the recent recovery in the Japanese economy is due in no small part to the rapid growth in economic relations between Japan and China, to a point where China has replaced the USA as Japan's largest single trading partner (Shorrock 2005). But Japan's declining economic importance to the region, especially when combined with the rapid rise of China, provides one part of a possible explanation for Japan's puzzling lack of political influence and leadership capacity in the region. And yet, Japan's own dependence on the region means that it cannot neglect, or at least attempt to play an influential role in East Asia. The contradictory nature of Japan's position in the region will be taken up in greater detail in the next chapter. At this stage, it is important to expand briefly on the analysis of the preceding chapter and say something about the way the region's other economies have been incorporated into the wider international economic system.

The first and second wave industrializing economies

As we have seen, the first (Northeast Asian) and second (Southeast Asian) waves of industrializing economies in East Asia 'took off' at different times; consequently, they have been incorporated into the global economy in rather different ways, too. Despite China's 'late-late' start, the sheer scale of its development arguably constitutes a third wave which, if sustained, will amount to a one-nation tsunami. All of the major East Asian economies eventually embarked on a course of export-oriented industrialization, but the fact that they did so at different times has had an impact on both the structures of their domestic economies and the way in which they have been incorporated into the wider international economic order. Korea, for example, was able to follow a broadly similar path to Japan, developing one of the world's largest shipbuilding industries, becoming a major steel producer, and – following the growth of the *chaebols* – establishing global brand names and a corporate presence in the process. Significantly, Korea also followed Japan's lead in relying much less on inflows of FDI than other East Asian countries to underpin the initial phases of this process, and it has only opened up to foreign capital inflows relatively recently (Islam and Chowdhury 2000). The consequences of this move are hotly debated, with some observers arguing that it undermined a highly effective developmental model and created the preconditions for Korea to be badly affected by the East Asian crisis (Wade and Veneroso 1998).

As Korea, Taiwan has also been highly successful in transforming the structure of domestic economic activity and turning itself into a manufacturing-, and latterly service-, oriented economy. Unlike Korea, however, Taiwan has been more open to foreign investment and used this as a vehicle to transfer technology. Taiwan is considered to have been 'East Asia's greatest success story', mainly because of the remarkable transformation in the structure of its economy, and the rapid rise of capital- and technology-intensive manufacturing at the centre of its export industries (Camilleri 2000: 84). The most important factor influencing Taiwan's recent development has been its burgeoning economic relationship with mainland China. But, before we consider that in any detail, it is important to note a distinctive feature of all the first-wave NICs: their heavy reliance on international trade. As Table 6.2 demonstrates, the NICs (including Singapore) are much more heavily integrated in, and exposed to, the international trading system than most of the Southeast Asian economies,[6] Japan or even China. Indeed, given Japan's historical importance economically in the region, it is remarkable how self-contained the Japanese economy remains, despite the continuing significance of the export sector in that country's overall economic performance. However, one negative consequence of this as far as Japan's overall regional significance is concerned is that Japan has not absorbed intra-regional exports in the way its economic size suggests it might have, which has caused irritation amongst its trade partners, especially at times of crisis (Lincoln 2004). China's much greater integration into the global trading system and the positive impact it has had on regional demand stands as a revealing comparison (Roland-Holst and Weiss 2005), and one with long-term implications for the two countries' relative influence.

It is also important to remember that the sheer scale of the Japanese and Chinese economies means that they have internal dynamics and

Table 6.2   Relative size of trade to GDP (Exports (imports) value/
nominal GDP, %)

	Exports		Imports	
	1985–87 Average	*1995–98 Average*	*1985–87 Average*	*1995–98 Average*
Japan	11.4	9.5	7.1	7
US	5.6	9.8	9.1	11.5
Euro area	12	11.4	11.5	11.1
East Asia	22.8	25.1	21.6	27.2
NICs (ex-Hong Kong)	44.5	38.8	40.5	42.9
ASEAN 4	27.2	39.2	20.1	38
China + Hong Kong	15	25.9	19.1	28.3
Latin America	12.8	12.1	8.3	13.9
Mercosur	9.6	6.2	5.2	6.7

Source: Adapted from Isogai and Shunichi, 'East Asia's intra- and inter-regional economic relations; data analyses on trade, direct investments and currency transactions', *International Department Working Paper Series* 00-E-4, International Department, Bank of Japan, Tokyo; using IMF Direction of Trade Statistics. Reproduced by permission.

potential strengths that are not applicable in other cases. The most extreme example of this possibility, perhaps, is Singapore, which is highly dependent on, and deeply integrated into, the international economic system. Not only did Singapore rely heavily on inflows of FDI to jump-start its industrialization process, but the nature of its integration has been heavily influenced by the nature of this investment and the MNCs that provide it as a consequence.[7] Singapore has successfully moved up the value-adding chain, turning itself into an exporter of sophisticated manufacturing products, especially in the information technology (IT) sector. Indeed, more than half its exports are now in this area. However, they are highly dependent on a limited number of markets, with over 25 per cent of exports going to the USA.[8] In such circumstances, the small Singaporean economy is especially vulnerable to the vicissitudes of the international economy generally and American markets in particular. Hong Kong's economic fate is also increasingly tied to one country, although these days, this has become an internal matter following its re-incorporation into the PRC. Although the scale of Hong Kong's investment flows to China are massive and atypical, they do highlight a more general point that is relevant to all the NICs: as the NICs have successfully industrialized and moved up the value chain, they have themselves become important sources of capital for Southeast Asia in particular (Isogai and Shibanuma no date).

The emerging regional division of labour is complex, but one in which Japan generally remains in an ascendant position, especially as a provider of technology-intensive capital goods (Hart-Landsberg and Burkett 1998). However, the emergence of the NICs as major sources of investment within the East Asian region is significant in consolidating not only investment linkages within the region, but also trade, too. Although the figures are significantly skewed by the Hong Kong–China relationship, the NICs' outward investment occurs overwhelmingly within the Asian region. The MNCs that have emerged from, say, Korea, Taiwan and Singapore have adopted what Dicken and Yeung (1999: 118) describe as a 'regional solution' to the challenge of economic restructuring and expansion. Rather than following Japan's pioneering lead and investing primarily in the lucrative markets of North America and Europe, the NICs have attempted to exploit 'local' advantages rather than attempt to compete with the established European and American MNCs on their home turf. One of the consequences of this process has been to entrench the position of the Southeast Asian economies at the bottom of the regional production hierarchy as the NICs export their low-end, less valuable, labour-intensive industries such as apparel, footwear and toys (Gereffi 1998: 50). These sorts of investment linkage between the first and second tier economies have, as the links between Japan and the first tier before it, contributed to the growth of intra-regional trade.

Despite a significant growth in intra-East Asian trade, however, which has expanded from 30.9 per cent in 1986 to 49.5 per cent in 1994 (Peng 2000: 176), the entire region remains highly dependent on external markets, especially America's. In this regard, the Malaysian economy is even more exposed to downturns in the American economy than Singapore's, with some 80 per cent of IT exports going to the USA.[9] This is especially important given that manufactured goods accounted for around 80 per cent of Malaysia's exports by the mid-1990s. Although Malaysia's industrialization process has been successful in many respects, it has been heavily reliant on imports of foreign capital and intermediate products, especially from Japan. As Islam and Chowdhury (2000: 229) point out, the heavy reliance on foreign investment and the concomitant repatriation of profits and dividends has led to continuing deficits in Malaysia's services trade. One of the strategies employed by Malaysia to encourage inward investment has been the establishment of export processing zones (EPZs), in which potential investors are offered major inducements including tax breaks and the provision of infrastructure. Although Malaysia's EPZ policy is generally considered to have been comparatively successful, it is thought to be partly responsible for the lack of industrial deepening noted in the last chapter. Only in the first wave of industrializing nations that followed Japan, such as Taiwan and Korea, was the EPZ strategy judged to be effective. In Indonesia and the Philippines, by contrast, it has generally failed to encourage widespread industrial development and deepening (Amirahmadi and Wu 1995; Hobday 2001).

The manner in which the economies of Southeast Asia have been integrated into the wider international order has consequently given rise to continuing doubts about the quality and depth of the industrialization process. Despite the fact that some countries, such as Malaysia, have been able to attract inflows of FDI into more sophisticated manufacturing processes, overall industrial development remains 'constrained by the interests and strategies of the multinational corporations' (Jomo 2004: 64). When added to the indigenous constraints imposed by Malaysia's ethnically-oriented developmental strategies, the prospects for 'rational' economic development in the 'national interest' look more remote. The development of an indigenous, 'Malaysian' car industry is indicative of how complex and politically (rather than economically) motivated such initiatives can be: not only was the quality of the agreement and technology transfer negotiated with the Japanese giant Mitsubishi that established the Proton debatable, but it was largely driven – if that is the right word – with little consultation by the then Prime Minister, Mahathir (Milne and Mauzy 1999: 65–6). The result has been an industry that is widely considered to be still technologically dependent on Japan and of questionable viability without continuing protection and assistance.[10] As we shall see in the next chapter, Malaysia's car industry is emblematic of a number of 'sensitive' industrial sectors across the region that have made the establishment of trade agreements in Southeast Asia inherently problematic. Indeed, the prospects for regional cooperation are constrained, and the historically low levels of intra-regional trade are explained, by the fact that the economies of Southeast Asia are inherently competitive, rather than complimentary (Chia 1999). In other words, the countries of Southeast Asia are frequently trying to establish themselves in precisely the same sorts of industries on the basis of similar comparative advantages, which their reliance on foreign capital does little to alleviate.

Even if there are continuing concerns about the impact of FDI on the course of the industrialization process in Southeast Asia, the region confronts a potentially more fundamental problem: the decline in its overall share of the FDI flowing into the East Asian region as a whole. Of the FDI that flows to East Asia, China has been absorbing ever greater quantities (UNCTAD 2005: 4). As Greg Felker (2003: 259) points out, Southeast Asia has been caught in what he calls a 'structural squeeze', between a rising China and the first-tier NICs; their failure to develop more sophisticated, high value-added manufacturing industries means that they risk being permanently eclipsed by the rise of China, which can offer potential investors all that the NICs can in terms of pliable cheap labour, but on an epic scale and with a potentially enormous internal market. While similar doubts have been raised about the nature of China's industrialization process, too, there is an emerging consensus that Southeast Asia's political and economic elites may have failed to adequately exploit what may prove to be a unique, unrepeatable histori-cal opportunity to consolidate the developmental process. As Felker observes:

> During the first decade of the post-Plaza FDI boom (1986–96), MNCs from the Triad and the [Northeast Asian] NICs greatly expanded their Southeast Asian operations, and introduced more advanced products and sophisticated processes. To a great extent, however, this dynamism represented an upgrading of the region's existing assembly role rather than a structural transformation. (Felker 2003: 261)

Countries such as Indonesia and the Philippines, which face particu-larly difficult developmental challenges, and which lack the kind of state capacity that exists in the first-tier NICs, may find it increasingly difficult to move up the hierarchy of regional production. This is an especially important consideration given that the state's legitimacy in the region has invariably been attached to its capacity to deliver rising living standards. Thailand highlights a more generalized dilemma in this regard: despite the fact that the industrialization process has been comparatively successful and the structure of the economy has been transformed, the nature of its integration with a market-oriented, neoliberal external order has tended to exacerbate the increasing polarization of income levels and life chances that is such a characteristic feature of the contem-porary international order more generally (Hewison 2006). This trend is also evident in Indonesia, the Philippines and Korea, where Haji and Zin (2005: 52) argue that 'the reduced role of government and the attendant increased role of the private sector have reversed the improving trend in income inequality'.

Given that 'unusually low and declining levels of inequality' have been identified as one of the hallmarks of the successful East Asian develop-mental experience (World Bank 1993: 29), any increase in potentially destabilizing social inequality has major implications for existent regimes in the region. The social dislocation and regime change that followed the Asian crisis serves as a powerful reminder of this possibility. Before we examine the crisis in any detail, though, we need to consider China's integration into the world economy, a country facing similar problems of social adjustment and transformation, but on an epic scale that has both regional and global implications.

The emergence of 'greater China'

As we saw in the last chapter, China's economic development has been largely caused (and deeply influenced) by its integration into the wider international system. Indeed, the relative lack of state capacity noted in the last chapter made China especially reliant on a variety of external forces to accelerate the pace of development and structural change. Whether it was the influence of organizations such as the WTO in encouraging domestic institutional change, or the impact of massive flows of FDI in accelerating industrial development, the influence of external actors has clearly been profound. However, the sheer scale of the transformation that has occurred in China means that its remarkable growth has begun to exercise a similarly significant impact on the outside world. And yet, for all the hyperbole that has accompanied the rise of China, we should acknowledge one important caveat at the outset: there is great difficulty in knowing precisely how big the Chinese economy actually is.[11] For example, Table 1.1 would seem to suggest that China is still a relatively small economy compared to Japan and the USA, but this is only the case if measured in current prices. If China's economy is measured in the arguably more revealing purchasing power parity terms, then its economy is already the second largest in the world and is possibly on track to overtake the USA sometime in the middle of the twenty-first century (Woodall 2004: 6). And yet, paradoxically enough, as Shaun Breslin (2005: 736) points out, 'even after two decades of double-digit growth, China's per capita income is still only around half of Russia's'.

It was for such reasons that some observers have argued that the importance of China was wildly overstated (Segal 1999). However, even in the relatively short time since Segal's article was published, the evidence about China's significance for the global economy has become increasingly compelling. Bezlova (2004), for example, estimates that despite China officially constituting only 4 per cent of the world economy, in 2003 China accounted for 7 per cent of global oil consumption, as well as 27 per cent of steel, 31 per cent of coal and 40 per cent of cement. China's steel production is now greater than Japan and the USA combined, and it is already a larger consumer of copper and aluminium than the USA; all this despite the continuing reality that 'China's per capita consumption of raw materials is still very modest compared to America' (Hale 2004: 140). As a result, optimists rejoice at the seemingly endless growth opportunities the China market seems to hold, which goes a long way towards explaining the remarkable amounts of FDI that have poured into China since the 1990s in particular, as Figure 6.1 indicates. Pessimists, by contrast, fret about the potential for conflict as the world's ever-expanding demand for energy – especially oil – meets a finite and possibly diminishing capacity to supply it. China is already the world's second largest oil consumer, but its consumption per head remains far lower than in the USA, where access to cheap oil remains an apparently non-negotiable part of American consumption patterns and a central component of American foreign policy (Klare 2004). As Table 6.3 suggests, China's demand for energy has grown dramatically and rapidly, which that helps to explain the recent spike in oil prices (a development with disturbing implications for the rest of Asia's generally oil-intensive, importing countries).[12]

There are, then, serious geopolitical and environmental doubts about the sustainability of China's rush for growth and the associated transformation in life-styles and consumption patterns that is likely to accompany it. These questions will be addressed in more detail in the final chapter. At present, it is important to detail the way in which China is integrated into the East Asian economy, as it highlights a number of

Figure 6.1   Asia: net private capital flows

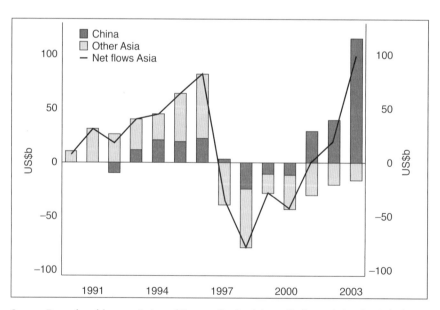

Source: Reproduced by permission of Reserve Bank of Australia from 'Asian Capital Flows', *Reserve Bank of Australia Bulletin*, August 2004: Graph 7, original sources of data CEIC: IMF; national sources.

Table 6.3 China's energy consumption trends

	1980	1985	1990	1995	2000	2001	2002	2003
Total	60,276	76,682	98,694	131,176	130,296	134,914	148,222	167,799
(growth rate)	4.9	5.2	5.9	-0.1	3.5	9.9	13.2	
Coal	43,519	58,125	75,202	97,857	86,126	88,099	97,219	112,627
(share)	72.2	75.8	76.2	74.6	66.1	65.3	65.6	67.1
(growth rate)	6	5.3	5.4	-2.5	2.3	10.4	15.8	
Oil	12,477	13,113	16,385	22,956	32,053	32,784	35,529	38,107
(share)	20.7	17.1	16.6	17.5	24.6	24.3	24	22.7
(growth rate)	1	4.6	7	6.9	2.3	8.4	7.3	
Natural gas	1,869	1,687	2,073	2,361	3,257	3,643	3,883	4,732
(share)	3.1	2.2	2.1	1.8	2.5	2.7	2.5	2.8
(growth rate)	-2	4.2	2.6	6.6	11.8	6.5	21.9	
Hydropower	2,411	3,757	5,034	8,002	8,860	10,388	11,591	12,333
(share)	4	4.9	5.1	6.1	6.8	7.7	7.8	7.4
(growth rate)	9.3	6	9.7	2.1	17.2	11.6	6.4	

Note: All data expressed in SCE (Standard Coal Equivalent); growth rate is the average annual growth rate; 'share' is share of total energy consumption. 'Share' = Share of total energy consumption.

Source: Reproduced from *White Paper on International Economy and Trade 2005 Overview*, July 2005, Ministry of Economy, Trade and Industry Japan: Table 2.1.122; original source of data: *China Statistical Yearbook*, National Bureau of Statistics of China.

issues that are likely to influence the course of development in East Asia, and which also have wider comparative significance.

Perhaps the most distinctive feature of 'China's' rise is that it is not something that has been confined to, or is a consequence of, events that have occurred within exclusively national borders. On the contrary, 'greater China' takes in Hong Kong, Taiwan and possibly even other elements of the 'overseas Chinese' diaspora. As we saw in the last chapter, there is a good deal of debate about the usefulness of this term, as it is rather loosely applied to the estimated 50 million or so ethnic Chinese resident in Asia outside China. Although the term 'overseas Chinese' may not be sufficiently nuanced to capture the wide variety of specific political and economic contexts in which Chinese-style capitalism is realized (Brown 1998), it is indicative of the distinctive form of economic organization associated with ethnic Chinese business, especially in Southeast Asia. Yet, while it is true that people who trace their ethnicity to China have come to assume a striking and disproportionate economic prominence in much of Southeast Asia in particular,[13] as Goodman (1997–8: 144) points out, 'it is not clear the Ethnic Chineseness is the most important predictor of their economic behaviour, let alone other kinds of activity'. Be that as it may, as far as the mainland is concerned, connections with Hong Kong and Taiwan (which have clearly been facilitated by common linguistic, cultural and commercial practices) have been especially important in channelling FDI into China and restructuring economic activity across the region.

At first glance, Hong Kong appears to be by far the biggest single source of FDI into China, and it clearly has been a crucially important part of the rapid, FDI-driven growth that has occurred on the mainland. Between 1979 and 2003, Hong Kong's average share of China's FDI inflows was over 40 per cent (Sung 2005: 27). However, this figure is misleading as Hong Kong funnels investment into China from tax havens in the Caribbean as well as from Taiwan. Consequently, Taiwan's share of China's FDI – a little over 7 per cent on average over the same period – is 'grossly understated because its capital is channelled to the mainland via third territories' (Sung 2005: 29). Whatever the precise measures of these flows may be, two points are abundantly clear. First, China's economic take-off has been powerfully fuelled by its relationship with Taiwan and Hong Kong and the capital they have directly or indirectly invested on the mainland. Second, the degree of economic integration that has occurred between the three elements of 'greater China' has blurred national economic boundaries and effectively constituted a major, trans-border 'growth triangle'.

While we need to be careful about employing essentialist and possibly racist stereotypes when talking about 'Chinese business' and the supposed commonalities in the Chinese diaspora, it is clear that Southeast Asian Chinese have been key players in what Yeung (2000a: 270) describes as a process of 'facilitating the rearticulation of their motherland, China, into the global economy'. This has occurred because Southeast Asian Chinese have become major investors in mainland China – establishing over 100,000 joint ventures with over \$50 billion of FDI – and because they have helped integrate the mainland into existent, global trade and financial networks, Yeung argues. What is clear is that since 1979, when the PRC began to establish the sorts of SEZs that were employed elsewhere in the region as part of the industrialization push (Crane 1990), manufacturing growth has occurred at an astonishing pace; it has, however, been primarily confined to the Pearl River delta adjacent to Hong Kong, taking in Shenzen and Guangzhou as well.[14] China now manufactures half of the world's cameras, 30 per cent of air conditioners and televisions, 25 per cent of washing machines and 20 per cent of refrigerators.[15] In 2004, China also overtook the USA to become the largest exporter of technology and telecoms goods,[16] confirming that the industrialization process is no longer confined to simple manufactures.

For all its undoubted importance in underpinning rapid economic development, however, the industrialization process and global integration have contributed to the unevenness of income distribution and overall levels of economic development that have become such a distinctive feature of China's recent development, and such a potentially explosive source of domestic inequality and discontent as a consequence (Miles 2002). Moreover, it is important to note that the manner of this foreign-dominated export-led industrialization process is placing even greater pressure on the SOEs and raises the same kinds of questions about the nature and depth of the industrialization process that were asked about Southeast Asia.[17]

Despite such concerns, China's rapid economic expansion is also redefining its external relations, too, and generally for the better. Despite both the well-known problems of doing business in China (at least, as far as many Western firms are concerned), and the fact that China has not always proved as profitable as many outsiders hoped,[18] many of the world's major MNCs (including General Motors, Philips, General Electric, Toshiba, Siemens and Motorola) have established operations there. This has a number of important consequences. First, it means that something like half of China's exports occur through joint ventures or foreign-owned enterprises. While this may not be a bad thing in itself, it is important to recognize, as Shaun Breslin points out, that the value-added that occurs within China of such exports is 'extraordinarily low', because many of the more valuable components and capital-intensive aspects of production occur *outside* China in places such as Japan.

Consequently, Breslin (2005: 743) argues, China acts as 'the manufacturing conduit through which the regional deficit is processed, with China running deficits with "supplier" states in East Asia, and surpluses with "demand" states in Europe and North America'. This is an especially important consideration given the importance attached to the 'problem' of the trade surplus with China amongst American policy-makers.[19] The reality, however, is that 'almost 60 percent of Chinese exports to the United States are produced by firms owned by foreign companies, many of them American ... Wal-Mart alone purchased $18 billion worth of Chinese goods in 2004, making it China's eighth-largest trading partner – ahead of Australia, Canada and Russia' (N. Hughes 2005: 94).

The second major point to make about the nature of China's trade, then, is not just that much of it is actually controlled by American companies and arguably good for 'the American economy', but that USA-based producers have an economic and *political* stake in good relations with China. Unlike Japan, which still has far lower levels of foreign investment and participation in its domestic economy, in the PRC there are many MNCs and external investors that can act as a potential constraint on the US government, and on any attempts to penalize China for its supposedly 'unfair' economic practices.

While there may still be questions about the nature, quality and depth of industrialization in China, its impact on the region and the world is much clearer: the sheer volume and importance of China's trade relations with Asia have not only made it a major engine of growth, but have also transformed its diplomatic position as well. China has adroitly consolidated its growing economic centrality in the region – especially with Southeast Asia – with a series of economic and diplomatic initiatives with ASEAN in particular (Ba 2003; Vatikiotis and Hiebert 2003). There have been widely held fears amongst many observers in Southeast Asia that China's rise is ultimately a negative for its smaller neighbours, who are locked in a zero-sum competition for foreign investment and markets. However, John Ravenhill's (forthcoming) detailed analysis of China's impact on the ASEAN economies makes it clear that China is, in fact, fostering a new division of labour in the region and encouraging the further development of the industrialization process there, further encouraging the growth of intra-industry trade in the process. Ravenhill also makes the important point that China has not attracted a share of regional FDI inflows that is disproportionate to the size of its economy, especially when some of the anomalies and distortions of China's FDI figures are taken into account. This is not only important for the course of regional economic integration, but it also has implications for China's political status if it becomes clear that it is a positive force as far as the rest of the region is concerned.

The implications of these agreements and their impact on China's place in the processes of regionalism will be taken up in the next chapter. At present, it is important to note that China's economic influence transcends the East Asian region and is having a marked impact – both positive and negative – on the wider international economy as well. On the one hand, China's unparalleled ability to produce cheap manufactured products has exerted downward pressure on the prices of consumer goods and helped create the remarkably benign inflation environment of recent times. On the other hand, however, this has created similar downward pressure on the wages of low-skilled labour in the OECD economies, as well as contributing to the growth of asset-price bubbles in the USA and elsewhere. Because China has been recycling its vast trade surpluses into American Treasury bonds, the excess liquidity this has created has caused an increase in the value of property and equity markets around the world, to say nothing of creating massive inter-dependency between the Chinese and American economies (Woodall 2004: 3–8). It is important to remember, of course, that it is the USA's budget deficits that are ultimately responsible for what look like unsustainable imbalances in the global economy, not China's.

The implications of this growing inter-dependency between the USA and East Asia will be taken up in the final part of this chapter. Before that, however, it is important to say something about the East Asian financial crisis, for not only was it a pivotal moment in the region's economic and political history, but it sheds a revealing light on the nature of the economic interaction between the region and the rest of the world, and also on the complex dynamics that underpin it.

The East Asian financial crisis and its aftermath

There is by now a voluminous literature that deals with the East Asian crisis, most of which rightly deals with those countries that bore the brunt of its impact: Indonesia, Thailand, Malaysia and – more surprisingly, perhaps – South Korea (see, for example, Haggard 2000; Noble and Ravenhill 2000; Pempel 1999; Robison *et al.* 2000). Rather than attempting to add significantly to that literature here, this section briefly notes some of the major impacts of the crisis while paying more attention to its longer-term implications for intra- and inter-regional relations. In this context, it is significant that all the major powers (Japan, China and the USA) played important roles in the way the crisis evolved, and may yet determine its long-term impact on the region's institutional architecture. Such institutional change may prove to be the most significant consequence of the crisis, despite the understandable attention given to its immediate effect on Southeast Asia in particular.

The impact of the crisis on regional institutional development will be given more extensive consideration in the next chapter. At this stage, it is important to note that the crisis affected the reputation and standing of the major powers in very different ways, and this has given a particular dynamic to processes of regionalism. In this regard, Japan suffered the greatest damage to its regional leadership ambitions and overall standing as a result of the crisis and its aftermath. Significantly, this process began well before the 'East Asian crisis' of 1997, suggesting that the region's economic problems were not confined to the four countries listed above, and that their antecedents can be found well before the events of the late 1990s. Japan, as we saw in the last chapter, had already experienced a 'crisis' of its own, albeit a slow-burning one that did not bring the country to its knees or affect employment and growth quite so dramatically.

What Japan's crisis did do, however, was to undermine the credibility of the 'Japanese model' on the one hand and – more importantly and tangibly – directly add to the underlying economic problems of the region, on the other. This happened in two principal ways: first, distressed Japanese banks were forced to begin repatriating capital from Asia to shore up their deteriorating, post-bubble balance sheets. Figure 6.2 dramatically illustrates the way in which Japanese bank lending began to decline well before the crisis. The net effect, King (2001: 440) argues, was to trigger the crisis 'inadvertently' as Japanese financial institutions reduced their exposure to Asia. The second problem Japan caused much of the region was a consequence of the steady decline in the value of the yen. What Robert Brenner (2002: ch. 4) calls 'the reverse Plaza Accord'[20] of 1995 saw the Japanese and American governments agree to allow the yen to decline in value, something that dramatically added to the competitiveness problems of neighbouring countries with pegged exchange rates, as we shall see. Furthermore, the possibility that Japan might play a positive role in soaking up exports from the region's distressed economies in the aftermath of the crisis was nullified by the impact of the crisis in Japan itself, where it further undermined domestic consumer confidence. Despite Japan's subsequent efforts to play a leadership role in post-crisis management (considered in more detail in the next chapter), the net impact of this period was to confirm the generally negative sentiment about its position, especially relative to China.

Changes in sentiment were not confined to views of Japan. Although the standing of some countries (such as China) may have actually been enhanced as a consequence of the crisis, there has been a more generalized and negative transformation of attitudes towards the region. In this regard, the abrupt change from 'miracle to meltdown' was more than a

Figure 6.2   Bank lending to Asia by source

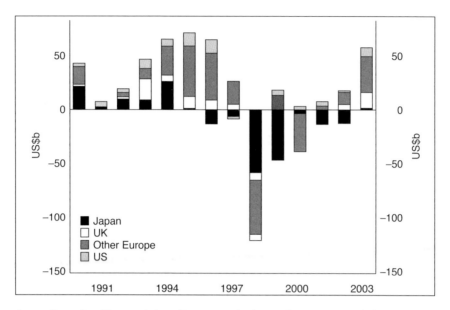

Source: Reproduced by permission of Reserve Bank of Australia 'Asian Capital Flows', *Reserve Bank of Australia Bulletin*, August 2004: Graph 4; original source of data Bank for International Settlements.

journalistic cliché: it was testimony to both the depth of the crisis itself and the manner in which much of East Asia suddenly fell out of favour with the 'international investment community'. In reality, of course, much of the international movements of mobile capital are determined by a relative handful of money market traders and mutual fund mangers who take advantage of profit opportunities rapidly and globally. Likewise, the 'miracle' economies are, as we have seen, a highly diverse group of countries with a variety of strengths and weaknesses, and different capacities to take advantage of the evolving international economic order. Such subtleties appeared not to figure in the calculations of the 'international investment community', however. At the heart of the massive, increasingly speculative and indiscriminate inflows of capital into the region was a 'faith in the immortality of the Asian miracle that led to excessive investment in a handful of cyclically sensitive export industries and in commercial construction' (Kenen 2001: 27). The crisis dramatically highlighted what could happen when small – and not so small, in Korea's case – economies became integrated into global circuits of financial capital and thus exposed to the actions and judgements of market actors beyond national control.

Thus, the most important difference between East Asia in the late

1990s and East Asia in the late 1970s was that many of the economies of the region had become increasingly open to inflows of highly mobile portfolio capital and short-term bank lending in a way that was not the case in the earlier period. Formerly, investment capital was primarily raised through high domestic savings or official government to government assistance. Gradually, however, governments across the region began to follow the neoliberal orthodoxy and open their capital accounts,[21] allowing much greater (and unregulated) movements of capital. Consequently, from the mid-1980s onwards, inflows of private capital grew much faster than government loans; by the mid-1990s, some 75 per cent of inflows were private, of which half was highly mobile portfolio capital (Beeson and Robison 2000; Winters 2000: 36). The other noteworthy feature of the borrowing patterns that emerged in the 1990s was how much of the debt incurred was short term.[22] Sceptics doubted the wisdom of this policy, arguing that in a region where savings were extremely high, productive investment could be financed from domestic sources with much less risk; the value of encouraging further inflows of mobile capital was debatable at best and likely to encourage increasingly speculative forms of investment (Wade and Veneroso 1998). Before trying to assess the merits of this strategy and the longer-term implications of this period, it is worth briefly rehearsing the main features of the crisis itself.

A region in crisis

Famously, the crisis began with a minor currency crisis in a relatively small, peripheral Southeast Asian economy. That Thailand could prove the catalyst for what would rapidly become a major regional – and eventually international – economic crisis, as its ripples spread outwards to Russia and Latin America, is remarkable and tells us something important about the nature of the contemporary international economy and its capacity to rapidly transmit 'shocks' around the world (Krugman 1999). While international economic integration may have major benefits in potentially allowing capital-poor countries access to foreign investment, it is also clear that economic shocks are capable of being transmitted much more rapidly and widely than they once were (Bryant 2003). Indeed, this is especially the case when the type of capital that is flowing to smaller developing economies is financial capital rather than the longer-term, far more stable foreign direct investment.

The trigger that caused the initial panic about Thailand (and the subsequent 'contagion' in Indonesia, Malaysia and Korea) was concern about the Thai government's ability to maintain its 'peg' to the value of the American dollar. As investors became concerned about the value of the *baht*, and thus the dollar value of their investments, a self-fulling panic ensued as they scrambled to withdraw. The Thai government was a victim of a problem that confronts even the most powerful governments, but which is especially acute for smaller economies that are regarded more speculatively (Beeson 1998). Although developing economies confront particularly challenging problems of risk and management, the difficulties of economic management and the consequences that flow from market-oriented policy settings are almost universal.[23] Policy-makers must contend with a well-known policy 'trilemma', or what Benjamin Cohen (1993) called an 'unholy trinity', in which they cannot simultaneously have independent monetary policies, fixed exchange rates and an open capital account. Because the Thai government had opened its capital account while trying to maintain a fixed exchange rate, it sacrificed control over monetary policy. Consequently, it was not able to use interest rates to control the domestic impact of massive capital inflows, which were simultaneously pushing up asset values and wages, fuelling a speculative construction boom, encouraging imports through increased liquidity and credit, and making Thai exports less competitive in the process.

What is striking and noteworthy in retrospect is that the structural imbalances in the Thai economy generally, and its exposure to short-term debt in particular, did not become causes of concern for outside investors sooner than they did. This is especially so given that the other problem pegged exchange rates had created was to encourage borrowing in American dollars. Confidence – misplaced as we now know – in the durability of the exchange rate against the dollar meant that many borrowers failed to 'hedge' their positions or insure against adverse currency movements (Jomo 1998: 6). When the baht and other regional currencies did collapse, many of the loans proved unserviceable.[24] It is testimony to the positive view of potential investors before the crisis hit that they ignored warning signs which should have urged caution. In other words, the herd-like behaviour that some observers take to be a positive force in encouraging 'good' policy-making (Friedman 2000) did not have a salutary influence before the crisis. On the contrary, it appears to have actively contributed to the very problems of cronyism and non-transparency that received so much retrospective attention. Indeed, the existence of 'strong' states and close government–business relations may have encouraged a 'moral hazard' problem on the part of international investors who were not only carried away by the general euphoria surrounding the Asian miracle, but who may have believed that states could and would indemnify them against any possible losses (Kenen 2001: 19).

Any such lingering expectations were, however, extinguished by the rapidity and extent of the panic that took hold. Across the five most badly affected economies – Thailand, Malaysia, Indonesia, the Philippines and Korea – a positive inflow of portfolio capital of over US$12 billion in 1996 turned into a negative outflow of over $11.5 billion in 1997 (Beeson and Robison 2000). On top of this, the currencies of Indonesia, Thailand, Malaysia, the Philippines, Korea, and even Singapore and Taiwan experienced major declines in value. In the case of Singapore and Taiwan, which were in comparatively good shape, and even in the Philippines, which was not as badly affected by the crisis,[25] this seemed like a case of guilt-by-association, rather than any specific failings on the part of these economies. The only East Asian countries not to experience the 'contagion effect' were Hong Kong and China. Significantly, neither of these countries had a tradable currency and they were thus insulated from the panic-stricken, herd-like behaviour that affected the rest of the region. As we shall see, this episode – especially China's decision not to devalue the yuan in response to currency collapses elsewhere – did much to improve its standing in the region and helps to explain the country's continuing nervousness about 'floating' its currency despite immense external pressure to do so (Eichengreen 2005).

Of the countries that did experience major currency movements, Indonesia was by far the most badly affected, with the rupiah losing about 80 per cent of its value in the first few months after the crisis. The upheaval this induced was not confined to the economic sphere, either. Unsurprisingly, perhaps, for a regime whose legitimacy was highly dependent on the delivery of rising living standards and economic stability, the crisis was catastrophic. At the urging of the IMF, and in an effort to restore confidence and stability, interest rates were pushed up to 65 per cent, and government spending – including politically-sensitive subsidies on staples such as cooking oil – was slashed in line with the IMF's standard austerity package (Bird 1996; Stiglitz 2002). The net effect was to compound an economic crisis with a political one. While many may celebrate the downfall of the autocratic Suharto regime which the crisis clearly brought about, it is important to recognize just how traumatic the impact of structural forces in the global economy and the direct intervention of external agencies (including the IMF) were in the life of a nominally sovereign nation. Thailand and Korea experienced similar changes of government as a direct consequence of the crisis. Again, while many might welcome the ascendancy of a political liberal such as Kim Dae-Jung, the impact of extraneous factors cannot be underestimated. In Korea's case, the key point to emphasize is that government liberalization of the financial sector, and a failure to exercise adequate supervision of the private sector, had established the preconditions for the subsequent economic and political crisis (Chang 1998).

Views about the merits of IMF crisis-management policies are emblematic of a fundamental division between those observers who attribute most weight to the sort of external systemic factors associated with 'globalization' discussed in Chapter 1 when explaining the crisis (Beeson 1998; Stiglitz 2002; Wade and Veneroso 1998; Winters 2000), and those who consider the crisis was primarily a consequence of failures of domestic governance and/or crony capitalism (Corsetti, Pesenti and Roubini 1999; Fischer 1998; Haggard 2000). Clearly, the sorts of reformist agendas and policy strategies that are proposed in the aftermath of the crisis will depend on the causal weight given to these factors. Even for those who take a multi-dimensional approach, such as that developed here, which sees the unfolding of the crisis as involving a complex interaction between structure and agency at a number of intersecting national, regional and global levels, some factors will be given more weight than others.

However, the IMF's privileging of internal factors meant it took the rather predictable view that the crisis was primarily a consequence of poor policy decisions and 'structural' problems within the affected economies. Consequently, in return for crisis management and a financial bail-out, the IMF insisted on far-reaching reform packages which were intended to break up the distinctive patterns of business–government relations that had developed across much of East Asia (Beeson 1999b). This was bad enough for many of the dominant political elites, of the region whose relationships were necessarily threatened by the proposed reforms. However, when it became increasingly clear that the IMF reform strategy was not only inappropriate and actually *contributing* to the crisis by dampening demand and undermining confidence in national financial systems (Stiglitz 2002: ch. 4), but that it was also being actively encouraged by an American government keen to exploit a possibly unique opportunity to force liberalization upon a recalcitrant region (Bello 1998), the depth of resentment intensified (Higgott 1998). It was in this atmosphere of generalized crisis, and unhappiness about the intrusive, insensitive role played by the IMF and the USA, which 'de facto largely dictates the IMF's policies' (Krugman 1999: 114), that Malaysia broke with the ruling orthodoxy and experimented with capital controls.[26]

A couple of points are worth briefly making about this interesting and illuminating episode. First, Malaysia's approach was something that the IMF – which had been an active proponent of precisely the sort of capital account liberalization that appeared to have undone the crisis economies – simply could not have contemplated or sanctioned. As Stephen Grenville[27] (2004: 82) astutely observes, 'It was a difficult time to acknowledge the danger of excessive flows, and to contemplate

restriction of inflows as part of crisis prevention would have been tanta-
mount to heresy.' In other words, the sort of ideational influences
discussed in Chapter 1 show a remarkable degree of continuity and
resilience, even in the face of powerful evidence as to their inappropri-
ateness. Second, at the very least, it is possible to argue that whatever the
motivation for Malaysia's apostasy – and a desire to shield extant
networks of political and economic power from external scrutiny and
reform was plainly a large part of it (Beeson 2000) – capital controls did
no harm, and may in fact have saved Malaysia from experiencing the sort
of economic trauma experienced by Indonesia.[28] Given that the crisis
sparked a major debate about the nature and role of the 'international
financial architecture', its role in the crisis, and the possible need for
reform (Armijo 2002), Malaysia's experiment also had significant
comparative importance, especially as far as other emerging economies
were concerned (B.J. Cohen 2000). The final point to make about the
Malaysian experience is that it exacerbated tensions between East Asia
and the USA, giving renewed life to Mahathir's aborted proposal for an
East Asian Economic Caucus (which would ultimately re-emerge as
ASEAN+3) and sparking interest in the possibility of developing regional
monetary mechanisms with which to ward off future crises.

Given that Joseph Stiglitz (2002: 99), the World Bank's former chief
economist considers that 'capital account liberalization was *the single
most important factor leading to the crisis*' (emphasis in original), it is
striking that the debate about the need to reform the international financial system has lost much of its momentum (Beeson and Bell 2005b). This
becomes less puzzling when we remember two things. First, financial
sector interests based in the USA have actively lobbied the American
government to promote further liberalization because, as Jagdish
Bhagwati points out, 'Wall Street's financial firms have obvious self-
interest in a world of free capital mobility since it only enlarges the arena
in which to make money' (Bhagwati 1998: 11). But the US government
has its own reasons for continuing to press for the continuing liberalization of global financial markets, despite growing doubts about the
wisdom of such policies for small, emerging economies with inadequate
regulatory capacity and poorly developed capital markets. The second
reason that the US government is an unequivocal supporter of the present
highly liberal international financial order is simply that it must. The
USA's expanding current account deficits leave it wholly dependent on
continuing inflows of capital – primarily from East Asia[29] – to finance its
trade and budget deficits. In what may prove to be a major long-term
development for the international economy, China has indicated that it
will diversify its massive foreign exchange reserves out of US dollar and
American bonds.[30] Equally significantly (and more worryingly from an

Table 6.4 Global foreign exchange reserves (end of 2004)

	Foreign exchange reserves ($ billion)	Of total global reserves (%)
Japan	833.9	21.6
NICs	676.5	17.6
ASEAN4	162.9	4.2
China	614.5	15.9
East Asia total	2,287.8	59.4
World total	3,853.7	100

Source: Adapted from *White Paper on International Economy and Trade 2005, Overview*, July 2005, Ministry of Economy, Trade and Industry, Japan: Figure 1.5.6.

American standpoint) there are indications that the Organization of the Petroleum Exporting Countries (OPEC) and Russia are filling this gap;[31] these are all countries with far less dependence on American markets than the East Asians. Without such inflows, not only will domestic interest rates be higher and consumption patterns at risk, but some of the more ambitious aspects of American foreign and strategic policy would be unsupportable (Ferguson and Kotlikoff 2003).

Thus, there are increasingly widely-held doubts about the sustainability of a situation in which 'Americans are spending over $700 billion a year more than their economy produces' (Beddoes 2005: 3). This raises a number of issues that are especially germane to post-crisis East Asia. First, there is an important, but oddly neglected normative question to be asked about the nature of capital flows between East Asia and the USA. As Robert Wade points out, the contemporary, American-dominated world economic order 'enables the USA, by many criteria the richest and most advanced country in the world, to borrow heavily from much poorer countries and to use the funds to sustain its pre-eminence and pursue foreign policy objectives that the lenders may not support' (Wade 2004: 244). It is not simply because such a relationship seems difficult to justify on ethical grounds that it is so jarring, but because 'private-sector investment in emerging Asia outside China has collapsed' (Beddoes 2005: 15). Investment levels in Southeast Asia have not regained their pre-crisis levels and, as Figures 6.1 and 6.3 demonstrate, capital continues to drain from much of the region outside China. Oddly enough, therefore, the economies of East Asia continue to pile up massive foreign exchange reserves as a consequence of their export-led recovery and industrialization strategies, as Table 6.4 demonstrates, however, this

Figure 6.3   Asia (excluding China): net private capital flows

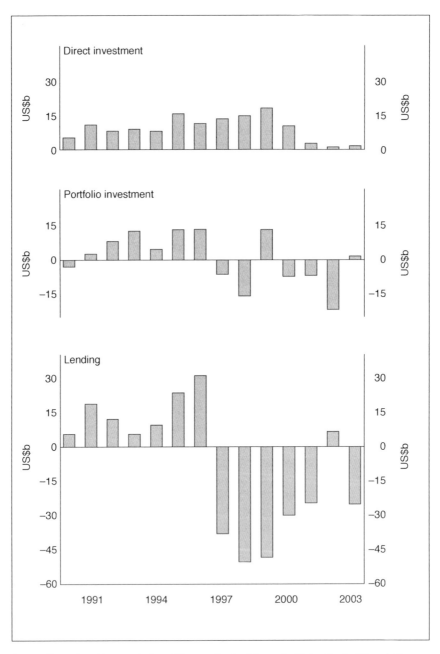

Source: Reproduced by permission of Reserve Bank of Australia 'Asian Capital Flows', *Reserve Bank of Australia Bulletin*, August 2004: Graph 9; original sources of data CEIC; IMF; national sources.

capital is not necessarily being invested locally, but is going offshore to fund America's shortfall in savings. As Andrew Crockett (2002) observes, 'it is hard to believe that East Asia should be an exporter of savings in the longer-term, or that the US deficit is indefinitely sustainable'.

Conclusion

Post-crisis East Asia is consequently characterized by a number of paradoxes. Although the USA currently retains a unique ability to exploit its pre-eminence,[32] the fact that it has to, and is increasingly reliant upon others to make up for its domestic economic shortcomings, is indicative of its relative decline (Ravenhill 2006). But America's reliance on, and interdependency with, East Asia is a two-way street: East Asian economies remain highly dependent on both continuing access to American consumer markets to underpin their export-led growth strategies, and on the ability of American consumers themselves to keep consuming. This relationship is usually analysed in terms of structural imbalances, the possible impact of rising interest rates, and the propensity for bubbles in the housing and equity markets to collapse, with potentially major implications for Asia. But it is worth noting in passing that there is something fundamentally inequitable and potentially unsustainable about the global economy if it is dependent on Americans consuming even more of the world's diminishing, finite resources than they already do. These issues will be taken up in the last chapter, as they play surprisingly little role in mainstream debates about the USA's relations with East Asia.

Thus far, East Asians have shown little capacity to exploit, or interest in exploiting, their potential structural leverage over the USA. This is somewhat surprising given the remarkable build-up in East Asia's foreign exchange reserves noted above. However, things may be changing as a consequence of both the crisis itself and a growing awareness of the potential efficacy of regional monetary mechanisms. Perhaps the most fundamental impact of the crisis was to heighten awareness about the possible costs, as well as the advantages of deeper integration into the global economy (Beeson 2003a). As we shall see in more detail in the next chapter, many of the most significant attempts at regional policy coordination have revolved around monetary cooperation and the desire to create regional crisis-management mechanisms. Not only might this provide greater economic stability, but it might also give a degree of political or institutional autonomy to a region increasingly conscious of its vulnerability to external economic and political forces.

There are, therefore, powerful practical and/or functional reasons driving greater cooperation in East Asia that flow directly from structural changes in the international economy. On the one hand, concern is increasingly being voiced about the willingness of Asian central banks to keep funding the US deficit because of doubts about the long-term position of the American economy and the value of dollar-denominated assets.[33] The danger for Asia, of course, is that its investors risk triggering the very crisis they fear if they appear to be acting on such concerns. On the other hand, there is a growing recognition that East Asian economies are not just failing to take advantage of their own remarkably high levels of savings, but that they are actively increasing the risks facing their economies by not developing adequate domestic or regional financial structures. As Jennifer Amyx points out: 'Many countries in East Asia maintain high savings rates but, because of the absence of stable long-term debt markets, the saving deposited into local banks tended to be funneled out to international financial centers and then back into the region as short-term currency loans' (Amyx 2005: 4). At present, therefore, East Asia has the worst of all worlds, gaining neither the benefits of its own savings nor the security of 'safe' investments. The attractions of developing a regional bond market in such circumstances are consequently manifold, as it might reduce exposure to unmanageable external risks while making capital more readily available within the region itself. Whether it is achievable is as much a political question as it is a 'technical' one, as we shall see in the next chapter.

In the longer term, therefore, the crisis had a number of important consequences for the region and its relationship with key external actors that merit re-emphasis. First, the relative standing of the East Asian region was undoubtedly diminished. If this was the consequence of a measured, well-informed reading of regional investment prospects on the part of key market participants, resulting in a more realistic and sustainable view of the former miracle economies, it might prove to be no bad thing. The signs are not good, however, as a 'China mania' appears to have replaced the more generalized East Asian variety, with China receiving an astounding 97 per cent of all net FDI in 2003. In an ominously familiar pattern, 60 per cent of foreign bank lending to China is now short term. However, lending and portfolio capital flows into China are only about half the size of FDI (Reserve Bank of Australia 2004: 59), so some of the more dangerous imbalances that characterized Southeast Asia before the crisis are not as evident. But the scale and increased importance of the Chinese economy means that a crisis there would have even more profound implications for both the regional and wider international economies. The situation in other parts of the region is equally concerning, with footloose, highly mobile, short-term capital flooding back into the region and pushing up equity markets in a manner that resembles the earlier crisis period.[34]

The second long-term impact of the crisis is more narrowly East Asian and is manifest in the growing interest in regional cooperation, especially in the area of finance. As we shall see in the next chapter, progress has been limited and there are formidable obstacles to this process, but the fact that such efforts are increasingly institutionalized and formalized is of potential long-term significance. At the very least, such initiatives add some weight to East Asian regionalism and have the potential to reshape relations with key extra-regional actors, including the USA and the IFIs. They also offer the possibility for East Asian countries more actively and assertively to manage the manner in which their economies are integrated into the wider global economy. Whether they are able to do so remains as much a political question as it is one of state capacity, and one that will be largely determined by the nature of intra- and inter-regional relationships and the historical factors that have shaped them.

Chapter 7

The Evolution of East Asian Regionalism

For a region that is so synonymous with difference and diversity, it is remarkable that *any* progress towards formal regional institutionalization should have occurred. After all, regionalism is associated with the self-conscious pursuit of political cooperation and coordination, something that the region's often traumatic history and the rather obsessive preoccupation with national sovereignty would seem to preclude. And yet, the reality is that not only is Southeast Asia home to one of the most enduring inter-governmental organizations outside Europe, ASEAN, but the region as a whole is displaying a much greater interest in the possibility of developing a wider, more ambitious and inclusive East Asian institutional architecture than history might lead us to expect. Potentially the most important of these initiatives, and the one with the capacity to give political expression to the idea of a discrete East Asian region, is ASEAN+3; consequently, it is given most attention in what follows. While it is still too early to say how the ASEAN+3 process – which involves China, Japan and South Korea in addition to the ASEAN countries – will evolve, or how it will fit in with other proposals such as the East Asian Summit, the very fact that *anything* is happening in a region with East Asia's history and renowned heterogeneity is interesting and worthy of further exploration. If East Asia can develop effective institutional forums to address collective action problems and give expression to some of the region's distinctive ideas about political, economic and security issues, this will be a development of long-term global significance.

To help make a judgement about the prospects for greater region-wide cooperation, it is important to look at the record of achievement so far. Consequently, I begin this chapter by looking at two of ASEAN+3's most important institutional precursors: ASEAN itself and the APEC forum. As we shall see, the former does have the great merit of being more authentically of the East Asian region in a way that the all-encompassing, amorphous APEC grouping never was or could be (Beeson 2006b). Both organizations have had their problems and neither bodes well for ASEAN+3's prospects (which helps to account for the high levels of scepticism surrounding this project: Hund 2003; Lincoln 2004).

Nevertheless, ASEAN+3 has developed a degree of momentum which suggests that there is a 'demand' for it, or something like it, on the part of many of the region's policy-making elites.[1] Whether this will prove sufficient to overcome some of the well-known tensions between the rival regional leadership aspirants, Japan and China, remains to be seen. What we can say, however, is that the USA may not be able to block such developments as easily as it did during the 1990s, when the former Malaysian Prime Minister, Mahathir, proposed an East Asian-style grouping which was effectively vetoed as a consequence of American opposition. I detail this episode and explain how the dynamics underpinning regional initiatives have changed in the intervening period.

Building on the earlier analyses of East Asia's distinct geostrategic position, I suggest that the course of institutional development in the region reflects, and is in some ways a response to, wider historical reconfigurations of international security, as well as the more obvious and important restructuring of the international political economy detailed in the preceding chapter. Indeed, when seen in this context, it is possible to argue that even if East Asian regionalism is not a certainty, neither is it as remote a possibility as it once seemed, and that the preconditions for greater East Asian cooperation excluding the United States are potentially in place. Moreover, it is also clear that China is becoming a more important influence on processes of regionalism, and in ways that threaten to permanently eclipse Japan's long-standing influence over processes of regionalization.

The world the Cold War made:[2] ASEAN and Southeast Asian regionalism

ASEAN is very much a product of the geopolitical circumstances described in Chapter 3. Its inauguration in 1967 occurred in the midst of the Cold War stand-off between the communist and capitalist powers, a confrontation that occasionally spilled over into actual conflict. The wars in Korea and Vietnam were vivid illustrations of the Cold War's potential to become 'hot' and move beyond ideological posturing, with catastrophic consequences for some of the countries of the region. Even where countries were not drawn directly into such conflicts, the possibility of domestic conflict or insurgency continued to haunt the region. The bloodbath associated with Suharto's rise to power and the crushing of the communist insurgency provided a salutary reminder to Southeast Asia's ruling elites about how precarious their hold on power was, and how traumatic regime change could be (see Cribb 1990). This combination of domestic fragility and a vulnerability to external forces that the individual countries of the region had little capacity to control or influence provided the catalyst for cooperation in Southeast Asia (Frost 1990). In many ways, it still does (Beeson 2002a).

ASEAN's original membership – Indonesia, Malaysia, Singapore, Thailand and the Philippines – represented the key countries of Southeast Asia, but from the outset their mutual relationships and the rationale for ASEAN itself were constrained by the overarching imperatives of the wider geopolitical context. The original Bangkok Declaration is a remarkably bland document that suggests that ASEAN's purpose will be to 'accelerate economic growth, social progress and cultural development in the region through joint endeavours in the spirit of equality and partnership in order to strengthen the foundation for a prosperous and peaceful community of South-East Asian Nations' (ASEAN 1967). Although the emphasis here and throughout the original Declaration is on encouraging economic development, prosperity and technical cooperation, the sub-text is all about enhancing security in what was seen as a fundamentally unstable and threatening regional environment. At one level, the catalyst for cooperation was transnational and geostrategic: the Vietnam War was at its height and profoundly affecting the foreign policy orientations and calculations of political elites across the region. At another level, however, the domestic spillover of Cold War conflicts and ideological struggles was focusing the attention of regional elites on mechanisms for strengthening domestic and regional stability. The need to reintegrate post-Sukarno Indonesia into the region in a manner that shored up both Indonesia's and the region's stability was paramount in the minds of Southeast Asian policy-makers.

Given the region's previous attempts at developing regionally-based institutions, there was initially no reason to suppose that ASEAN would endure. The Association of Southeast Asia (ASA) between Thailand the Philippines and Malaysia was derailed by the conflict between the Philippines and Malaysia over the disputed territory of Sabah. Similarly, the short-lived MAPHILINDO initiative between Malaysia, the Philippines and Indonesia was undermined by the perception that it was primarily a device with which to frustrate the emergence of the proposed Malaysian Federation. Despite the failure of these initiatives, they did pave the way for the development of ASEAN which drew on some of these earlier organizations' principles, especially ASA's 'institutional formlessness and lack of binding obligations' (Weatherbee 2005: 69). This sort of structure and institutional logic has been the hallmark of ASEAN; it has also been both a key to its longevity and a source of its ineffectiveness.

Despite all the talk about economic and technical cooperation, ASEAN's principal attraction in the eyes of its original members lay in its potential to enhance domestic and regional security, whilst simultaneously providing a forum within which to manage potentially fractious intra-regional relations. With the memories of *Konfrontasi* between Malaysia and Indonesia still fresh,[3] and Singapore feeling vulnerable following its expulsion from the Malaysian Federation, ASEAN members were understandably preoccupied with managing their inter-relationships and domestic security. The salience of strategic issues was given further weight following the enunciation of the Nixon Doctrine in 1969 and the possible winding back of America's strategic commitment to the region (Yahuda 2004). At the very least, the ASEAN grouping had the potential to give its members a greater collective presence and an enhanced capacity to respond to common threats. That it has rarely been able to do so tells us much about the challenges that continue to constrain regional cooperation.

Paradoxically, ASEAN's most distinctive institutional and ideational contribution has been central to its longevity, but also the principal reason for its ineffectiveness: the so-called 'ASEAN Way'. Although it is not clear where the term came from and precisely what it means, the ASEAN Way is, according to Acharya (2001: 63), 'a term favoured by the ASEAN leaders themselves to describe the process of intra-mural interaction and to distinguish it from other, especially Western, multilateral settings'. As Acharya (2001: 64) further points out, it is indicative of a '*process* of regional interactions and cooperation based on discreteness, informality, consensus building and non-confrontational bargaining styles' (emphasis in original). Not only is there very little chance of regional elites losing 'face' in such circumstances, but it is a modus operandi that is contrasted favourably with what is seen as an adversarial and excessively legalistic Western model.

At the centre of the ASEAN Way is the principle of non-interference in the domestic affairs of other member countries. However, it is precisely ASEAN's apparent inability to address contentious issues that makes it ineffective according to some critics (Narine 1999; Smith and Jones 1997). The possible limitations of the ASEAN Way have been highlighted by some of ASEAN's more liberal members, such as Thailand, which have advocated developing a more 'flexible' approach to intra-regional relations that would allow comment on the domestic affairs of other members (Haacke 1999). There also appears to be an increased willingness on the part of some members to overcome ASEAN's institutional limitations by employing more legalistic strategies and involving international institutions in the resolution of economic and territorial disputes within the Southeast Asian region (Kahler 2000), in a tacit acknowledgement of ASEAN's limitations.

There are a number of important issues that ASEAN's history highlights, that have implications for the future of East Asian regionalism more generally, and for comparisons with other organizations such as APEC. First, can indigenously developed norms and practices of socialization actually influence the behaviour of states, either in East Asia or elsewhere? Here the evidence is mixed. On the one hand, Charrier (2001) has persuasively argued that the very existence of ASEAN as an institution and the repeated elite-level interactions this has fostered have actually gone a long way to bringing the idea of a Southeast Asian region into being through sheer repetition and habituation. Similarly, Acharya (2004) has argued that ASEAN norms of consultation and consensus have become part of the institutional make-up of organizations such as the ARF, and have ultimately affected the behaviour of even the most powerful countries, such as the USA. On the other hand, of course, it is possible to cite numerous examples of unilateral American behaviour that takes little notice of even the closest allies' wishes, which has become especially apparent in the 'war on terror' and its impact on Southeast Asia (Beeson 2004b). Moreover, as we saw in Chapter 3, ASEAN's finest diplomatic hour – the resolution of the Cambodian conflict – was successful because its goals coincided with, and furthered the preferences of, the USA and China, and not because their behaviour was changed by ASEAN.

The second major issue that ASEAN highlights is about the role of less powerful nations in the evolution of wider regional processes. Although it needs to be acknowledged that there has not been a conflict between members since ASEAN's inauguration (Kivimaki 2001), its record of achievement is modest and its future uncertain. While it is impossible to know whether intra-regional conflict might have occurred in the absence of ASEAN, it seems reasonable to assume that its existence and the institutionalization and regularization of intra-regional relations and interactions has contributed to stability in Southeast Asia. And yet, ASEAN's capacity to shape regional outcomes and behaviour looks certain to be eroded. On the one hand, the steady expansion of ASEAN's original membership[4] means that it may prove increasingly difficult to socialize new members (such as Burma) into 'good' behaviour, or to implement initiatives among members with limited state capacity (Narine 1999). On the other hand, the emergence of more encompassing institutions (such as ASEAN+3) threatens to make ASEAN a less influential caucus within a larger entity.

ASEAN's efforts to facilitate economic integration suggest that its economic initiatives may fare little better than its political ones. Given the original priority attached to 'accelerating economic growth', it is surprising that trade and investment initiatives have not enjoyed a more prominent place in ASEAN's developmental priorities. Yet, when

we remember that ASEAN's 'real' motivation was originally geopolitical and strategic rather than economic, this is perhaps unsurprising.
Likewise, the fact that Southeast Asia's primary trade links lay outside
the region and that its economies were inherently competitive also
made intra-regional cooperation more difficult. But in the aftermath of
the Cold War, when economic issues increasingly displaced strategic
ones on the agendas of policy-makers everywhere (Luttwak 1990),
ASEAN was forced to give much greater attention to facilitating
economic development and cooperation. In this regard, the development of the ASEAN Free Trade Area (AFTA) was 'as much about building post-Cold War cohesion and increasing ASEAN's credibility as it
was an attempt to boost the region's gross domestic product'
(Henderson 1999: 22).

Bowles and MacLean (1996) suggest three factors underpinned
AFTA's development. First, changes in the international political economy – especially the Plaza Accord discussed in previous chapters, and
the formation of trade blocs in other parts of the world – combined to
reconfigure the external political and economic environment within
which the ASEAN economies operated. Second, Bowles and MacLean
argue that ASEAN needed to reinvent itself and develop a new *raison
d'être* in a reconfigured geopolitical environment in which former
strategic imperatives were no longer as compelling. Finally, they stress
the importance of 'a shift in the internal power structures within the
ASEAN states toward business interests' (Bowles and MacLean 1996:
331). Given the privileging of business interests that has characterized
the developmental strategies of so many East Asian nations, this may
seem an unremarkable observation. But, as we saw in earlier chapters,
there has been a steady reconfiguring of state–business links across the
region as indigenous businesses have become more integrated into the
wider world economy. As Richard Stubbs (2000) points out, the underlying political dynamic in many Southeast Asian nations has changed
as the relative influence of economic nationalists and internationally-
oriented advocates of liberalization has shifted decisively in favour of
the latter, giving AFTA the requisite political momentum to, at least,
become a key part of the region's policy agenda.

Although most analyses of AFTA have unsurprisingly focused on its
impact on trade liberalization and the difficulties it has experienced in
actually realizing its original, highly ambitious tariff reduction
agenda,[5] Helen Nesadurai points out that a regional investment strategy was also an important part of the AFTA process. Indeed, she makes
it clear that the ASEAN states attempted to privilege indigenous
investors over FDI, using regional strategies and agreements as a way
of accommodating global forces and pressures. In this regard, what

Nesadurai (2003: 99) calls 'developmental regionalism' offered a way of countering the 'hegemony of foreign MNCs', and was sharply at odds with the sort of 'open regionalism' that was being promoted by IFIs such as APEC, which were more attuned to the dominant Washington Consensus. Seen in this way, AFTA may have had a dual appeal for the political elites of Southeast Asia: on the one hand, it acted as a signalling device to foreign investors that the region was still broadly committed to the principles of trade integration and liberalization (Bowles 2000), and keen to facilitate regionally-oriented FDI;[6] on the other hand, however, within this broader trade-oriented framework, the potential for creative political 'intervention' and investment guidance still existed.

The other point to emphasize is that the reform agenda was not necessarily an inevitable threat to those political and economic interests that were capable of responding proactively to the seemingly inevitable reformist and competitive pressures. On the contrary, while some of the pressures associated with globalization are necessarily universal, the way nationally embedded actors respond to them is not. Etel Solingen (2004) has detailed how 'internationalizing constituencies' in various Southeast Asian countries were able to take advantage of international restructuring to consolidate their position and power. Even where individual leaders may have been toppled, as in Indonesia, the underlying patterns of power and interest remained largely intact or were actually consolidated as they moved to exploit new opportunities. As Kanishka Jayasuriya points out:

> Trade liberalization or open economic policies have served to consolidate a particular economic and political bargain between a politically connected non-tradable sector and an open-orientated export sector. From the late 1980s the state-led development projects gave way to a system of *nomenklatura* capitalism: powerful domestic cartels connected to the ruling apparatus of political power. (Jayasuriya 2003: 350)

This '*nomenklatura* capitalism', or the close connections between political elites and economically insulated cartels, has often been able to adjust to the changing international circumstances and respond positively to initiatives such as AFTA. For all of AFTA's problems with implementation, delayed timetables and problems with 'sensitive' industries, therefore, it becomes easier to understand why it continued to enjoy support within the region. It also becomes easier to understand why other institutions had less appeal.

The post-Cold War and the rise and fall of Asia Pacific Economic Cooperation

When the Asia Pacific Economic Cooperation forum was inaugurated in 1989, it looked like an idea whose time had come. With the Cold War at an end and economic issues increasingly central parts of foreign policy agendas throughout the world, the establishment of an organization that was intended to facilitate trade relations between the eastern and western sides of the Pacific seemed timely and appropriate. Initially, the prospects for APEC seemed relatively bright, and its inauguration in 1989 was accompanied by much hyperbole and optimism, especially in Australia and Japan, which had done more than any other countries to bring the APEC initiative to fruition. That such hopes and ambitions have generally not been realized tells us much about the difficulties of institutional consolidation in East Asia and beyond, and provides an insight into the sort of problems that may confront other initiatives similar to ASEAN+3.

The fact that it was Japan and Australia that provided much of the intellectual capital and political leadership for APEC is in itself revealing. Both countries were concerned about the development of trade blocs elsewhere and the possibility of being locked out of key markets, as well as with their relationship to the rapidly expanding East Asian region upon which both were dependent in different ways (Beeson and Yoshimatsu 2006). Despite its own flagrant shortcomings as a genuine free trader (Lincoln 1990), Japan had assiduously promoted the idea of a Pacific free trade area for many years (Korhonen 1994). While such an arrangement was clearly in its interests, as it was reliant on continuing access to protectionist North American markets to underpin its own economic model, it is significant that Japan's diplomatic ambitions then, as now, were hamstrung by history. In such circumstances, the Japanese encouraged Australia to take the running in promoting a new economic grouping dedicated to trade promotion and liberalization (Funabashi 1995).

Australia had its own reasons for being enthusiastic abut being a member of an institution that included its key trade partners. Indeed, so significant were trade relations considered to be during the 1980s by Australia's then Labour government that former Prime Minister Bob Hawke's original proposal did not even include its key strategic partner, the USA.[7] While such an omission is unthinkable in the contemporary geopolitical environment under Australia's current Liberal government (Beeson 2003b), it is indicative of the concern Australian officials felt in the late 1980s about the possibility of being excluded from a region upon which Australia's economic future was increasingly dependent. Although the principal driving force for this re-orientation may have been material

and manifest in Australia's rapidly expanding resource exports to industrializing Asia, it also had a crucially important ideational dimension: not
only was Australia involved in a long-term national discussion about
identity, multi-culturalism and relations with the region, but the nature
of that 'engagement' with Asia was the product of a highly influential,
long-running public policy debate (Beeson 1999b; Keating 2000). This
debate was not only significant from an Australian perspective, but also
helped to influence the development of regional relations and patterns of
institutionalization more generally.

One of the most distinctive features of APEC's initial emergence was
the role played by an array of path-breaking institutions and individuals that helped shape economic debates in Australia and the wider
region. A number of 'track two' organizations[8] composed of various
combinations of academics, business figures and government officials
played a pivotal role in developing and actively championing a set of
beliefs that would eventually become part of APEC's agenda (see, for
example, Drysdale and Garnaut 1993). Central in this context were
arguments about the merits of economic integration, trade liberalization and a form of 'open regionalism' that did not discriminate against
outsiders. These individuals and organizations effectively constituted
an 'epistemic community',[9] assiduously promoting ideas that would
ultimately – it was hoped – be translated into public policy across the
region's mercantilist and comparatively closed economies in East Asia.
John Ravenhill's definitive study of APEC concludes that the Pacific
Trade and Development Conference (PAFTAD) played an especially
influential role in driving the APEC process forward, without which it
would 'probably not' have developed in the way it did (Ravenhill 2001:
88). And yet, despite the undoubted influence of such organizations and
the enthusiasm of their participants, the actual appeal of the ideas they
promoted and their capacity to be seamlessly translated into public
policy across the region always seemed overstated (Beeson 1996).

One of the key difficulties that has confronted APEC from its inception has been differences between its Anglo–American and Asian
members about the content and nature of the reform process. It is
rather ironic, therefore, that one of the reasons that APEC's trade liberalization agenda has proved hard to implement is that – in line with
ASEAN's modus operandi and in order to gain the support of Asian
members – all agreements within APEC are consensual and voluntary.
Similarly, APEC's secretariat (like ASEAN's, but unlike the EU's) is tiny,
and has no capacity to enforce agreements or ensure member compliance. These underlying realities are reflected in APEC's distinctive
reformist discourse, with its relance on 'concerted unilateralism',
which effectively recognized that many Asian governments were reluc-

tant to sign up to binding agreements. As Ravenhill (2001: 142–3) points out, this is a major practical and conceptual problem for an agenda premised on the supposed merits of mutually-beneficial trade liberalization: 'essentially, APEC's members are left to decide for themselves what their obligations are and when they will aspire to meet them' (Ravenhill 2001: 163). Not only is the contrast with the WTO – replete as it is with enforcement mechanisms and binding obligations – stark and revealing, but it begs the question of what purpose APEC serves, given the existence of a more powerful inter-governmental body with a similar reform agenda.

As has ASEAN, therefore, APEC has attempted to reinvent itself and broaden the scope of its activities beyond the narrow, technocratic preoccupation with trade liberalization: this agenda elicited less than universal enthusiasm in East Asia. One rather paradoxical consequence of this move is that APEC's greatest weakness could also become its greatest asset. One of the criticisms that has dogged APEC from the outset has revolved around the nature of its membership. APEC's original membership[10] included countries with little in common other than a fairly arbitrary relationship to the 'Asia-Pacific' region. This membership has been further expanded, or diluted, by the accession of a number of new entrants, including Russia (a country with only the most marginal claims to membership of a nominally 'regional' body). Russia's inclusion, which Paul Keating (1998), a former Australian Prime Minister and APEC advocate, described as an 'act of economic vandalism', tells us a number of things about regionalism in the Asia-Pacific generally and about APEC's development in particular.

First, the USA was always unconvinced about APEC and its voluntaristic style, and was willing to use it opportunistically or trade it off as part of its global strategic calculus.[11] Second, the composition of 'regional' organizations and the nature of regional identity itself is ultimately arbitrary (Woodside 1993). In this regard, though, as we shall see, some definitions of regions seem more 'authentic' and resonate more strongly than others. And yet, it is precisely APEC's diversity and broad member base that gives it a potentially unique role in the life of the 'Asia-Pacific': only APEC brings together the leaders of all the key regional economies, including Japan, China and the USA, in the same forum as Taiwan, as well as the Southeast Asian countries that are currently the focus of so much strategic angst. Consequently, some of the most recent APEC Leaders' Meetings have been preoccupied with such things as the war on terror, peace-keeping in East Timor, and the proliferation of weapons of mass destruction in the region, rather than the arcane challenges of promoting trade liberalization.

After APEC?

It is a measure of APEC's increasing irrelevance and its inability to pursue its original goals that multilateral trade liberalization is no longer a major part of regional diplomacy. Indeed, the most important development as far as trade relations are concerned, both within East Asia and within the more broadly conceived Asia-Pacific region, has been the rapid growth of *bilateral* trade agreements. In this regard, APEC's record of non-achievement is partly to blame. Some member countries were concerned about APEC's inability to deliver trade liberalization, while others – especially Korea and Japan – were concerned that it might force them to open politically sensitive domestic sectors to external competition (Ravenhill 2003: 300). Either way, support for APEC waned. When combined with the failure of both the WTO and AFTA to promote trade liberalization, the attractions of bilateral preferential trade deals increased (partly through example). As Christopher Dent (2003) points out, the growth in bilateral trade agreements rapidly gained a self-sustaining momentum from the late 1990s. Significantly, Singapore was an especially prominent exponent of bilateral trade agreements, being unhappy with the pace of trade liberalization in the region, but non-threatening for other potential partners concerned about reciprocal access to their own protected agricultural sectors. Although the USA was relatively slow in jumping on the bilateral bandwagon, it has recently become heavily involved in such initiatives and its efforts to link this to wider security objectives look likely to entrench this approach for the foreseeable future (Beeson 2006c; Higgott 2004).

The diminished importance of multilateralism has implications that extend beyond APEC, although the credibility of this institution seems certain to be permanently undermined by recent developments. APEC's reduced influence is also emblematic of a lack of leadership and support for multilateralism on the part of the USA (Webber 2001), without which such organizations will have little chance of success.[12] While the growing preference for unilateral and bilateral policy options can be seen as part of a more general foreign policy re-orientation on the part of the current Bush administration (Beeson and Higgott 2005; Daalder and Lindsay 2003), in an East Asian context it is also allowing China to assume a much more prominent position as a consequence. As Alice Ba (2003) has astutely pointed out, China's free trade agreement with ASEAN seems certain to consolidate its position in Southeast Asia and counter the USA's hegemonic influence in the region. The fact that US Secretary of State, Condoleezza Rice, chose not to attend the recent ASEAN Summit in Vientiane was widely seen as a significant downgrading of American interest in the region, and one that compared unfavourably with China's assiduous courting of its Southeast Asian neighbours.[13]

Thus, despite APEC's attempts to reinvent itself as a quasi-security organization, it already looks like a body whose time has passed. In part, this can be attributed to the narrowness of its initial agenda: not only did some of APEC's original supporters overestimate the intrinsic appeal of the rather technocratic discourse that surrounded its original trade liberalization blueprint, but they seriously underestimated the political obstacles that confronted its implementation. Powerful vested interests, especially in agriculture and uncompetitive manufacturing industries, were always going to make compliance problematic. Likewise, the recurring divisions that distinguish East Asian and Anglo–American approaches to policy content and application were always likely to make consensus difficult; the non-binding nature of commitments could only paper over such cracks. In any case, for much of the East Asian part of the Asia-Pacific region the focus of policy attention is no longer on trade but on investment and the flows of capital that played such a destabilizing role in the East Asian crisis (Hamilton-Hart 2004). Indeed, what arguably sealed APEC's fate was its own invisibility in the aftermath of the East Asian crisis, and the fatal lack of support from an American government that has often preferred other mechanisms through which to pursue its foreign policy objectives (Beeson 1999b). It is important to recognize – as governments in the region increasingly have – that the USA enjoys the privilege of pursuing what Richard Haas, Director of Policy Planning at the State Department, described as 'a la carte multilateralism' when it suits its purposes (cited in Pempel 2004: 27). It is precisely such inconsistent and opportunistic behaviour that has led even prominent realists to recognize that American policy may be undermining its own position and actually contributing to the growth of an alternative, more coherent East Asian position (Brzezinski 2004: 127).

The emergence of East Asian regionalism

As we saw in Chapter 2, the idea of a distinct East Asian region dominated by either China or, more recently, Japan, is not a new phenomenon. What is different about today's East Asian regional order, however, is that both the regional giants are strong at the same time and actively competing to assert themselves (an unprecedented development in regional history). The interaction between Japan and China, and their capacity to accommodate or adjust to the ambitions and development of each other will be one of the defining dynamics of the East Asian region in the twenty-first century; but it is a dynamic that will be overlaid by the influence of an international order that remains dominated by the USA. Just how important and influential the USA will continue to be is a matter of debate, but it clearly still has the capacity to influence the course of regional development in East Asia. To gain some impression about the nature of its influence and the way American foreign policy towards the region is evolving, it is useful to revisit briefly a recent abortive effort to initiate an distinctively East Asian grouping.

One of the most important, prominent and outspoken advocates of the 'Asianisation of Asia' (Funabashi 1993) and the promotion of Asian values has been Malaysia's former Prime Minister, Mahathir. As a tangible expression of this impulse, Mahathir promoted the idea of an exclusively 'Asian' trading bloc from the early 1990s onwards. Although the proposed East Asian Economic Caucus (EAEC) was never actually realized, it paved the way for ASEAN+3 and included all of the countries that would eventually constitute the new grouping: that is, the ASEAN countries, plus China, Japan and South Korea. For Mahathir, the key to the development of an exclusively East Asian bloc was Japan, an idea he developed in a co-authored volume with the prominent Japanese nationalist, Ishihara Shintaro.[14] Given Mahathir's admiration of Japan, his 'Look East' policy, his well-known antipathy towards the West, and the importance of the Japanese economy to Malaysia and the rest of the region, such views are unsurprising. What is more surprising, perhaps, was Japan's complete inability to fulfil the sort of leadership role Mahathir envisioned. Despite what Glenn Hook (1999: 226) describes as Mahathir's ' "love call" from the "periphery" to the "core" ', Japan studiously ignored his overtures and declined the opportunity to play a leadership role in the region.

Malaysia's proposal was met with outright hostility from the USA, which was concerned about the development of an exclusive regional bloc over which it might have little influence. In Mark Berger's (1999: 1,026) view, the failure of Mahathir's initiative at this time 'symbolised the limits to any and all regional challenges to US hegemony in the Asia-Pacific'. Japan's failure to accept Malaysia's invitation can be easily explained: its reactive foreign policy, sensitivities about its war-time role within the region, and above all its continuing strategic and economic dependence on the USA meant that it was incapable of doing otherwise (Drifte 1996: 143). What requires explanation now, though, is why the sort of East Asian regionalism that Mahathir championed has re-emerged under the banner of ASEAN+3. More pointedly, why is Japan now an active participant in such a grouping, and why does American opposition appear to have diminished?

In the context of the long-term development of the region as a more distinct whole with common interests and issues to confront, it is impossible to overstate the importance of the financial crisis of the late 1990s. Not only did this radically affect the way in which regional political and economic elites perceived their relationship to each other, but it also had a major impact on relations between the region and external actors. As we saw in the last chapter, the crisis and the subsequent role of the IFIs and the USA profoundly influenced East Asian views about the global economy and the region's relationship with it. At one level, this was manifest in an increased interest in developing cooperative mechanisms and strategies with which to manage the region's integration with the wider international economy. At another level, the reconfigured nature of intra- and inter-regional relations was evident in Japan's evolving policy stance. As Terada (2003) points out, one of the most important developments in this regard was 'Japan's realization that a consensus had developed that the time was ripe to create East Asian regionalism solely to tackle regional problems'. That Japan's initial leadership forays were squashed by the USA and its institutional allies should not obscure the fact that Japan's post-crisis policy has been characterized by a number of attempts to play a leadership role in the region (Hughes 2000). The other factor driving this process has been China's highly successful attempts to consolidate its influence in Southeast Asia. Again, the fact that Japan's efforts to establish similar free trade deals with ASEAN have not met with as much success as China's may be less important in the longer term than the underlying dynamic that is fuelling their respective diplomatic efforts.

Before considering how this competition for regional influence is playing itself out in any detail, though, it is important to try to answer the other question that is posed by EAEC/ASEAN+3's re-emergence: why has the USA adopted a less obstructionist position on this occasion? Michael Wesley suggests the Bush administration is relaxed about the re-emergence of a more exclusive form of East Asian regionalism because it has historically been able to assert itself through extant multi-lateral and bilateral channels in East Asia, and because the new regionalism 'had showed itself to US policy makers to be incapable of constituting a challenge to US power' (Wesley 2006: 66). Given the formidable obstacles that regional initiatives need to overcome and the strength of the USA's ties with Japan in particular, such a view seems plausible enough. America's preoccupation with Iraq, the war on terror, and an increasingly fractious relationship with Europe may also have made East Asia less of a priority for the USA. Whatever weight we give to causes, however, recent events have created a set of circumstances in which East Asian regionalism has gained additional momentum.

The development of monetary regionalism

The conspicuous failure of both APEC and ASEAN to provide leadership and support to the region's distressed economies in the aftermath of the crisis significantly diminished both organizations and made it increasingly clear that, if East Asians were to manage their own financial affairs, they would need to develop new mechanisms with which to do it. This perception was reinforced by two other developments, one long term, the other short. First, the principal focus of policy attention for many of the region's political and economic elites has shifted from trade to finance (Dieter and Higgott 2003), in line with a general transformation of East Asia's links with the global economy generally and as a consequence of the East Asian financial crisis in particular. The other factor which made it clear that East Asia lacked the political weight to independently manage regional financial relations was the fate of Japan's Asian Monetary Fund (AMF) initiative.

Japan's original proposal for an AMF involved it providing US$100 billion as the basis of an assistance package for economies suffering from speculative attacks on their currencies or balance of payments difficulties. Despite being widely welcomed in East Asia,[15] the proposal was vigorously opposed and effectively vetoed by both the IMF and the USA who were concerned that it would undermine their authority and control in the region (Stiglitz 2002: 112). This was an especially sensitive issue given the widespread perception that the conditionality attached to AMF loans would be a less stringent and invasive than those of the IMF (Chang and Rajan 2001). It was, of course, for precisely these reasons that the IMF and the USA were so hostile to it. Despite the fact that Japan's initial attempt at regional leadership collapsed in the face of this opposition, for some observers this period marked a watershed in inter-regional relations generally and between the USA and Japan in particular. In Katada's (2002) opinion, Japanese policy-makers:

became more interested in taking a leadership role to define and strengthen regional monetary cooperation in reaction to the way the United States and the IMF handled the Asian financial crisis . . . The idea behind these monetary initiatives is to reduce or balance Asian countries' current heavy reliance on the US dollar. Both of these initiatives appear as a large step towards the institutionalization of Asian economic regionalization in a pure 'Asian' form rather than an 'Asia-Pacific' one (which would include the major presence of the United States. (Katada 2002: 86)

Significant though this development is in terms of the evolution of both intra- and inter-regional relations, we need to be careful not to over-state its importance: not only was the original initiative squashed, but subsequent developments have been carefully crafted to comply with, and implicitly recognize the authority of, the overarching policy approach of the IMF. For example, the ASEAN Surveillance Process that was established as part of the 'Manila Framework' initiative devised by regional central bankers and finance ministers in the aftermath of the crisis was intentionally designed to be 'complimentary to the surveillance exercise undertaken by the IMF' (Manupipatong 2002: 112). In other words, the dominant paradigm overseen by the IFIs and promoted by the USA remained in place and provided the foundation for subsequent developments.

Similar constraints can be seen in the Chiang Mai Initiative (CMI), the most significant proposal to emerge in the area of monetary cooperation. The CMI is essentially a revival and expansion of Japan's aborted AMF proposal. If successfully realized, it has the potential both to reinforce and give direct expression to regionally-based cooperative processes such as ASEAN+3, and to provide a degree of stability to the region's fragile financial structures. The CMI had two main components: an expanded currency swap arrangement amongst the ASEAN countries and a network of bilateral swap agreements and a repurchase arrangement involving all 13 ASEAN+3 countries. There are, however, some significant limitations within the CMI. On the one hand, the available bail-out funds (US$1 billion) in the intra-ASEAN system are relatively small and still reliant on the IMF to provide back-up in the event of their proving inadequate. On the other hand, there are differences amongst members between those (such as Malaysia) who favour breaking ties with the IMF, and those (such as Singapore and Brunei) who are concerned about being committed to bailing-out their impoverished neighbours (Park and Wang 2005). This latter concern has also afflicted the wider ASEAN+3 strand of the CMI, with both Japan and China being concerned to ensure that any bilateral swap agreements (BSAs) they agreed to were linked to IMF conditionality (Ravenhill 2002: 192).

Consequently, some commentators have suggested that the CMI is too small to have much impact and that its bilateral structures do little to further the course of regional integration and cooperation (Lincoln 2004: 220–1). Clearly, there is something in such criticisms, but the fact that monetary cooperation continues to enjoy the support of regional governments and is a focus of continuing attention and policy interaction is not without significance either, especially in a region with little history of (or capacity for) these sorts of technically challenging, politically contentious cooperative interactions. C. Randall Henning has undertaken one of the most detailed analyses of the CMI and its impact, and it is worth quoting at length from his judicious overview:

The CMI does not create a new institution, nor does it pool the reserves of countries in the region under central management. Contrary to the hopes of enthusiasts for regional cooperation, the CMI does not even mobilize a substantial fraction of the foreign exchange reserves of the Northeast Asian three [China, Japan, and South Korea] . . . At the same time, the CMI provides the financial resources that are collectively important [and perhaps] more important, the bilateral swap arrangements provide a focus for concrete negotiations, periodic reviews among officials within the region, and the basis for building serious policy dialogue. These advances are in fact path-breaking: officials within the region have never before had such intensive, continuous negotiations and policy dialogue on a regional basis on monetary and financial matters. (Henning 2002: 29)

As Jennifer Amyx (2004a: 8) observes, despite some formidable implementation problems, 'the simple *process* of negotiating and concluding the BSAs has had a major impact on the ability of countries in the region to fend off future speculative attacks by giving rise to dense networks of communication between central bankers and finance ministers in the region' (Amyx 2004b: 8; emphasis in original). In this context, there are striking parallels between the interactions under way in the economic sphere and the sorts of confidence-building measures and socialization processes we saw in the security arena in Chapter 3. Given that economic crises have – thus far, at least – been catalysts for greater cooperation rather than confrontation, it is not entirely fanciful to suggest that the complex nature of regional–global interaction may actually be a spur to processes of regionalism. This certainly seems to have been the underlying dynamic driving the development of the ASEAN+3 process.

ASEAN+3

If the number of emerging diplomatic initiatives, groupings and proposed institutions is any indication, East Asian regionalism is, in the words of former Indonesian foreign minister Ali Alatas (2001), 'an idea whose time has come'. As yet, however, it is unclear which – if any – of the alternatives on offer is likely to prove the most important and durable. The inaugural meeting of the East Asian Summit (EAS) was held in Kuala Lumpur in December 2005, but produced little of substance. However, it was noteworthy for the fact that it contained a number of 'outsiders' including Australia, New Zealand and India, but not the United States, which was conspicuous by its absence. While this may have been symbolically significant, a number of key participants (such as Malaysia and China) saw the EAS as something of a distraction from the activities of

ASEAN+3. Indeed, it was noteworthy that the EAS unequivocally endorsed ASEAN+3 as the 'main vehicle' for achieving the longer-term goal of developing an East Asian Community (ASEAN 2005: 1). Consequently, despite the existence of a number of other initiatives and the difficulty of knowing what the relationship will be between the various bodies, it is useful to concentrate on ASEAN+3 as it is the most developed and unambiguously East Asian grouping developed thus far, and provides a useful insight into the prospects for East Asian regional initiatives more generally.

As noted above, ASEAN+3 is essentially Mahathir's EAEC grouping by another name, and contains all the countries in the original proposal. The re-badged grouping emerged as a consequence of an inter-regional dialogue with Europe, which convened under the banner of the Asia-Europe Meeting (ASEM). While ASEM may not have achieved anything terribly significant in itself, it did have the important long-term effect of consolidating the idea of East Asia as a coherent, collective actor with a distinct identity and one with the potential to counter-balance American hegemony (Camroux and Lechervy 1996). As we saw in Chapter 1, this sort of identity-building process is a vital precursor to the institutionalization of regional processes. This is a not insignificant development when we remember that Japan is a prominent member of ASEAN+3. The principal reason behind Japan's change of heart and willingness to participate in ASEAN+3 was its growing rivalry with China and the latter's agreement to accept ASEAN's invitation to participate in informal talks during the 1997 ASEAN Summit in Kuala Lumpur (Stubbs 2002: 443).

The catalyst for consolidating and formalizing this nascent grouping was the East Asian crisis. The crisis effectively dispelled any doubts about the desirability of some sort of grouping with which to address more narrowly conceived East Asian concerns. From 1998 onwards, ASEAN+3 summits have been held in conjunction with regular ASEAN summits, maintaining the appearance, if not the reality, that ASEAN remained the driving force of the emerging grouping. Following an APEC precedent, at the instigation of South Korean President Kim Dae-Jung, an East Asian Vision Group (EAVG) was established in 1998 to develop a blueprint for further cooperation under ASEAN+3 auspices. The EAVG, which was composed of independent experts, reported to an East Asia Study Group (EASG) composed of senior officials from member countries. The culmination of this welter of bureaucratic activity was the EASG's Final Report which spells out an agenda of 'concrete measures' that ASEAN+3 could and should undertake (EASG 2002). These recommendations revolve primarily around economic, financial, political and security, environmental and energy, as well as 'social, cultural and educational', cooperation.

Those who are optimistic about ASEAN+3's prospects suggest that, as with the evolution of monetary cooperation, the *process* is crucial. In this context, Nick Thomas (2002: 17) argues that the expansion of the meetings of ASEAN officials to include their counterparts in Northeast Asia is 'the most significant development in regional politics', and one that could presage the development of European-style policy coordination in the longer term. Richard Stubbs (2002) makes an even bolder set of claims about the prospects for ASEAN+3, arguing that the region's history and development are actually sources of common identity rather than an inevitable focus of dispute and division. In support of this thesis, he suggests that the distinctive institutions associated with Asian forms of capitalism, the historical circumstances from which they developed, and the values that distinguished them provide the basis for an emerging sense of regional, *Asian* identity.

Even if ASEAN+3 proves not to be the vehicle to carry the process of East Asian regionalism forward, the idea that there are a number of underlying drivers of regional integration with the capacity to overcome long-standing animosities is shared by other astute observers of regional development. T.J. Pempel, for example, suggests that in addition to the formal governmental processes and the integrative impact of Asian MNCs, regionalism is being consolidated by what he describes as 'ad hoc problem-oriented coalitions' of public and private sector organizations designed to tackle issues such as the SARS emergency, water management, energy issues and other trans-boundary problems. Consequently, Pempel (2005a: 256) argues that an exclusive focus on formal, inter-governmental cooperation as a measure of the prospects for regional consolidation is misconceived as 'the most overt and explicitly political institutions of East Asian regionalism are but a small part of the cumulative linkages that have developed across the region'.

This is a particularly important observation when we consider that the prospects for formal regional cooperation would seem especially bleak because of the deterioration in relations between Japan and China and, to a lesser extent, between Japan and South Korea. At the centre of the recent tensions between the Northeast Asian powers have been the long-standing sensitivities about Japan's historical role in the region. While it may be a truism that history inevitably shapes the present, and that East Asia's history is especially inauspicious in this regard, what has recently inflamed relations has been Prime Minister Koizumi's repeated visits to the Yakasuni Shrine, a symbol of Japanese militarism that infamously contains the remains of 14 'Class A' war criminals. At one level, this could be seen as simply an error of judgement or insensitivity about the symbolic importance of such visits as far as China is concerned, which regards them as 'antagonistic' acts.[16] Even if China's outrage is inflated for domestic purposes and a convenient way of damaging Japan's diplomatic ambitions,[17] it is important to recognize just how virulent anti-Japanese sentiment is in China, and what a potent force nationalism has been historically in that country. What is even more surprising and troubling, perhaps, is that reciprocal anti-Chinese feeling is growing in Japan[18] (ostensibly a beacon for democratic stability in the region) and that nationalism is becoming a stronger, more popular force within the LDP.[19] It is possible that the atmosphere surrounding Japan's relations in the region may change dramatically following Koizumi's expected departure from the political scene, and there are signs of that such a process may already be under way (Masaki 2005a). However, it is also apparent that anti-Chinese feeling may be becoming entrenched in the top levels of Japan's foreign policy-making establishment.[20]

The key question confronting not just Japan and China, therefore, but also the region more generally, is whether the increasingly important, mutually beneficial effects of greater economic integration can overcome deep-seated, long-standing political and strategic rivalries. Whatever the future of East Asian regionalism proves to be, it is worth remembering that asking a similar question about the future of Franco–German relations in the late 1940s might have evinced similar levels of scepticism to those that revolve around the prospects for East Asian regionalism (Hund 2003; Lincoln 2004; Ravenhill 2001). What we can say is that the growth of intra-regional trade and investment, or regionalization, is likely to give continuing momentum to the more formal processes of regionalism. What is most striking in this context is that, as we saw in the last chapter, Japan's importance to the region is declining relative to China's, and this may have long-term implications for the form that regional initiatives take. This is especially the case as a result of China's increasingly sophisticated diplomacy which is calculated to convince its neighbours about the non-threatening implications of its 'peaceful rise'.[21] It is also diminishing the influence and importance of the USA as it does so,[22] which ought to consolidate the importance of East Asian (as opposed to Asia-Pacific) organizations.

Thus, the possible evolution of East Asian regionalism is unclear and the evidence somewhat contradictory. On the one hand, there are many reasons for doubting whether East Asia's major powers can achieve a minimal working relationship, let alone provide the sort of individual or – even less likely – joint leadership that might drive the East Asian regionalism process forward. On the other hand, it seems that competition between China and Japan may actually be encouraging the development of a dense web of bilateral trade deals that is effectively 'networking the region' (Dent 2003),[23] and forcing closer ties and working relations between even testy neighbours such as China and Japan.[24] Likewise, the momentum that has been achieved in monetary cooperation via the ASEAN+3-sponsored CMI suggests that the demand for regional institutions and cooperation to resolve 'technical' problems is likely to grow despite intra-regional enmities. In the longer term, the very process involved in establishing such relationships may be as important as any specific outcomes they may deliver, as the remarkable transformation in the style and content of Chinese diplomacy since it became enmeshed in international institutions reminds us.

The future of East Asian regionalism will be taken up in the concluding chapter. The point to make at this stage is that the excess of institutional development and experimentation that is under way at the moment suggests that such initiatives are seen as potentially useful by regional policy-makers. It remains to be seen how the underlying region will be defined or the primary purpose to which such organizations will be put. But the disappointing record of the technocratic, issue-oriented APEC forum suggests that any future organization will need to have a more overtly political purpose and much stronger sense of regional identity and ownership if it is to enjoy the support of its members.

Conclusion

In the complex, multi-level dialectical interaction that constitutes global–regional–national relations as outlined in Chapter 1, we saw that regional processes can be a response to, or shaped by, global processes. The position of the state in such circumstances remains critical as a mediator of external pressures. Although such processes have gone less far in East Asia than in the EU, it is clear that even in supposedly sovereignty-obsessed East Asia cooperative attitudes and more flexible positions are emerging as a direct consequence of the challenges of globalization (Acharya 2002). The critical challenge for an East Asian region in which, for some countries, nation-building is still a relatively new and incomplete project is to accommodate external pressures – be they regional or global – while maintaining internal stability and coherence (Rozman 2004). Even those countries with the most established and enduring identities, such as Japan and especially China, must find ways of reconciling these competing pressures whilst simultaneously managing sometimes fractious international relations. Without wanting to underestimate the difficulties involved in this task, the ever-present possibility of miscalculation, or some completely unforeseen contingent circumstance, there are some encouraging indications as far as the development of East Asian regionalism is concerned.

There is, as we have seen, substantial evidence about the 'socializing' effects of institutionalized interaction on member states. For all the limited capacity of the ASEAN Secretariat to compel members to behave in particular ways, it is clear that continual interaction has gone a long way towards building trust and confidence in Southeast Asia. While Burma's continuing recalcitrance reminds us of the limits of this strategy, China's diplomatic charm offensive and the apparent change in its overall behaviour suggests that such socializing influences can be effective and significant. There is also a general recognition of the importance of economic stability and development for a region where regime legitimacy is frequently measured primarily in material terms. Regional institutions offer one way of managing and stabilizing such relations. While the degree of institutionalization and regularization on intra-regional relations in East Asia is a long way short of the EU, it has already become highly unlikely, if not quite unthinkable, that Japan and China could seriously contemplate war as a method of solving their fractious relations. The reality is that both parties would have far too much to lose and nothing to gain from such an outcome in the present circumstances. Much hinges on the sustainability of East Asia's remarkable growth, which all parties have a stake in seeing continue. Unfortunately for the region, the ability of various countries across the region to manage such a feat, and thus stabilize the existing order, may depend on more than state capacity, technocratic competence and functional intra-regional relations.

Chapter 8

East Asian Futures

Despite the fact that there are formidable obstacles confronting either the development of an EU-style regional organization in East Asia, or the sort of close relationships that have made the EU possible, East Asian regionalism is an idea that refuses to go away. While the degree of institutionalization and international coordination in an organization such as ASEAN+3 is nothing like as great as in the EU (Beeson and Jayasuriya 1998; Katzenstein 2005), as we saw in the last chapter there have been some noteworthy developments in the those areas where cooperation is arguably most pragmatically desirable. Seen in the long-term development of a region famous for its heterogeneity, its privileging of national sovereignty, and its mutual distrust and hostility, to say nothing of several of the bloodiest confrontations of the twentieth century, the bland-sounding (sometimes eye-glazing) efforts of regional officials to facilitate economic cooperation should not be underestimated. Not only do they help to build transnational relationships between key regional political and economic elites (Evans 2005), but they are also suggestive of a broader recognition of the importance of continuing economic development for the region as a whole. Throughout East Asia, economic development has conferred a performance legitimacy on regional governments that means political elites may have little choice other than to cooperate if they are to ensure the continuation of the development process in an era where 'global' forces and transborder economic integration mean that international coordination is a necessity rather than an option. The only question is what form it assumes.

Speculation about the future is necessarily a foolhardy enterprise, but it is made especially challenging by the complexity of the multi-dimensional factors that are likely to shape East Asia's possible future directions. While most attention has been given to the important economic drivers that have encouraged political cooperation in East Asia, the situation is even more complex than it may seem at first glance. Not only is the precise form of any putative regional institution still not certain, but neither are its constituent members. Even if the most important forms of institutionalization take place on the basis of an East Asian rather than an Asia-Pacific identity, relations between East Asia's major powers – China and Japan – remain unsettled and confrontational, and complicated by their respective relationships with the USA. These relationships would be complex and difficult to manage even if they were confined to narrowly conceived economic issues; unfortunately, they are not. In this context, it is important to recognize, as I have argued throughout this book, that the economic developments that have been the primary focus of attention in much of East Asia's recent history occur within a specific geopolitical context. In this regard, broadly conceived security issues are a major determinant of political relations as well as intra- and inter-regional economic connections. Consequently, East Asia's future development and its relations with other parts of the world are going to be determined by more than questions of economic efficiency and functional necessity.

The potentially mutually constitutive and constraining nature of economic, political and strategic factors was most dramatically evident in the context of the Cold War, when any possibility of developing an East Asian regional entity or identity was foreclosed. Even though the sort of ideological divisions that characterized this period have largely disappeared, this has not engendered some sort of Fukuyama-esque era of political and economic homogeneity. On the contrary, the political systems and even the economic structures of East Asia continue to display striking differences in their underlying organizational rationales and dynamics (Orrù, Biggart and Hamilton 1991). The logic of path-dependency and the embedded nature of particular vested interests and existing power structures suggests that such differences will not be easily eroded or rapidly disappear (Beeson 2002b). This is an especially important consideration when we remember that China, the country that is arguably doing most to redefine the East Asian region, is still nominally a 'communist' country, and one with a limited capacity to make the transition to a fully market-oriented economy, even if its ruling elites wished to do so.

If one prediction looks relatively uncontroversial it is that China, for better or worse, is likely to exert the greatest influence over the course of East Asian development in the foreseeable future. In the most optimistic reading of this process, China's 'peaceful rise' continues, generating rising living standards for its own population and an ever-expanding market for its neighbours. The process of political change already under way goes on, as an increasingly well-educated, politically-savvy citizenry encourages further domestic political reform and greater participation in inter-governmental institutions – institutions over which China comes to play a role in keeping with its growing economic and demographic weight. While this might strike some as an excessively Panglossian picture, there are substantial grounds for optimism as far as China is concerned. After all, it has *already* completely overturned expectations and preconceptions about the possible course of development in a country that was, until recently, synonymous with poverty and underdevelopment. Indeed, the recent history of China suggests that human beings generally seem to have a much better understanding of the prerequisites of the development process than they have ever done before, and that development really is – to some extent, at least – a 'technical' challenge that requires some fairly basic but achievable interventions if it is to occur (Sachs 2005).

All things being equal, therefore, we might expect that, at current rates of development and economic expansion, much of China's population could expect to enjoy living standards similar to those of other parts of developing Asia within a few decades. And yet, China faces developmental challenges that are historically unprecedented and on such a scale that they are profoundly affecting not just the economic development of the region, but the physical environment of which it is a part. The great tragedy as far as China – and the rest of the developing world, for that matter – is concerned is that, at the very moment when China's people appear to have made great strides towards solving the problem of economic development, there are fundamental doubts about its sustainability. Not only is China's breakneck development placing possibly unsupportable strains on the natural environment, but it is unclear where the resources and energy will come from to supply China's gargantuan appetites. In other words, China's remarkable and welcome growth, which has excited such optimism, may be creating the preconditions for major domestic instability and a possible clash with external interests in a zero-sum scramble for rapidly diminishing resources. In this final chapter, therefore, we need to consider whether East Asia and the world in general face an environmental crunch that makes the prospects for international cooperation and harmony an insubstantial pipe-dream, or whether institutionalized cooperative efforts offer the only feasible way of managing such challenges and are thus the key to the region's future development.

Return of the resource curse?

Making sense of the environmental constraints that face East Asia and the world more generally is complicated by the degree of uncertainty and unpredictability about some of the most basic issues. Disagreement is so widespread and ideologically-loaded that it is difficult for even the specialist to make definitive judgements about the implications of complex phenomena such as climate change. Furthermore, judgements about the 'value' of the natural environment inevitably have a subjective

dimension that tends to reflect the physical, political and economic position of the observer. Whether developing countries have any less right to
do what they want to with 'their' resources than the West did is still a
moot point, even if the disastrous consequences of such exploitation are
becoming all too clear. What we can say is that human beings would seem
entitled to certain universal basic rights simply on the basis of their
humanity and that the same standards and principles should apply everywhere (Shue 1980).

In this context, we ought to keep in mind one of the recurring themes
of this book: history matters. Going early in the industrialization process
had major advantages,[1] not the least of which was the capacity ruthlessly
to exploit the environment before the implications and limits of such
actions became all too apparent. Britain, the USA and the other early
industrializing countries, along with the corporations that developed
within them, enjoyed significant 'first mover advantages' in establishing
dominant positions in an emerging global economy (Chandler 1990; H.J.
Chang 2002). Crucially, they were able to ravage their own environments
as they 'developed' free of the global constraints that are now becoming
clearer. Anyone who has read Charles Dickens knows that Britain's
economic rise generated problems of social dislocation and environmental degradation similar to those afflicting China and the developing
world today. In Britain's case, economic development clearly gave it the
wherewithal to 'solve' some of its own environmental problems in ways
that seem impossible today. It was able to do so at least in part by exploiting the resources of the developing world (Blaut 1993). Britain was also
able to export some of its surplus population in ways that are simply not
possible now. Indeed, it is important to remember that, for all the talk
about globalization, labour migration is generally far more tightly
controlled and much less significant than it was when the early industrializing nations were taking off (James 2001). The physical and political
circumstances confronting would-be industrializing nations now are
consequently very different from those that confronted Britain, or even
Japan, when they undertook similar processes.

Nevertheless, many in the developing world consider (with some justification, perhaps) that the developed world got where it is by a fairly
ruthless approach to the environment and its exploitation, so why
shouldn't they? There are two important differences now, of course, that
highlight the importance of timing in the development process and in
determining the historical distribution of the world's resources. On the
one hand, globalization has made it dramatically clear just how small the
world is and how limited its resources are. Environmental issues are
inescapably planetary in scope, and there is consequently a concomitant
consciousness and a regulatory imperative that was simply not present

during earlier periods of industrialization. Not only are the governments of countries in the developing world consequently urged to uphold their responsibilities as custodians of irreplaceable fauna and flora – in a way the West never did at a similar stage of the development process – but it is painfully clear that many of the superficially attractive economic practices that underpinned the West's rise are simply environmentally and possibly economically unsustainable in the long run (Hawken 2005). The other thing that is different now is what might be described as the 'logic of exploitation': the governments of many of the countries that are under most pressure to exploit their natural resources frequently only have limited control over their own assets, or are constrained by their relationships with external economic actors.

The extent and potentially destructive nature of these relationships can be seen in the impact of what Peter Dauvergne (1997) describes as 'Japan's ecological shadow', or the impact that the Japanese economy has on the natural environment outside Japan itself. Dauvergne details the way in which Japanese multi-national corporations dominate the trade in tropical timber in Southeast Asia, utilizing their overwhelming economic leverage ruthlessly to exploit the region's natural resources. As one resource is exhausted, Japan's locust-like MNCs simply move on to the next, systematically working their way through the forests of countries such as Indonesia, the Philippines and Papua New Guinea in a process that is emblematic of a number of the political and economic processes outlined in earlier chapters: Japan's own highly successful development process has created an insatiable appetite for resource inputs; and the strategies and structures of its MNCs, the logic of resource security and the simple capacity to manipulate indigenous economic and political actors across the region has led to a brilliantly effective capacity to exploit the region's resources to satisfy such demand. In this regard there is, as Bryant and Parnwell (1996: 9) point out, an 'essential continuity of processes and practices' between the colonial period and the present, even if some of the actors and methodologies have changed. Indeed, in Japan's case, the strategy of out-sourcing environmental degradation was pioneered during the Tokugawa dynasty (Diamond 2005: 300).

For much of the region, then, environmental exploitation at the hands of outsiders is simply part of a continuing historical pattern. What is different now, of course, is the scale and 'efficiency' of the exploitation, something that is dramatically exacerbated by relentless population growth. Aat Vervoorn (1998) uses the example of Java to illustrate in microcosm (if that is the right way to describe an island with a population of more than 100 million) many of the problems that afflict developing East Asia more generally. Despite internal migration programmes, this fertile island can no longer support its burgeoning population; despite high rainfall it experiences water shortages and flash-flooding as a consequence of massive deforestation. Add to this, massively depleted fish stocks around a coastline formerly rich in sea-life, and cities so over-crowded they are becoming dysfunctional, and you have a sense of some of the problems confronting much of the region. In such circumstances, the surprise is that there has not been more civil disturbance and social dislocation as a consequence of the deteriorating environment. The impact on the regional environment was bad enough while Japan was the only 'successful' source of resource demand. Now that it has been joined by China, the situation could prove catastrophic. Before considering China's impact on its own and the global environment in any detail, it is worth spelling out some of the more sobering facts about East Asia's general situation.

Perhaps the most implacable dynamic exacerbating all of the region's environmental problems is the relentless population growth that contin-ues across most of the region. It is not simply the rapid growth of Asia's population that is potentially such a problem, but that Asia is following a well-trodden path to development that inevitably has major environ-mental impacts. Millions of people are moving off the land into increas-ingly massive cities and attempting to pursue a Western, consumerist life-style. That such a life may be permanently beyond the reach of many of them does little to stop the overall trend and adds to the demands on the natural environment. Seen in this context, the recent hand-wringing in Japan and elsewhere about the decline in the size of its population becomes rather puzzling: if population growth and consumerism really are at the heart of the planet's environmental problems, then a relative decrease in the impact of Japan's ecological shadow and resource usage should be welcomed, not feared. It is testimony to the power of contem-porary growth-oriented economic discourses and traditional notions of security that this alternative reading of Japanese demographics is gener-ally not given much of an airing.

When we consider the litany of sobering statistics that describes East Asia's environmental circumstances, it becomes clear that at some stage some of the more traditional notions of development, national security and transnational relations will have to be rethought. Although the rate of population expansion in Southeast Asia is slowing, the degradation of the environment continues. Over 50 million hectares of land in Southeast Asia are now 'severely affected' by declines in soil fertility as a consequence of erosion, water-logging, salinity and overuse (Elliott 2004: 183). The deforestation noted above continues at a rapid rate, especially in Indonesia, but also in Malaysia, Burma, Thailand and the Philippines (UN 2000: 27). Some 95 per cent of the original 'frontier forests' have disappeared from the region, which has had a dramatic impact on biodiversity and environmental stability. Indonesia and the Philippines, for example, are becoming especially prone to catastrophic flooding. Remarkably enough for such a lush region, Indonesia is also plagued by forest fires which are deliberately started as a quick way of clearing land for palm oil plantations. The central government has shown little capacity to control them,[2] despite the fact that they are becoming a growing source of irritation to Indonesia's neighbours who have to live with the massive air pollution this causes (see Cotton 1999).

Tension between East Asian neighbours has also been growing as a consequence of more fundamental questions of water usage. Population pressures are a main contributor to the growing demands on fresh water supplies as it is used to irrigate farmland. In Asia as a whole, per capita water availability has declined by between 40 and 65 per cent since 1950 (Dupont 2001: 117).[3] Emblematic of this problem is the potentially intractable conflict that has emerged over water usage around the Mekong River Basin. The Mekong is vital for Cambodia, Laos, Thailand and Vietnam, and they signed an agreement in 1995 to cooperate in its use and management. But the fact that China did not sign this agreement profoundly undermines its potential effectiveness, as China is the country with the largest capacity to control the river's flow (Dupont 2001: 129). Indeed, the scale of China's developmental needs and impacts are so extensive that they merit separate consideration as they highlight many of the broader challenges facing the region.

Is the planet big enough for China?

China's capacity to manage some of the formidable challenges associated with continuing the process of economic development has implications that extend well beyond its own borders. The sheer scale of China's economic expansion and concomitant energy needs mean that it inevitably has a major impact on East Asia and the rest of the world. If China's population were to achieve First World living standards, it would 'approximately double the entire world's human resource and environmental impact' (Diamond 2005: 373). Evidence of its ecological footprint already extends right across the Pacific, and its rapidly growing demand for oil and other resources has had a major impact on global commodity prices. The most important question as far as the future of the region and the international system more generally is concerned is whether competition for crucial but diminishing resources can be managed within market-based processes, or whether it will spill over into outright conflict and 'resource wars' (Klare 2002). We have already seen in earlier chapters just how dramatic China's growth and its concomitant need for energy and industrial raw materials has been (Hale 2004). As Table 6.3 indicated, China's consumption of key resources, including oil, gas and coal, continues to grow rapidly. There are two major consequences of China's development that are significant when thinking about the possible future of the East Asian region: the impact on the environment, and the geopolitical consequences of growing competition for scarce resources. Unless the 'externalities' associated with China's industrialization process can be successfully managed, the political and social stability of China itself and its bold experiment in capitalist economics will be in doubt.

As far as the environment is concerned, as in much of Southeast Asia, the evidence is alarming and rapidly getting worse. Although China's consumption of oil and gas attracts most attention because of its potential security implications, it is important to note that there is an even more fundamental domestic constraint on its ability to sustain current levels of growth and economic expansion: water. It is estimated that 70 per cent of China's waterways and lakes are polluted, a problem exacerbated by high-profile chemical spills that further degrade supplies and even spill over into neighbouring countries.[4] China relies on underground water supplies to meet nearly 70 per cent of its drinking water needs, but an estimated 90 per cent of such supplies to China's cities are polluted.[5] In addition, some 360 million Chinese rural residents lack access to safe drinking water, a problem compounded by illegal dumping into rivers that local officials appear unwilling or unable to stop.

Even though the Chinese government has made significant progress in curbing population growth, many demographic problems are 'locked-in' and its population is still expected to reach 1.5 billion within the next decade or so, presenting the PRC government with formidable logistical problems (Brown 1995). This would be challenge enough if China's population was still living the 'traditional' life-style of grinding rural poverty but, when much of the population aspires to Western-style consumerism, the implications are profound and very possibly unachievable, let alone sustainable. Not only are China's cities becoming gridlocked as a consequence of rapidly rising levels of car ownership, but such life-style changes are also adding to China's already massive levels of carbon dioxide (CO_2) production from coal, its principal energy source. Indeed, it is suggested that growth of emissions in China will 'dwarf any cuts in CO_2 that the rest of the world can make'.[6] Some 400,000 people die prematurely in China each year as a direct consequence of air pollution, and on some days 25 per cent of the particulate matter above Los Angeles can be traced directly to China.[7]

It is possible to pile up these sorts of statistics until they become mind-numbing and incomprehensible in their sheer scale and possible implications. The general point to make is that collectively, as Elizabeth Economy's (2004: 25) carefully researched study makes clear, 'China's environmental problems now have the potential to bring the country to its knees economically.' The problem is not simply demographic, Economy (2004: 9) argues, but a consequence of 'centuries of rampant, sometimes wilful, destruction of the environment'. As in the West, China's leaders have often had a frontier mentality that has seen the environment as something to be systematically and ruthlessly exploited. The difference now, of course, is that there are no new resources to discover and exploit, and no possibility of exporting significant numbers of people to virgin territories. This fundamental physical constraint is not only limiting the options available to Chinese leaders, but it is also intensifying the competition for the finite resources that do remain available.

It has become increasingly obvious that there is a potentially catastrophic mismatch between global energy demand and the planet's capacity to sustain it, a possibility that is especially clear in the context of oil production. Whether the 'topping point' or 'peak oil' production capacity has already been reached, or will arrive in a decade or so, there is general agreement that there will be a progressive, overall decline in oil production very soon (Leggett 2005). The potential implications of this are enormous and seem not to have been as widely recognized or debated as we might have hoped or expected. China is already the second largest consumer of oil after the USA, and the growth of car ownership and energy-intensive industries such as steel, aluminium and plastics will see this demand continue to escalate.[8] At the very least, the basis of China's industrial expansion will be threatened by rising costs and uncertain supply. This is significant enough in itself, given the central importance of economic performance in legitimating the continuing supremacy of the CCP. However, it is an issue of major international significance given the implications of a possible collapse in China's existing regime and the growing international competition for energy.

It is this latter issue that has the potential to undermine both China's stability and the peaceful development of East Asia more generally. The key international challenge in this context is managing China's relationship with the USA, which remains by far the largest consumer of energy generally and oil in particular. Indeed, so central has access to oil become that energy issues have become one of the defining policy concerns of all US governments. It is not necessary to be a conspiracy theorist to recognize that one of the increasingly pivotal roles of the American military is to ensure access to oil supplies, an idea that was articulated in the so-called 'Carter Doctrine' as long ago as 1980 (Klare 2004).[9] Many in

China certainly believe that the principal reason for the USA's invasion of Iraq was 'ensuring oil supplies', and that 'the US ability to dominate world affairs would be greatly reduced if it fails to control the Middle East'.[10]

Even if America's invasion of Iraq was about more than just oil, in an East Asian context, what is significant is that China's leaders have responded to the changing international political and energy environment by employing the same sort of approach to energy security that Japan has employed for a number of decades. China has been establishing closer ties with key sources of oil, such as Russia and Iran. Not only does this mark an important shift in the geopolitical relations of Central Asia, but it also explains why China is reluctant to condemn Iran's nuclear programme in a way that much of the 'international community' and the USA might like (Gundzik 2005). Significantly, China is consolidating these relationships by constructing pipelines through Kazakhstan and by investing in major energy assets overseas (Engdahl 2005). So extensive have China's overseas investments become that the state-owned China National Offshore Oil Corporation even attempted to buy an American oil company, Unocal. Interestingly, in a display of neomercantilist protectionism that was more reminiscent of Japan's developmental state than the supposed home of free enterprise and competition, the purchase was effectively blocked by Congressional opposition.[11] It is also significant and revealing that the importance of oil in particular, and energy supplies more generally, has been one of the few issues on which Japan has been willing to stand up to US pressure and chart its own diplomatic course in defiance of US wishes.[12]

The coming war with China?

There is no shortage of alarming scenarios that can be developed about the future of East Asia and the possibility of a conflict involving China. While the causes of such a clash are generally thought to revolve around the 'Taiwan problem' (Carpenter 2006), a conflict over the control of diminishing energy supplies – without which any industrial economy as currently configured will rapidly grind to a halt – looks a more credible long-term prospect. After all, the Taiwan issue has been problematic for half a century without generating outright conflict, and the increasing economic integration between the two neighbours ought to make conflict less, rather than more, likely. Securing energy supplies, on the other hand, looks like an issue that will grow in importance, making conflict in disputed areas – such as the potentially resource-rich South China Sea – more likely (Collins 2003).

Is a conflict between China and the USA, or any of the other East Asian nations inevitable? Before considering the more familiar political and strategic aspects of this issue, it is worth saying something about the underlying geophysical dynamics and constraints that appear to make growing friction, if not outright conflict, more likely. Vaclav Smil's exhaustive survey of global energy supplies makes it clear that, despite the fact that energy consumption and economic development are closely correlated, the end of cheap oil is not *necessarily* a 'harbinger of unimaginable civilizational difficulties' (Smil 2003: 212). The good news, as Smil points out, is that human beings have successfully shifted from social orders based on different forms of energy utilization in the past, so there is no reason to suppose this cannot happen again in the future. Somewhat surprisingly, there is no shortage of feasible ideas about how such a paradigm shift might be achieved.[13] The bad news – according to Smil, at least – is that there is likely to be a difficult transition period while this occurs and that, in any case, demographic pressures, the limitations of other energy supplies, and the need rapidly to reduce reliance on existing greenhouse gas-producing energy supplies means that there will still be a need for a *reduction* of per capita energy consumption in the West of the order of 25–35 per cent.[14]

Even if Smil's claims about the relationship between energy consumption and the environment are accepted as correct – and there is, of course, a powerful and articulate pro-business lobby arguing that it is not (Lomborg 2001) – it will strike some readers as unrealistic and fanciful to expect any change in social and economic organization of this magnitude. Not only is the PRC leadership effectively locked into a legitimacy-conferring growth paradigm that is heavily dependent on cheap energy and massive resource inputs to sustain it, but so too is the United States. For decades, the USA has made securing future energy supplies a key component of its foreign and security policies, and the current Bush administration shows little evidence of breaking with this tradition[15] despite the recent acknowledgement of the problems that flow from America's 'addiction to oil'.[16] Indeed, the growing securitization of American foreign policy under George W. Bush has produced a situation in which 'senior officials appear to believe that the use of military force is not just legitimate but also an *effective* response to foreign threats to the flow of petroleum' (Klare 2004: 24; emphasis in original). While recent events in Iraq would seem to suggest that such thinking is seriously misguided, the point to emphasize here is that it is the USA rather than China that has shown the greatest willingness of late to resort to military means to underwrite the seemingly non-negotiable elements of its domestic political economy and broader social relations.

Given that the USA is so often taken as the indispensable bedrock upon which East Asian stability rests, America's greater recourse to military options in foreign policy is not insignificant. As we saw in Chapter

3, even before the 'war on terror' America's strategic position in the region was already being assessed more critically; its increasing willingness to act unilaterally in pursuit of narrowly conceived national interests will have done nothing to diminish that trend. And yet, paradoxically enough, East Asia is actually encouraging 'bad' behaviour on America's part: the greater economic inter-dependency between East Asia and the USA detailed in earlier chapters allows the USA to consume an ever more disproportionate share of the world's finite and diminishing resources, and to do so with credit obtained in Asia. While the normative aspects of a relationship in which some of the world's wealthiest individuals borrow from the poorest to continue their environmentally destructive life-styles are troubling enough, more immediately it looks unsustainable for more mundane and technocratic reasons. The conventional economic wisdom suggests that the scale of America's budgetary liabilities will trigger a major 'correction' at some stage, with potentially profound implications for East Asia in particular and the global economy more generally.[17] Not only is the value of dollar-denominated assets likely to be seriously eroded in such a crisis, but America's seemingly insatiable consumers may finally be forced to change their ways as a consequence of rising interest rates.

As we saw in earlier chapters, the scale of East Asia's reliance on American markets makes this a nightmarish prospect, and helps to explain the continuing willingness of East Asian lenders to keep channelling funds into the USA: if they cease to do so, they risk triggering the very crisis they fear. One way out of this structurally embedded dependence is to increase the importance of intra-East Asian trade and investment. This is already happening thanks to the dramatic rise of China, although Japan has also played an important part in this processes as we have seen. The question now is whether such intra-regional processes will intensify and make the region less dependent on external markets and capital flows. This is why the issue of environmental sustainability becomes so crucial: all other things being equal, it is not unreasonable to expect that China's economic development would continue (and even accelerate) as the benefits of greater investment in infrastructure, education and production create a virtuous circle of rising living standards and expanding markets. This would inevitably have the effect of making East Asia generally less dependent on the USA. Even if some of this new-found wealth and economic strength is diverted into re-equipping the Chinese military, the logic of inter-dependence would suggest that China's leaders might be even more unwilling to jeopardize economic development in the same way that (most of) their counterparts in the West are.

Again, such views will strike some as hopelessly naïve and at odds with influential readings of history, which suggest that a materially grounded continuing struggle for survival in a relentlessly competitive and anarchical international system is the only thing of which we can be certain. There is clearly something in this, especially when the dominant mode of economic and social organization is predicated on the exploitation of rapidly diminishing resources. This is not to argue, however, that capitalism is solely responsible for, or uniquely antithetical to, environmental sustainability, as some have suggested (see O'Connor 1994): the 'socialist' regimes of the Soviet Union and China were hardly bywords for concerned stewardship of the global commons. But it is clear that industrialization and the growth of larger, consumer-oriented societies is potentially unsustainable if they are predicated upon the dominant Western model (Hawken 2005). The 'ecological footprint' of the wealthy parts of the world, including Japan, Europe and especially the United States, continues to expand and consume an ever more disproportionate and 'unfair' share of the planet's resources (Worldwatch Institute 2006). The shift to a 'lighter' economy based on computers, services and lower levels of resource utilization means little if consumption patterns remain the same. In other words, we cannot assume that rising living standards will necessarily or automatically allow countries to 'fix' environmental problems. Thus, it is difficult to imagine how China and India will possibly be able to follow the extant Western model with today's populations, let alone with those of 20 or 30 years' time.

Consequently, 'realists' and environmental-conflict analysts such as Homer-Dixon (1999) may be right, and the twenty-first century will be characterized by an increasingly intense and possibly violent struggle over the planet's diminishing resources. However, not only would there be no long-term winners in such a process, but the delicate webs of inter-dependency that distinguish the contemporary international economic order would also be rent asunder. The history of East Asia provides powerful reminders of how important such inter-connections are, and how dangerous, and ultimately self-destructive, it can be to break them. The rise of China, as Japan before it, has been dependent on its integration into an existing order that allowed it to develop and prosper; without such an order, development would certainly have been slower and possibly may not have occurred at all. In Japan's case, its most recent rise was preceded by an equally spectacular and painful 'fall', in which its misguided, militarily-inspired pursuit of resource security caused it to start a war it had no chance of winning, which achieved nothing but the destruction of its own economy. It should no longer be necessary for every nation to discover for itself how futile such behaviour is, and that the lesson of Japan's pre- and post-war experiences demonstrate unequivocally that a 'peaceful rise' really is the only way to sustain prosperity, even in a world of limited resources.

If such lessons have been learned and the benefits of inter-dependence are clear to the region's policy-makers (clearly a big 'if'), then the sort of institutions that have been developed in East Asia over the last few decades have a potentially important role to play. 'Objectively', it really is rather preposterous that, for example, impoverished nations such as Indonesia and the Philippines should think of increasing defence spending to defend 'their' assets in the South China Sea. Not only would such an endeavour be unlikely to succeed or deter potential adversaries (China presumably), but it would divert vital spending from national development. Likewise, even if China were able to secure possession of such an area through force of arms, the implications for relations with the USA and the impact of such a development on the wider international economy are potentially catastrophic. Clearly, all sides have a vested interest in attempting to resolve such issues peacefully, and it is in this context that regional institutions can play such a critical part.

The rise of an institutionalized East Asia and the decline of American influence?

It is not clear at this stage which institutions will emerge as the most important, which countries will be in them, or precisely what the geographical extent of the region such institutions represent will be. Given the need to accommodate a more powerful China and the possible advantages that might flow from having a regional institutional identity that did *not* include the USA – at least, as far as China is concerned – then the consolidation of some sort of East Asian grouping is certainly possible. There are, of course, a number of factors that will inhibit such a development, most obviously the existence of close American allies in East Asia such as Japan, who would be loath to see ties with the USA endangered, or American influence eclipsed by China. And yet, given Japan's capacity to alienate its neighbours and its inability to provide regional leadership of its own, it may find itself having to go along with some sort of China-centric regional order or risk being marginalized in a more self-consciously realized 'East Asia'.

When speculating about the future of East Asia, one of the few things we can be sure of is that, as in the twentieth century, much will depend on the actions of the United States. Indeed, the actions of the current Bush administration have helped to undermine the credibility of multi-lateral institutions such as APEC, and made the development of more exclusive East Asian institutions more attractive (Beeson 2006b). But, it is quite possible that a new administration may be more enthusiastic about multi-lateralism, and keener on formal mechanisms with which to manage inter-regional relations. If so, then the prospects for the peaceful resolution of key issues of resource exploitation and inter-dependency will obviously be brighter. American leadership at a global level will plainly continue to exert a powerful influence everywhere, but especially in an East Asian region that is vulnerable to changes in America's economic circumstances or foreign policy. Having said that, one thing seems equally clear: America's capacity to shape the international order unilaterally and militarily seems certain to diminish. Not only has the USA been unable to impose a military 'solution' in Iraq (Packer 2005), but the sorts of relationships that Kent Calder (1996) predicted would emerge as a consequence of Asia's evolving energy and resource needs have indeed developed; China (and even Japan) have become closer to 'rogue' regimes such as Iran as a consequence of their implacable energy demands. But, the development of relations that do not revolve around the USA is not necessarily a bad thing: the recent agreement between China and India to cooperate on the acquisition of third-country oil assets, might – if it holds – provide a very different model for pursuing resource security,[18] and one that stands in stark contrast to that of the USA.

The other reason for supposing that the USA may come to exert less of an influence over even its most ardent and unequivocal allies, such as Japan, is that it is simply not as economically important to the region as it once was (Ravenhill 2006). While it is true that the USA remains a vital market for East Asia, it is also becoming a potential source of instability as the basis of its economic importance – American consumerism – becomes increasingly environmentally damaging and economically unsustainable. America's current position is fraught with troubling environmental and geostrategic implications, and rests on a potentially fragile economic base. At some stage, economic orthodoxy suggests there will be a 'correction' and the USA's budgetary and trade deficits will be reduced (Brenner 2002; Garten 2005). When coupled with the apparently inexorable rise of China, a reconfiguring of intra- and inter-regional relationships consequently no longer looks as fanciful as it once did.

While the sceptics may be right to draw attention to the modest record of collaborative achievement and institutional development in East Asia thus far, we should not write off East Asian institutionalization too quickly: for all the undoubted inadequacies of ASEAN and the ARF, there has not been a major war involving the members of either group since their inauguration. Although this may not yet constitute a full-blown security community, and while the process of confidence-building, socialization and norm construction may be a bit difficult to quantify, it is not unreasonable to claim that such processes must have had *some* impact in decreasing the likelihood of conflict in a region that many continue to insist is inherently conflict-prone and unstable. Indeed, it is important to note that the only countries that have directly participated in both the region's major recent conflicts in Korea and Vietnam have been the USA and its trusted ally, Australia; both external powers and supposedly forces for stability. Given the USA's repeated violent intrusions into the region, it is rather surprising that so many in East Asia continue to believe that the USA is such a stabilizing force, or that they are incapable of peacefully managing their own affairs without the assistance of an American hegemon.

Things may be changing, however. We have seen how much China has been transformed over the last few decades, both internally and as an increasingly effective diplomatic force in the region. China is of central economic importance to all of East Asia including Japan, and has become more deeply integrated into the region's policy networks and less threatening to its neighbours as a consequence. True, many will cling to the American security blanket as a way of off-setting China's pre-eminence, but given how recently China's rise has taken place, this is not altogether surprising. In the longer term, *all other things being equal*, it seems certain that China's influence can only grow and that its position will be consolidated in the evolving regional institutional architecture (Shambaugh 2005). It is should also be remembered that when seen in the longer historical context of Asian civilization, East Asia has been more stable and peaceful when China has been strong and at the centre of regional affairs (Kang 2003a; Katzenstein 2005).

The key question in the long term is whether China – and the rest of developing Asia, for that matter – can sustain the development process. Here, the issues would seem less technocratic or geopolitical, and much more to do with the fundamental carrying capacity of the planet. Limiting population growth and managing the transition from one industrial, developmental and environmentally sustainable paradigm to another will be the central challenge. East Asia's distinctive, frequently bloody history serves as a powerful reminder that violent solutions to energy insecurity are simply not feasible (as Japan's abortive attempts to dominate resource-rich Southeast Asia demonstrated). But Japan also demonstrates what a remarkable transformation can occur in people's views about militarism and nationalism. There is, of course, no guarantee that even the Japanese will not succumb to such destructive manias again in the future. This is where regional institutions have the potential to play such a critical role. East Asia and Western Europe are, of course, very different places (Higgott 1995; Katzenstein 2005), and there is no reason to expect that East Asian institutions will inevitably or exactly replicate the European experience; but it is remarkable what a pacifying impact the process of institutionalized intra-regional relations has had on Europe. True, many Europeans are not enamoured of the European project (European Commission 2000), and even fewer consider themselves to be 'Europeans' rather than citizens of a particular nation, but it has become quite simply unthinkable that any of the more long-standing members of the EU would seriously think of going to war with each other.

This is why the project of East Asian regionalism remains so important. For all the inefficiencies, excesses, infringements of national sovereignty and all the other costs of inter-dependence, if the ultimate pay-off of regional institutionalization is a more peaceful, more cooperative and perhaps more prosperous region, it will be a remarkably small price to pay. Given the scale of the challenges the region faces, it is an investment that ought to be made, even if the short-term results are uncertain and contentious. Without such institutions, the chances of resolving major tensions over energy security and environmental sustainability are reduced, and threaten to undermine some of the very real gains the region as a whole has made over the past 50 years or so.

Notes

1 Conceptualizing East Asia: From the Local to the Global

1 'The West' is an unsatisfactory but useful shorthand for those countries and values that were initially associated with Western Europe, the Enlightenment and the development of political liberalism, and which are now championed primarily by the United States. For different views, see Huntington (1996) and Hall (1996).

2 For a contemporary review of this literature, see Rosamond (2005).

3 The literature on globalization is enormous. Good introductions are provided by Held *et al.* (1999) and Scholte (2000).

4 The GATT was replaced by the World Trade Organization (WTO) in 1995. Significantly, the WTO has far greater enforcement powers than the essentially voluntaristic GATT, although this has not meant that free trade has become universally entrenched or that tariff barriers have disappeared. See Das (2003).

5 Unless otherwise indicated, the 'post-war period' refers to post 1945, the consolidation of American hegemony and the acceleration of globalization processes.

6 It is important to note that this schema should not be drawn too sharply as there are significant differences in the nature of investment and trade linkages, with the latter being more diffuse and less concentrated than the former. See Poon, Thompson and Kelly (2000).

7 The World Bank (1993) did most to popularize the notion of the East Asian 'miracle' with its landmark account of the region's remarkable development.

8 The capital account records the movement of short- and long-term capital in and out of a country. It is worth pointing out that the IMF's role as a champion of financial liberalization is a relatively new one that reflects major changes in the international political economy. Until the early 1970s, the IMF's job had been to manage a system of 'pegged' exchange rates. See Pauly (1997).

9 The idea of the 'Third World' is increasingly considered to be unhelpful as it agglomerates disparate experiences and no longer accurately reflects the nature of the post-Cold War international order and the complex realities within it. See Berger (2004a).

10 The modern state is generally taken to have emerged from the Treaty of Westphalia of 1648, which ended the Thirty Years War and recognized the principle of state sovereignty and enshrined state borders secured by law. It

became the dominant form of political organization as a consequence of a process of institutional competition because it offered specific organizational political, economic and strategic advantages. See Spruyt (1994). For an important reinterpretation of this process and period, see Teschke (2003).

11   It is important to emphasize that states come in a variety of forms and that many are 'failing' or lacking in domestic competence and capacity. Historically, East Asia has contained examples of some of the most able and interventionist states, such as Japan, as well as some of the least able and dependent, such as Cambodia.

12   The East Asian crisis is a painful reminder of the reality that market sentiment can change remarkably quickly and that massive, rapid outflows of mobile capital can devastate small economies.

13   Interestingly, the present Bush administration is something of an exception in the depth of its ideological commitment to tax rates at all costs, which has major implications for the stability of global economic and interregional relations. See Chapter 6.

2   The Weight of History

1   Modelski and Thompson (1996) persuasively argue that the foundations of 'globalization' and the sort of rapid economic development that characterizes the modern era were laid down in Sung dynasty China some 1,000 years ago.

2   The Mandate of Heaven was based on the belief that a ruler enjoyed the blessing of the deity, an idea with powerful legitimating potential for the ruling elite. The loss of heaven's mandate was thought to be manifest in an increase in natural disasters and a breakdown of social order.

3   The extent of China's naval capacity and the extent of their withdrawal from the world is symbolized in the voyages of Grand Eunuch Zheng He, who was commanded to survey China's trade routes in the early fifteenth century. His armada consisted of over 300 vessels, including some of the largest ever built. Zheng travelled as far as India and Africa.

4   China's examination system provided a degree of social mobility through competitive entry to the civil service and thus the gentry, who constituted the governing elite between the autocracy and the peasantry. See Hsü (1983).

5   The Manchus originated in the Jurched tribes of Manchuria. The key historical point is that not only was a small group able to supplant the Ming dynasty, but that 'in reality they remained conquerors', and consequently suspicious of the Chinese, something that contributed to the Qing dynasty's ultimate demise. See Hsü (1983: 446–7).

6   The main differences of interpretation revolve around the importance of economic, political and strategic factors, the benefits that accrue to the imperial power, and the damage this inflicts on the development of the

peripheral power. The relevant literature is vast, but for useful perspectives see Hobsbawm (1987) and Doyle (1986).

7   From Marco Polo onwards, European interest in China had been intense. Chinese intellectual ideas, especially Confucianism, made a substantial impact on Europe and can be seen in the writings of Montesquieu and the ideas of the Physiocrats. See Fairbank, Reischauer and Craig (1965: 64–6).

8   The self-strengthening movement developed in the latter half of the nineteenth century. It was led by prominent scholar-officials such as Zeng Guofan and Li Hongzhang, and was intended to adopt and learn from the West's technological expertise, but this inevitably led to a wider importation of Western ideas, some of which were political and contributed to undermining the old order. The contrast with Japan's much more successful borrowing from the West is revealing and instructive.

9   The tributary system was series of practices through which China managed its external affairs, in which barbarian states accepted their subordinate position and paid homage through gifts and emissaries to the Chinese imperial order. The pay-off for the subordinates was access to Chinese trade and reciprocal bribes. See Hamashita (1994).

10 Historically there has been a fundamental congruence between the modernization process, especially the development of a complex industrial society, and nationalism, which has provided an especially powerful force for organizing social and material resources. See Gellner (1983).

11 The May the Fourth Movement refers specifically to a massive student demonstration in Peking in 1919 in response to Japan's 'Twenty-one Demands' which were endorsed by the Versailles Conference following the First World War. The long-term impact of the May the Fourth Movement was to spark a more generalized intellectual revolution in China. See Fitzgerald (1996).

12 'China must cut farming population, says OECD', Financial Times, 14 November 2005.

13 Taiwan was formerly known as Formosa and is sometimes called 'Chinese Taipei', in deference to mainland China's sensitivities about its status.

14 Even before the fall of the Tokugawa, Japan had sent a number of missions abroad to study European styles of political, economic and, especially, military organization. These were subsequently expanded as the modernization push gained momentum.

15 Many Japanese were unhappy about the impact of the reform process, and not just marginalized feudal lords. Some samurai were concerned about the impact of Western-style reform on traditional Japanese values, especially their own loss of status.

16 As part of this comprehensive programme of occupation and exploitation, more than 300,000 Japanese actually emigrated to Manchuria during the 1930s.

17 For an interesting discussion of both Japan's war-time thinking about the West, and more recent usages of these sorts of discursively constructed cultural binaries, see Burma and Margalit (2004).

18 By contrast, Christianity's introduction to the region in concert with

growing European trade links was more systematic, but only became dominant in the Philippines where the Spanish colonizers had significant state support and the experience of Latin American colonization to draw on.

19   Patron–client ties or patrimonialism, refers to the personal ties and loyalties that exist between superiors and subordinates, and which may be the basis of power and patronage when part of a wider social and political system. See Brown (1994: 114–17).

20   Broadly, formal rationality refers to the techniques by which ends are achieved, and substantive rationality to the norms and values that underpin such endeavours.

21   On the rivalries between the European powers that formed the backdrop of this period of colonial expansion, see Tarling (1966).

22   Saigon was re-named Ho Chi Minh City following the communist takeover of the South.

23   These intense, long-standing regional rivalries are also important in explaining contemporary tensions and problems in the region, as we shall see in subsequent chapters.

24   This way of conceptualizing relations between the developed economies of the imperial powers and the emerging colonial economies is drawn from analyses based in world systems theory, and captures something important about the enduring 'structural' nature of the relationship. See Chase-Dunn (1998).

25   This process was instrumental in cementing the dominant economic position of Chinese immigrants, the consequences of which are taken up in later chapters.

26   The *mestizos* are people of mixed Chinese–native parentage.

3   Geopolitics and Security

1   But for an important exception, see Stubbs (2005).

2   Whereas Agnew uses an essentially Marxist framework, Bobbitt's book is an amalgam of liberal and realist ideas that highlight the way in which particular national and international orders are constitutionalized.

3   For a provocative discussion of the 'geography of thought', see Nisbett (2003).

4   The Korean peninsula remained divided along the 38th parallel as a consequence of a war-time agreement between the Soviet Union and the United States.

5   The JSDF were originally intended, as the name implies, for strictly defensive purposes, although it has never been entirely clear what this might mean in practice. In 1976, Prime Minister Miki placed a 1% ceiling on Japanese defence spending although, given the dramatic expansion of the Japanese economy, this has still made Japan one of the world's most significant potential military powers.

6   ABRI (Angkatan Bersenjata Republik Indonesia) is the former name of the

Indonesian armed forces, which were was re-named the TNI (Tentara Nasional Indonesia) in 1999.

7   As Chapter 6 makes clear, this does not mean that these states do not have highly effective domestic security regimes.

8   Burma's military regime had originally been called the State Law and Order Restoration Council (SLORC). In 1997, on the advice of a public relations firm, the junta re-badged itself as the SPDC.

9   It is widely believed that Japan could become a nuclear power very rapidly, if it chose to. It should also be noted that despite the constitutional checks on Japan's aggressive intent, it is the world's largest defence spender, and has a formidable 'defensive' capability.

10 Although there are some surprising similarities in the views of historical-materialists and realists, the latter would expect all states to behave in a similar fashion and be driven by similar goals, whereas Marxists would consider capitalist states to be especially aggressive and expansionary as a consequence of their need to try and resolve internal 'contradictions'. See Doyle (1997).

11 Status quo powers are, as the name suggests, content with the prevailing order and not intent on changing it. China's rise generally, and its unhappiness about the status of Taiwan in particular, lead some observers to suggest that it is a non-status quo power and therefore a potential source of instability. See Johnston (2003a).

12 Of course, the Vietnam War, or the American War, as the Vietnamese know it, had an even more profound impact on Vietnam, as well as Laos and Cambodia which were also extensively bombed. For the definitive discussion of the Vietnam War's significance, see Kolko (1985).

13 Before his election and the attacks of September 11 that triggered the radical change of direction in foreign policy, Bush was a foreign policy neophyte who argued that the USA needed to take a 'humbler' approach to its dealings with other countries. See Daalder and Lindsay (2003).

14 See, 'Economic ties binding Japan to rival China', *New York Times*, 31 October 2005.

15 An important contemporary focus of national sensitivity and strategic significance is the territorial dispute between China and Japan in the East China Sea. Both countries have deployed naval craft in the area to reinforce their claims to the potentially rich oil and gas reserves there. See 'Oil and gas in troubled waters', *The Economist*, 8 October 2005.

16 There is plausible evidence to suppose that recent anti-Japanese demonstrations in China were at least tolerated, if not orchestrated, by the PRC government. Embarrassing Japan about its war record and 'insensitivity' also provides a way for China to undermine Japan's long-held goal of attaining a permanent seat on the UN Security Council, whilst simultaneously reinforcing its own position as the premier East Asian nation in international affairs. See 'UN power play drives China protests', *International Herald Tribune*, 12 April 2005.

17 These issues are explored in more detail in Chapter 6, which highlights the way Japan's leadership initiatives at the regional level have been thwarted by the Americans.

18   In addition to the ASEAN countries themselves, the ARF initially included seven 'dialogue partners' (the USA, Japan, South Korea, Australia, New Zealand, Canada and the European Union), and was subsequently expanded in 1993 to include China, Russia and Papua New Guinea, as well as Vietnam and Laos, who were not at that stage members of ASEAN itself. It was formally established in 1994.

19   Vietnam invaded Cambodia in 1978. Its installation of a sympathetic regime presented a major challenge for ASEAN and its capacity to deal with conflict in Southeast Asia. Vietnam saw this as a way of curbing Chinese expansionism and resolving a destabilizing domestic conflict. The fact that ASEAN was instrumental in engineering a peaceful withdrawal by Vietnam is seen by ASEAN as a triumph of ASEAN-style diplomacy and cooperation. See Acharya (2001)

20   US Secretary of State Condoleezza Rice's decision not to attend the ASEAN Summit in Laos was taken as an indication of the USA's declining commitment to the region. See 'ASEAN members worried by Rice's decision to skip talks', *International Herald Tribune*, 22 July 2005.

21   Authoritative surveys by the Pew Research Center indicated that support for (and trust in) the United States had deteriorated across the world. Support for the USA in Indonesia, the largest Muslim country in the world, had collapsed from 61 to 15% in 2003. See Pew Research Center (2003).

22   China's political leaders have, since the 2003 National People's Congress, been promoting the idea of China's 'peaceful rise', or the idea that China can become a great power without inevitably disrupting the prevailing order or causing war. See Yahuda (2004: 305–10).

23   There is evidence of a third position emerging within the Bush administration that favours a 'hedging' strategy based on the belief that China is being transformed and constrained by its integration into the international system in a way that favours the USA's long-term interests: 'The panda hedgers', *International Herald Tribune*, 5 October 2005.

24   Recent attempts by the USA to get South Korea to impose sanctions on the North appear to have further soured relations between Seoul and Washington: 'Pressure from US angers S Korea', *The Australian*, 26 January 2006.

25   There is also a similar dispute between Vietnam and China over control of the Paracel Islands.

26   There have, however, been a number of incidents involving the Chinese navy and various regional powers; these have the potential to become more serious. See Klare (2002).

27   China's rapid economic development is remarkable and in many ways welcome, but it is having a profound, disastrous and potentially unsustainable impact on its own and the global environment, the implications of which are explored in the concluding chapter. See 'China crisis: threat to the global environment', *The Independent*, 20 October 2005.

28   Donald Rumsfeld (2005) epitomized this approach in a speech that accused the Chinese of clandestinely increasingly military spending despite an absence of threats: a remarkably myopic and unsympathetic view given

China's history, America's overwhelming military dominance, and its own
rapidly expanding military budget.

29 See Leftwich (2000) for an illuminating comparison of African and East
Asian developmental outcomes.

30 In 2003, for example, the number of people killed by terrorist actions was
about one-third of Australia's annual road toll and a fraction of China's.
See 'New 2003 data: 625 terrorism deaths, not 307', *Washingtonpost.com*,
23 June 2005.

31 See note 21.

4 Nationalism, Domestic Politics and Asian Values

1 For a useful discussion of state strength in the international context and an
explanation of the difficulty many non-Western states have in shaping the
international regulatory architecture, see Volgy and Bailin (2003).

2 Modernization theories were developed, in part at least, as a response to
what were then the influential Marxist interpretations of development and
non-development. Modernization theorists such as Walt Rostow argued
that institutional modernization was the key to economic development
'take-off' – in ways that are still current in contemporary debates. See Mark
Berger (2004b) for an excellent overview of the modernization theory and
its ideological significance.

3 Democracy is surprisingly hard to define, especially at a time when global
processes are eroding the autonomy and authority of states (even if democratically elected). However, there is an assumption that this will involve
some sort of procedural minimums involving, 'rule by the people', a capacity for them to formally express their political preferences, and a regular
turn-over of political elites. On democratic forms, see Held (1987). On the
'structural' constraints that economic power present to 'authentic' democracy, see Bowles and Gintis (1996). On the capacity of global forces to
undermine democracy, see Cerny (1999).

4 As I explain in subsequent chapters, there are major environmental
constraints on the economic development process in parts of the region that
make this goal anything but certain.

5 This possibility has assumed new theoretical and ideological significance as a
consequence of the occupation of Iraq. However, a number of commentators
have pointed out that both Germany and Japan had much more conducive
preconditions for post-war reconstruction and democratization than Iraq.
'Rebuilding Iraq on the cheap?', *Christian Science Monitor*, 15 July 2004.

6 However, Stockwin (2002) argues that, despite Japan's obvious shortcomings, it still qualifies as an authentic democracy.

7 It should be noted that in some ways this marked a return to business as
usual, as organized labour had been denied the sort of representation
enjoyed by business and agricultural interests in formulating national
policy. See Pempel and Tsunekawa (1979).

8   The potential impact of the larger geopolitical context was apparent in the Security Treaty crisis of 1960, which marked another major turning point in Japanese politics and international relations. In 1958, the government of Kishi Nobusuke began negations with the USA to revise the 1951 Security Treaty in an effort to give Japan greater autonomy without reducing America's military commitment to Japan's defence. The new agreement was violently opposed by Left-wing militants, but ultimately rammed through Parliament, simultaneously undermining the strength and credibility of the socialists, while unifying the LDP – despite the major tensions the agreement created.

9   'Koizumi's new party', *International Herald Tribune*, 29 September 2005.

10 Japan's unusual voting system included single non-transferable votes and multi-member constituencies, and meant that voters had only one preference, but constituencies typically returned three, four or five members. Because individual parties might return more than one successful candidate from each electorate, candidates from the same party competed amongst themselves to try to maximize their share of the party's overall vote. To distinguish themselves from each other, they frequently resorted to what were little more than bribes to lock in personal support. The consequence of this, of course, was to entrench the role and importance of 'money politics'. However, there have been significant attempts to overhaul this system, and it is important to acknowledge that it is widely considered that there is far less corruption now than there once was (Curtis 1999: 165).

11 See 'Koizumi's new party', *International Herald Tribune*, 29 September 2005.

12 This is how Robert Wade (1990) describes pre-democratic government in Taiwan.

13 See 'Dancing with the enemy: a survey of Taiwan', *The Economist*, 15 January 2005.

14 The 'domino theory' suggested that Southeast Asian nations were structurally vulnerable to communist predation and would collapse one after another unless forcibly opposed by America. See Rotter (1987).

15 For two important accounts, see Cribb (1990) and Elson (2001).

16 The five principles were: 'Belief in the One and Only God'; Just and Civilized Humanity'; 'the Unity of Indonesia'; 'Democracy Guided by the Inner Wisdom in the Unanimity Arising out of Deliberation amongst Representatives'; and 'Social Justice for the Whole People of Indonesia'.

17 This has now changed and the present incumbent, Yudhoyono, was directly elected in a process that was widely seen as fair and transparent.

18 Under Suharto, Golkar was the dominant political party and contained representatives of key 'functional' groups such as military officers, civil servants and trade unions, in a highly effective, if politically unrepresentative, corporatist structure.

19 Since Suharto's downfall, Indonesia has had four leaders: Habbibie, Wahid, Megawati and the current President Yudhoyono.

20 'Democracy the Indonesian way', *The Australian*, 19–20 June 2004: 29.

21 When Ho Chi Minh declared independence – prematurely, as it turned out

– in North Vietnam following the Second World War, he laced his speech with quotations from Thomas Jefferson. Significantly, Ho's friendly, potentially conflict-avoiding, overtures to the USA were rebuffed on the grounds of anti-communism. See Rotter (1987: 100–1).

22 The incumbent president, Arroyo, has been embroiled in a long-running scandal about her apparent interference in the electoral process, something that has undermined the legitimacy of an administration already damaged by the perception that it engineered a constitutional coup to overthrow the government of former President Estrada (who remains popular with the poor). See Hutchison (2006).

23 Every village in Thailand was promised 1 million *baht* if TRT was elected, extra to additional health care spending.

24 At the time of writing, Thaksin appeared to be about relinquish his position in the face of extensive demonstrations about his alleged corrupt business dealings and anti-democratic practices. It remains to be seen whether this will mark the end of either his influence and political career, or the nexus between political and economic power.

25 Under the Nominated Member of Parliament scheme, for example, government appointed experts choose candidates for short-term appointments to Parliament.

26 'The changing of the guard: A survey of Malaysia', *The Economist*, 15 April 2003: 3.

27 The financial crisis of 1998 created major tensions between Mahathir and his deputy, Anwar Ibrahim, about economic management and relations with the IFIs which culminated in Anwar's downfall and jailing in highly contentious circumstances. See Khoo (2003).

28 Equally significantly, Badawi has suggested that Malays will no longer be the beneficiaries of positive discrimination, but will have to cope with the proverbial 'level playing field': 'Malays losing privileges', *Australian Financial Review*, 1 August 2003.

29 'Taking anger out of politics', *Far Eastern Economic Review*, 19 February 2004.

30 Despite its diminutive stature, Timor excites a good deal of scholarly and diplomatic interest. For a good background discussion, see Cotton (2004).

31 The Cultural Revolution began as a leadership purge, but quickly became a mass movement with a momentum of its own. The key point to emphasize is that, unlike the 'Great Leap Forward' (considered in the next chapter), the Cultural Revolution was an essentially a political rather than an economic phenomenon. See Robinson (1971).

32 It should also be noted that when one of the principal 'others' against which Chinese nationalism is defined is Japan and its war-time record, then the prospects for regional cooperation are not auspicious. See 'Beijing stokes Japan hatred', *The Australian*, 18 April 2005.

33 It is important to note that control of the provinces remains a challenge for the central government, especially as many are the size of European countries and some are enjoying rapid economic development that encourages greater independence. See Goodman (1997).

34   One of the first initiatives of the new communist government was to develop an elaborate nomenclature of class positions with which to categorize the entire population and indicate its status as members of the proletariat or 'class enemies'. See Lawrence (1998: 13–14).

35   Deng fell out of favour during the Cultural Revolution when Mao saw him as a threat to his authority and was only rehabilitated in 1974. See Chang (1988).

36   The Gang of Four were led by Mao's widow Jiang Qing and were removed from power following Mao's death, subjected to show trials and largely blamed for the excesses of the Cultural Revolution. Their trials were major public events and effectively marked the end of the more radical, ideologically-inspired phase of the Cultural Revolution.

37   'China's communists try to decide what they stand for', *New York Times*, 1 May 2002.

38   As we shall see in the next chapter, such pressures are not confined to encouraging political liberalization, but the political constitution and legal structures of the PRC as well.

39   Part of this has been a concerted campaign against the media. See 'Former rival helps Hu solidify grip on China', *International Herald Tribune*, 25 September 2005.

40   These points draw heavily on Dupont (1996: 16), Ingleson (1996: 257) and Robison (1996: 310–11), .

41   There are signs, however, that much of this criticism is for domestic consumption in the USA, and that China's increased economic importance has made American officials less critical elsewhere: 'In Asia, a different Bush message', *International Herald Tribune*, 15 November 2005.

42   'Meeting the superpower', *The Economist*, 19 November: 11.

43   This is clearly an idea that appears to China as it tries to counter the USA's ideational hegemony. See 'Cultivating "East Asian values"', *China Daily*, 6 March 2005.

44   'In Asia, a different Bush message', *International Herald Tribune*, 15 November 2005.

5   East Asia's Developmental States

1   The high-growth era lasted from 1955 until 1973, and marked the period when the developmental state was at the height of its interventionist powers.

2   It is worth noting in passing that List's ideas also exerted considerable influence in the United States when it was going through a similar developmental stage. Alexander Hamilton, first Secretary of the Treasury, was an admirer of List's ideas and used them as the basis of his highly interventionist strategies for promoting American economic development. The idea that America prospered solely because of market forces is consequently a myth that has been – possibly conveniently – forgotten by subsequent

generations of policy-makers: see H.J. Chang (2002). On Hamilton, his ideas and place in American development, see Chernow (2004).

3   There is, of course, a good deal of difference between the sort of liberal ideas that became part of economic and political discourse in the nineteenth and twentieth centuries, and the practice of both by the leading powers of the day. As noted earlier, both Britain and the USA were champions of liberal principles, but neither has resiled from using mercantilist techniques or national economic leverage when it suited them. See H.J. Chang (2002).

4   I am indebted to Aurelia George Mulgan for encouraging me to clarify this point in particular and the overall argument of the chapter more generally. The usual caveats apply, of course.

5   It should be emphasized that this consensus had its coercive elements, as we saw in Chapter 2 when I detailed the manner in which Japanese organized labour was suppressed in the war's aftermath.

6   Japan experienced a period of 'price destruction' during the 1990s, when prices fell, consumer sentiment remained negative, and a lack of domestic demand reflected and added to Japan's other economic problems.

7   Foreign pressure, especially from the USA, has been decisive in shaping Japanese public policy, something that is an outcome of the historical and strategic factors discussed in earlier chapters. The fact that the Japanese have a word for it – *gaiatsu* – is revealing in itself. See George (1997) and Schoppa (1997).

8   It should be noted that the situations of Japan in the 1980s and China now are quite different, however, despite the similarity in American policies. China is a far more open economy than Japan was, and is far more reliant on American investment and market access. Not only is a revaluation of the yuan unlikely to fix the 'problem' of the trade deficit, but it might do significant damage to the Chinese economy as well. See 'This time, history isn't repeating', *International Herald Tribune*, 16 October 2005.

9   See 'Aphorisms and suspicions', *The Economist*, 19 November 2005: 21–3.

10   This strategy was widely employed in the region, but it is fatally undermined by financial sector liberalization. On the role of financial repression in East Asian development, see the World Bank (1993: 237–9).

11   Aurelia George Mulgan makes the point that Japan's internationally competitive sectors ceased to receive government support once they were established and self-sustaining (personal communication). The net effect of this was to concentrate government assistance on the least competitive industries.

12   Japan's *keiretsu* networks and major corporations generally have long-term relationships with small-scale producers which give them a good deal of flexibility, facilitate the celebrated just-in-time delivery system, and provide a shock absorber in times of economic down-turn. See Sakai (1990).

13   One of the most distinctive features of the *keiretsu* groups was the existence of a 'main bank' within the overall corporation. The bank would be a key source of capital for member companies, a relationship that was reinforced by cross-shareholdings and board representation. See Gerlach (1992).

14   See 'Mindset', *The Economist*, 23 October 1999; Pempel (1999).

15   The impact and extent of the overseas Chinese is outlined in more detail in the next chapter.
16   This influential thesis was in some ways a forerunner of the globalization paradigm, and argued that the restructuring of international production was allowing mobile MNCs to take advantage of an international pool of labour.
17   Amsden (2001: 282) argues that all late-developing economies have to make a 'profound choice' between relying on foreign MNCs or attempting to develop indigenous firms to compete internationally. Singapore's limited scale may have effectively precluded the latter option.
18   The most important of the so-called regional growth triangles by far is that covering China, Hong Kong and Taiwan, and is considered in more detail in the next chapter. On growth triangles more generally, see Chen and Kwan (1997).
19   Rentier classes derive their wealth, as the name suggests, from rents, bonds and unearned income.
20   'Malays losing privileges', *Australian Financial Review*, 1 August 2003.
21   The Great Leap Forward began at Mao's behest in 1958 and was intended to speed up the transition from socialism to communism by collectivizing agriculture, while the control of industry was decentralized. The breakdown in centralized decision-making this caused led to a major famine and discredited the entire process.
22   This phrase refers to the implicit relationship between the state and the people in which the former guarantees the latter's well-being.
23   It is currently estimated that there are some 20 million unemployed urban workers with a further 160 million surplus agricultural workers in China, adding to the massive internal migration that is a major, potentially destabilizing, social force. 'China's jobless could spark crisis in region', *Straits Times*, 1 May 2002. It is estimated that over 40 million workers have lost their jobs as a consequence of the restructuring of the SOEs. 'Mao's heirs face fiscal shock', *Australian Financial Review*, 6 November 2002.
24   There are signs that this may be changing, however, as the polarizing social impacts of rapid economic and regulatory reform become more apparent: 'A sharp debate erupts in China over ideologies', *New York Times*, 12 March 2006.
25   While no one knows quite how extensive non-performing loans may be, estimates of 25 per cent of GDP are common.

6   East Asia in a Global Economy

1   On dependent development, see Hoogvelt (2001). On the nature of core–periphery relations, see Chase-Dunn (1998). What both these perspectives have in common are pessimistic expectations about the prospects for development as a consequence of the structurally embedded, essentially exploitative relationships that exist between different parts of the world.

2 The 'value chain' refers to the way in which products become more valuable as they are transformed from basic commodities to finished manufactured products. More highly-paid jobs and wealth-creating processes are generally found nearer to the point of completion, making such activities a key focus of industry policies. The existence of established companies, and even national economies, makes it much harder for new entrants to break into the more lucrative aspects of the value-creating process, however. See Kaplinsky (2000).

3 Raw material suppliers such as Indonesia are an exception to this general pattern.

4 I am indebted to John Ravenhill for alerting me to the significance of this.

5 For a more general discussion of MNC strategies, see Dunning (1988).

6 Malaysia is an important exception to this pattern, as is Singapore which is included in the NICs for the purposes of this discussion.

7 Significantly, much of Singapore's investment has come from the USA, which reinforces its dependence on, and orientation to, American markets.

8 'Submerging again?', *The Economist*, 31 March 2001: 71–2.

9 Ibid.

10 'Proton's future creates rift in Malaysia', *Financial Times*, 20 July 2005.

11 'How cooked are the books?', *The Economist*, 16 March: 35–6.

12 'Pump priming', *The Economist*, 2 October 2004: 27–8.

13 Linda Lim (1996) estimates that ethnic Chinese business interests amount for only 4 per cent of Indonesia's population and yet control 75 per cent of private sector economic activity, with similar ratios in the Philippines (2 per cent to 40 per cent), Thailand (10 per cent to 85 per cent), and Malaysia (30 per cent to 65 per cent).

14 'A new workshop of the world', *The Economist*, 12 October 2002: 25–6.

15 'The world's factory floor', *Australian Financial Review*, 11 October 2002: 72)

16 'Digital dragon', *The Economist*, 17 December 2005.

17 'China now a key profit source for MNCs', *Asia Times*, 24 September 2005.

18 'China: enter at your own risk', *Australian Financial Review*, 17 May 2002.

19 America's trade deficit with China was set to top $200 billion in 2005. 'Meeting the superpower', *The Economist*, 19 November 2005. Significantly, the USA has begun to employ precisely the same sorts of quota and targets to restrict the flow of Chinese exports that it employed – without success – against Japan in the 1980s: 'US, China stitch up landmark trade deal', *The Australian*, 11 November 2005.

20 US policy-makers were increasingly concerned about the performance of the Japanese economy – especially in the aftermath of a financial crisis in Mexico – and agreed to the devaluation in an effort to ward off a possible crisis in Japan, too.

21 The capital account records the movement of long- and short-term capital in and out of a country. During the 1990s in particular, governments across the world allowed capital to move more freely and with fewer controls. Problems can emerge when inflows are too extensive to be used 'prudently', leading to speculative investment and problems of 'moral hazard' where

capital is allocated on the basis of connections rather than economic efficiency. See Kenen (2001).

22 By 1996, Indonesia's short-term debt was 56.7 per cent of overall liabilities,
South Korea's was 58.5 per cent, Thailand's 67.2 per cent, and Malaysia's
a massive 70.1 per cent. See Haggard (2000: 18).

23 Almost, but not quite: the USA continues to enjoy unique privileges that
flow from being able to pay its debts in its own currency. See Cohen (1998).

24 It is important to note that the IMF bail-out package was largely intended
to protect the positions of outside investors, raising major questions about
'moral hazard'. See Stiglitz (2002).

25 That the Philippines was less badly affected by the crisis is not testimony to
strong fundamentals of sound economic policy-making, but more to the
fact that they had received far less investment than their neighbours, had
generally poorer economic outcomes, and thus had less far to fall. See Bello
(2000).

26 During this period, Malaysia restricted capital moments in and out of the
country and did not allow the *ringgit* to be traded on international capital
markets.

27 Stephen Grenville is the Deputy Governor of the Reserve Bank of Australia
and his comments mark a revealing division between national monetary
authorities even in the pro-market, Anglo–American economies.

28 In this regard, it is worth noting that Malaysia's stance enjoyed the support
of some economically-orthodox, high-profile commentators from outside
East Asia. See, for example, Krugman (1999) and Stiglitz (2002).

29 Japan has long been a major source of capital inflows into the USA, but
China has also become increasingly important, investing the bulk of its
approximately $500 billion foreign exchange reserves in American
Treasury bonds. See Woodall (2004).

30 'China hints at shift from greenback', *Weekend Australian*, 7–8 January
2006: 31.

31 'OPEC, Russia to pick up US deficit slack', *Weekend Australian*, 7–8
January 2006: 32.

32 For an interesting and original exploration of the structural power
American indebtedness confers upon the USA, see Seabrooke (2001).

33 'Ballooning US foreign debt spells trouble for Asia', *Straits Times*, 12
September 2003: 21.

34 'Hot money returns to Asia', *International Herald Tribune*, 20 October
2003.

7 The Evolution of East Asian Regionalism

1 Liberal theorists such as Robert Keohane (1982) argued that the demand
for international institutions would increase as a consequence of their functional utility and a decline in US hegemony. While the extent of American
decline remains hotly contested, Keohane was clearly right in suggesting

that it would be an important factor in shaping the course of regional institutional development.

2 This phrase is borrowed from Cronin's (1996) excellent analysis of the Cold War.

3 Indonesia challenged the legitimacy of the newly independent Malaysia but its decision to renounce the confrontational approach 'served as a model for its neighbours and raised the possibility of a regional order based on the non-use of force in inter-state relations': Acharya (2001: 49).

4 In addition to the original members, ASEAN has expanded to include Brunei, Vietnam, Laos, Cambodia and, most contentiously, Burma.

5 AFTA was originally intended to reduce tariffs on manufactured exports to 0–5 per cent by 2008. This agenda was expanded to include a range of agreements on services, trade, investment and agricultural products. Despite the crisis, there is still a general commitment to adhere to the agreements, although there is still some flexibility in 'sensitive' industries and sectors. See Nesadurai (2003).

6 The elimination or reduction of internal trade barriers within the ASEAN grouping made the sort of cross-border production strategies employed by Japanese car manufacturers discussed in the last chapter more feasible and attractive.

7 This may reflect the rather ill-considered, ad hoc nature of the original proposal that Hawke launched on a visit to Seoul. See Funabashi (1995: 55).

8 Amongst the most significant were the Pacific Basin Economic Council, the Pacific Economic Cooperation Council and the Pacific Trade and Development Conference. See Woods (1993).

9 Ernst Haas (1990) suggests that an epistemic community is 'composed of professionals . . . who share a commitment to a common causal model and a common set of political values. They are united by a belief in the truth of their model and a commitment to translate this truth into public policy.'

10 APEC's original membership included the members of ASEAN, plus Australia, New Zealand, the USA and Canada. In 1991, China, Hong Kong and Taiwan (styled 'Chinese Taipei' in deference to PRC sensitivities) joined. In 1993, Mexico and Papua New Guinea joined, Chile in 1994, with Peru, Russia and Vietnam joining in 1997.

11 Russian membership of APEC, which was supported by the USA despite Australian protests, appears to have been a trade-off for it not objecting to the eastward expansion of NATO: 'US imperatives rule in maturing APEC', *The Australian*, 27 November 1997.

12 The authority of a number of other key international organizations, such as the United Nations, has been similarly undermined by a lack of US support, despite the fact that it is becoming increasingly apparent that they remain crucially important elements of the contemporary international order and frequently operate to further American interests. See Tucker and Hendrickson (2004).

13 'Asean members worried by Rice's decision to skip talks', *International Herald Tribune*, 22 July 2005.

14   See Mahathir and Ishihara (1995). For an important discussion of the background to these developments and their impact on APEC in particular, see Berger (1999).
15   Significantly, however, China was, at best, lukewarm about the idea, something that seriously undermined the prospects for a coherent regional response. See Amyx (2004b).
16   'Japan is not helping ties with China', *People's Daily*, 29 December 2004.
17   It seems clear that anti-Japan demonstrations in China have occurred with the tacit approval (if not the connivance) of the government. One motivation may be to thwart Japan's bid for a permanent seat on the UN Security Council: 'UN power play drives China protests', *International Herald Tribune*, 12 April 2005.
18   'Poll shows Japan's hardening attitude to China', *Financial Times*, 14 December 2005.
19   'A sign of Japan's decline', *Japan Times*, 3 November 2005.
20   'Foreign ministry mind set: "Hate China" ', *Japan Times*, 11 June 2005.
21   'China seeks to reassure on "peaceful development" ', *International Herald Tribune*, 25 April 2005.
22   'China eroding US dominance', *Asia Times*, 8 December 2005.
23   'Fear of losing out to China prompts FTA stampede', *Japan Times*, 10 September 2004.
24   'Economic ties binding Japan to rival China', *New York Times*, 31 October 2005.

8   East Asian Futures

1   Indeed, according to Jared Diamond (1998), going early in the civilizational process is a big advantage, too, and one that locks in historical patterns of domination and subordination.
2   The fact that the logging industry is notoriously corrupt and receives protection from the police and the military does not help. See Guerin (2005a).
3   The potential for conflict is highlighted in the tensions between Singapore and Malaysia, as Singapore remains heavily dependent on its neighbour for supplies of water.
4   'China water supplies: a continuing threat', *International Herald Tribune*, 11 January 2006.
5   'Fears over Chinese water supply', *BBC News*, 28 December 2005.
6   'China crisis: threat to the global environment', *The Independent*, 20 October 2005.
7   China's next big boom could be foul air', *New York Times*, 30 October 2005.
8   'China's voracious appetite is for energy is eating into global capacity and sending prices skywards', *Financial Times*, 21 May 2004.

9   Then President Carter committed the USA to using 'any means necessary' to protect oil flows and supplies in the Persian Gulf.

10 'Oil and votes, two factors fuelling the war', *People's Daily*, 21 March 2003.

11 'US firms fear revenge after China's lost oil bid', *International Herald Tribune*, August 2005.

12 For example, Japan is investing heavily in Iranian oil production despite American efforts to block the deal. See Hanson (2004).

13 In one of the most important and optimism-inducing analyses of energy and resource use, Hawken, Lovins and Lovins (1999) lay out a blueprint for dramatically reducing future environmental depletion, mainly by making better use of existing assets.

14 The latest evidence suggests that the impact of global warming may be more severe and catastrophic than previously thought, and its impacts may already be irreversible: 'Stark warning over climate change', *BBC News*, 30 January 2006.

15 For an important statement of the dilemmas facing the USA as far as its reliance on foreign energy supplies are concerned, and a blueprint for what the USA should do about this, see the report of the National Energy Policy Development Group (NEPDG 2001), chaired by Vice President Dick Cheney.

16 As *The Economist* (4 February 2006) pointed out, despite Bush's State of the Union rhetoric, the reality is that 'Bush is still avoiding most of the regulations that might actually encourage the market to ditch dirty technologies in favour of clean ones. And he is still avoiding any attempt to make Americans pay the true cost of the oil they guzzle.'

17 'Still gushing forth', *The Economist*, 5 February 2005; 'US threat to world economy', *The Australian*, 9 January 2004.

18 'China and India: bidding partners, at least on paper', *International Herald Tribune*, 20 January 2006.

References

Abernathy, David B. (2000) *Global Dominance: European Overseas Empires, 1415–1980* (New Haven: Yale University Press).

Acharya, Amitav (2005) 'The Bush Doctrine and Asian regional order', in Gurtov, M. and Van Ness, P. (eds), *Confronting the Bush Doctrine: Critical Views from the Asia-Pacific* (London: RoutledgeCurzon): 203–26.

Acharya, Amitav (2004) 'How ideas spread: whose norms matter? Norm localization and institutional change in Asian regionalism', *International Organization*, 58: 239–75.

Acharya, Amitav (2002) 'Regionalism and the emerging world order', in Breslin, S., Hughes, C., Phillips, N. and Rosamond, B. (eds), *New Regionalisms in the Global Political Economy* (London: Routledge): 20–32.

Acharya, Amitav (2001) *Constructing a Security Community in Southeast Asia: ASEAN and the Problem of Regional Order* (London: Routledge).

Acharya, Amitav (2000) *The Quest for Identity: International Relations of Southeast Asia* (Singapore: Oxford University Press).

Adler, E. and Barnett, M. (1998) 'A framework for the study of security communities', in Adler, E. and Barnett, M. (eds), *Security Communities* (Cambridge: Cambridge University Press): 29–65.

Agnew, John (2005) *Hegemony: The New Shape of Global Power* (Philadelphia, PA: Temple University Press).

Agnew, John (1994) 'The territorial trap: the geographical assumptions of international relations theory', *Review of International Political Economy*, 1 (1): 53–80.

Ahmad, Sameena (2004) 'Behind the mask: a survey of business in China', *The Economist*, 20 March.

Alagappa, Muthiah (2003) 'Managing Asian security: competition, cooperation, and evolutionary change', in Alagappa, M. (ed.) *Asian Security Order: Instrumental and Normative Features* (Stanford, CA: Stanford University Press): 571–606.

Alagappa, Muthiah (2001) 'Introduction: presidential election, democratization, and cross-Strait relations', in Alagappa, M. (ed.), *Taiwan's Presidential Politics* (Armonk, NY: M.E. Sharpe): 3–47.

Alagappa, Muthiah (1998) 'Asian practice of security: key features and explanations', in Alagappa, M. (ed.), *Asian Security Practice: Material and Ideational Influences* (Stanford, CA: Stanford University Press): 611–76.

Alagappa, Muthiah (ed.) (1995) *Political Legitimacy in Southeast Asia: The Quest for Moral Authority* (Stanford, CA: Stanford University Press).

Alatas, Ali (2001) *'ASEAN Plus Three' Equals Peace Plus Prosperity* (Singapore: Institute of Southeast Asian Studies).

Amirahmadi, Hooshang and Wu, Weiping (1995) 'Export processing zones in Asia', *Asian Survey*, 35 (9): 828–49.

Amsden, Alice H. (2001) *The Rise of 'The Rest': Challenges to the West from Late-Industrializing Economies* (Oxford: Oxford University Press).

Amsden, Alice H. (1995) 'Like the rest: South-east Asia's "late" industrialization', *Journal of International Development*, 7 (5): 791–9.

Amsden, Alice H. (1989) *Asia's Next Giant: South Korea and Late Industrialization* (New York: Oxford University Press).

Amyx, Jennifer (2005) 'What motivates regional financial cooperation in East Asia today?', *Asia Pacific Issues*, 76 (Honolulu: East West Centre).

Amyx, Jennifer A. (2004a) *A Regional Bond Market for East Asia? The Evolving Political Dynamics of Regional Financial Cooperation*, Pacific Economic Paper 343 (Canberra: Australian National University).

Amyx, Jennifer (2004b) 'Japan and the evolution of regional financial arrangements in East Asia', in Krauss, E.S. and Pempel, T.J. (eds), *Beyond Bilateralism: US–Japan Relations in the New Asia-Pacific* (Stanford, CA: Stanford University Press): 198–218.

Anderson, Benedict (1988) 'Cacique democracy and the Philippines: origins and dreams', *New Left Review*, 169: 3–31.

Anderson, Benedict (1983) *Imagined Communities* (London: Verso).

Anderson, Benedict (1972) *Java in a Time of Revolution: Occupation and Resistance*, 1944–1946 (Ithaca, NY: Cornell University Press).

Arase, David (1995) *Buying Power: The Political Economy of Japan's Foreign Aid* (Boulder, CO: Lynne Rienner).

Arase, David (1994) 'Public–private sector interest coordination in Japan's ODA', *Pacific Affairs*, 67 (2): 171–99.

Armijo, Leslie Elliott (2002) ''The terms of the debate: what's democracy got to do with it?', in Armijo, L.E. (ed.), *Debating the Global Financial Architecture* (New York: New York State University): 2–62.

Arthur, Brian (1989) 'Competing technologies, increasing returns, and lock-in by historical events', *Economic Journal*, 99: 116–31.

ASEAN (2005) Kuala Lumpur Declaration on the ASEAN Plus Three Summit, Kuala Lumpur, 12 December. Available at: http://www.aseansec.org/18036.htm

ASEAN (1967) *The ASEAN Declaration*, available at: http://www.aseansec.org/1629.htm

Ash, Timothy G (2004) *Free World: America, Europe, and the Surprising Future of the West* (New York: Random House).

Ayoob, Mohammed (2005) 'The future of political Islam: the importance of external variables', *International Affairs*, 81 (5): 951–61.

Ba, Alice D. (2003) 'China and Asean: reinvigorating relations for a 21st-century Asia', *Asian Survey*, 43 (4): 622–47.

Bagchi, A.K. (2000) 'The past and the future of the developmental state', *Journal of World Systems Research*, Summer /Fall: 398–442.

Balassa, Bela (1988) 'The lessons of East Asian development: an overview', *Economic Development and Cultural Change*, 36 (3): S273–90.

Barber, Benjamin R. (2001) *Jihad vs McWorld* (New York: Ballantine Books).

Barnett, Michael and Finnemore, Martha (2004) *Rules for the World: International Organizations in Global Politics* (Ithaca, NY: Cornell University Press).

Beasley, W.G. (1993) *The Rise of Modern Japan: Political, Economic, and Social Change since 1850* (London: Weidenfeld & Nicolson).

Beasley, W.G. (1989) 'Meiji political institutions', in Jansen, M.B. (ed.), *The Cambridge History of Japan, Volume 5: The Nineteenth Century* (Cambridge: Cambridge University Press): 618–73.

Beddoes, Zanny Minton (2005) 'The great thrift shift: a survey of the world economy', *The Economist*, 24 September.

Beeson, Mark (2006a) 'American ascendancy: conceptualising contemporary hegemony', in Beeson, M. (ed.), *Bush and Asia: America's Evolving Relations with East Asia* (London: RoutledgeCurzon): 3–23.

Beeson, Mark (2006b) 'American hegemony and regionalism: the rise of East Asia and the end of the Asia-Pacific', *Geopolitics*, 11 (4): 1–20.

Beeson, Mark (2006c) 'Does hegemony still matter? Revisiting regime formation in the Asia-Pacific', in Nesadurai, Helen E.S. (ed.), *Globalisation and Economic Security in East Asia: Governance and Institutions* (London: RoutledgeCurzon): 183–99.

Beeson, Mark (2006d) 'Southeast Asia and the international financial institutions', in Rodan, G., Hewison, K. and Robison, R. (eds), *The Political Economy of South-East Asia: An Introduction*, 3rd edn (Melbourne: Oxford University Press): 238–55.

Beeson, Mark (2006e) 'The rise of the "neocons" and the evolution of American foreign policy', in Hadiz, Vedi (ed.), *Empire, Neoliberalism, and Asia* (London: Routledge): 69–82.

Beeson, Mark (2005a) 'Politics and markets in East Asia: is the developmental state compatible with globalisation?', in Stubbs, Richard and Underhill, Geoffrey R.D. (eds), *Political Economy and the Changing Global Order*, 3rd edn (Ontario: Oxford University Press): 443–53.

Beeson, Mark (2005b) 'Re-thinking regionalism: Europe and East Asia in comparative historical perspective', *Journal of European Public Policy*, 12 (6): 969–85.

Beeson, Mark (2004a) 'The rise and fall (?) of the developmental state: the vicissitudes and implications of East Asian interventionism', in Low, L. (ed.), *Developmental States: Relevant, Redundant or Reconfigured?* (New York: Nova Science): 29–40.

Beeson, Mark (2004b) 'US hegemony and Southeast Asia: the impact of, and limits to, American power and influence', *Critical Asian Studies*, 36 (3): 323–54.

Beeson, Mark (2003a) 'ASEAN Plus Three and the rise of reactionary regionalism', *Contemporary Southeast Asia*, 25 (2): 251–68.

Beeson, Mark (2003b) 'Australia's relationship with the United States: the case for greater independence', *Australian Journal of Political Science*, 38 (3): 387–405.

Beeson, Mark (2003c) 'East Asia, the international financial institutions and regional regulatory reform: a review of the issues', *Journal of the Asia Pacific Economy*, 8 (3): 305–26.

Beeson, Mark (2003d) 'Japan's reluctant reformers and the legacy of the developmental state', in Cheung, A. and Scott, I. (eds), *Governance and Public Sector Reform in Post-Crisis Asia: Paradigm Shift or Business as Usual?* (London: Curzon Press): 25–43.

Beeson, Mark (2003e) 'Sovereignty under siege: globalisation and the state in Southeast Asia', *Third World Quarterly*, 24 (2): 357–74.

Beeson, Mark (2002a) 'Southeast Asia and the politics of vulnerability', *Third World Quarterly*, 23 (3): 549–64.

Beeson, Mark (2002b) 'The more things change . . .? Path dependency and convergence in East Asia', in Beeson, M. (ed.), *Reconfiguring East Asia: Regional Institutions and Organisations after the Crisis* (London: RoutledgeCurzon): 246–56.

Beeson, Mark (2001a) 'Globalisation, governance, and the political-economy of public policy reform in East Asia', *Governance: An International Journal of Policy, Administration and Institutions*, 14 (4): 481–502.

Beeson, Mark (2001b) 'Japan and Southeast Asia: the lineaments of quasi-hegemony', in Rodan, Garry, Hewison, Kevin and Robison, Richard (eds), *The Political Economy of South-East Asia: An Introduction*, 2nd edn (Melbourne: Oxford University Press): 283–306.

Beeson, Mark (2000) 'Mahathir and the markets: globalisation and the pursuit of economic autonomy in Malaysia', *Pacific Affairs*, 73 (3): 335–51.

Beeson, Mark (1999a) *Competing Capitalisms: Australia, Japan and Economic Competition in the Asia Pacific* (London: Macmillan).

Beeson, Mark (1999b) 'Reshaping regional institutions: APEC and the IMF in East Asia', *Pacific Review*, 12 (1): 1–24.

Beeson, Mark (1998) 'Indonesia, the East Asian crisis, and the commodification of the nation-state', *New Political Economy*, 3 (3): 357–74.

Beeson, Mark (1996) 'APEC: nice theory, shame about the practice', *Australian Quarterly*, 68 (2): 35–48.

Beeson, Mark and Bell, Stephen (2005a) 'Structures, institutions and agency in the models of capitalism debate', in Phillips, Nicola (ed.), *Globalising International Political Economy* (Basingstoke: Palgrave Macmillan): 116–40.

Beeson, Mark and Bell, Stephen (2005b) 'The G20 and the politics of international financial sector reform: robust regimes or hegemonic instability?', CSGR Working Paper 174/05, Warwick University, September. Available at: http://www2.warwick.ac.uk/fac/soc/csgr/research/working-papers/2005/wp17405.pdf

Beeson, Mark and Berger, Mark T. (2003) 'The paradoxes of paramountcy: regional rivalries and the dynamics of American hegemony in East Asia', *Global Change, Peace and Security*, 15 (1): 27–42.

Beeson, Mark and Higgott, Richard (2005) 'Hegemony, institutionalism and US foreign policy: theory and practice in comparative historical perspective', *Third World Quarterly*, 26 (7): 1,173–88.

Beeson, Mark and Islam, Iyanatul (2005) 'Neoliberalism and East Asia: Resisting the Washington Consensus', *Journal of Development Studies*, 41 (2): 197–219.

Beeson, Mark and Jayasuriya, Kanishka (1998) 'The political rationalities of regionalism: APEC and the EU in comparative perspective', *Pacific Review*, 11 (3): 311–36.

Beeson, Mark and Robison, Richard (2000) 'Introduction: interpreting the crisis', in Robison, R. *et al.* (eds), *Politics and Markets in the Wake of the Asian Crisis* (London: Routledge): 3–24.

Beeson, Mark and Yoshimatsu, Hidetaka (2006) 'Asia's odd men out: Australia, Japan, and the politics of regionalism', CSGR Working Paper 196/06, Warwick University, March 2006. Available at: http://www2.warwick.ac.uk/fac/soc/csgr/research/workingpapers/2006/ wp 19606.pdf/

Bell, Stephen (2005) 'How tight are the policy constraints: the policy convergence thesis, institutionally situated actors and expansionary monetary policy in Australia', *New Political Economy*, 10 (1): 68–91.

Bell, Stephen and Feng, Steven (forthcoming) 'IT infrastructure policy and the politics of trade opening in post-WTO China: the second image reversed?', *Review of International Political Economy*.

Bello, Walden (2000) 'The Philippines: the making of a neo-clasical tragedy', in Robison, R. *et al.* (eds), *Politics and Markets in the Wake of the Asian Crisis* (London: Routledge): 238–57.

Bello, Walden (1998) 'East Asia: On the eve of the great transformation?', *Review of International Political Economy*, 5 (3): 424–44.

Bello, Walden and Poh, Li Kheng (1998) *A Siamese Tragedy: Development and Disintegration in Modern Thailand* (London: Zed Books).

Beresford, Melanie (2006) 'Vietnam: the transition from central planning', in Rodan, G., Hewison, K. and Robison, R. (eds), *The Political Economy of South-East Asia: An Introduction*, 3rd edn (Melbourne: Oxford University Press): 195–218.

Berger, Mark T. (2004a) 'After the Third World? History, destiny and the fate of Third Worldism', *Third World Quarterly*, 25 (1): 9–39.

Berger, Mark T. (2004b) *The Battle for Asia: From Decolonization to Globalization* (London: RoutledgeCurzon).

Berger, Mark T. (1999) 'APEC and its enemies: the failure of the new regionalism in the Asia-Pacific', *Third World Quarterly*, 20 (5): 1,013–30.

Berger, Suzanne and Dore, Ronald (eds.) (1996) *National Diversity and Global Capitalism* (Ithaca, NY: Cornell University Press).

Bernard, Mitchell and Ravenhill, John (1995) 'Beyond product cycles and flying geese: regionalization, hierarchy, and the industrialization of East Asia', *World Politics*, 47: 179–210.

Bertrand, Jacques (1998) 'Growth and democracy in Southeast Asia', *Comparative Politics*, 30 (3): 355–75.

Bevacqua, Ron (1998) 'Whither the Japanese model: the Asian economic crisis and the continuation of Cold War politics in the Pacific Rim', *Review of International Political Economy*, 5 (3): 410–23.

Bezlova, Antoaneta (2004) 'The dragon stirs in a wary world', *Asia Times*, 25 December, available at: http://www.atimes.com

Bhagwati, Jagdish (1998) 'The capital myth', *Foreign Affairs*, 77 (3): 7–12.

Bird, Graham (1996) 'The IMF and developing countries: a review of the evidence and policy options', *International Organization*, 50 (3): 477–511.

Blaut, J.M. (1993) *The Colonizer's View of the World* (New York: Guilford Press).

Bleiker, Roland (2005) *Divided Korea: Toward a Culture of Reconciliation* (Minneapolis, MN: University of Minnesota Press).

Bobbitt, Philip (2002) *The Shield of Achilles: War, Peace and the Course of History* (New York: Knopf).

Boli, J. and Thomas, G.M. (1999) 'INGOs and the organisation of world culture', in Boli, J. and Thomas, G.M. (eds), *Constructing World Culture: International Nongovernmental Organizations Since 1875* (Stanford, CA: Stanford University Press): 13–48.

Boot, Max (2002) *The Savage Wars of Peace: Small Wars and the Rise of American Power* (New York: Basic Books).

Booth, Anne (1999) 'Development: Achievement and weakness', in Emmerson, D. (ed.), *Indonesia beyond Suharto* (Armonk, NY: M.E. Sharpe): 109–35.

Booth, Ken and Trood, Russell (eds) (1999) *Strategic Cultures in the Asia-Pacific Region* (London: Macmillan).

Boucher, Richard (2005) *Joint statement of the US–Japan Security Consultative Committee* (Washington, DC: US Department of State).

Bowie, Alasdair and Unger, Danny (1997) *The Politics of Open Economies: Indonesia, Malaysia, the Philippines and Thailand* (Cambridge: Cambridge University Press).

Bowles, Paul (2002) 'Asia's post-crisis regionalism: bringing the state back in, keeping the (United) States out', *Review of International Political Economy*, 9 (2): 244–70.

Bowles, Paul (2000) 'Regionalism and development after (?) the global financial crises', *New Political Economy*, 5 (3): 433–55.

Bowles, S. and Gintis, H. (1996) *Democracy and Capitalism* (New York: Basic Books).

Bowles, Paul and MacLean, Brian (1996) 'Understanding trade bloc formation: the case of the ASEAN Free Trade Area', *Review of International Political Economy*, 3 (2): 319–48.

Boyer, Robert and Hollingsworth, J.R. (1997) 'From national embeddedness to spatial nestedness', in Hollingsworth, J.R. and Boyer, R. (eds), *Contemporary Capitalism: The Embeddedness of Institutions* (Cambridge: Cambridge University Press): 433–84.

Braithwaite, John and Drahos, Peter (2000) *Global Business Regulation* (Cambridge: Cambridge University Press).

Brenner, Neil (1999) 'Beyond state-centrism? Space, territoriality, and geographical scale in globalization studies', *Theory and Society*, 28: 39–78.

Brenner, Robert (2002) *The Boom and the Bubble* (London: Verso).

Breslin, Shaun (2005) 'Power and production: rethinking China's global economic role', *Review of International Studies*, 31: 735–53.

Breslin, Shaun and Higgott, Richard (2000) 'Studying regions: learning from the old, constructing the new', *New Political Economy*, 5 (3): 333–52.

Brown, C. (1998) ' "Overseas Chinese" business in South East Asia', in Sheridan, K. (ed.), *Emerging Economic Systems in Asia* (St Leonards: Allen & Unwin): 208–27.

Brown, David (1994) *The State and Politics in Southeast Asia* (London: Routledge).

Brown, Lester (1995) *Who will Feed China? Wake-up Call for a Small Planet* (London: Earthscan).

Bryan, Dick (1995) *The Chase across the Globe: International Accumulation and the Contradictions for the Nation State* (Boulder, CO: Westview Press).

Bryant, Ralph C. (2003) *Turbulent Waters: Cross-Border Finance and International Governance* (Washington, DC: Brookings Institution).

Bryant, Raymond L. and Parnwell, Michael J.G. (1996) 'Introduction: politics, sustainable development and environmental change in Southeast Asia', in Bryant, R.L. and Parnwell, M. (eds) *Environmental Change in South-east Asia: People, Politics, and Sustainable Development* (London: Routledge): 1–20.

Brzezinski, Zbigniew (2004) *The Choice: Global Domination or Global Leadership* (New York: Basic Books).

Buchanan, Paul G. and Nicholls, Kate (2003) 'Labour politics and democratic transition in South Korea and Taiwan', *Government and Opposition*, 38 (2): 203–37.

Burke, Anthony and McDonald, Matt (eds) (2006), *Critical Security in the Asia Pacific* (Manchester: Manchester University Press).

Burma, Ian and Margalit, Avishai (2004) *Occidentalism: The West in the Eyes of its Enemies* (New York: Penguin).

Bush, George W. (2005) 'President discusses freedom and democracy in Kyoto Japan, The White House, 18 November. Available at: http://www.whitehouse.gov/news/releases/2005/11/print/20051116-6.html

Buzan, Barry (1995) 'The level of analysis problem in international relations reconsidered', in Booth, K. and Smith, S. (eds), *International Relations Theory Today*, (Oxford: Polity Press): 198–216.

Buzan, Barry and Waever, Ole (2003) *Regions and Powers: The Structure of International Security* (Cambridge: Cambridge University Press).

Calder, Kent E. (2004) 'Securing security through prosperity: the San Francisco System in comparative perspective', *Pacific Review*, 17 (1): 135–57.

Calder, Kent E. (1996) *Asia's Deadly Triangle: How Arms, Energy and Growth Threaten to Destabilize Asia Pacific* (London: Nicholas Brealey).

Calder, Kent E. (1988a) *Crisis and Compensation: Public Policy and Public Stability in Japan* (Princeton, NJ: Princeton University Press).

Calder, Kent E. (1988b) 'Japanese foreign economic policy formation: explaining the reactive state', *World Politics*, 40 (4): 25–54.

Callon, Scott (1995) *Divided Sun: MITI and the Breakdown of Japanese High-Tech Policy, 1975–1993* (Stanford, CA: Stanford University Press).

Camilleri, Joseph A. (2000) *States, Markets and Civil Society in Asia Pacific* (Northampton: Edward Elgar).

Cammack, Paul (2003) 'The governance of global capitalism: a new materialist perspective', *Historical Materialism*, 11 (2): 37–59.

Camroux, David and Lechervy, C. (1996) ' "Close encounter of the Third Kind?" The inaugural Asia-Europe meeting of March 1996', *Pacific Review*, 9 (3): 442–53.

Caporaso, J.A. (1996) 'The European Union and forms of state: Westphalian, regulatory or post-modern?', *Journal of Common Market Studies*, 34 (1): 29–51.

Carlile, Lonny E. (1998) 'The politics of administrative reform', in Carlile, L.E. and Tilton, M.C. (eds), *Is Japan Really Changing its Ways? Regulatory Reform and the Japanese Economy* (Washington, DC: Brookings Institute): 76–110.

Carlile, Lonny E. and Tilton, Mark C. (1998) 'Regulatory reform and the developmental state', in Carlile, L.E. and Tilton, M.C. (eds), *Is Japan Really Changing its Ways? Regulatory Reform and the Japanese Economy* (Washington, DC: Brookings Institute): 197–218.

Carpenter, Susan (2003) *Special Corporations and the Bureaucracy: Why Japan Can't Reform* (Basingstoke: Macmillan).

Carpenter, Ted G. (2006) *America's Coming War with China: A Collision Course over Taiwan* (Basingstoke: Palgrave Macmillan).

Case, William (2002) *Politics in Southeast Asia: Democracy or Less* (London: RoutledgeCurzon).

Castells, Manuel (1992) 'Four Asian tigers with a dragon head', in Applebaum, R.P and Henderson, J. (eds), *States and Development in the Asian Pacific Rim* (Newbury Park, CA: Sage): 33–70.

Cerny, Philip G. (2005) 'Power, markets and accountability: the development of multi-level governance in international finance', in Baker, Andrew, Hudson, Alan and Woodward, Richard (eds), *Governing Global Finance: International Political Economy and Multi-Level Governance* (London: Routledge): 24–48.

Cerny, Philip G. (1999) 'Globalization and the erosion of democracy', *European Journal of Theoretical Research*, 36: 1–26.

Cerny, Philip G. (1996) 'International finance and the erosion of state policy capacity', in Gummett, P. (ed.), *Globalisation and Public Policy* (Cheltenham: Edward Elgar): 82–104.

Cerny, Philip G. (1995) 'Globalization and the changing logic of collective action', *International Organization*, 49 (4): 595–625.

Cerny, Philip G. (1991) 'The limits of deregulation: transnational interpenetration and policy change', *European Journal of Political Research*, 19: 173–96.

Chai-Anan Samudavanija (1993) 'The new military and democracy in Thailand', in Diamond, L. (ed.), *Political Culture and Democracy in Developing Countries* (Boulder, CO: Lynne Rienner): 269–87.

Chaibong, Hahm (2005) 'The two South Koreas: a house divided', *Washington Quarterly*, 28 (3): 57–72.

Chalk, Peter (2001) 'Separatism and Southeast Asia: the Islamic factor in Southern Thailand, Mindanao, and Aceh', *Studies in Conflict and Terrorism*, 24: 241–69.

Chandler, Alfred (1990) *Scale and Scope: The Dynamics of Industrial Capitalism* (Cambridge, MA: Harvard University Press).

Chang, David Wen-Wei (1988) *China under Deng Xiaoping: Political and Economic Reform* (New York: St Martin's Press).

Chang, Gordon G. (2002) *The Coming Collapse of China* (London: Arrow).

Chang, Ha-Joon (2002) *Kicking Away the Ladder: Development Strategy in Historical Perspective* (London: Anthem Books).

Chang, Ha-Joon (2000) 'Globalization, transnational corporations, and economic development: can the developing countries pursue strategic industry policy in a globalizing world economy?', in Baker, D., Epstein, G. and Pollin, R. (eds), *Globalization and Progressive Economic Policy* (Cambridge: Cambridge University Press).

Chang, Ha-Joon (1998) 'Korea; the misunderstood crisis', *World Development*, 26 (8): 1555–61.

Chang, Li Lin and Rajan, Ramkishen S. (2001) 'The economics and politics of monetary regionalism in Asia', *ASEAN Economic Bulletin*, 18 (1): 103–18.

Charrier, Philip (2001) 'ASEAN's inheritance: The regionalization of Southeast Asia, 1941–61', *Pacific Review*, 14 (3): 313–38.

Chase-Dunn, Christopher (1998) *Global Formation: Structures of the World Economy* (Lanham, MD: Rowan & Littlefield).

Chen, Edward and Kwan, C.H. (eds) (1997) *Asia's Borderless Economy: The Emergence of Sub-Regional Zones* (St Leonards, NSW: Allen & Unwin).

Chernow, Ron (2004) *Alexander Hamilton* (Harmondsworth: Penguin).

Chia, Siow Yue (1999) 'Trade, foreign direct investment and economic development of Southeast Asia', *Pacific Review*, 12 (2): 249–70.

Chin, Mikyung (2003) 'Civil society in South Korean democratization', in Arase, D. (ed.), *The Challenge of Change: East Asia in the New Millennium* (Berkeley, CA: Institute of East Asian Studies): 201–14.

China Internet Information Centre (2005) *Building of Political Democracy in China*, available at: http://english.people.com.cn/whitepaper/democracy/democracy.html

Choi, Jang Jip (1995) 'Political cleavages in South Korea', in Koo, H. (ed.), *State and Society in Contemporary Korea* (Ithaca, NY: Cornell University Press): 13–50.

Christensen, Thomas J. (1999) 'China, the US–Japan alliance, and the security dilemma in East Asia', *International Security*, 23 (4): 49–80.

Christie, Clive J. (1996) *A Modern History of Southeast Asia* (London: I.B. Tauris).

Chung, Chin-Wee (1986) 'The evolution of political institutions in North Korea', in Scalapino, R.A., Sato, S. and Wanandi, J. (eds), *Asian Political Institutionalization* (Berkeley, CA: Institute of East Asian Studies): 18–41.

Ciccantell, Paul S. and Stephen G. Bunker (2004) 'The economic ascent of China and the potential for restructuring the capitalist world-economy', *Journal of World Systems Research*, 10 (3): 565–89.

Cochrane, Joe (2002) 'A military mafia', *Newsweek*, 26 August.

Cohen, Benjamin J. (2000) 'Taming the Phoenix? Monetary governance after the crisis', in Noble, G.W. and Ravenhill, J. (eds), *The Asian Financial Crisis and the Architecture of Global Finance* (Cambridge: Cambridge University Press): 192–212.

Cohen, Benjamin J. (1998) *The Geography of Money* (Ithaca, NY: Cornell University Press).

Cohen, Benjamin J. (1993) 'The triad and the Holy Trinity: lessons for the Pacific region', in Higgottt, R., Leaver, R. and Ravenhill, J. (eds), *Pacific Economic Relations in the 1990s: Cooperation or Conflict?* (Boulder, CO: Lynne Rienner): 133–58.

Cohen, Stephen and Zysman, John (1987) *Manufacturing Matters: The Myth of the Post-Industrial Economy* (New York: Basic Books).

Cohen, Warren I. (2000) *East Asia at the Center* (New York: Columbia University Press).

Collins, Alan (2003) *Security and Southeast Asia: Domestic, Regional, and Global Issues* (Boulder, CO: Lynne Rienner).

Connors, Michael (2006) 'Thailand and the United States: beyond hegemony?', in Beeson, M. (ed.), *Bush and Asia: America's Evolving Relations with East Asia* (London: RoutledgeCurzon): 128–44.

Corsetti, Giancarlo, Pesenti, Paolo and Roubini, Nouriel (1999) 'What caused the Asian currency and financial crisis', *Japan and the World Economy*, 11: 305–73.

Cotton, James (2004) *East Timor, Australia and Regional Order: Intervention and its Aftermath in Southeast Asia* (London: RoutledgeCurzon).

Cotton, James (1999) 'The "haze" over Southeast Asia: challenging the ASEAN mode of regional engagement', *Pacific Affairs*, 72 (3): 331–51.

Crane, George T. (1990) *The Political Economy of China's Special Economic Zones* (Amonk, NY: M.E. Sharpe).

Crane, K., Cliff, R., Mederios, E., Mulvenon, J. and Overholt, W. (2005) *Modernizing China's Military: Opportunities and Constraints* (Santa Monica, CA: Rand Corporation).

Cribb, Robert (ed.) (1990) *The Indonesian Killings of 1965–1966: Studies from Java and Bali* (Clayton, Victoria: Centre of SE Asian Studies, Monash University).

Crockett, Andrew (2002) 'Capital flows in East Asia since the crisis', Speech to the ASEAN Plus Three Deputies, Beijing, 11 October.

Cronin, James E. (1996) *The World the Cold War Made: Order, Chaos, and the Return of History* (London: Routledge).

Crouch, Harold (1996) *Government and Society in Malaysia* (St Leonards, NSW: Allen & Unwin).

Crouch, Harold (1985) *Economic Change, Social Structure and the Political System in Southeast Asia: Philippine Development Compared with other ASEAN Countries* (Singapore: Institute of Southeast Asian Studies).

Cumings, Bruce (2004) *North Korea: Another Country* (Melbourne: Scribe).

Cumings, Bruce (1997a) 'Japan and Northeast Asia into the Twenty-first century', in Katzenstein, P.J. and Shiraishi, T. (eds), *Network Power: Japan and Asia* (Ithaca, NY: Cornell University Press): 136–68.

Cumings, Bruce (1997b) *Korea's Place in the Sun: A Modern History* (New York: W.W. Norton).

Cumings, Bruce (1990) *The Origins of the Korean War: Volume II, The Roaring Cataract of 1947–50* (Princeton, NJ: Princeton University Press).

Cumings, Bruce (1984) 'The origins and development of Northeast Asian political economy: industrial sectors, product cycles, and political consequences', *International Organization*, 38 (1): 1–40.

Curtis, Gerald L. (1999) *The Logic of Japanese Politics: Leaders, Institutions, and the Limits of Change* (New York: Columbia University Press).

Daalder, Ivo H. and Lindsay, James M. (2003) *America Unbound: The Bush Revolution in Foreign Policy* (Washington, DC: Brookings Institution).

Das, Dilip (2003) *WTO: The Doha Agenda, The New Negotiations on World Trade* (London: Zed Books).

Dauvergne, Peter (1997) *Shadows in the Forest: Japan and the Politics of Timber in Southeast Asia* (Cambridge, MA: MIT Press).

Deng, Yong (2001) 'Hegemon on the offensive: Chinese perspectives on US global strategy', *Political Science Quarterly*, 116 (3): 343–65.

Dent, Christopher M. (2003) 'Networking the region? The emergence and impact of Asia-Pacific bilateral free trade agreement projects', *Pacific Review*, 16 (1): 1–28.

Diamond, Jared (2005) *Collapse: How Societies Choose to Fail or Survive* (London: Allen Lane).

Diamond, Jared (1998) *Guns, Germs and Steel: A Short History of Everybody for the Last 13,000 Years* (London: Vintage).

Diamond, Larry (2001) 'Anatomy of an electoral earthquake: how the KMT lost and the DPP won the 2000 Presidential election', in Alagappa, M. (ed.), *Taiwan's Presidential Politics* (Armonk, NY: M.E. Sharpe): 48–87.

Dick, Howard (2002) 'Corruption and good governance: the new frontier of social engineering', in Lindsey, T. and Dick, H. (eds), *Corruption in Asia: Rethinking the Governance Paradigm* (Leichhardt: Federation Press): 71–86.

Dicken, Peter (1998), *Global Shift: Transforming the World Economy* (London: Paul Chapman).

Dicken, Peter and Yeung, Henry Wai-chung (1999) 'Investing in the future: East Asia firms in the global economy', in Olds, K., Kong, L., Kelly, P. and Yeung, H.W. (eds), *Globalisation and the Asia-Pacific* (London: Routledge): 106–28.

Dieter, Herbert and Higgott, Richard (2003) 'Exploring alternative theories of economic regionalism: from trade to finance in Asian co-operation?', *Review of International Political Economy*, 10 (3): 430–54.

Ding, X.L. (2000) 'Informal privatisation through internationalization: the rise of nomenklatura capitalism in China's offshore businesses', *British Journal of Political Science*, 30: 121–46.

Dittmer, Lowell (2003) 'Leadership change and Chinese political development', *China Quarterly*, 176: 904–25.

Dittmer, Lowell (2002) 'Modernizing Chinese informal politics', in Unger, J. (ed.), *The Nature of Chinese Politics: From Mao to Jiang* (Armonk, NY: M.E. Sharpe): 3–37.

Dore, Ronald (1986) *Flexible Rigidities: Industrial Policy and Structural Adjustment in the Japanese Economy 1970–80* (Stanford, CA: Stanford University Press).

Doremus, Paul N., Keller, William W., Pauly, Louis W. and Reich, Simon (1999) *The Myth of the Global Corporation* (Princeton, NJ: Princeton University Press).

Doronila, Amando (1985) 'The transformation of patron–client relations and its political consequences in postwar Philippines', *Journal of Southeast Asian Studies*, March: 89–97.

Dower, John (1995) *Japan in War and Peace* (London: HarperCollins).

Dower, John W. (1986) *War Without Mercy: Race and Power in the Pacific War* (New York: Pantheon).

Doyle, Michael (1997) *Ways of War and Peace: Realism, Liberalism, and Socialism* (New York: Norton).

Doyle, Michael W. (1986) *Empires* (Ithaca, NY: Cornell University Press).

Dreyer, June T. (2000) *China's Political System: Modernization and Tradition* (London: Macmillan).

Drezner, Daniel (2001a) 'Globalization and policy convergence', *International Studies Review*, 3 (1): 53–78.

Drezner, Daniel (2001b) 'State structure, technological leadership and the maintenance of hegemony', *Review of International Studies*, 27: 3–25.

Drifte, Reinhard (1996) *Japan's Foreign Policy: From Economic Superpower to What Power?* (Basinstoke and New York: Macmillan/St Martin's Press).

Drysdale, Peter and Garnaut, Ross (1993) 'The Pacific: an application of a general theory of economic integration', in Bergsten, C.F. and Noland, M. (eds), *Pacific Dynamism and the International Economic System* (Washington, DC: Institute for International Economics): 183–223.

Duffield, Michael (2002) *Global Governance and the New Wars* (London: Zed Books).

Dunning, John H. (2000) 'Globalization and the new geography of foreign investment', in Woods, N. (ed.), *The Political Economy of Globalization* (London: Macmillan): 20–53.

Dunning, John H. (1988) *Explaining International Production* (London: Unwin Hyman).

Dupont, Alan (2001) *East Asia Imperilled: Transnational Challenges to Security* (Cambridge: Cambridge University Press).

Dupont, Alan (1996) 'Is there an "Asian Way"?', *Survival*, 38 (2): 13–33.

EASG (2002) *Final Report of the East Asia Study Group*, ASEAN+3 Summit, Phnom Penh.

Eastman, Lloyd E. (1986) 'Nationalist China during the Nanking decade 1927–1937', in Fairbank, John K. and Feurwerker, Albert (eds), *The Cambridge History of China, Volume 13: Republican China 1912–1949* (Cambridge: Cambridge University Press): 116–67.

Eccleston, Bernard (1995) *State and Society in Post-War Japan* (Cambridge: Polity Press).

Economy, Elizabeth C. (2004) *The River Runs Black: The Environmental Challenge to China's Future* (Ithaca, NY: Cornell University Press).

Edwardes, Michael (1961) *Asia in the European Age, 1498–1955* (London: Thames & Hudson).

Eichengreen, Barry (2005) 'China's new exchange rate regime', *Current History*, 104 (683): 264–7.

Eichengreen, B. and Kenen, P.B. (1994) 'Managing the world economy under the Bretton Woods system: an overview', in Kenen, P.B. (ed.), *Managing the World Economy: Fifty Years after Bretton Woods* (Washington: Institute for International Economics): 3–57.

Eldridge, Philip J. (2002) *The Politics of Human Rights in Southeast Asia* (London: Routledge).

Elliott, Lorraine (2004) 'Environmental challenges, policy failure and regional dynamics in Southeast Asia', in Beeson, M. (ed.), *Contemporary Southeast Asia: Regional Dynamics, National Differences* (Basingstoke: Palgrave Macmillan): 178–97.

Elson, Robert E. (2005) 'Constructing the nation: ethnicity, race, modernity and citizenship in early Indonesian thought', *Asian Ethnicity*, 6 (3): 145–60.

Elson, Robert E. (2004) 'Reinventing a region: Southeast Asia and the colonial experience', in Beeson, M. (ed.), *Contemporary Southeast Asia: Regional Dynamics, National Differences* (Basingstoke: Palgrave Macmillan): 15–29.

Elson, Robert E. (2001) *Suharto: A Political Biography* (Cambridge: Cambridge University Press).

Elson, Robert E. (1999) 'International commerce, the state and society: economic and social change', in Tarling, N. (ed.), *The Cambridge History of Southeast Asia, Volume 3, From c. 1800 to the 1930s* (Cambridge: Cambridge University Press): 127–92.

Emmerson, Donald K. (1988) 'The military and development in Indonesia', in Dwinandono, J.S. and Cheong, T.M. (eds), *Soldiers and Stability in Southeast Asia* (Singapore: Institute of Southeast Asian Studies): 107–30.

Emmerson, Donald K. (1984) 'Southeast Asia: What's in a Name?', *Journal of Southeast Asian Studies*, 15 (1): 1–21.

Emmott, Bill (2005) 'The sun also rises: a survey of Japan', *The Economist*, 8 October.

Engdahl, F. William (2005) 'China lays down the gauntlet in energy war: the geopolitics of oil, Central Asia and the United States', *Asia Times*, 22 December, available at: http://www.atimes.com.

Ernst, Dieter (2000) 'Evolutionary aspects: the Asian production networks of Japanese electronics firms', in Borrus, M., Ernst, D. and Haggard, S. (eds), *International Production Networks in Asia: Rivalry or Riches?* (London: Routledge): 80–109.

Etō, Shinkichi (1986) 'China's international relations 1911–1931', in Fairbank, John K. and Feurwerker, Albert (eds), *The Cambridge History of China, Volume 13: Republican China 1912–1949* (Cambridge: Cambridge University Press): 74–115.

European Commission (2000) *Standard Eurobarometer: Public Opinion in the European Union*, 52 (Brussels: European Commission).

Evans, Paul (2005) 'Between regionalism and regionalization: policy networks and the nascent East Asian institutional identity', in Pempel, T.J. (ed.), *Remapping East Asia: The Construction of a Region* (Ithaca, NY: Cornell University Press): 195–215.

Evans, Peter (1998) 'Transferable lessons? Re-examining the institutional prerequisites for East Asian economic policies', *Journal of Development Studies*, 34 (6): 66–87.

Evans, Peter (1995) *Embedded Autonomy: States and Industrial Transformation* (Princeton, NJ: Princeton University Press).

Evans, Peter, Rueschemeyer, D. and Skocpol, T. (eds) (1985) *Bringing the State Back In* (Cambridge: Cambridge University Press).

Fairbank, John K. (1994) *China: A New History* (Cambridge, MA: Harvard University Press).

Fairbank, John K., Reischauer, Edwin O. and Craig, Albert M. (1965) *East Asia: The Modern Transformation* (Boston, MA: Houghton Mifflin).

Farrell, Roger (2000) 'Japanese foreign direct investment in the world economy 1951–1997', *Pacific Economic Papers*, 299 (Canberra: Australia–Japan Research Centre).

Fawcett, Louise (1995) 'Regionalism in historical perspective', in Fawcett, L. and Hurrell, A. (eds), *Regionalism in World Politics: Regional Organization and International Order* (Oxford: Oxford University Press): 9–36.

Felker, Greg (2003) 'Southeast Asian industrialisation and the changing global production system', *Third World Quarterly*, 24 (2): 255–82.

Feng, Hui (2006) *The Politics of China's Accession to the World Trade Organisation: The Dragon Goes Global* (London: Routledge)

Ferguson, Niall (2002) *Empire: The Rise and Demise of the British World Order and the Lessons for Global Power* (New York: Basic Books).

Ferguson, Niall and Kotlikoff, Laurence J. (2003) 'Going critical: American power and the consequences of fiscal overstretch', *National Interest*, 73: 22–32.

Fewsmith, Joseph (2001) 'The political and social implications of China's accession to the WTO', *China Quarterly*, 167: 573–91.

Fischer, Stanley (1998) 'The Asian crisis: a view from the IMF', Address to Bankers' Association, Washington, DC, 22 January.

Fitzgerald, John (1996) *Awakening China: Politics, Culture, and Class in the Nationalist Revolution* (Stanford, CA: Stanford University Press).

Fong, Glen (1998) 'Follower at the frontier: international competition and Japanese industrial policy', *International Studies Quarterly*, 42: 339–66.

Frank, André Gunder and Gills, Barry K. (1993) *The World System: Five Hundred Years or Five Thousand?* (London: Routledge).

Frank, Andre Gunder (1998) *ReOrient: Global Economy in the Asian Age* (Berkeley, CA: University of California).

Friedberg, Aaron (1993–4) 'Ripe for rivalry: prospects for peace in a multi-polar Asia', *International Security*, 18 (3): 5–33.

Friedman, David (1988) *The Misunderstood Miracle: Industrial Development and Political Change in Japan* (Ithaca, NY: Cornell University Press).

Friedman, Edward (2000) 'Since there is no East and there is no West, how could either be the best?', in Jacobsen, M. and Bruun, O. (eds), *Human Rights and Asian Values: Contesting National Identities and Cultural Representations in Asia* (London: Curzon): 21–42.

Friedman, Thomas (2000) *The Lexus and the Olive Tree* (London: HarperCollins).

Froebel, Folker, Heinrichs, Jürgen and Kreye, Otto (1980) *The New International Division of Labour* (Cambridge: Cambridge University Press).

Frost, Frank (1990) 'Introduction: ASEAN since 1967 – origins, evolution and recent developments', in Broinowski, A. (ed.), *ASEAN into the 1990s* (London: Macmillan): 1–31.

Fry, Gerald W. and Faming, Manyooch Nitnoi (2001) 'Laos', in Heenan, P. and Lamontagne, M. (eds), *The Southeast Asia Handbook* (Chicago, IL: Fitzroy Dearborn): 145–56.

Fukuyama, Francis (2004) *State-Building: Governance and Order in the 21st Century* (Ithaca, NY: Cornell University Press).

Fukuyama, Francis (1995) *Trust: The Social Virtues and the Creation of Prosperity* (London: Hamish Hamilton).

Fukuyama, Francis (1992) *The End of History and the Last Man* (New York: Avon Books).

Funabashi, Yoichi (1995) *Asia Pacific Fusion: Japan's Role in APEC* (Washington, DC: Institute for International Economics).

Funabashi, Yoichi (1993) 'The Asianisation of Asia', *Foreign Affairs*, 72 (5): 75–85.

Fung, Edmund (1995) 'Chinese nationalism in the twentieth century', in Mackerras, Colin (ed.), *Eastern Asia* (Melbourne: Longman): 175–88.

Gaddis, John Lewis (1997) *We Now Know: Rethinking Cold War History* (Oxford: Oxford University Press).

Gaddis, John Lewis (1982) *Strategies of Containment: A Critical Appraisal of Postwar American Security Policy* (Oxford: Oxford University Press).

Gaddis, John Lewis (1972) *The United States and the Origins of the Cold War, 1941–1947* (New York: Columbia University Press).

Gangopadhyay, Partha (1998) 'Patterns of trade, investment and migration in the Asia-Pacific region', in Thompson, G. (ed.), *Economic Dynamism in the Asia-Pacific* (London: Routledge): 20–54.

Garrett, Banning (2001) 'China faces, debates, the contradictions of globalization', *Asian Survey*, 41 (3): 409–27.

Garrett, Geoffrey (1998) *Partisan Politics in the Global Economy* (Cambridge: Cambridge University Press).

Garten, Jeffrey E. (2005) 'The global economic challenge', *Foreign Affairs*, 84 (1): 37–48.

Gellner, Ernest (1983) *Nations and Nationalism* (Princeton, NY: Princeton University Press).

George, Aurelia (1997) 'The role of foreign pressure (gaiatsu) in Japan's agricultural trade liberalization', *Pacific Review*, 10 (2): 165–209.

George Mulgan, Aurelia (2006) 'Japan and the Bush agenda: alignment of divergence?', in Beeson, M. (ed.), *Bush and Asia: America's Evolving Relations with East Asia* (London: RoutledgeCurzon): 109–27.

George Mulgan, Aurelia (2005) *Japan's Interventionist State: The Role of the MAFF* (London: RoutledgeCurzon).

Gereffi, Gary (1998) 'More than the market, more than the state: global commodity chains and industrial upgrading in East Asia', in Chan, S. and Clark, C. (eds), *Beyond the Developmental State: East Asia's Political Economies Reconsidered* (London: Macmillan): 38–59.

Gereffi, Gary (1995) 'Global production systems and third world development', in Stallings, B. (ed.), *Global Change, Regional Response: The New International Context of Development* (Cambridge: Cambridge University Press): 100–42.

Gereffi, Gary and Wyman, D.L. (eds) (1990) *Manufacturing Miracles: Paths of Industrialization in Latin America and East Asia* (Princeton, NJ: Princeton University Press).

Gerlach, Michael (1992) *Alliance Capitalism: The Social Organization of Japanese Business* (Berkeley, CA: University of California).

Gersham, John (2002) 'Is Southeast Asia the second front?', *Foreign Affairs*, 81 (4): 60–74.

Gerschenkron, Alexander (1966) *Economic Backwardness in Historical Perspective* (Cambridge, MA: Belknap Press).

Giddens, Anthony (1985) *The Nation State and Violence* (Cambridge: Polity Press).

Gill, Stephen (1995) 'Globalization, market civilization, and disciplinary neoliberalism', *Millennium*, 24 (3): 399–423.

Glassman, Jim (2006) 'US foreign policy and the war on terror in Southeast Asia', in Rodan, Garry, Hewison, Kevin and Robison, Richard (eds) *The Political Economy of South-East Asia: An Introduction*, 3rd edn (Melbourne: Oxford University Press): 219–37.

Godement, François (1997) *The New Asian Renaissance: From Colonialism to the Post-Cold War* (London: Routledge).

Goh, Evelyn (2004) 'The ASEAN Regional Forum in United States East Asian strategy', *Pacific Review*, 17 (1): 47–69.

Gold, Thomas B. (1986) *State and Society in the Taiwan Miracle* (Armonk, NY: M.E. Sharpe).

Goldstein, Avery (2001) 'The diplomatic face of China's grand strategy: a rising power's emerging choice', *China Quarterly*, 168: 835–63.

Gomez, E.T. and Jomo, K.S. (1997) *Malaysia's Political Economy: Politics, Patronage and Profits* (Cambridge: Cambridge University Press).

Gong, Gerrit W. (1984) *The Standard of 'Civilisation' in International Society* (Oxford: Clarendon Press).

Gonzalez, Joaquin L. (2001) 'Philippines: counting people power', in Funston, J. (ed.), *Government and Politics in Southeast Asia* (London: Zed Books): 252–90.

Goodman, David S.G. (1997–8) 'Are Asia's "ethnic Chinese" a regional-security threat?', *Survival*, 39 (4): 14–55.

Goodman, David S.G. (1997) 'China in reform: the view from the provinces', in Goodman, D.S.G. (ed.), *China's Provinces in Reform: Class, Community and Political Culture* (London: Routledge): 1–20.

Gordon, A. (1993) 'Contests for the Workplace', in Gordon, A. (ed.), *Postwar Japan as History* (Berkeley, CA: University of California): 373–94.

Gordon, David M. (1994) 'Twixt cup and the lip: mainstream economics and the formation of economic policy', *Social Research*, 61 (1): 1–29.

Green, Michael (2001) *Japan's Reluctant Realism: Foreign Policy Challenges in an Era of Uncertain Power* (New York: Palgrave).

Green, Stephen and Liu, Guy S. (2005) 'China's industrial reform strategy: retreat and retain', in Green, S. and Liu, G.S. (eds), *Exit the Dragon? Privatization and State Control in China* (London: Chatham House): 15–41.

Grenville, Stephen (2004) 'The IMF and the Indonesian crisis', *Bulletin of Indonesian Economic Studies*, 40 (1): 77–94.

Gries, Peter Hays (2004) *China's New Nationalism: Pride, Politics and Diplomacy* (Berkeley: University of California Press).

Guerin, Bill (2005a) 'Indonesia targets timber trafficking racket', *Asia Times*, 26 February, available at: http://www.atimes.com

Guerin, Bill (2005b) 'Yudhoyono's bumpy first year', *Asia Times*, 28 October, available at: http://www.atimes.com

Gundzik, Jephraim P. (2005) 'The ties that bind China, Russia and Iran', *Asia Times*, 6 June, available at: http://www.atimes.com

Haacke, Jurgen (1999) 'The concept of flexible engagement and the practice of enhanced interaction: intramural challenges to the "ASEAN way"', *Pacific Review*, 12 (4): 581–611.

Haas, Ernst B. (1990) *When Knowledge is Power: Three Models of International Organizations* (Berkley, CA: University of California).

Haas, Ernst B. (1968) *The Uniting of Europe: Politics, Social and Economic Forces, 1950–1957* (Stanford, CA: Stanford University Press).

Haas, Ernst B. (1964) *Beyond the Nation State: Functionalism and International Organization* (Stanford, CA: Stanford University Press).

Hadiz, Vedi (2004a) 'Decentralization and democracy in Indonesia: a critique of neo-institutionalist perspectives', *Development and Change*, 35 (4): 697–718.

Hadiz, Vedi (2004b) 'The politics of labour movements in Southeast Asia', in Beeson, M. (ed.), *Contemporary Southeast Asia: Regional Dynamics, National Differences* (Basingstoke: Palgrave Macmillan): 118–35.

Haggard, Stephan (2000) *The Political Economy of the Asian Financial Crisis* (Washington, DC: Institute for International Economics).

Haggard, Stephan (1990) *Pathways from the Periphery: The Politics of Growth in the Newly Industrialising Countries* (Ithaca, NY: Cornell University Press).

Haggard, S. and Kaufman, R. (1995) *The Political Economy of the Democratic Transitions* (Princeton, NJ: Princeton University Press).

Haji, Ragayah and Zin, Mat (2005) 'Income distribution in East Asian developing countries: recent trends', *Asian-Pacific Economic Literature*, 19 (2): 36–54.

Hale, David (2004) 'China's growing appetites', *National Interest* (76): 137–47.

Hall, Peter A. (1999) 'The political economy of Europe in an era of interdependence', in H. Kitschelt, Lange, P., Marks, G. and Stephens, J.D. (eds), *Continuity and Change in Contemporary Capitalism* (Cambridge: Cambridge University Press): 135–163.

Hall, Peter A. (1986) *Governing the Economy: The Politics of State Intervention in Britain and France* (Oxford: Oxford University Press).

Hall, Peter A. and Soskice, David (2001) 'An introduction to the varieties of capitalism', in Hall, P.A. and Soskice, D. (eds), *Varieties of Capitalism: The Institutional Foundations of Comparative Advantage* (Oxford: Oxford University Press): 1–68.

Hall, Rodney B. (2003) 'The discursive demolition of the Asian development model', *International Studies Quarterly*, 47: 71–99.

Hall, Stuart (1996) 'The West and the rest: discourse and power', in Hall, S. and Gieben, B. (eds), *Formation of Modernity* (Cambridge: Polity Press): 275–332.

Hamashita, Takeshi (1994) 'The tribute trade system and modern Asia', in Latham, A.J.H. and Kawakatsu, H. (eds), *Japanese Industrialization and the Asian Economy* (London: Routledge): 91–107.

Hamilton, Gary (1994) 'Civilizations and the organization of economies', in Smelser, N.J. and Swedberg, R. (eds), *The Handbook of Economic Sociology* (Princeton, NJ: Princeton University Press): 183–205.

Hamilton-Hart, Natasha (2005) 'Terrorism and Southeast Asia: expert analysis, myopia and fantasy', *Pacific Review*, 18: 303–25.

Hamilton-Hart, Natasha (2004) 'Capital flows and financial markets in Asia: national, regional, or global?', in Krauss, E.S and Pempel, T.J. (eds), *Beyond Bilateralism: US–Japan Relations in the New Asia-Pacific* (Stanford, CA: Stanford University Press): 133–53.

Hanson, Richard (2004) 'Japan, Iran sign major oil deal, US dismayed', *Asia Times*, 20 February, available at: http://www.atimes.com

Harris, S. and Mack, A. (1997) 'Security and economics in East Asia', in Harris, S. and Mack, A. (eds), *Asia-Pacific Security: The Economics-Politics Nexus* (St Leonards: Allen & Unwin): 1–29.

Harrison, Lawrence E. and Huntington, Samuel P. (eds) (2000) *Culture Matters: How Values Shape Human Progress* (New York: Basic Books).

Hart-Landsberg, Martin and Burkett, Paul (1998) 'Contradictions of capitalist industralization in East Asia: a critique of "flying geese" theories of development', *Economic Geography*, 74 (2): 87–110.

Hartcher, Peter (1997) *The Ministry* (Sydney: HarperCollins).

Harvey, David (1988) *The Condition of Postmodernity: An Enquiry into the Origins of Cultural Change* (Oxford: Basil Blackwell).

Hatch, Walter and Yamamura, Kozo (1996) *Asia in Japan's Embrace: Building a Regional Production Alliance* (Cambridge: Cambridge University Press).

Hawes, Gary (1987) *The Philippine State and this Marcos Regime: The Politics of Export*, (Ithaca: Cornill University Press).

Hawken, Paul (2005) *The Ecology of Commerce: A Declaration of Sustainability* (New York: Collins).

Hawken, Paul, Lovins, Amory and Lovins, L. Hunter (1999) *Natural Capitalism: Creating the Next Industrial Revolution* (Boston, MA: Little, Brown).

Hedman, Eva-Lotta E. (2001) 'The Philippines: not so military, not so civil', in Alagappa, M. (ed.), *Coercion and Governance: The Declining Political Role of the Military in Asia* (Stanford, CA: Stanford University Press): 165–86.

Heginbotham, Eric and Samuels, Richard J. (1998) 'Mercantile realism and Japanese foreign policy', *International Security*, 22 (4): 171–203.

Heginbotham, Eric and Twomey, Christopher P. (2005) 'America's Bismarkian Asia policy', *Current History*, 104 (683): 243–50.

Heilbroner, Robert (1990) 'Analysis and vision in the history of modern economic thought', *Journal of Economic Literature*, 38: 1,097–114.

Heilbroner, Robert (1985) *The Nature and Logic of Capital* (New York: W.W. Norton).

Held, David (2004) 'Democratic accountability and political effectiveness from a cosmopolitan perspective', *Government and Opposition*, 39 (2): 364–91.

Held, David (1995) *Democracy and the Global Order* (Cambridge: Polity Press).

Held, David (1987) *Models of Democracy* (Oxford: Polity Press).

Held, David, McGrew, Anthony, Goldblatt, David and Perraton, Jonathan (1999) *Global Transformations* (Stanford, CA: Stanford University Press).

Helleiner, Eric (1994) *States and the Reemergence of Global Finance* (Ithaca, NY: Cornell University Press).

Hemmer, Christopher and Katzenstein, Peter J. (2002) 'Why is there no NATO in Asia? Collective identity, regionalism, and the origins of multilateralism', *International Organization*, 56 (3): 575–607.

Henderson, Jeannie (1999) *Reassessing ASEAN*, Adelphi Paper, vol. 328 (New York: Oxford University Press).

Henning, C. Randall (2002) *East Asian Financial Cooperation* (Washington, DC: Institute for International Economics).

Hernandez, Carolina G. (1986) 'Political institution building in the Philippines', in Scalapino, R.A., Sato, S. and Wanandi, J. (eds), *Asian*

Political Institutionalization (Berkeley, CA: Institute of East Asian Studies): 261–87.

Hettne, Björn (1999) 'Globalization and the new regionalism: the second great transformation', in Hettne, B., Inotai, A. and Sunkel, O. (eds), *Globalism and the New Regionalism* (London: Macmillan): 1–24.

Hettne, Björn and Söderbaum, Fredrick (2002) 'Theorizing the rise of regioness', in Breslin, S., Hughes, C. and Philips, N. (eds), *New Regionalisms in the Global Political Economy* (London: Routledge): 33–47.

Hewison, Kevin (2006) 'Thailand: boom, bust, and recovery', in Rodan, G., Hewison, K. and Robison, R. (eds), *The Political Economy of South-East Asia: An Introduction*, 3rd edn (Melbourne: Oxford University Press): 72–106.

Hewison, Kevin (2001) 'Thailand's capitalism: development through boom and bust', in Rodan, G., Hewison, K. and Robison, R. (eds), *The Political Economy of South-east Asia* (Melbourne: Oxford University Press): 71–103.

Hewison, Kevin (1999) 'Political space in Southeast Asia: "Asian-style" and other democracies', *Democratization*, 6 (1): 224–45.

Hewison, Kevin (1989) *Bankers and Bureaucrats: Capital and the Role of the State in Thailand* (New Haven: Yale University Press).

Higgott, Richard (2004) 'US foreign policy and the "securitization" of economic globalization', *International Politics*, 41 (2): 147–75.

Higgott, Richard A. (1998) 'The Asian economic crisis: a study in the politics of resentment', *New Political Economy*, 3 (3): 333–56.

Higgott, Richard A. (1995) 'Economic cooperation in the Asia Pacific: a theoretical comparison with the European Union', *Journal of European Public Policy*, 2 (3): 361–83.

Hilley, John (2001) *Malaysia: Mahathirism, Hegemony, and the New Opposition* (London: Zed Books).

Hirst, Paul and Thompson, Grahame (1996) *Globalization in Question* (Oxford: Polity Press).

Hobday, Mike (2001) 'The electronics industries of the Asia-Pacific: exploiting international production networks for economic development', *Asian Pacific Economic Literature*, 15 (1): 13–29.

Hobsbawm, Eric (1994) *Age of Extremes: The Short Twentieth Century 1914–1991* (London: Weidenfeld & Nicolson)

Hobsbawm, Eric (1987) *The Age of Empire* (London: Weidenfeld & Nicolson).

Hobson, John M. (2004) *The Eastern Origins of Western Civilization* (Cambridge: Cambridge University Press).

Hobson, John M. (2003) 'Disappearing taxes or the "race to the middle"? Fiscal policy in the OECD', in Weiss, Linda (ed.), *States in the Global Economy: Bringing Domestic Institutions Back In* (Cambridge: Cambridge University Press): 37–57.

Hodgson, Geoffrey M. (1996) 'Varieties of capitalism and varieties of economic theory', *Review of International Political Economy*, 3 (3): 380–433.

Hogan, Michael J. (1998) *A Cross of Iron: Harry S. Truman and the Origins of the National Security State 1945–1954* (Cambridge: Cambridge University Press).

Homer-Dixon, Thomas F. (1999) *Environment, Scarcity, and Violence* (Princeton, NJ: Princeton University Press).

Hoogvelt, Ankie (2001) *Globalization and the Postcolonial World*, 2nd edn (Baltimore, MD: Johns Hopkins University Press).

Hook, Glenn (1999) 'The East Asian economic caucus: a case of reactive subregionalism?', in Hook, G. and Kearns, I. (eds), *Subregionalism and World Order* (London: Macmillan): 223–45.

Hsiao, Frank S.T., Hsiao, Mei-chu W. and Yamashita, Akio (2003) 'The impact of the US economy on the Asia-Pacific region: does it matter?', *Journal of Asian Economics* 14: 219–41.

Hsü, Immanuel (1983) *The Rise of Modern China*, 3rd edn (Hong Kong: Oxford University Press).

Huang, Ray (1997) *China: A Macro History* (Armonk, NY: M.E. Sharpe).

Hughes, Christopher W. (2005) *Japan's Re-emergence as a 'Normal' Military Power*, Adelphi Paper 368–9 (London: Routledge).

Hughes, Christopher W. (2000) 'Japanese policy and the East Asian currency crisis: abject defeat or quiet victory?', *Review of International Political Economy*, 7: 219–53.

Hughes, Neil C. (2005) 'A trade war with China?', *Foreign Affairs*, 84 (4): 94–106.

Hund, Markus (2003) 'ASEAN Plus Three: towards a new age of pan-East Asian regionalism? A sceptic's appraisal', *Pacific Review*, 16 (3): 383–417.

Hundt, David (2005) 'The end of the affair? The dynamics of the Korean developmental alliance', Unpublished PhD thesis, University of Queensland.

Hunt, Michael H. (1987) *Ideology and US Foreign policy* (New Haven, CT: Yale University Press).

Huntington, Samuel P. (1996) 'The West unique, not universal', *Foreign Affairs*, 75 (6): 28–46.

Huntington, Samuel P. (1991) *The Third Wave: Democratization in the Late Twentieth Century* (Norman, OK: University of Oklahoma Press).

Hurrell, Andrew (1995) 'Explaining the resurgence of regionalism in world politics', *Review of International Studies*, 21: 331–58.

Hutchcroft, Paul D. (1999) 'Neither dynamo nor domino: reforms and crises in the Philippine political economy', in Pempel, T.J. (ed.), *The Politics of the Asian Economic Crisis* (Ithaca, NY: Cornell University Press): 163–83.

Hutchcroft, Paul D. (1998) *Booty Capitalism: The Politics of Banking in the Philippines* (Ithaca, NY: Cornell University Press).

Hutchcroft, Paul D. (1997) 'The politics of privilege: assessing the impact of rents, corruption, and clientelism on Third World development', *Political Studies*, 45: 639–58.

Hutchcroft, Paul D. (1994) 'Booty capitalism: business-government relations in the Philippines', in MacIntyre, A. (ed.), *Business and Government in Industrializing Asia* (St Leonards, NSW: Allen & Unwin): 216–43.

Hutchison, Jane (2006) 'Poverty of politics in the Philippines', in Rodan, G., Hewison, K. and Robison, R. (eds), *The Political Economy of South-East Asia: An Introduction*, 3rd edn (Melbourne: Oxford University Press): 39–71.

Huxley, Tim and Willett, Susan (1999) *Arming East Asia*, Adelphi Paper 329 (London: International Institute of Strategic Studies).

Ikenberry, G. John (2001a) *After Victory: Institutions, Strategic Restraint, and the Rebuilding of Order After Major Wars* (Princeton. NJ: Princeton University Press).

Ikenberry, G. John (2001b) 'American power and the empire of capitalist democracy', *Review of International Studies*, 27: 191–212.

Ikenberry, G. John and Mastanduno, Michael (2003) 'Conclusion: the United States and stability in East Asia', in Ikenberry, G.J. and Mastanduno, M. (eds), *International Relations Theory and the Asia-Pacific* (New York: Columbia University Press): 421–39.

Ingleson, John (1996) 'The "Asian ethic"', in Bell, R., McDonald, T. and Tidwell, A. (eds), *Negotiating the Pacific Century: The 'New' Asia, the United States and Australia* (St Leonards, NSW: Allen & Unwin): 251–67.

Iriye, Akira (1989) 'Japan's drive to great power status', in Jansen, M.B. (ed.), *The Cambridge History of Japan, Volume 5: The Nineteenth Century* (Cambridge: Cambridge University Press): 721–82.

Iriye, Akira (1981) *Power and Culture: The Japanese–American War, 1941–1945* (Cambridge, MA: Harvard University Press).

Iriye, Akira (1967) *Across the Pacific: An Inner History of American–East Asian Relations* (New York: Harbinger).

Islam, Iyanatul and Chowdhury, Anis (2000) *Asia-Pacific Economies: A Survey* (London: Routledge).

Isogai, Takashi and Shibanuma, Shunichi (no date) 'East Asia's intra- and inter-regional economic relations: data analyses on trade, direct investments and currency transactions', *International Department Working Paper Series*, 00-E-4 (Tokyo: Bank of Japan).

Jain, Purnendra (1997) 'Party politics at the crossroads', in Jain, P. and Inoguchi, T. (eds), *Japanese Politics Today: Beyond Karaoke Democracy?* (Melbourne: Macmillan): 11–29.

James, Harold (2001) *The End of Globalization: Lessons from the Great Depression* (Cambridge, MA: Harvard University Press).

Jansen, Marius B. (1989) 'The Meiji Restration', in Jansen, M.B. (ed.), *The Cambridge History of Japan, Volume 5: The Nineteenth Century* (Cambridge: Cambridge University Press): 308–66.

Jayasuriya, Kanishka (2003) 'Embedded mercantilism and open regionalism: the crisis of a regional political project', *Third World Quarterly*, 24 (2): 339–55.

Jayasuriya, Kanishka (2001) 'Globalization and the changing architecture of the state: the regulatory state and the politics of negative co-ordination', *Journal of European Public Policy*, 8 (1): 101–23.

Jayasuriya, Kanishka (1999) 'Globalization, law, and the transformation of sovereignty: the emergence of global regulatory governance', *Indiana Journal of Global Legal Studies*, 6 (2): 425–55.

Jayasuriya, Kanishka (1996) 'The rule of law and capitalism in East Asia', *Pacific Review*, 9 (3): 367–88.

Jessop, Bob (2003) *The Future of the Capitalist State* (Cambridge: Polity Press).

Jesudason, J.V. (1989) *Ethnicity and the Economy: The State, Chinese Business, and Multinationals in Malaysia* (Singapore: Oxford University Press).

Joffe, Josef (1995) ' "Bismarck" or "Britain"? Toward an American grand strategy after bipolarity', *Foreign Affairs*, 14 (4): 94–117.

Johnson, Chalmers (2000) *Blowback: The Costs and Consequences of American Empire* (London: Little, Brown).

Johnson, Chalmers (1999) 'The developmental state: odyssey of a concept', in Woo-Cumings, M. (ed.), *The Developmental State* (Ithaca, NY: Cornell University Press): 32–60.

Johnson, Chalmers (1987) 'Political Institutions and Economic performance: the government–business relationship in Japan, South Korea, and Taiwan', in Deyo, F. (ed.), *The Political Economy of the New Asian Industrialism* (Ithaca, NY: Cornell University Press): 136–64.

Johnson, Chalmers (1982) *MITI and the Japanese Miracle: The Growth of Industry Policy 1925–1975* (Stanford, CA: Stanford University Press).

Johnson, Chalmers (1962) *Peasant Nationalism and Communist Power: The Emergence of Revolutionary China, 1937–1945* (Stanford, CA: Stanford University Press).

Johnston, Alastair I. (2003a) 'Is China a status quo power?', *International Security*, 27 (4): 5–56.

Johnston, Alastair I. (2003b) 'Socialization in international institutions: the ASEAN way and international relations theory', in Ikenberry, G.J. and Mastanduno, M. (eds), *International Relations and the Asia-Pacific* (New York: Columbia University Press): 107–62.

Johnston, Alastair I. (1999) 'Realism(s) and Chinese security policy in the post-Cold War period', in Kapstein, E.B. and Mastanduno, M. (eds), *Unipolar Politics: Realism and State Strategies after the Cold War* (New York: Columbia University Press): 261–318.

Johnston, Alastair I. (1995) *Cultural Realism: Strategic Culture and Grand Strategy in Chinese History* (Princeton, NJ: Princeton University Press).

Jomo, K.S. (2004) 'Southeast Asian developmental states in comparative East Asian perspective', in Low, L. (ed.), *Developmental States: Relevant, Redundant or Reconfigured?* (New York: Nova Science): 57–77.

Jomo, K.S. (2001) 'Introduction: growth and structural change in the second-tier Southeast Asian NICs', in Jomo, K.S. (ed.), *Southeast Asia's Industrialization: Industrial Policy, Capabilities and Sustainability* (Basingstoke: Palgrave Macmillan): 1–29.

Jomo, K.S. (1998) 'Introduction: financial governance, liberalization and crises in East Asia', in Jomo, K.S. (ed.), *Tigers in Trouble* (London: Zed Books): 1–32.

Jomo, K.S. (1997) *Southeast Asia's Misunderstood Miracle: Industrial Policy and Economic Development in Thailand, Malaysia and Indonesia* (Boulder, CO: Westview Press).

Jones, David Martin (1998) 'Democratization, civil society, and illiberal middle class culture in Pacific Asia', *Comparative Politics*, 30 (2): 147–69.

Jones, Eric (1981) *The European Miracle: Environments, Economies and Geopolitics in the History of Europe and Asia* (Cambridge: Cambridge University Press).

Kagan, Robert (2004) 'America's legitimacy crisis', *Foreign Affairs*, 83 (2): 65–87.

Kahler, Miles (2000) 'Legalization as a strategy: the Asia-Pacific case', *International Organization*, 54 (3): 549–71.

Kakuchi, Suvendrini (2003) 'Japan strives to adapt to a strong China', *Asia Times*, 2 April, available at: http://www.atimes.com

Kaldor, Mary (2001) *New and Old Wars: Organized Violence in a Global Era* (Stanford, CA: Stanford University Press).

Kang, Choi (1999) 'Korea: a tradition of peace – the danger of war', in Booth, Ken and Trood, Russell (eds), *Strategic Cultures in the Asia-Pacific Region* (London: Macmillan): 93–108.

Kang, David C. (2003a) 'Getting Asia wrong: the need for new analytical frameworks', *International Security*, 27 (4): 57–85.

Kang, David C. (2003b) 'International relations theory and the second Korean war', *International Studies Quarterly*, 47: 301–24.

Kang, David C. (2003c) 'Transaction costs and crony capitalism in East Asia', *Comparative Politics*, 35 (4): 439–58.

Kang, David C. (2002) *Crony Capitalism: Corruption and Development in South Korea and the Philippines* (Cambridge: Cambridge University Press).

Kaplinsky, Raphael (2000) 'Globalisation and unequalisation: what can be learned from value chain analysis?', *Journal of Development Studies*, 37 (2): 117–46.

Katada, Saori N. (2002) 'Japan and Asian monetary regionalisation: cultivating a new regional leadership after the Asia financial crisis', *Geopolitics*, 7 (1): 85–112.

Katz, Richard (1998) *Japan: The System That Soured* (Armonk, NY: M.E. Sharpe).

Katzenstein, Peter J. (2005) *A World of Regions: Asia and Europe in the American Imperium* (Ithaca, NY: Cornell University Press).

Katzenstein, Peter J. (1996) *Cultural Norms and National Security: Police and Military in Postwar Japan* (Ithaca, NY: Cornell University Press).

Kausikan, Bilahari (1993) 'Asia's Different Standard', *Foreign Policy*, 92: 24–41.

Keating, Paul (2000) *Engagement: Australia faces the Asia Pacific* (Sydney: Macmillan).

Keating, Paul (1998) 'The perilous moment: Indonesia, Australia and the Asian crisis', Public Lecture at the University of New South Wales, 25 March.

Kenen, Peter B. (2001) *The International Financial Architecture: What's New? What's Missing* (Washington, DC : Institute for International Economics).

Kennedy, Paul (1989) *The Rise and Fall of Great Powers: Economic Change and Military Conflict from 1500 to 2000* (London: Fontana).

Keohane, Robert O. (1982) 'The demand for international regimes', *International Organization*, 36 (25): 325–55.

Khoo, Boo Teik (2006) 'Malaysia: balancing development and power', in Rodan, G., Hewison, K. and Robison, R. (eds), *The Political Economy of South-East Asia: An Introduction*, 3rd edn (Melbourne: Oxford University Press): 168–94.

Khoo, Boo Teik (2003) *Beyond Mahathir: Malaysian Politics and its Discontents* (London: Zed Books).

Khoo, Boo Teik (1995) *Paradoxes of Mahthirism* (Oxford: Oxford University Press).

Kim Dae-Jung (1994) 'Is culture destiny? The myth of Asia's anti-democratic values', *Foreign Affairs*, 73 (6): 189–93.

Kindleberger, Charles P. (1996) *Manias, Panics, and Crashes: A History of Financial Crises* (New York: John Wiley).

Kindleberger, Charles P. (1973) *The World in Depression 1929–1939* (Berkeley: University of California Press).

King, Michael R. (2001) 'Who triggered the Asian financial crisis?', *Review of International Political Economy*, 8 (3): 438–66.

Kivimaki, Timo (2001) 'The long peace of ASEAN', *Journal of Peace Research*, 38 (1): 5–25.

Klare, Michael T. (2004) *Blood and Oil: How America's Thirst for Petrol is Killing Us* (Harmondsworth: Penguin).

Klare, Michael T. (2002) *Resource Wars: The New Landscape of Global Conflict* (New York: Metropolitan).

Kohli, Atul (1999) 'Where do high-growth political economies come from? The Japanese lineage of Korea's "developmental state"', in Woo-Cumings, M. (ed.), *The Developmental State* (Ithaca, NY: Cornell University Press): 93–136.

Kolko, Gabriel (1997) *Vietnam: Anatomy of a Peace* (London: Routledge).

Kolko, Gabriel (1985) *Anatomy of a War: Vietnam, the United States, and the Modern Historical Experience* (New York: Pantheon).

Korbin, Stephen J. (2002) 'Economic governance in an electronically networked global economy', in Hall, R.B. and Bierstecker, T.J. (eds), *The Emergence of Private Authority in Global Governance* (Cambridge: Cambridge University Press): 43–75.

Korhonen, Pekka (1997) 'Monopolising Asia: the politics of metaphor', *Pacific Review*, 10 (3): 347–65.

Korhonen, Pekka (1996) 'The Pacific age in world history', *Journal of World History*, 7 (1): 41–70.

Korhonen, Pekka (1994) *Japan and the Pacific Free Trade Area* (London: Routledge).

Krauss, Ellis S. (1992) 'Political economy: policymaking and industrial policy in Japan', *PS: Political Science & Politics* (March): 44–57.

Krauthammer, Charles (1990–1) 'The unipolar moment', *Foreign Affairs*, 70 (1): 23–33.

Kristol, William and Kagan, Robert (1996) 'Toward a neo-Reaganite foreign policy', *Foreign Affairs*, 75 (4): 18–32.

Krugman, Paul (1999) *The Return of Depression Economics* (Harmondsworth: Penguin).

Krugman, Paul (1986) 'Introduction: new thinking about trade theory', in Krugman, Paul (ed.), *Strategic Trade Policy and the New International Economics* (Cambridge, MA: MIT Press).

Kunz, Diane B. (1997) *Butter and Guns: America's Cold War Economic Diplomacy* (New York: Free Press).

Kwan, C.H. (2001) *Yen Bloc: Toward Economic Integration in Asia* (Washington, DC: Brookings Institute).

LaFeber, W. (1997) *The Clash: US–Japanese Relations Throughout History* (New York: W.W. Norton).

Lake, David A. (1999) *Entangling Relations: America's Foreign Policy and its Century* (Princeton, NJ: Princeton University Press).

Lampton, David M. (2001) 'China's foreign and national security policy-making process: Is it changing, and does it matter?', in Lampton, David M. (ed.), *The Making of Chinese Foreign and Security Policy in the Era of Reform* (Stanford, CA: Stanford University Press): 1–36.

Lapavitsas, C. (1997) 'Transition and crisis in the Japanese financial system: an analytical overview', *Capital & Class*, 62: 21–47.

Lardy, Nicholas R. (2002) *Integrating China into the Global Economy* (Washington, DC: Brookings Institute).

Lardy, Nicholas R. (1998) *China's Unfinished Economic Revolution* (Washington, DC: Brookings Institution).

Latham, Robert (1997), *The Liberal Moment: Modernity, Security, and the Making of Postwar International Order* (New York: Columbia University Press).

Lawrence, Alan (1998) *China under Communism* (London: Routledge).

Lee, Chung H. (1992) 'The government, financial system, and large private enterprises in the economic development of South Korea', *World Development*, 20 (2): 187–97.

Leffler, Melvyn P. (1992) *A Preponderance of Power: National Security, the Truman Administration, and the Cold War* (Stanford, CA: Stanford University Press).

Leftwich, Adrian (2000) *States of Development: On the Primacy of Politics in Development* (Oxford: Polity Press).

Leggett, Jeremy (2005) *The Empty Tank: Oil, Hot Air, and the Coming Global Financial Catastrophe* (New York: Random House).

Legewie, Jochen (1999) 'Manufacturing strategies for Southeast Asia after the crisis: European, US and Japanese firms', *Business Strategy Review*, 10 (4): 55–64.

Leifer, Michael (1996) *The ASEAN Regional Forum*, Adelphi Paper, vol. 302. (London: International Institute for Strategic Study).

Leigh, M. (1992) 'Politics, bureaucracy, and business in Malaysia: realigning the eternal triangle', in MacIntyre, A. and Jayasuriya, K. (eds) *The Dynamics of Economic Policy Reform in South-east Asia and the Southwest Pacific* (Melbourne: Oxford University Press): 115–23.

Leyshon, Andrew (1994) 'Under pressure: finance, geo-economic competition and the rise and fall of Japan's postwar growth economy', in Corbridge, S., Martin, R. and Thrift, N. (eds), *Money, Power and Space* (Oxford: Basil Blackwell): 116–45.

Liddle, R. William (1999) 'Regime: The New Order', in Emmerson, D.K. (ed.), *Indonesia Beyond Suharto* (Armonk, NY: M.E. Sharpe): 39–70.

Lieberthal, Kenneth G. (1995) *Governing China from Revolution through Reform* (New York: W.W. Norton).

Lieberthal, Kenneth G. (1992) 'Introduction: the "fragmented authoritarianism" model and its limitations', in Lieberthal, K.G. and Lampton, D.M. (eds), *Bureaucracy, Politics, and Decision Making in Post-Mao China* (Berkeley, CA: University of California Press): 1–30.

Liew, Leon (2001) 'What is to be done? WTO, globalisation and state–labour relations in China', *Australian Journal of Politics and History*, 47 (1): 39–60.

Lim, Linda C. (1996) 'The evolution of Southeast Asian business systems', *Journal of Asian Business*, 12 (1): 51–74.

Lin, Yi-min (2003) 'Economic institutional change in post-Mao China: reflections on the triggering, orienting, and sustaining mechanisms', in So, A.Y. (ed.), *China's Developmental Miracle: Origins, Transformations, and Challenges* (Armonk, NY: M.E. Sharpe): 29–57.

Lincoln, Edward J. (2004) *East Asian Economic Regionalism* (Washington, DC: Brookings Institution).

Lincoln, Edward J. (2001) *Arthritic Japan: The Slow Pace of Economic Reform in Japan* (Washington, DC: Brookings Institute).

Lincoln, Edward J. (1990) *Japan's Unequal Trade* (Washington, DC: Brookings Institute).

Lipschutz, R.D. (1992) 'Reconstructing world politics: The emergence of global civil society', *Millennium*, 21 (3): 389–420.

Liu, Alan P.L. (1996) *Mass Politics in the People's Republic: State and Society in Contemporary China* (Boulder, CO: Westview Press).

Lomborg, B. (2001) *The Skeptical Environmentalist* (Cambridge, MA: Cambridge University Press).

Low, D.A. (1991) *Eclipse of Empire* (Cambridge: Cambridge University Press).

Lu, Ning (2001) 'The central leadership, supraministry coordinating bodies, state council ministries, and party departments', in Lampton, D.M. (ed.), *The Making of Chinese Foreign and Security Policy in the Era of Reform* (Stanford, CA: Stanford University Press): 39–60.

Lu, Ya-li (1991) 'Political developments in the Republic of China', in Robinson, T.W. (ed.), *Democracy and Development in East Asia* (Washington: AEI Press): 35–48.

Luttwak, Edward (1990) 'From geopolitics to geo-economics', *National Interest* (Summer): 17–23.

Machado, Kit G. (1992) 'ASEAN state industrial policies and Japanese regional production strategies: the case of Malaysia's motor vehicle industry', in Clark, C. and Chan, S. (eds), *The Evolving Pacific Basin in the Global Political Economy* (Boulder, CO: Lynne Rienner): 169–202.

MacIntyre, Andrew (1994) 'Power, prosperity and patrimonialism: business and government in Indonesia', in MacIntyre, A. (ed.), *Business and Government in Industrializing Asia* (St Leonards, NSW: Allen & Unwin): 244–67.

Mahathir, Mohamad bin (1998 [1970]) *The Malay Dilemma* (Kuala Lumpur: Times Books).

Mahathir, Mohamad bin (1997) 'The Asian values debate', *Perdana Papers* (Kuala Lumpur: ISIS).

Mahathir, Mohamad bin and Ishihara, Shintaro (1995) *The Voice of Asia: Two Leaders Discuss the Coming Century* (Tokyo: Kondansha International).

Mahbubani, K. (1995) 'The Pacific Impulse', *Survival*, 37 (1): 105–20.

Maisrikrod, Surin and McCargo, Duncan (1997) 'Electoral politics: commercialization and exclusion', in Hewison, Kevin (ed.), *Political Change in Thailand: Democracy and Participation* (London: Routledge): 132–48.

Mann, Michael (1993) *The Sources of Social Power: The Rise of Classes and Nation States, 1760–1914* (Cambridge: Cambridge University Press).

Manupipatong, W. (2002) 'The ASEAN surveillance process and the East Asian Monetary Fund', *ASEAN Economic Bulletin*, 19 (1): 111–22.

Martinez, Patricia A. (2001) 'The Islamic state or the state of Islam in Malaysia', *Contemporary Southeast Asia*, 23 (3): 474–503.

Marx, Karl and Engels, Friedrich (1978 [1872]) 'Manifesto of the Communist Party', in Tucker, R.C. (ed.), *The Marx-Engels Reader*, 2nd edn (New York: W.W. Norton): 469–500.

Masaki, Hisane (2005a) 'Japan's opposition leader seeks to woo China', *Asia Times*, 6 December. Available at: http://www.atimes.com

Masaki, Hisane (2005b) 'Koizumi plays it his way', *Asia Times*, 10 October, available at: http://www.atimes.com

Mastanduno, Michael (2002) 'Incomplete hegemony and security order in the Asia-Pacific', in Ikenberry, G.J. (ed.), *America Unrivalled: The Future of the Balance of Power* (Ithaca, NY: Cornell University Press): 181–210.

Mathews, Jessica (1997) 'Power shift', *Foreign Affairs*, 76 (1): 50–66.

May, R.J., Lawson, Stephanie and Selochan, Viberto (1998) 'Introduction: democracy and the military in comparative perspective', in May, R.J. and Viberto, S. (eds), *The Military and Democracy in Asia and the Pacific* (Bathurst: Crawford House): 1–28.

McCloud, Donald G. (1995) *Southeast Asia: Tradition and Modernity in the Contemporary World* (Boulder, CO: Westview Press).

McCormack, Gavan (2004) 'Remilitarizing Japan', *New Left Review*, 29: 29–45.

McCormack, Gavan (1996) *The Emptiness of Japanese Affluence* (St Leonards, NSW: Allen & Unwin).

McDougall, Walter A. (1997) *Promised Land, Crusader State: The American Encounter with the World since 1776* (Boston, MA: Mariner Books).

McMahon, Robert J. (1999) *The Limits of Empire: The United States and Southeast Asia since World War II* (New York: Columbia University Press).

McNeil, William H. (1982) *The Pursuit of Power* (Chicago: University of Chicago Press).

Mearsheimer, John J. (2001) *The Tragedy of Great Power Politics* (New York: W.W. Norton).

Migdal, Joel S. (1994) 'The state in society: an approach to struggles for domination', in Migdal, Joel S., Kohli, Atul and Shue, Vivienne (eds), *State Power and Social Forces: Domination and Transformation in the Third World* (Cambridge: Cambridge University Press): 7–34.

Migdal, Joel S. (1988) *Strong States and Weak Societies: State–Society Relations and State Capabilities in the Third World* (Princeton, NJ: Princeton University Press).

Miles, James (2002) 'Out of puff: a survey of China', *The Economist*, 15 June.

Miles, James (2000–1) 'Chinese nationalism, US policy and Asian security', *Survival*, 42 (4): 51–71.

Millar, T.B. (1978) *Australia in Peace and War: External Relations 1788–1977* (Canberra: Australian National University Press).

Milliband, Ralph (1991) *Divided Societies: Class Struggle in Contemporary Capitalism* (Oxford: Oxford University Press).

Milne, R.S. and Mauzy, Diane K. (1999) *Malaysian Politics under Mahathir* (London: Routledge).

Milner, Helen V. and Keohane, Robert O. (1996) 'Internationalization and domestic politics: an introduction', in Keohane, R.O. and Milner, H.V. (eds), *Internationalization and Domestic Politics* (New York: Cambridge University Press): 3–24.

Milward, Alan S. (1984) *The Reconstruction of Western Europe, 1945–51* (Berkeley, CA: University of California Press).

Ministry of Economy, Trade and Industry (2005) *White Paper on International Economy and Trade 2005* (Tokyo: Ministry of Economy, Trade and Industry).

Mishima, Ko (2005) 'After the victory, can Koizumi deliver?', *Far Eastern Economic Review*, 168 (8): 13–17.

Mitrany, David (1965) 'The prospect of integration: federal or functional?', *Journal of Common Market Studies*, 4 (2): 119–49.

Mochizuki, Mike M. (2004) 'Terms of engagement: the US–Japan alliance and the rise of China', in Krauss, E.S and Pempel, T.J (eds), *Beyond Bilateralism: US–Japan Relations in the New Asia-Pacific* (Stanford, CA: Stanford University Press): 87–114.

Mochizuki, Mike M. (1995) 'Japan as an Asia-Pacific power', in Ross, R. (ed.), *East Asia in Transition: Toward a New Regional Order* (Singapore: Institute of Southeast Asian Studies): 124–59.

Modelski, George and Thompson, William (1996) *Leading Sectors and World Powers: The Coevolution of Global Economics and Politics* (Columbia: University of South Carolina Press).

Moore, Barrington (1973) *Social Origins of Dictatorship and Democracy* (Harmondsworth: Penguin).

Moore, Thomas G. (2002) *China in the World Market: Chinese Industry and International Sources of Reform in the Post-Mao Era* (Cambridge: Cambridge University Press).

Moravsik, Andrew (1998) *The Choice for Europe: Social Purpose and State Power from Messina to Maastricht* (Ithaca, NY: Cornell University Press).

Morris-Suzuki, Tessa (1994) *The Technological Transformation of Japan: From the Seventeenth to the Twenty-first Century* (Cambridge: Cambridge University Press).

Morris-Suzuki, Tessa (1989) *A History of Japanese Economic Thought* (London: Routledge).

Morriss, Peter (1997) 'Roh regrets: leadership, culture and politics in South Korea', *Crime, Law and Social Change*, 28: 39–51.

Murphy, Alexander B. (2004) 'Forum: is there a politics to geopolitics?', *Progress in Human Geography*, 28 (5): 619–40.

Murphy, R. Taggart (1997) *The Weight of the Yen* (New York: W.W. Norton).

Narine, Shaun (1999) 'ASEAN into the twenty-first century: problems and prospects', *Pacific Review*, 12 (3): 357–80.

Nathan, Andrew J. and Gilley, Bruce (2002) 'The fourth generation', *Australian Financial Review*, 11 October.

Nathan, Andrew J. and Ross, Robert S. (1997) *The Great Wall and the Empty Fortress: China's Search for Security* (New York: W.W. Norton).

Neher, Clark D. (2001) 'Burma', in Heenan, P. and Lamontagne, M. (eds), *The Southeast Asia Handbook* (Chicago, IL: Fitzroy Dearborn): 157–64.

NEPDG (2001) *National Energy Policy* (Washington, DC: National Energy Policy Development Group).

Nesadurai, Helen E.S. (2006) 'Malaysia and the United States: rejecting dominance, embracing engagement', in Beeson, M. (ed.), *Bush and Asia: America's Evolving Relations with East Asia* (London: RoutledgeCurzon).

Nesadurai, Helen E.S. (2003) *Globalisation, Domestic Politics and Regionalism: The ASEAN Free Trade Area* (London: Routledge).

Nester, William (1992) *Japan and the Third World: Patterns, Power, Prospects* (New York: St Martin's Press).

Nisbett, Richard E. (2003) *The Geography Thought: How Asians and Westerners Think Differently . . . and Why* (New York: Free Press).

Noble, Gregory W. (1999) *Collective Action in East Asia: How Ruling Parties Shape Industrial Policy* (Ithaca, NY: Cornell University Press).

Noble, Gregory W. and Ravenhill, John (eds) (2000) *The Asian Financial Crisis and the Architecture of Global Finance* (Cambridge: Cambridge University Press).

O'Brien, Richard (1992) *Global Financial Integration: The End of Geography* (London: Royal Institute of International Affairs).

Ockey, James (2001) 'Thailand: the struggle to redefine civil-military relations', in Alagappa, M. (ed.), *Coercion and Governance: The Declining Political Role of the Military in Asia* (Stanford, CA: Stanford University Press): 187–208.

O'Connor, Martin (ed.) (1994) *Is Capitalism Sustainable? Political Economy and Politics of Ecology* (New York: Guilford Press).

Odgaard, Liselotte (2001) 'Deterrence and cooperation in the South China Sea', *Contemporary Southeast Asia*, 23 (2): 292–306.

Office of the Secretary of Defence (2005) *Annual Report to Congress on the Military Power of the People's Republic of China*. Available at: http://www.defese.gov/news/Jul2005/d20050719china.pdf

Ohmae, Kenichi (1996) *The End of the Nation State: The Rise of the Regional Economies* (London: Harper Collins).

Ohmae, Kenichi (1990) *The Borderless World: Power and Strategy in the Interlinked Economy* (New York: Harper Business).

Okimoto, Daniel (1989) *Between MITI and the Market: Japanese Industrial Policy for High Technology* (Stanford, CA: Stanford University Press).

Oman, Charles (1994) *Globalisation and Regionalisation: The Challenge for Developing Countries* (Paris: OECD).

Orrù, M., Biggart, N.W. and Hamilton, G.G. (1991) 'Organizational isomorphism in East Asia', in Powell, W.W. and DiMaggio, P.J. (eds), *The New Institutionalism in Organizational Analysis* (Chicago, IL: University of Chicago Press): 361–89.

Ó Tuathail, Gearóid (1996) *Critical Geopolitics* (London: Routledge).

Packer, George (2005) *The Assassin's Gate: America in Iraq* (New York: Farrar, Strauss & Giroux).

Park, Yung Chul and Wang, Yunjong (2005) 'The Chiang Mai Initiative and beyond', *World Economy*, 28 (1): 91–101.

Parry, J.H. (1971) *Trade and Dominion: The European Overseas Empires in the Eighteenth Century* (London: Phoenix Press).

Pasuk, Phongpaichit and Baker, Chris (2004) *Thaksin: The Business of Politics in Thailand* (Chiang Mai: Silkworm Books).

Pauly, L.W. (1997) *Who Elected the Bankers? Surveillance and Control in the World Economy* (Ithaca, NY: Cornell).

Peet, Richard (1991) *Global Capitalism: Theories of Social Development* (London: Routledge).

Pempel, T.J. (2005a) 'Conclusion: tentativeness and tensions in the construction of an Asian region', in Pempel, T.J. (ed.), *Remapping East Asia: The Construction of a Region* (Ithaca, NY: Cornell University Press): 256–75.

Pempel, T.J. (2005b) 'Firebreak: East Asia institutionalizes its finances', Paper presented to Regionalization and the Taming of Globalisation? Conference, University of Warwick, October.

Pempel, T.J. (2004) 'Challenges to bilateralism: changing foes, capital flows, and complex forums', in Krauss, E.S. and Pempel, T.J. (eds), *Beyond Bilateralism: US–Japan Relations in the New Asia-Pacific* (Stanford, CA: Stanford University Press): 1–33.

Pempel, T.J. (ed.) (1999) *The Politics of the Asian Economic Crisis* (Ithaca, NY: Cornell University Press).

Pempel, T.J. (1998) *Regime Shift: Comparative Dynamics of the Japanese Political Economy* (Ithaca, NY: Cornell University Press).

Pempel, T.J. and Tsunekawa, K. (1979) 'Corporatism without labour? The Japanese anomaly', in Schmitter, P.C. and Lembruch, G. (eds), *Trends Toward Corporatist Intermediation* (Beverly Hills, CA: Sage): 231–70.

Peng, Dajin (2000) 'The changing nature of East Asia as an economic region', *Pacific Affairs*, 73 (2): 171–91.

Petri, Peter A. (1992) *The East Asian Trading Bloc: An Analytical History*, Department of Economics, Brandeis University.

Pew Research Centre (2003) *Views of a Changing World 2003* (Washington, DC: Pew Research Center). Available at: http://people-press.org/reports/display.php3?ReportID=185>

Phillips, Kevin (2004) *American Dynasty: Aristocracy, Fortune, and the Politics of Deceit in the House of Bush* (New York: Viking).

Pasuk, Phongpaichit and Baker, Chris (2004) *Thaksin: The Business of Politics in Thailand* (Chiang Mai: Silkworm Books).

Pasuk, Phongpaichit and Piriyarangsan, Sungsidh (1994) *Corruption and Democracy in Thailand* (Chiang Mai: Silkworm Books).

Pieterse, Jan Nederveen (2004) *Globalization or Empire?* (London: Routledge).

Pirie, Iain (2005) 'The new Korean state', *New Political Economy*, 10 (1): 25–42.

Polanyi, Karl (1957) *The Great Transformation: The Political and Economic Origins of Our Time* (Boston, MA: Beacon Press).

Polidano, C. (2000) 'Measuring public sector capacity', *World Development*, 28 (5): 805–22.

Pomeranz, Kenneth (2000) *The Great Divergence* (Princeton, NJ: Princeton University Press).

Pomeranz, Kenneth and Topik, Steve (1999) *The World That Trade Created: Society, Culture, and the World Economy* (Armonk, NY: M.E. Sharpe).

Poon, Jessie, Thompson, Edmund R. and Kelly, Philip F. (2000) 'Myth of the triad? The geography of trade and investment "blocs" ', *Transactions of the Institute of British Geographers*, 25: 427–44.

Porter, M., Takeuchi, H. and Sakakibara, M. (2000) *Can Japan Compete?* (London: Macmillan).

Potter, Pitman B. (2001) 'The legal implications of China's accession to the WTO', *China Quarterly*, 167: 592–609.

PRC (2005) *Building of Political Democracy in China* (Beijing: Information Office of the State Council of the People's Republic of China).

PRC (2000) 'The one-China principle and the Taiwan issue', *Beijing Review*, 6 March: 16–24.

Prestowitz, Clyde (2003) *Rogue Nation: American Unilateralism and the Failure of Good Intentions* (New York: Basic Books).

Prybyla, Jan S. (1991) 'Economic developments in the Republic of China', in

Robinson, Thomas W. (ed.), *Democracy and Development in East Asia* (Washington, DC: AEI Press): 49–74.

Przeworski, Adam, Alvarez, M.E., Cheibub, J.A. and Limongi, F. (2000) *Democracy and Development: Political Institutions and Well-Being in the World, 1950–1990* (Cambridge: Cambridge University Press).

Putnam, Robert D. (1992) *Making Democracy Work: Civic Traditions in Modern Italy* (Princeton, NJ: Princeton University Press).

Pye, Lucian (1990) 'China: Erratic state, frustrated society', *Foreign Affairs*, 69 (4): 56–74.

Pye, Lucian (1985) *Asian Power and Politics: The Cultural Dimensions of Authority* (Cambridge, MA: Harvard University Press).

Pyle, Kenneth B. (1988) 'Japan, the world, and the Twenty-first century', in Inoguchi, T. and Okimoto, D. (eds), *The Political Economy of Japan: Volume 2, The Changing International Context* (Stanford, CA: Stanford University Press): 446–86.

Rasiah, Rajah and Shari, Ishak (2001) 'Market, government and Malaysia's new economic policy', *Cambridge Journal of Economics*, 25: 57–78.

Ravenhill, John (forthcoming) 'Is China an economic threat to Southeast Asia', *Asian Survey*.

Ravenhill, John (2006) 'US economic relations with East Asia: from hegemony to complex interdependence?', in Beeson, M. (ed.), *Bush and Asia: America's Evolving Relations with East Asia* (London: RoutledgeCurzon): 42–63.

Ravenhill, John (2003) 'The new bilateralism in the Asia-Pacific', *Third World Quarterly*, 24 (2): 299–317.

Ravenhill, John (2002) 'A three bloc world? The new East Asian regionalism', *International Relations of the Asia Pacific*, 2 (2): 167–95.

Ravenhill, John (2001) *APEC and the Construction of Pacific Rim Regionalism* (Cambridge: Cambridge University Press).

Ravenhill, John (1995) 'Competing logics of regionalism in the Asia-Pacific', *Journal of European Integration*, 18: 179–99.

Redding, Gordon (2002) 'The capitalist business system of China and its rationale', *Asia Pacific Journal of Management*, 19: 221–49.

Reich, Robert (1991) *The Work of Nations: Preparing Ourselves for 21st-Century Capitalism* (New York: Vintage Books).

Reid, Anthony (2000) *Charting the Shape of Early Modern Southeast Asia* (Singapore: Institute of Southeast Asian Studies).

Reid, Anthony (1999), 'Economic and social change, c. 1400–1800', in Tarling, Nicholas (ed.), *The Cambridge History of Southeast Asia, Volume 2* (Cambridge: Cambridge University Press): 116–63.

Reinicke, Wolfgang H. (1998) *Global Public Policy: Governing Without Government?* (Washington, DC: Brookings Institute).

Reserve Bank of Australia (2004) *Reserve Bank of Australia Bulletin*, August (Sydney: Reserve Bank of Australia).

Riggs, Fred (1966) *Thailand: The Modernization of a Bureaucratic Polity* (Honolulu: East–West Center Press).

Roberti, Mark (1996) *The Fall of Hong Kong: China's Triumph and Britain's Betrayal* (New York: Wiley).

Robinson, Thomas W. (1971) *The Cultural Revolution in China* (Berkeley, CA: University of California Press).

Robison, Richard (1997) 'Politics and markets in Indonesia's post-oil era', in Rodan, Garry, Hewison, Kevin and Robison, Richard (eds), *The Political Economy of South-East Asia: An Introduction* (Melbourne: Oxford University Press): 29–63.

Robison, Richard (1996) 'The politics of "Asian values" ', *Pacific Review*, 9 (3): 309–27.

Robison, Richard, Beeson, M., Jayasuriya, K. and Kim, H.-R. (eds) (2000) *Politics and Markets in the Wake of the Asian Crisis* (London: Routledge).

Robison, Richard and Hadiz, Vedi R. (2004) *Reorganising Power in Indonesia: The Politics of Oligarchy in an Age of Markets* (London: RoutledgeCurzon).

Rodan, Garry (2006) 'Singapore: globalization, the developmental state and politics', in Rodan, G., Hewison, K. and Robison, R. (eds), *The Political Economy of South-East Asia: An Introduction*, 3rd edn (Melbourne: Oxford University Press): 136–67.

Rodan, Garry (2005) *Transparency and Authoritarian Rule in Southeast Asia* (London: Routledge).

Rodan, Garry (1997) 'Singapore: Globalisation and the politics of economic restructuring', in Rodan G., Hewison, K. and Robison, R. (eds), *The Political Economy of Southeast Asia*, 2nd edn (Melbourne: Oxford University Press): 138–77.

Rodan, Garry (1996a) 'State–society relations and political opposition in Singapore', in Rodan, G. (ed.), *Political Oppositions in Industrializing Asia* (London: Routledge): 95–127.

Rodan, Garry (1996b) 'The internationalization of ideological conflict: Asia's new significance', *Pacific Review*, 9 (3): 328–51.

Rodan, Garry (1989) *The Political Economy of Singapore's Industrialization* (London: Macmillan).

Rodan, Garry and Hewison, Kevin (2004) 'Closing the circle? Globalization, conflict, and political regimes', *Critical Asian Studies*, 36 (3): 383–404.

Roland-Holst, David and Weiss, John (2005) 'People's Republic of China and its neighbours: evidence on regional trade and investment effects', *Asian-Pacific Economic Literature*, 19 (2): 18–35.

Rosamond, Ben (2005) 'The uniting of Europe and the foundation of EU studies: revisiting the neofunctionalism of Ernst B. Haas', *Journal of European Public Policy*, 12 (2): 1–18.

Rosecrance, Richard (1986) *The Rise of the Trading State: Commerce and Conquest in the Modern World* (New York: Basic Books).

Ross, Michael L. (1999) 'The political economy of the resource curse', *World Politics*, 51: 297–322.

Rotter, Andrew J. (1987) *The Path to Vietnam: Origins of the American Commitment to Southeast Asia* (Ithaca, NY: Cornell University Press).

Roy, Denny (2003) 'China's reaction to American predominance', *Survival*, 45 (3): 57–78.

Rozman, Gilbert (2004) *Northeast Asia's Stunted Regionalism: Bilateral Distrust in the Shadow of Globalisation* (Cambridge: Cambridge University Press).

Rueschemeyer, Dietrich, Stephens, Evelyne H. and Stephens, John D. (1992) *Capitalist Development and Democracy* (Cambridge: Polity Press).

Ruggie, John Gerard (1993) 'Territoriality and beyond: problematizing modernity in international relations', *International Organization*, 47 (1): 139–74.

Ruigrok, Winfried and van Tulder, Rob (1995) *The Logic of International Restructuring* (London: Routledge).

Rumsfeld, Donald (2005) Speech to the International Institute for Strategic Studies, 4 June, Singapore.

Sachs, Jeffrey D. (2005) *The End of Poverty: Economic Possibilities for our Time* (New York: Penguin).

Saich, Tony (2004) *Governance and Politics of China*, 2nd edn (Basingstoke: Palgrave Macmillan).

Said, Edward (1985) *Orientalism* (Harmondsworth: Penguin).

Sakai, Kuniyasu (1990) 'The feudal world of Japanese manufacturing', *Harvard Business Review* (Nov./Dec.).

Salisbury, Harrison E. (1992) *The New Emperors: Mao & Deng, A Dual Biography* (London: HarperCollins).

Samuels, Richard J. (1994) *Rich Nation, Strong Army: National Security and the Technological Transformation of Japan* (Ithaca, NY: Cornell University Press).

Samuels, Richard J. (1987) *The Business of the Japanese State: Energy Markets in Comparative and Historical Perspective* (Ithaca, NY: Cornell University Press).

Samuels, Warren (1991) ' "Truth" and "discourse" in the social construction of economic reality: an essay on the relation of knowledge to socio-economic policy', *Journal of Post Keynesian Economics*, 13 (4): 511–24.

SarDesai, D.R. (1997) *Southeast Asia: Past and Present*, 4th edn (Boulder, CO: Westview Press).

Saxenian, A.-L. (1994) *Regional Advantage: Culture and Competition in Silicon Valley and Route 128* (Cambridge: Cambridge University Press).

Sayer, Derek (1991) *Capitalism and Modernity: An Excursus on Marx and Weber*: (London: Routledge).

Schaede, Ulrike (1995) 'The "old boy" network and government–business relationships in Japan', *Journal of Japanese Studies*, 21 (2): 293–317.

Schaller, Michael (1997) *Altered States: The United States and Japan since the Occupation* (New York: Oxford University Press).

Schlesinger, Jacob M. (1999) *Shadow Shoguns: The Rise and Fall of Japan's Postwar Political Machine* (Stanford, CA: Stanford University Press).

Schoppa, Leonard J. (1997) *Bargaining with Japan: What American Pressure Can and Cannot Do* (New York: Columbia University Press).

Schmitter, P. (1979) 'Still the Century of Corporatism?', in Schmitter, P. (ed.), *Trends Toward Corporatist Intermediation* (Beverly Hills, CA: Sage): 7–48.

Scholte, Jan Aart (2000) *Globalization: A Critical Introduction* (Basingstoke: Palgrave Macmillan).

Seabrooke, Leonard (2001) *US Power in International Finance* (Basingstoke: Palgrave Macmillan).

Searle, Peter (1999) *The Riddle of Malaysian Capitalism* (St Leonards, NSW: Allen & Unwin).

Segal, Adam (2003) *Chinese Military Power* (New York: Council on Foreign Relations).

Segal, Gerald (1999) 'Does China matter?', *Foreign Affairs*, 78 (5): 24–36.

Segal, Gerald (1995) 'What is Asian about Asian security?' in Rolfe, J. (ed.) *Unresolved Futures: Comprehensive Security in the Asia-Pacific* (Wellington, NZ: Centre of Security Studies): 107–20.

Sen, Amartya (1999) 'Human rights and economic achievements', in Bauer, J.R. and Bell, D.A. (eds), *The East Asian Challenge for Human Rights* (Cambridge: Cambridge University Press): 88–99.

Shambaugh, David (2005) 'Return to the middle kingdom? China and Asia in the early twenty-first century', in Shambaugh, D. (ed.), *Power Shift: China and Asia's New Dynamics* (Berkeley, CA: University of California Press): 23–47.

Shambaugh, David (1999) 'China's military views the world', *International Security*, 24 (3): 52–79.

Shambaugh, David (1996) 'Containment or engagement of China? Calculating Beijing's responses', *International Security*, 21 (2): 180–210.

Shambaugh, David (1994) 'Growing strong: China's challenge to Asian security', *Survival*, 36 (2): 43–59.

Shih, Chih-yu (2005) 'Breeding a reluctant dragon: can China rise into partnership and away from antagonism?', *Review of International Studies*, 31: 755–74.

Shin, Doh Chull, Park, C.-M., Hwang, A.-R., Lee, H.-W. and Jang, J. (2003) 'The democratization of mass political orientations in South Korea', *International Journal of Public Opinion Research*, 15 (3): 265–84.

Shirk, Susan L. (1993) *The Political Logic of Economic Reform in China* (Berkeley, CA: University of California Press).

Shorrock, Tim (2005) 'Bright side to Sino–Japanese ties', 15 December. Available at: http://www.atimes.com

Shue, Henry (1980) *Basic Rights: Subsistence, Affluence, and US Foreign Policy* (Princeton, NJ: Princeton University Press).

Simon, Sheldon (1998) 'Security prospects in Southeast Asia: collaborative efforts and the ASEAN Regional Forum', *Pacific Review*, 11 (2): 195–212.

Sinclair, Timothy J. (2005) *The New Masters of Capital: American Bond Rating Agencies and the Politics of Creditworthiness* (Ithaca, NY: Cornell University Press).

Skocpol, Theda (1985) 'Bringing the state back in: strategies of analysis in current research', in Evans, P.B., Rueschemeyer, D. and Skocpol, T. *Bringing the State Back In* (Cambridge: Cambridge University Press): 3–37.

Slater, Dan (2003) 'Iron cage in an iron fist: authoritarian institutions and the personalization of power in Malaysia', *Comparative Politics*, 36 (1): 81–101.

Smil, Vaclav (2003) *Energy at the Crossroads: Global Perspectives and Uncertainties* (Cambridge, MA: MIT Press).

Smith, Anthony D. (1998) *Nationalism and Modernism* (London: Routledge).

Smith, M.L. and Jones, D.M. (1997) 'ASEAN, Asian values and Southeast Asian security in the new world order', *Contemporary Security Policy*, 18 (3): 126–56.

Smith, Tony (1994) *America's Mission: The United States and the Worldwide Struggle for Democracy in the Twentieth Century* (Princeton, NJ: Princeton University Press).

So, Alvin Y. (2003) 'Introduction: rethinking the Chinese developmental miracle', in So, A.Y. (ed.), *China's Developmental Miracle: Origins, Transformations, and Challenges* (Armonk, NY: M.E. Sharpe): 3–26.

Sohn, Hak-Kyu (1989) *Authoritarianism and Opposition in South Korea* (London: Routledge).

Solingen, Etel (2004) 'Southeast Asia in a new era: domestic coalitions from crisis to recovery', *Asian Survey*, 44 (2): 189–212.

Spruyt, Hendrik (1994) *The Sovereign State and its Competitors* (Princeton, NJ: Princeton University Press).

Stafford, D. (1997) 'Malaysia's New Economic Policy and the global economy: the evolution of ethnic accommodation', *Pacific Review*, 10 (4): 556–80.

Steven, Rob (1990) *Japan's New Imperialism* (London: Macmillan).

Stiglitz, Joseph E. (2002) *Globalization and its Discontents* (New York: Norton).

Stiglitz, Joseph E. (2001) 'From miracle to recovery: lessons from four decades of East Asia experience', in Stiglitz, J.E. and Yusuf, S. (eds), *Rethinking the East Asia Miracle* (Oxford: Oxford University Press): 509–26.

Stilwell, Frank (2002) *Political Economy: The Contest of Economic Ideas* (Melbourne: Oxford University Press).

Stockwell, A.J. (1999) 'Southeast Asia in war and peace: the end of European colonial empires', in Tarling, N. (ed.) *The Cambridge History of Southeast Asia* (Cambridge: Cambridge University Press): 1–58.

Stockwin, J.A.A. (2002) 'Reshaping Japanese politics and the question of democracy', *Asia-Pacific Review*, 9 (1): 45–59.

Stockwin, J.A.A. (1999) *Governing Japan: Divided Politics in a Major Economy* (Oxford: Blackwell).

Strange, Susan (1998) *Mad Money: When Markets Outgrow Governments* (Ann Arbor, MI: University of Michigan Press).

Strange, Susan (1997) 'The future of global capitalism; or, will divergence persist forever?', in Crouch, C. and Streeck, W. (eds) *Political Economy of Modern Capitalism: Mapping Convergence and Diversity* (London: Sage): 183–91.

Strange, Susan (1996) *The Retreat of the State: The Diffusion of Power in the World Economy* (Cambridge: Cambridge University Press).

Strange, Susan (1987) 'The persistent myth of lost hegemony', *International Organization*, 41 (4): 551–74.

Stubbs, Richard (2005) *Rethinking Asia's Economic Miracle* (Basingstoke: Palgrave).

Stubbs, Richard (2002) 'ASEAN Plus Three: Emerging East Asian Regionalism?', *Asian Survey*, 42 (3): 440–55.

Stubbs, Richard (2000) 'Signing on to liberalisation: AFTA and the politics of regional economic cooperation', *Pacific Review* (13) 2: 297–318.

Suh, Dae-sook (1988) *Kim Il Sung: The North Korean Leader* (New York: Columbia University Press).

Sung, Yun-Wing (2005) *The Emergence of Greater China: The Economic Integration of Mainland China, Taiwan and Hong Kong* (Basingstoke: Palgrave Macmillan).

Sutcliffe, Bob and Glyn, Andrew (1999) 'Still underwhelmed: indicators of globalization and their misinterpretation', *Review of Radical Political Economics*, 31 (1): 111–32.

Swaine, Michael D. (2004) 'Trouble in Taiwan', *Foreign Affairs*, 83 (2): 30–49.

Tabb, William K. (1995) *The Postwar Japanese System: Cultural Economy and Economic Transformation* (New York: Oxford University Press).

Tai, Ming Cheung (2001) 'The influence of the gun: China's central military commission and its relationship with the military, Party, and state decision-making systems', in Lampton, D.M. (ed.), *The Making of Chinese Foreign and Security Policy in the Era of Reform* (Stanford, CA: Stanford University Press): 61–90.

Tan, Andrew (2000) *Intra-ASEAN Tensions*, Adelphi Discussion Paper, vol. 84 (London: Royal Institute of International Affairs).

Tanter, Richard (2005) 'With eyes wide shut: Japan, Heisei militarization, and the Bush Doctrine', in Gurtov, M. and Van Ness, P. (eds), *Confronting the Bush Doctrine: Critical Views from the Asia-Pacific* (London: RoutledgeCurzon): 153–80.

Tanter, Richard (1990) 'Oil, IGGI and US hegemony: the global pre-conditions for Indonesian rentier-militarization', in Budiman, A. (ed.) *State and Civil Society in Indonesia*, (Melbourne: Monash Papers on Southeast Asia): 51–93.

Tarling, Nicholas (2001) *Imperialism in Southeast Asia* (London: RoutledgeCurzon).

Tarling, Nicholas (1998) *Nations and States in Southeast Asia* (Cambridge: Cambridge University Press).

Tarling, Nicholas (1966) *A Concise History of Southeast Asia* (New York: Praeger).

Terada, Takashi (2003) 'Constructing an "East Asia" concept and growing regional identity: from EAEC to ASEAN+3', *Pacific Review*, 16 (2): 251–77.

Terrill, Ross (2003) *The New Chinese Empire: And What it Means for the United States* (New York: Basic Books).

Terry, Edith (2002) *How Asia Got Rich: Japan, China, and the Asian Miracle* (Armonk, NY: M.E. Sharpe).

Teschke, Benno (2003) *The Myth of 1648: Class, Ecopolitics and the Making of Modern International Relations* (London: Verro).

Thomas, Nick (2002) 'From ASEAN to an East Asian community? The role of functional cooperation', *Working Paper Series*, 28 (July), Southeast Asia Research Centre, Hong Kong.

Thomas, Nicholas (1999) *Democracy Denied: Identity, Civil Society and Illiberal Democracy in Hong Kong* (Aldershot: Ashgate).

Thomson, James C., Stanley, Peter W. and Perry, John Curtis (1981) *Sentimental Imperialists: The American Experience in East Asia* (New York: Harper & Row).

Thurborn, Elizabeth and Weiss, Linda (2006) 'Investing in openness: the evolution of FDI strategy in South Korea and Taiwan', *New Political Economy*, 11 (1): 1–22.

Tilly, Charles (1990) *Coercion, Capital, and European States* (Oxford: Basil Blackwell).

Tilly, Charles (1984) *Big Structures, Large Processes, Huge Comparisons* (New York: Russell Sage Foundation).

Tow, William (2001) *Asia-Pacific Strategic Relations: Seeking Convergent Security* (Cambridge: Cambridge University Press).

Trocki, Carl A. (1999) 'Political structures in the nineteenth and early twentieth centuries', in Tarling, N. (ed.), *The Cambridge History of Southeast Asia, Volume 3, From c. 1800 to the 1930s* (Cambridge: Cambridge University Press): 75–126.

Tucker, Robert W. and Hendrickson, David C. (2004) 'The sources of American legitimacy', *Foreign Affairs*, 83 (6): 18–32.

UN (2000) *State of the Environment in Asia and the Pacific, 2000* (New York: United Nations).

UNCTAD (United Nations Conference on Trade and Development) (2005) *World Investment Report 2005: Transnational Corporations and the Internationalization of R&D*, (New York: United Nations).

Underhill, Geoffrey R.D. (2001) 'State, market, and global political economy: Genealogy of an (inter-?) discipline', *International Affairs*, 76 (4): 805–24.

Underhill, Geoffrey R.D. and Zhang, Xiaoke (2005) 'The changing state-market condominium in East Asia: rethinking the political underpinnings of development', *New Political Economy*, 10 (1): 1–24.

US Government (2002) *National Security Strategy of the USA* (Washington, DC: The White House).

Vandergeest, Peter (1993) 'Constructing Thailand: regulation, resistance and citizenship', *Comparative Studies in Society and History*, 35 (1): 133–58.

van Ness, Peter (2006) 'Bush's search for absolute security and the rise of China', in Beeson, M. (ed.), *Bush and Asia: America's Evolving Relations with East Asia* (London: RoutledgeCurzon): 97–108.

van Wolferen, Karel (1989) *The Enigma of Japanese Power: People and Politics in a Stateless Nation* (London: Papermac).

Vatikiotis, Michael R.J. (1996) *Political Change in Southeast Asia* (London: Routledge).

Vatikiotis, Michael R.J. and Hiebert, Murray (2003) 'How China is building an empire', *Far Eastern Economic Review*: 30–3.

Vervoorn, Aat (1998) *ReOrient: Change in Asian Societies* (Melbourne: Oxford University Press).

Vogel, Steven K. (1996) *Freer Markets, More Rules: Regulatory Reform in Advanced Industrial Countries* (Ithaca, NY: Cornell University Press).

Volgy, Thomas J. and Bailin, Alison (2003) *International Politics and State Strength* (Boulder, CO: Lynne Rienner).

Wade, Robert H. (2004) 'Bringing economics back in', *Security Dialogue*, 35 (2): 243–9.

Wade, Robert (2002) 'US hegemony and the World Bank: the fight over people and ideas', *Review of International Political Economy* 9 (2): 215–43.

Wade, Robert (1996) 'Japan, the World Bank, and the art of paradigm maintenance: the East Asian Miracle in political perspective', *New Left Review*, 217: 3–36.

Wade, Robert (1990) *Governing the Market: Economic Theory and the Role of Government in East Asian Industrialization* (Princeton, NJ: Princeton University Press).

Wade, Robert and Veneroso, Frank (1998) 'The Asian crisis: the high debt model versus the Wall Street–Treasury–IMF complex', *New Left Review*, 228: 3–23.

Wallace, William (1999) 'The sharing of sovereignty: the European paradox', *Political Studies*, 47: 503–21.

Wallace, William (1995) Regionalism in Europe: Model or exception?', in Fawcett, L. and Hurrell, A. (eds), *Regionalism in World Politics: Regional Organization and International Order* (Oxford: Oxford University Press): 201–27.

Waltz, Kenneth N. (1993) 'The emerging structure of international politics', *International Security*, 18 (2): 44–79.

Waltz, Kenneth N. (1979) *Theory of International Politics* (New York: McGraw-Hill).

Watson, Adam (1992) *The Evolution of International Society* (London: Routledge).

Watson Andaya, Barbara (1999) 'Religious developments in Southeast Asia, c. 1500–1800', in Tarling, Nicholas (ed.), *The Cambridge History of Southeast Asia, Volume 2* (Cambridge: Cambridge University Press): 164–227.

Weatherbee, Donald E. (2005) *International Relations in Southeast Asia: The Struggle for Autonomy* (Lanham, MD: Rowman & Littlefield).

Webber, Douglas (2001) 'Two funerals and a wedding? The ups and downs of regionalism in East Asia and Asia-Pacific after the Asian crisis', *Pacific Review*, 14 (3): 339–72.

Weiss, Linda (2003) 'Is the state being "transformed" by globalisation?', in Weiss, L. (ed.) *States in the Global Economy: Bringing Domestic Institutions Back In*, (Cambridge: Cambridge University Press): 293–317.

Weiss, Linda and Hobson, John M. (1995) *States and Economic Development: A Comparative Historical Analysis* (Oxford: Polity Press).

Wesley, Michael (2006) 'The dog that didn't bark: the Bush administration and East Asian regionalism', in Beeson, M. (ed.), *Bush and Asia: America's Evolving Relations with East Asia* (London: Routledge): 64–79.

White, Gordon (1993) *Riding the Tiger: The Politics of Economic Reform in Post-Mao China* (Stanford, CA: Stanford University Press).

Whitley, Richard (1999) *Divergent Capitalisms: The Social Structuring and Change of Business Systems* (Oxford: Oxford University Press).

Whitley, Richard (1990) 'Eastern Asian Enterprise Structures and the Comparative Analysis of Forms of Business Organization', *Organization Studies*, 11 (1): 47–74.

Williamson, John (1994) 'In search of a manual for Technopols', in J. Williamson (ed.), *The Political Economy of Policy Reform* (Washington, DC: Institute for International Economics): 11–28.

Williamson, Oliver E. (1985) *The Economic Institutions of Capitalism: Firms, Markets, Relational Contracting* (New York: Free Press).

Willmott, H.P. (1982) *Empires in the Balance* (Annapolis, MD: Naval Institute Press).

Wingfield, Tom (2002) 'Democratization and economic crisis in Thailand', in Gomez, E.T. (ed.), *Political Business in East Asia* (London: Routledge): 250–300.

Winters, Jeffrey A. (2000) 'The financial crisis in Southeast Asia', in Robison, R. *et al.* (eds), *Politics and Markets in the Wake of the Asian Crisis* (London: Routledge): 34–52.

Winters, Jeffrey A. (1996) *Power in Motion: Capital Mobility and the Indonesian State* (Ithaca, NY: Cornell University Press).

Wittkopf, Eugene R. and McCormick, James M. (eds) (2004) *The Domestic Sources of American Foreign Policy*, 4th edn (Lanham, MD: Rowman & Littlefield).

Wolters, O.W. (1999) *History, Culture, and Region in Southeast Asian Perspectives* (Singapore: ISEAS).

Wolf, Eric R. (1969) *Peasant Wars of the Twentieth Century* (New York: Harper & Row).

Wong, R. Bin (1997) *China Transformed: Historical Change and the Limits of the European Experience* (Ithaca, NY: Cornell University Press).

Woo, Jung-en (1991) *Race to the Swift: State and Finance in Korean Industrialization* (New York: Columbia University Press).

Woo-Cumings, Meredith (1999) 'Introduction: Chalmers Johnson and the politics of nationalism and development', in Woo-Cumings. M. (ed.), *The Developmental State* (Ithaca, NY: Cornell University Press): 1–31.

Woo-Cumings, Meredith (1997) 'Slouching toward the market: the politics of financial liberalization in South Korea', in Loriaux, M., Cumings, M., Calder, K.E., Maxfield, S. and Preez, S.A., *Capital Ungoverned: Liberalizing Finance in Interventionist States* (Ithaca, NY: Cornell University Press): 57–91.

Wood, Christopher (1992) *The Bubble Economy: The Japanese Economic Collapse* (London: Sidgwick & Jackson).

Wood, Ellen Meiksins (2002) *The Origin of Capitalism* (London: Verso).

Woodall, Pam (2004) 'The dragon and the eagle: a survey of the world economy', *The Economist*, 2 October.

Woods, Lawrence (1993) *Asia-Pacific Diplomacy: Nongovernmental Organizations and International Relations* (Vancouver: University of British Columbia Press).

Woods, Ngarie (1995) 'Economic ideas and international relations: beyond rational neglect', *International Studies Quarterly*, 39: 161–80.

Woodside, A. (1993) 'The Asia-Pacific idea as a mobilisation myth', in Dirlik, A. (ed.), *What is a Rim? Critical Perspectives on the Pacific Region Idea* (Boulder, CO: Westview Press): 13–28.

World Bank (1997) *World Development Report 1997: The State in a Changing World* (New York: Oxford University Press).

World Bank (1993) *The East Asian Miracle: Economic Growth and Public Policy* (Oxford: Oxford University Press).

Worldwatch Institute (2006) *State of the World 2006* (Washington, DC: Worldwatch Institute).

Wright-Neville, David (2004) 'Dangerous dynamics: activists, militants and terrorists in Southeast Asia', *Pacific Review*, 17 (1): 27–46.

Wu, Baiyi (2001) 'The Chinese security concept and its historical evolution', *Journal of Contemporary China*, 10 (27): 275–83.

Wyatt-Walter, Andrew (1995) 'Regionalism, globalization, and world economic order', in Fawcett, L. and Hurrell, A. (eds) *Regionalism in World Politics: Regional Organization and International Order* (Oxford: Oxford University Press): 74–121.

Yahuda, Michael (2004) *The International Politics of the Asia-Pacific*, 2nd edn (London: RoutledgeCurzon).

Yahuda, Michael (2000) 'The changing faces of Chinese nationalism: the dimension of statehood', in Leifer, M. (ed.), *Asian Nationalism* (London: Routledge): 21–37.

Yahuda, Michael (1997) 'How much has China learned about interdependence?', in Goodman, D. and Segal, G. (eds), *China Rising: Nationalism and Interdependence* (London: Routledge): 6–26.

Yeung, Henry Wai-chung (2000a) 'Economic globalization, crisis and the emergence of Chinese business communities in Southeast Asia', *International Sociology*, 15 (2): 266–87.

Yeung, Henry Wai-chung (2000b) 'The dynamics of Asian business systems in a globalizing era', *Review of International Political Economy*, 7 (3): 399–433.

Yoshihara, Kunio (1988) *The Rise of Ersatz Capitalism in Southeast Asia* (Manila: Manila University Press).

Yoshimatsu, Hidetaka (2005) 'Japan's Keidanren and free trade agreements', *Asian Survey*, 45 (2): 258–78.

Yoshimatsu, Hidetaka (2002) 'Preferences, interests, and regional integration: the development of the ASEAN industrial cooperation arrangement', *Review of International Political Economy*, 9: 123–49.

Young, Louise (1998) *Japan's Total Empire: Manchuria and the Culture of Wartime Imperialism* (Berkeley, CA: University of California).

Young, Susan (1997) 'The private sector in China's economic reforms', in Hudson, C. (ed.), *The China Handbook* (Chicago, IL: Fitzroy Dearborn): 150–61.

Yuan, Jing-dong (2005) 'Hu goes to the Hermit Kingdom', *Asia Times*, 27 October, available at: http://www.atimes.com

Zakaria, Fareed (2004) *The Future of Freedom: Illiberal Democracy at Home and Abroad* (New York: W.W. Norton).

Zakaria, Fareed (1994) 'Culture is destiny: a conversation with Lee Kuan Yew', *Foreign Affairs*, 73 (2): 109–26.

Zhang, Yongjin (1991) 'China's entry into international society: beyond the standard of civilisation', *Review of International Studies*, 17: 3–16.

Zheng, Yongnian and Lye, Liang Fook (2005) 'Political legitimacy in reform China: between economic performance and democratization', in White, L. (ed.), *Legitimacy: Ambiguities of Political Success or Failure in East and Southeast Asia* (Hackersack, NJ: World Scientific): 183–214.

Zysman, John (1996) 'The myth of the 'global' economy: enduring national foundations and emerging regional realities', *New Political Economy*, 1 (2): 157–84.

Zysman, John (1983) *Governments, Markets, and Growth: Financial Systems and the Politics of Industrial Change* (Ithaca, NY: Cornell University Press).

Index